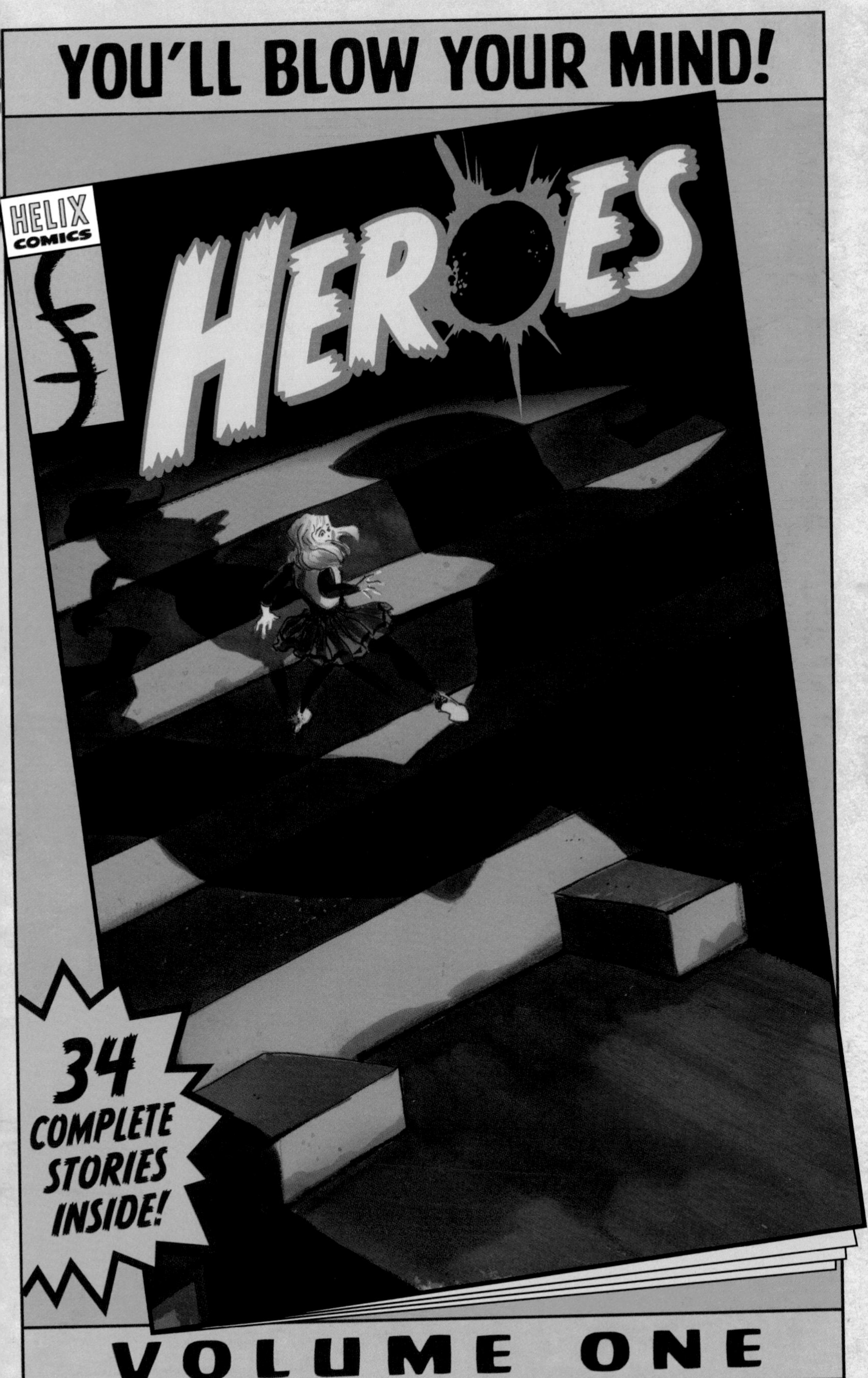
YOU'LL BLOW YOUR MIND!
HELIX COMICS
HEROES
34 COMPLETE STORIES INSIDE!
VOLUME ONE

CONTENTS

CREDI

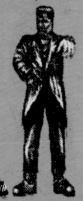

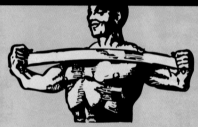

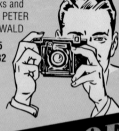

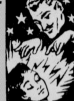

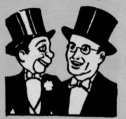

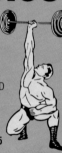

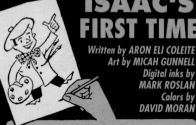

CONTENTS

CREDITS

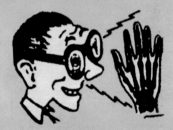

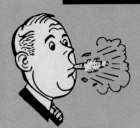

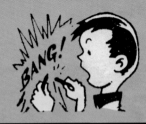

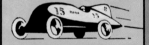

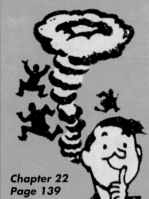

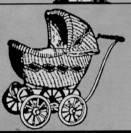

WAR BUDDIES

MONEY BACK GUARANTEE

SIX CHAPTERS LONG

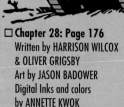
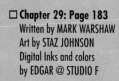

STRING THEORY

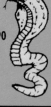

WALLS

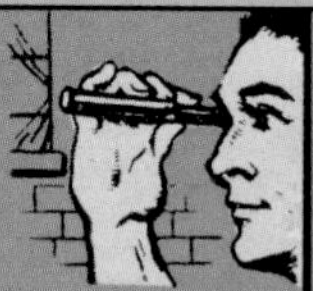

Written by JOE POKASKI

THE DEATH OF HANA GITELMAN

Lettering and Design by JOHN ROSHELL of COMICRAFT

Collected Edition Dustjacket
A by **ALEX ROSS**

Collected Edition Dustjacket
B by **JIM LEE**

Paintings by **TIM SALE
& DAVE STEWART**

Special thanks to FRANK MASTROMAURO & NANCI QUESAD

The Folks From Helix Comics:
**Aron Eli Coleite • Joe Pokaski • Jesse Alexander
Jeph Loeb • Chuck Kim • Mark Warshaw**

NATURALLY NIFTY, NEWSY, NONDESCRIPT NONSENSE ABOUT OUR NUTTY NON-ENTITIES!

HEROES, published by WildStorm Productions. 888 Prospect St. #240, La Jolla, CA 92037. Compilation, cover art, chapter break art, interview and introduction copyright © 2007 Universal Studios Licensing LLLP. Heroes is a trademark and copyright of NBC Studios, Inc. All rights reserved. SUPERMAN #1 is ™ and © DC Comics. Used with permission. Originally published at www.nbc.com/Heroes/novels © 2006, 2007, NBC Studios, Inc.

WildStorm and logo are trademarks of DC Comics. The stories, characters, and incidents mentioned in this magazine are entirely fictional.

Printed on recyclable paper. WildStorm does not read or accept unsolicited submissions of ideas, stories or artwork. Printed in the United States.

DC Comics, a Warner Bros. Entertainment Company.

HARDCOVER
Alex Ross cover
ISBN-10: 1-4012-1705-2
ISBN-13: 978-1-4012-1705-1

Jim Lee cover
ISBN-10: 1-4012-1709-5
ISBN-13: 978-1-4012-1709-9

SOFTCOVER
ISBN-10: 1-4012-1707-9
ISBN-13: 978-1-4012-1707-5

MASSIVELY MIGHTY MASTHEAD:

JIM LEE
Editorial Director

JOHN NEE
VP—Business Development

HANK KANALZ
VP—General Manager:
WildStorm and
Collected Edition Editor

KRISTY QUINN and
MICHAEL McCALISTER
Collected Edition
Assistant Editors

ED ROEDER
Art Director

PAUL LEVITZ
President & Publisher

GEORG BREWER
VP—Design & DC Direct
Creative

RICHARD BRUNING
Senior VP—
Creative Director

PATRICK CALDON
Executive VP—
Finance & Operations

CHRIS CARAMALIS
VP—Finance

JOHN CUNNINGHAM
VP—Marketing

ALISON GILL
VP—Manufacturing

PAULA LOWITT
Senior VP—Business &
Legal Affairs

MARYELLEN McLAUGHLIN
VP—Advertising & Custom
Publishing

GREGORY NOVECK
Senior VP—Creative Affairs

SUE POHJA
VP—Book Trade Sales

CHERYL RUBIN
Senior VP—
Brand Management

JEFF TROJAN
VP—Business Development:
DC Direct

BOB WAYNE
VP—Sales

JUMP, MAGAZINE, SUNDAY.

THESE THREE WORDS describe a big part of my childhood and my imagination. They are three manga magazines published weekly in Japan. Even after coming to America at the age of six, I read the imported magazines and they defined a good part of my adolescence. These magazines printed stories by everyone from great classical authors like Osamu Tezuka and Fujio Akatsuka, to contemporary masters like Naoki Urasawa, Akira Toriyama, and Rumiko Takahashi, just to name a few. The artists always brought stories and characters that reflected our current culture and times to the page. We grew with them and they grew with us.

Manga, like graphic novels or any piece of art, has many unique powers. It can unite us and inspire us. Through these art forms, we share a common bond, a passion that we could all lose ourselves in. It was always fascinating to me that every Tuesday when the weekly SHONEN JUMP came out, all the businessmen, in their suits and ties, would pick up a JUMP from a kiosk. They would ride the subways or buses, all silent, just immersing themselves in

the world of manga. At that moment, these grown men were all experiencing the same thing. Manga is part of the Japanese culture and it defines a lot of who I am. At times it would be my romantic consultant, reading stories about a shy boy who is trying to muster the courage to ask a girl out. It would be my teacher as it pontificated on potential disruptions to the space/time continuum. It would be my hero as it continued to inspire me with journeys and tales of bravery and adventure. Sure, at lot of what I've "learned" isn't too applicable in real life, or would sometimes invite a slap in the face, but it enhanced my imagination and enriched our creativity.

We've all been affected by graphic novels in one form or another. As we grow, become adults, and gain responsibility, mangas are where I can find sanctuary and still be a kid. Imagination flows and it's a comfort to know that there are many, many others out there—from all walks of life—enjoying the same experience. If you're a kid, enjoy it. Savor it. Hold on to your imagination and your dreams. You can make a world

a different place—but it begins with you. If you're an adult, enjoy. Relax. Let yourself be a kid again. Take a vacation and let your mind wander in the magical world of graphic novels. No one can stop us from learning. No one can stop us from dreaming. No one can stop us from believing.

Tim Kring created a beautiful world, laden with rich stories and deep characters. Many artists came together under his vision to create a fantastical piece of television called HEROES. What you see on television is a reflection of all the hard work put in by hundreds of people. But a mere television show couldn't contain us. There still are more stories to tell, that we *wanted* to tell but couldn't given the medium. Fortunately, we can share and expand through a different medium. We present you these graphic novels to help add another dimension to the HEROES universe. We hope you enjoy it and let yourself get lost in the HEROES world.

For Charlie,
Hiro Nakamura
(Masi Oka)

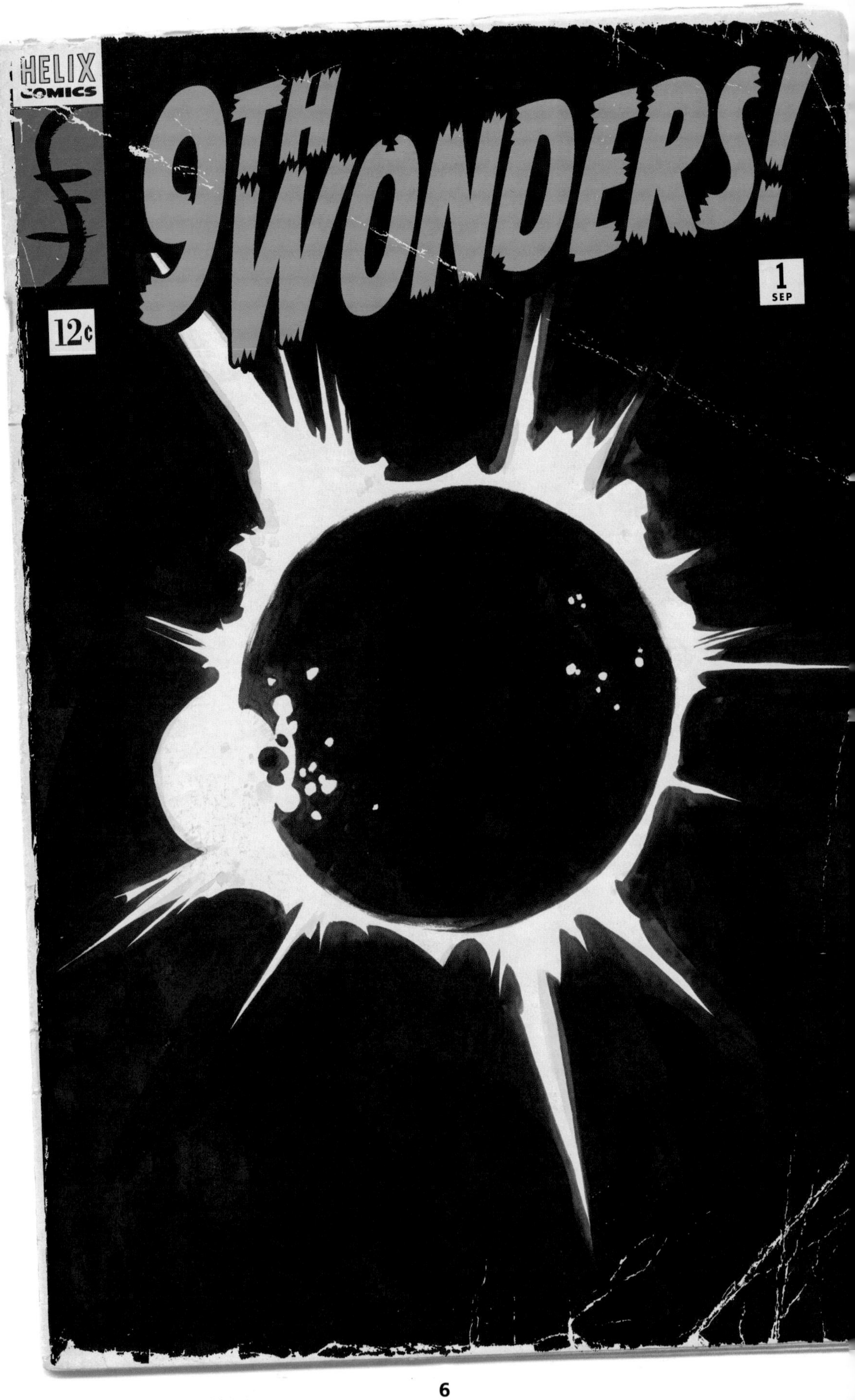
HELIX
COMICS
9TH WONDERS!
1
SEP
12¢

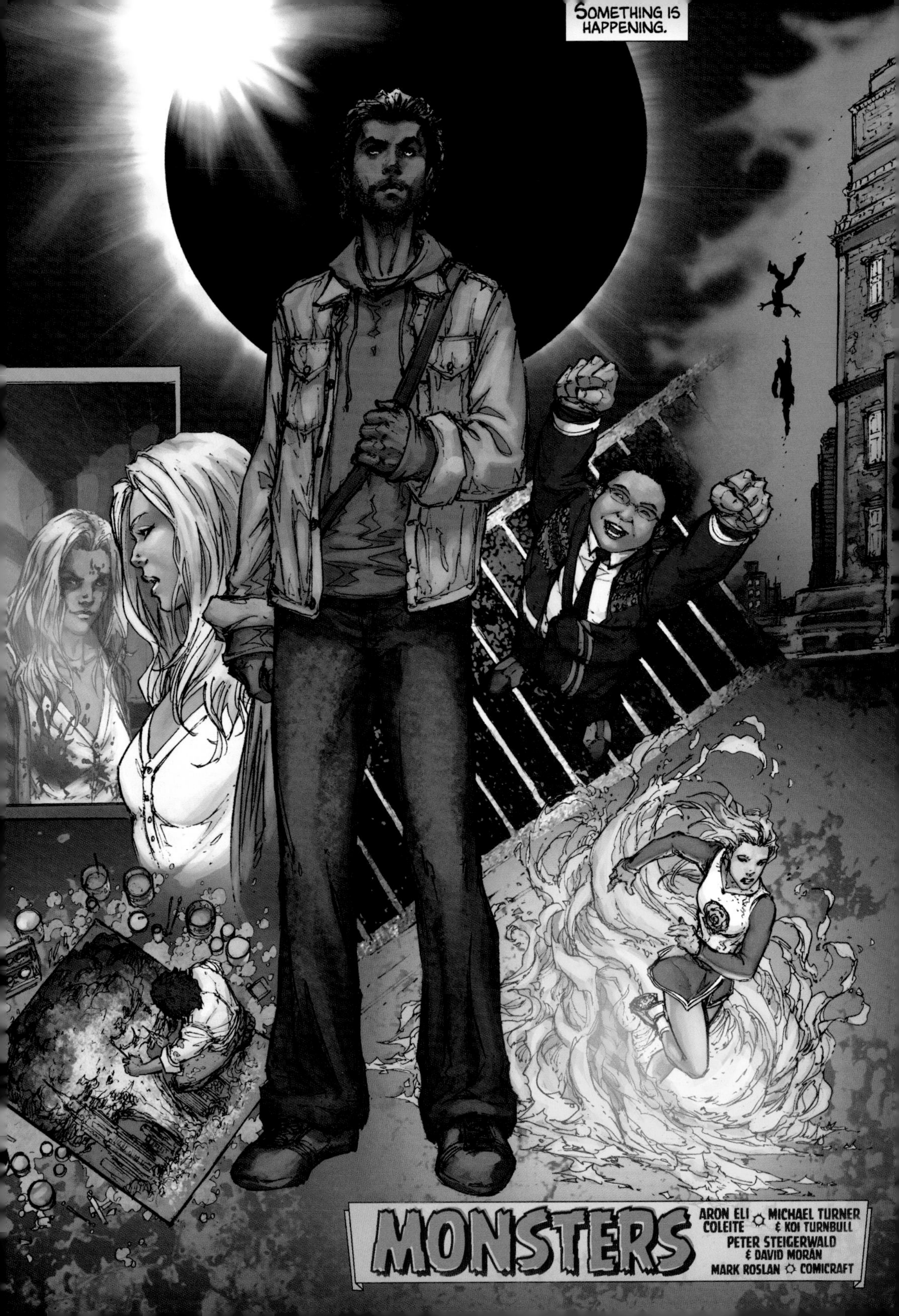
SOMETHING IS HAPPENING.
MONSTERS
ARON ELI COLEITE
MICHAEL TURNER & KOI TURNBULL
PETER STEIGERWALD & DAVID MORÁN
MARK ROSLAN
COMICRAFT

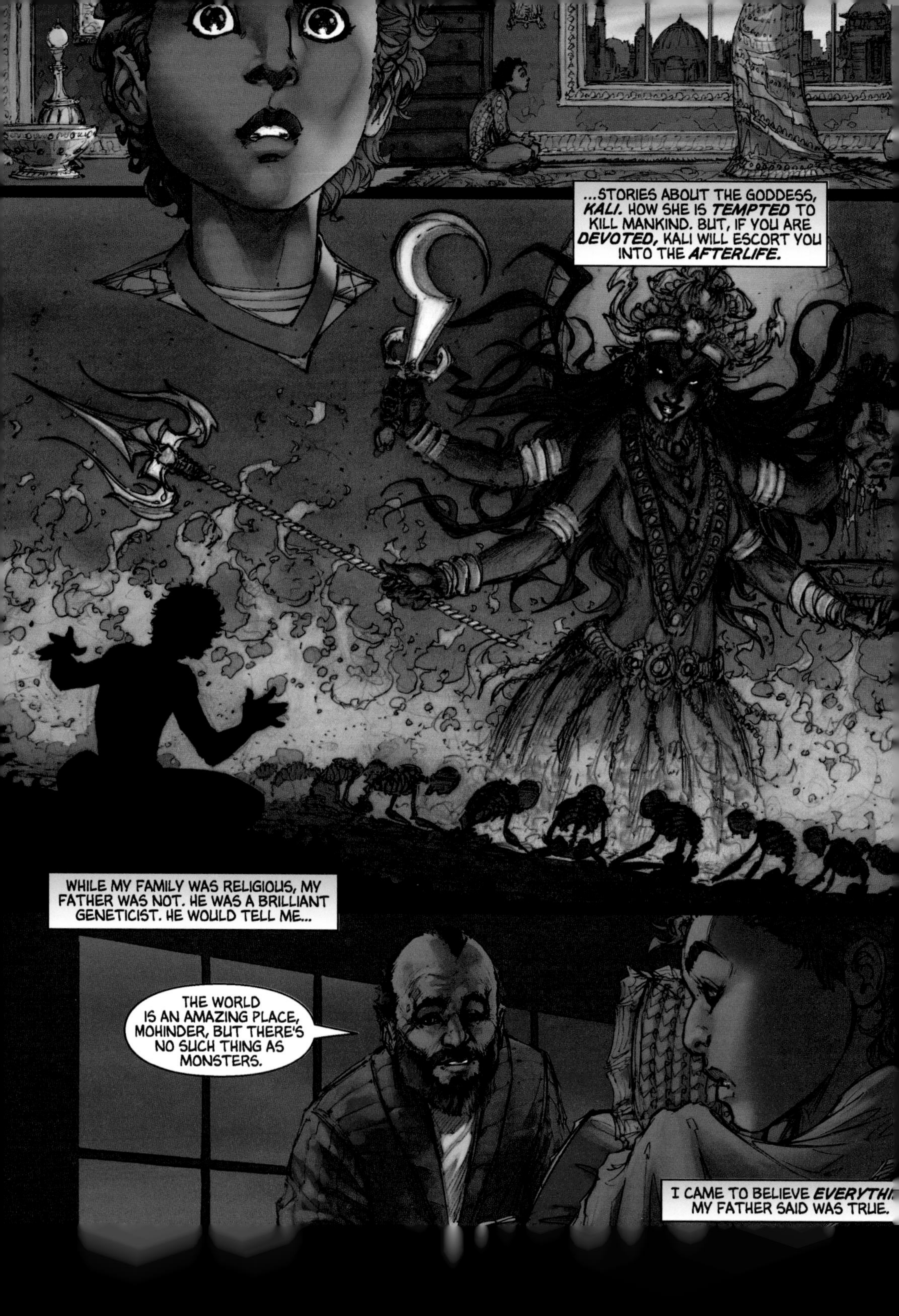
...STORIES ABOUT THE GODDESS, *KALI.* HOW SHE IS *TEMPTED* TO KILL MANKIND. BUT, IF YOU ARE *DEVOTED,* KALI WILL ESCORT YOU INTO THE *AFTERLIFE.*
WHILE MY FAMILY WAS RELIGIOUS, MY FATHER WAS NOT. HE WAS A BRILLIANT GENETICIST. HE WOULD TELL ME...
THE WORLD IS AN AMAZING PLACE, MOHINDER, BUT THERE'S NO SUCH THING AS MONSTERS.
I CAME TO BELIEVE *EVERYTHI* MY FATHER SAID WAS TRUE.

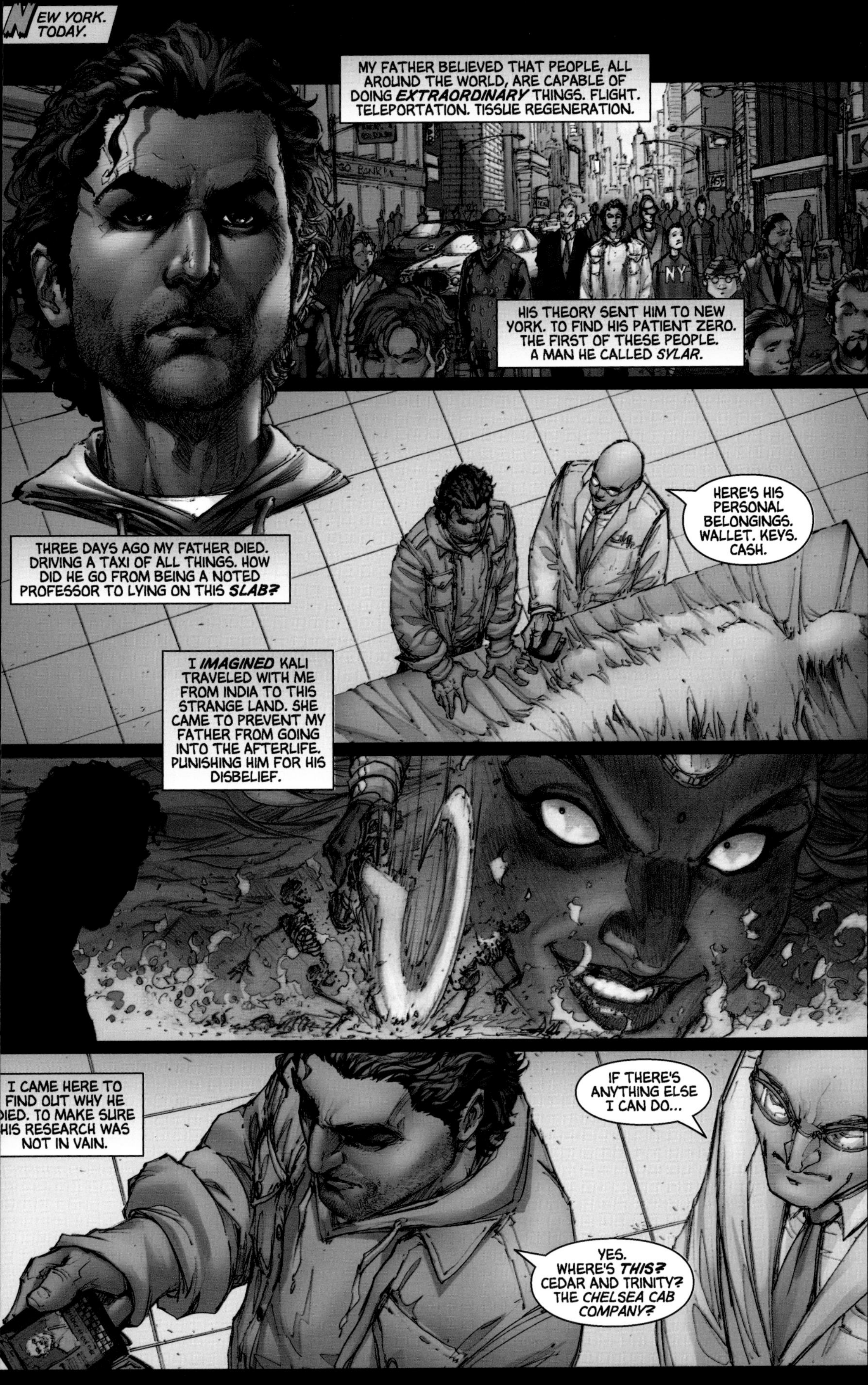
NEW YORK. TODAY.
MY FATHER BELIEVED THAT PEOPLE, ALL AROUND THE WORLD, ARE CAPABLE OF DOING EXTRAORDINARY THINGS. FLIGHT. TELEPORTATION. TISSUE REGENERATION.
HIS THEORY SENT HIM TO NEW YORK. TO FIND HIS PATIENT ZERO. THE FIRST OF THESE PEOPLE. A MAN HE CALLED SYLAR.
THREE DAYS AGO MY FATHER DIED. DRIVING A TAXI OF ALL THINGS. HOW DID HE GO FROM BEING A NOTED PROFESSOR TO LYING ON THIS SLAB?
HERE'S HIS PERSONAL BELONGINGS. WALLET. KEYS. CASH.
I IMAGINED KALI TRAVELED WITH ME FROM INDIA TO THIS STRANGE LAND. SHE CAME TO PREVENT MY FATHER FROM GOING INTO THE AFTERLIFE. PUNISHING HIM FOR HIS DISBELIEF.
I CAME HERE TO FIND OUT WHY HE DIED. TO MAKE SURE HIS RESEARCH WAS NOT IN VAIN.
IF THERE'S ANYTHING ELSE I CAN DO...
YES. WHERE'S THIS? CEDAR AND TRINITY? THE CHELSEA CAB COMPANY?

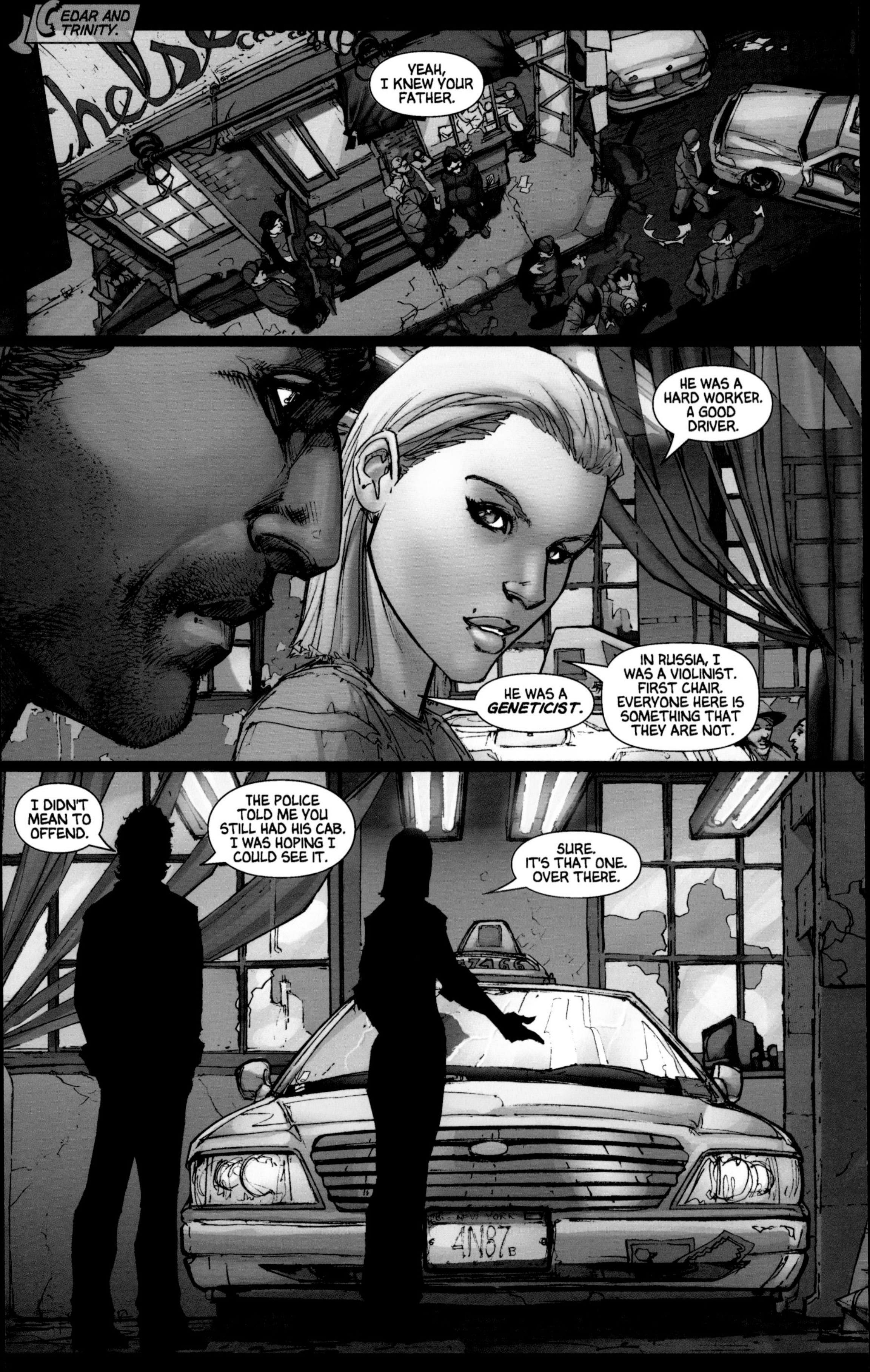
CEDAR AND TRINITY.
YEAH, I KNEW YOUR FATHER.
HE WAS A HARD WORKER. A GOOD DRIVER.
HE WAS A GENETICIST.
IN RUSSIA, I WAS A VIOLINIST. FIRST CHAIR. EVERYONE HERE IS SOMETHING THAT THEY ARE NOT.
I DIDN'T MEAN TO OFFEND.
THE POLICE TOLD ME YOU STILL HAD HIS CAB. I WAS HOPING I COULD SEE IT.
SURE. IT'S THAT ONE. OVER THERE.
4N87 B

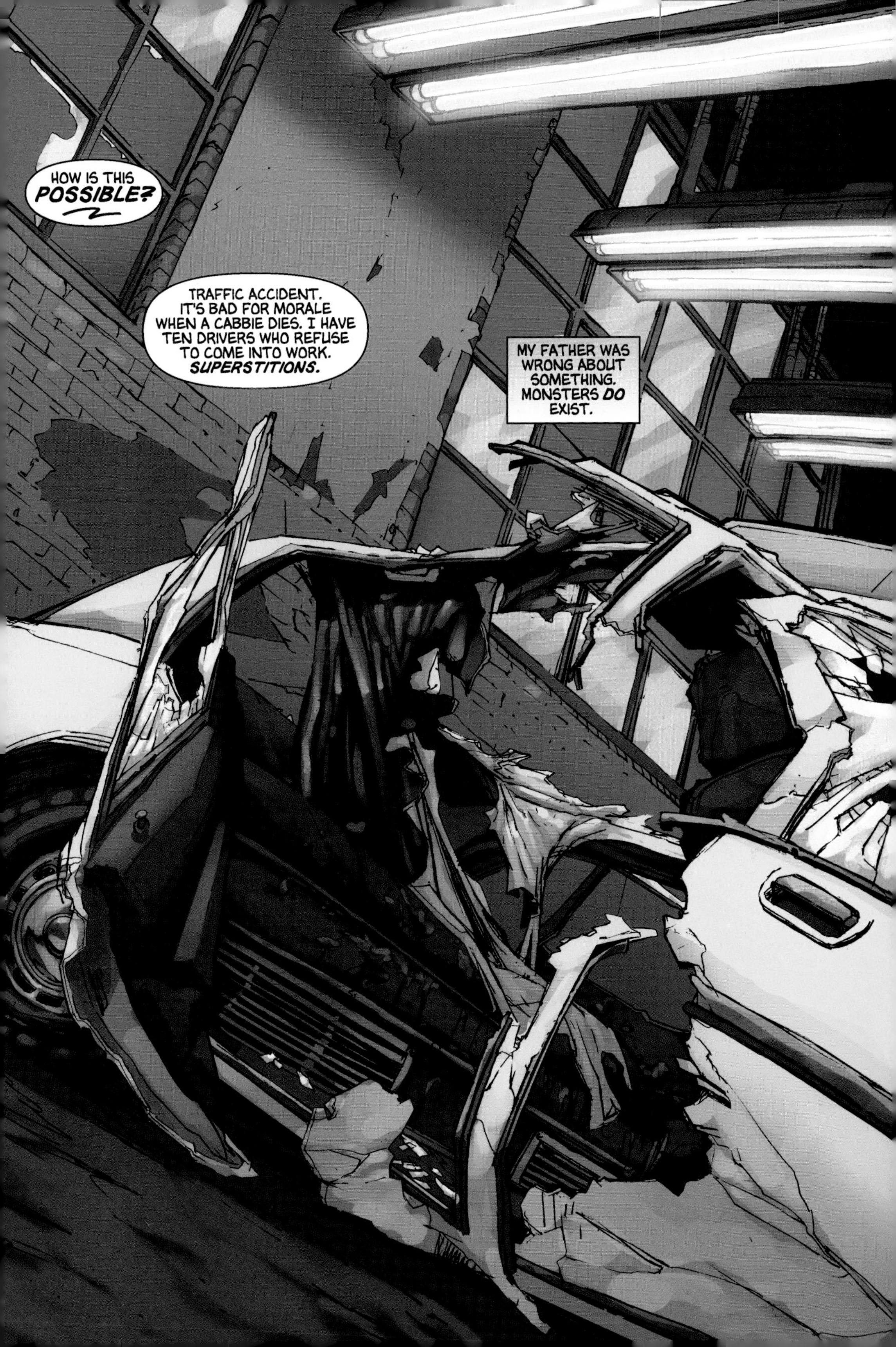
HOW IS THIS POSSIBLE?
TRAFFIC ACCIDENT. IT'S BAD FOR MORALE WHEN A CABBIE DIES. I HAVE TEN DRIVERS WHO REFUSE TO COME INTO WORK. SUPERSTITIONS.
MY FATHER WAS WRONG ABOUT SOMETHING. MONSTERS DO EXIST.

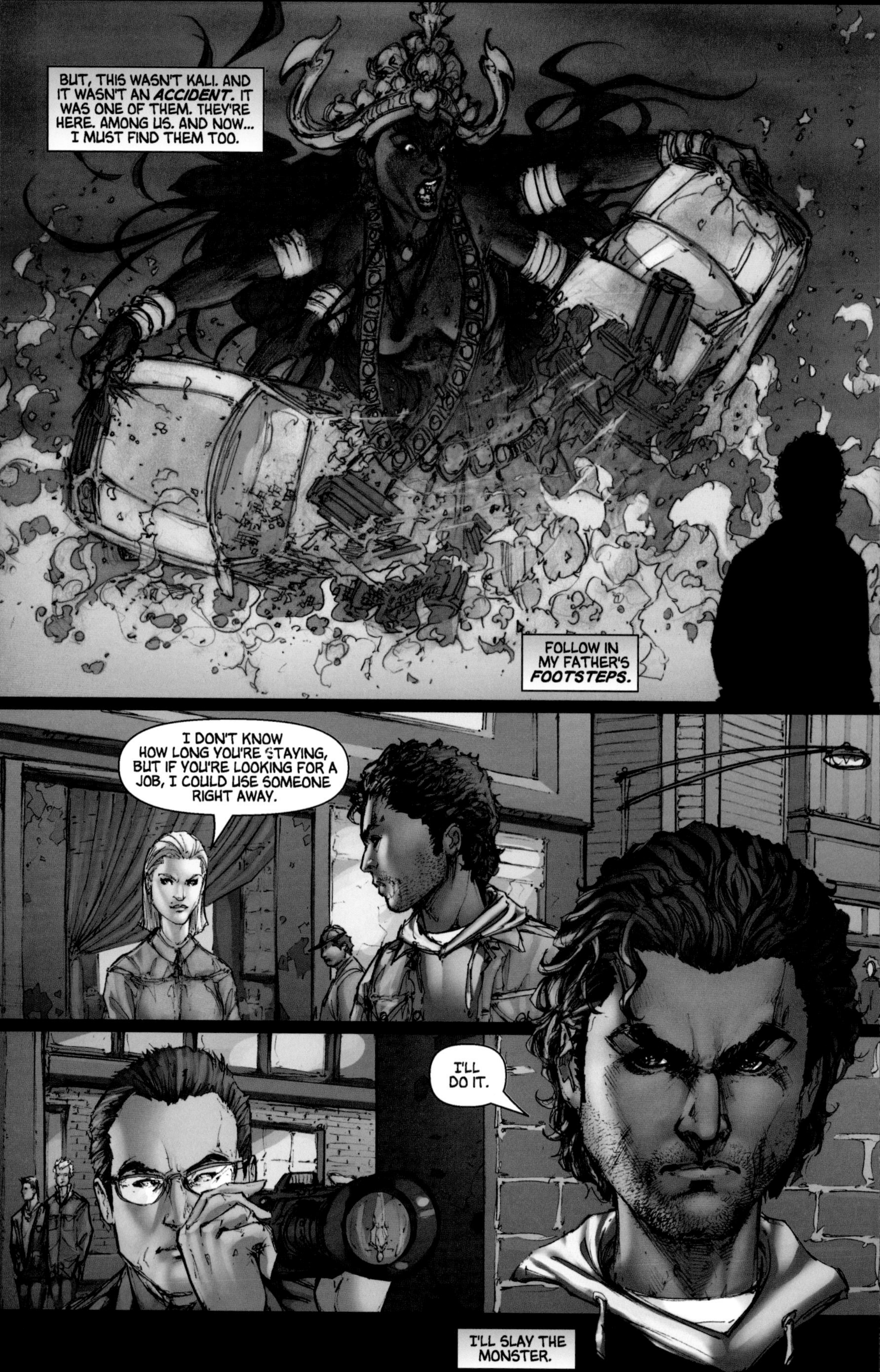
BUT, THIS WASN'T KALI. AND IT WASN'T AN *ACCIDENT*. IT WAS ONE OF THEM. THEY'RE HERE. AMONG US. AND NOW... I MUST FIND THEM TOO.
FOLLOW IN MY FATHER'S *FOOTSTEPS.*
I DON'T KNOW HOW LONG YOU'RE STAYING, BUT IF YOU'RE LOOKING FOR A JOB, I COULD USE SOMEONE RIGHT AWAY.
I'LL DO IT.
I'LL SLAY THE MONSTER.

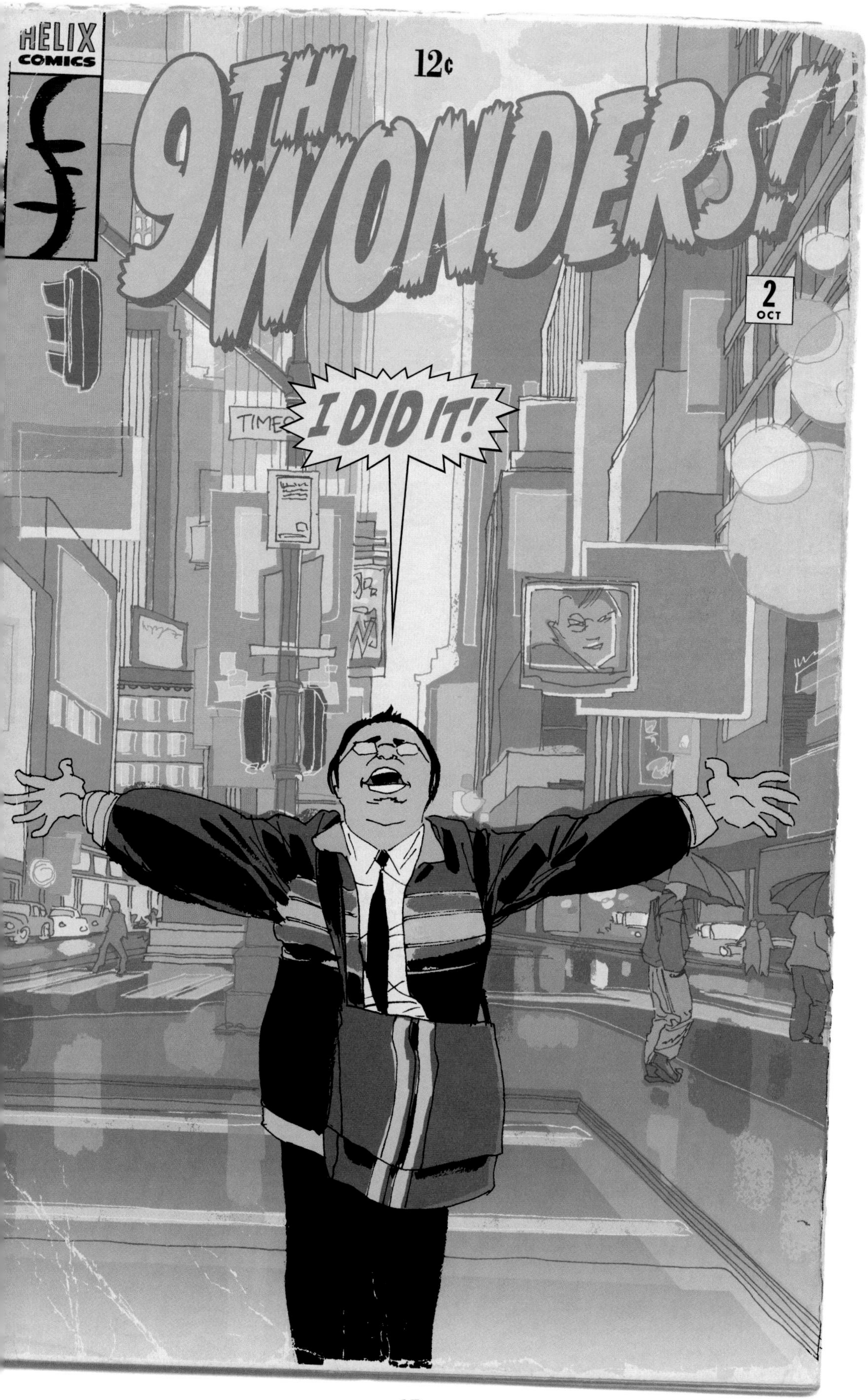
HELIX COMICS
12¢
9TH WONDERS!
2 OCT
TIMES
I DID IT!

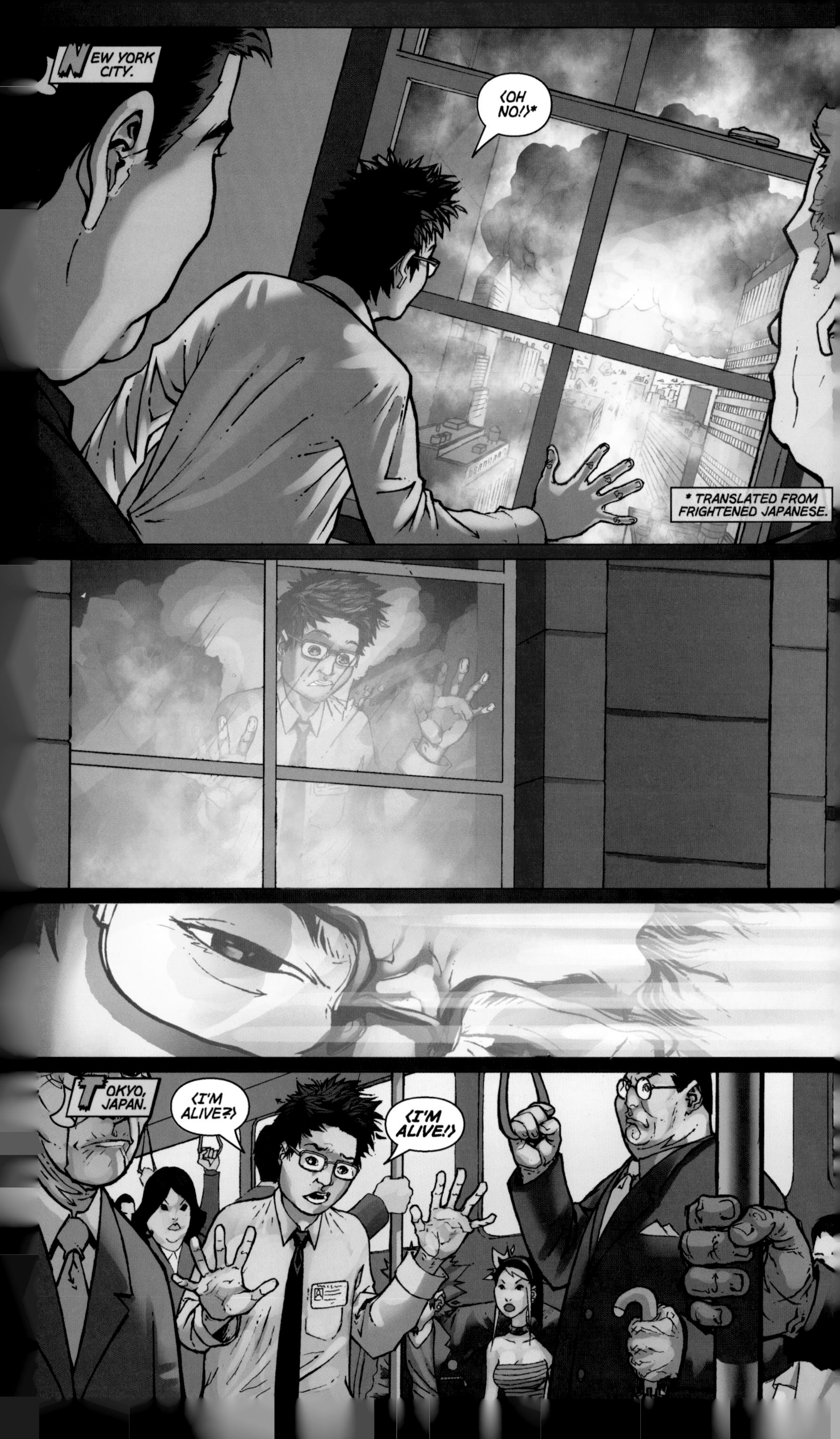
NEW YORK CITY.
‹OH NO!›*
* TRANSLATED FROM FRIGHTENED JAPANESE.
TOKYO, JAPAN.
‹I'M ALIVE?›
‹I'M ALIVE!›

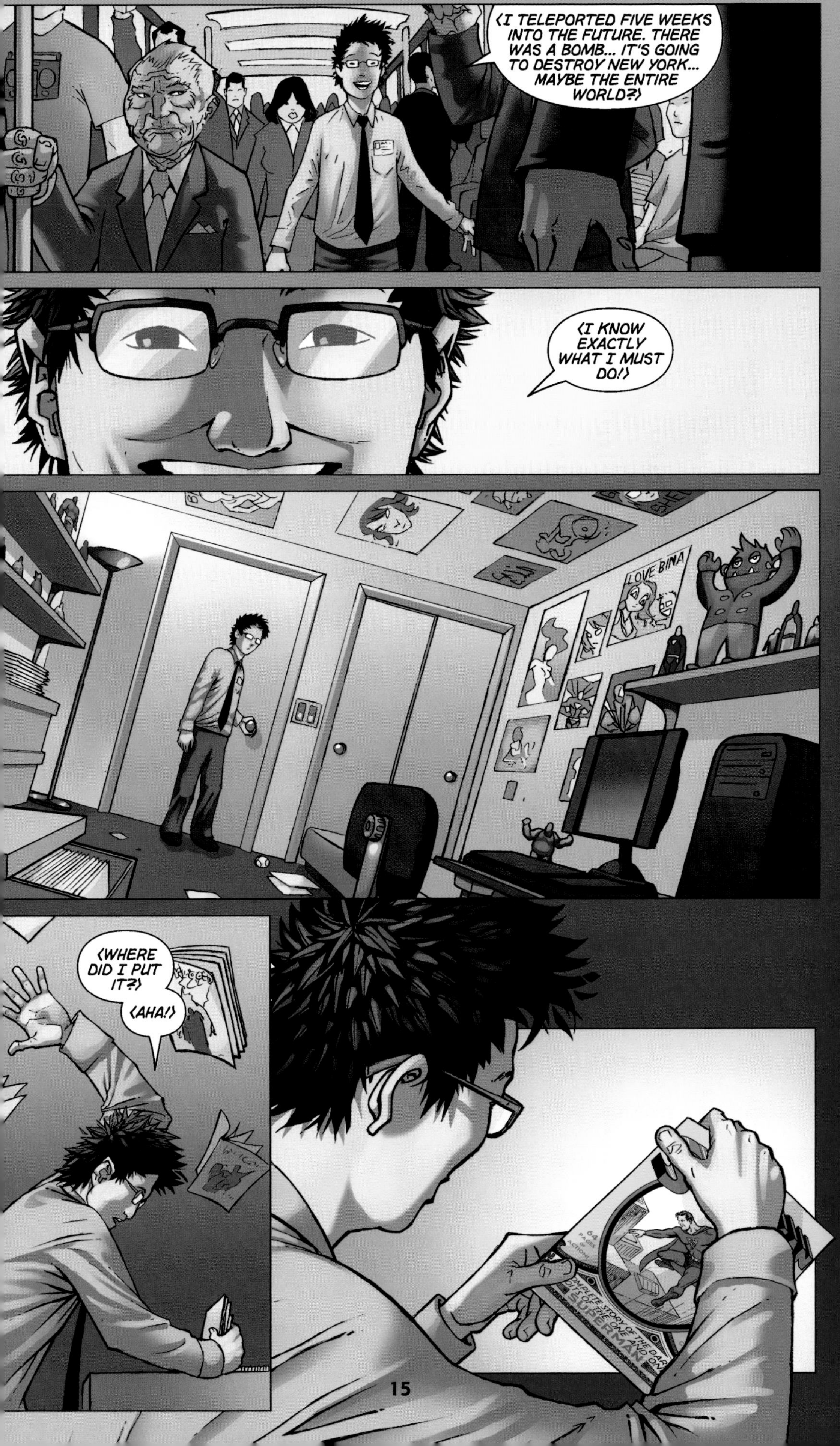
‹I TELEPORTED FIVE WEEKS INTO THE FUTURE. THERE WAS A BOMB... IT'S GOING TO DESTROY NEW YORK... MAYBE THE ENTIRE WORLD?›
‹I KNOW EXACTLY WHAT I MUST DO!›
LOVE BINA
‹WHERE DID I PUT IT?›
‹AHA!›
64 PAGES OF ACTION!
COMPLETE STORY OF THE DAR... OF THE ONE AND ON...
SUPERMAN

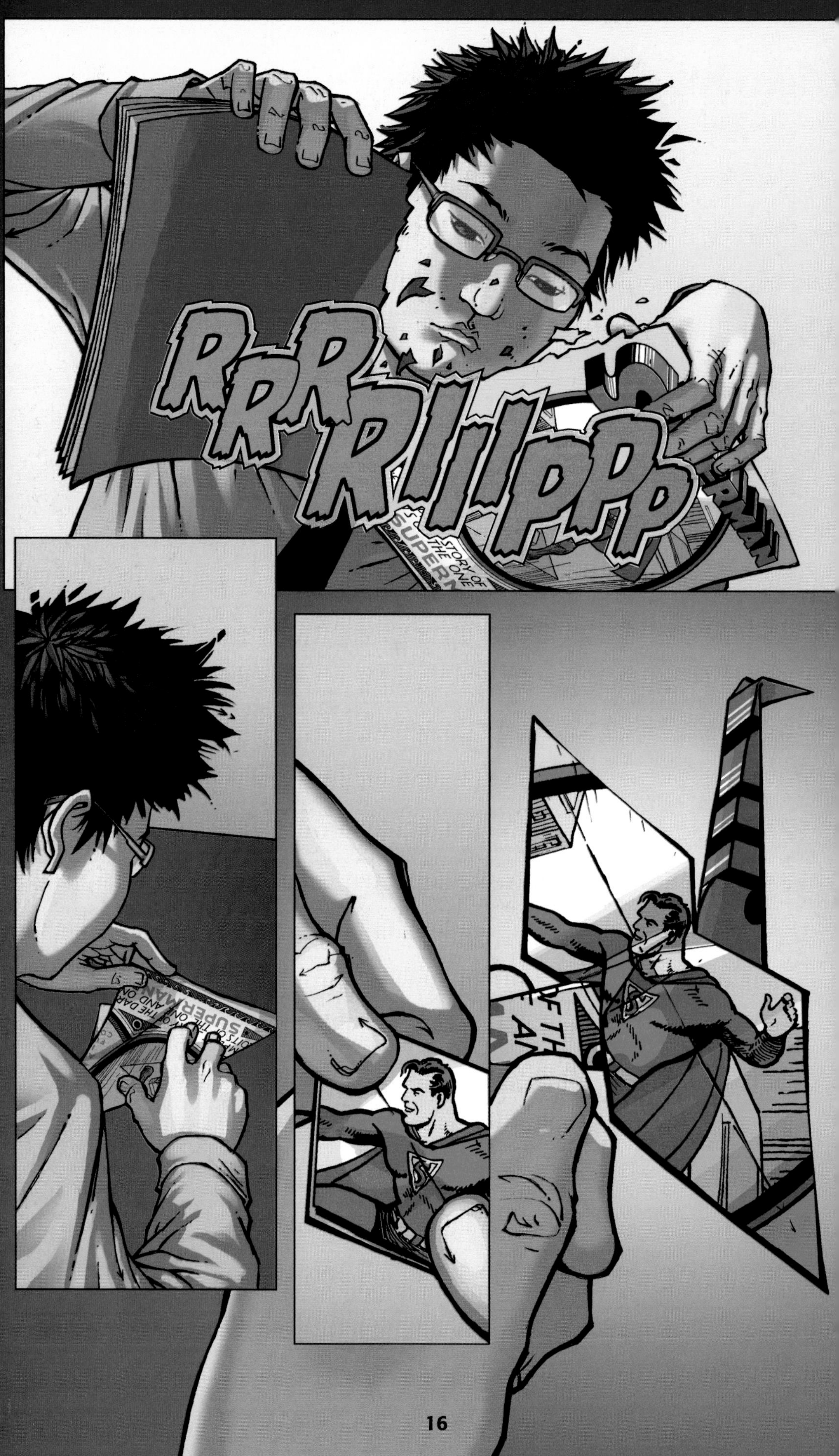
RRRRIIPPP

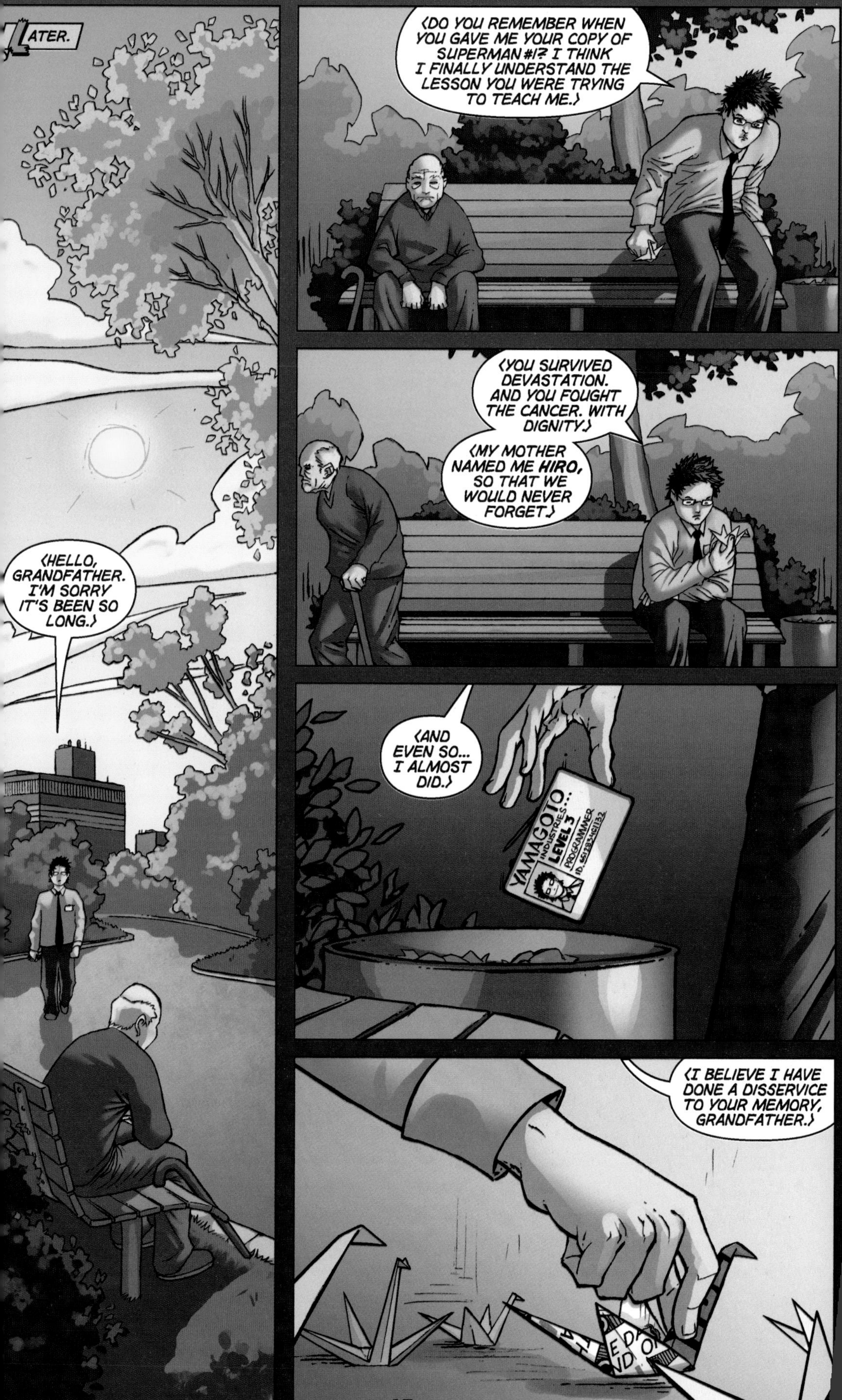
LATER.
⟨HELLO, GRANDFATHER. I'M SORRY IT'S BEEN SO LONG.⟩
⟨DO YOU REMEMBER WHEN YOU GAVE ME YOUR COPY OF SUPERMAN #1? I THINK I FINALLY UNDERSTAND THE LESSON YOU WERE TRYING TO TEACH ME.⟩
⟨YOU SURVIVED DEVASTATION. AND YOU FOUGHT THE CANCER. WITH DIGNITY.⟩
⟨MY MOTHER NAMED ME HIRO, SO THAT WE WOULD NEVER FORGET.⟩
⟨AND EVEN SO... I ALMOST DID.⟩
YAMAGOTO INDUSTRIES... LEVEL 3 PROGRAMMER
⟨I BELIEVE I HAVE DONE A DISSERVICE TO YOUR MEMORY, GRANDFATHER.⟩

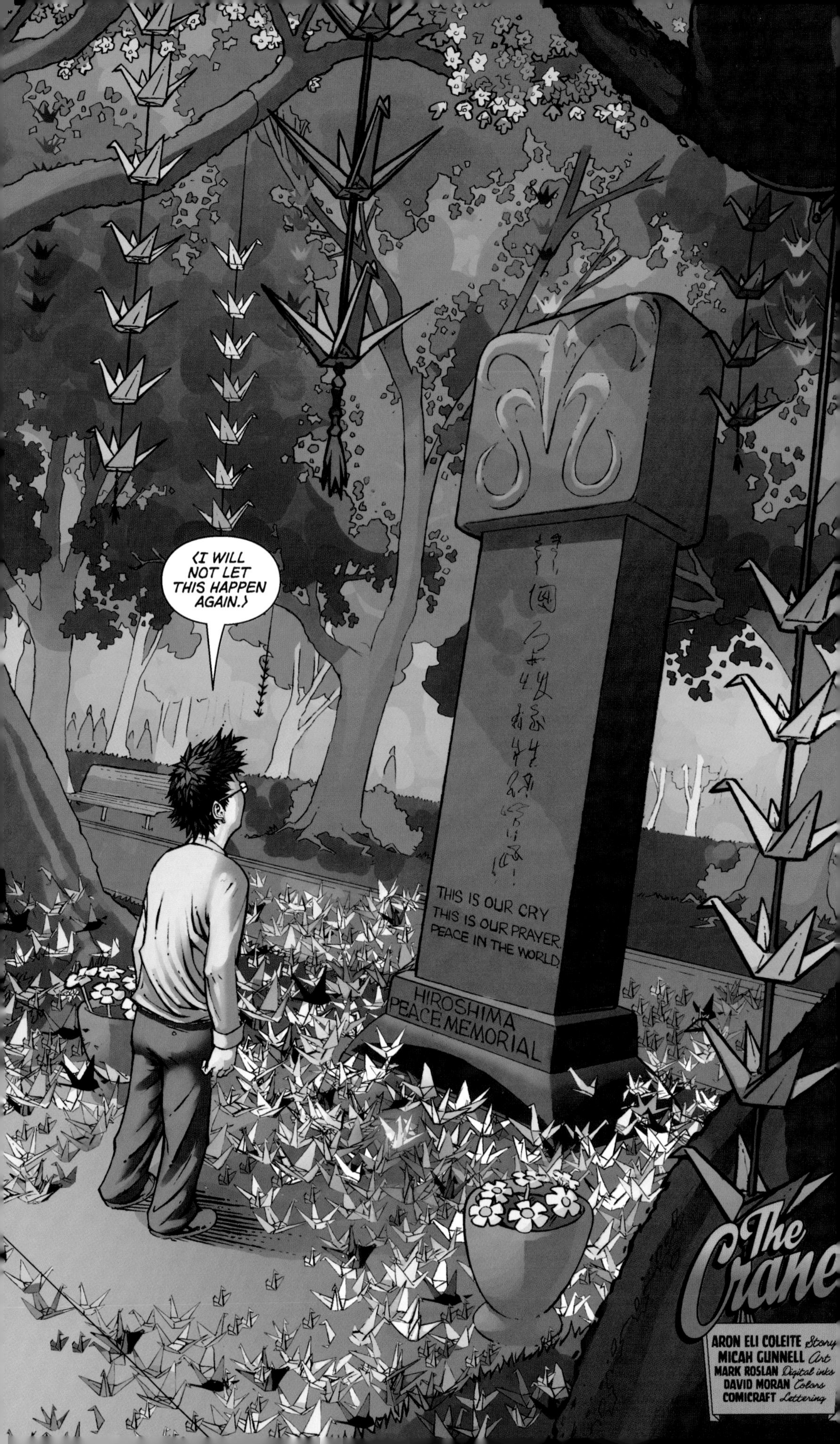

⟨I WILL NOT LET THIS HAPPEN AGAIN.⟩
THIS IS OUR CRY
THIS IS OUR PRAYER.
PEACE IN THE WORLD.
HIROSHIMA PEACE MEMORIAL
The Crane
ARON ELI COLEITE Story
MICAH GUNNELL Art
MARK ROSLAN Digital inks
DAVID MORAN Colors
COMICRAFT Lettering

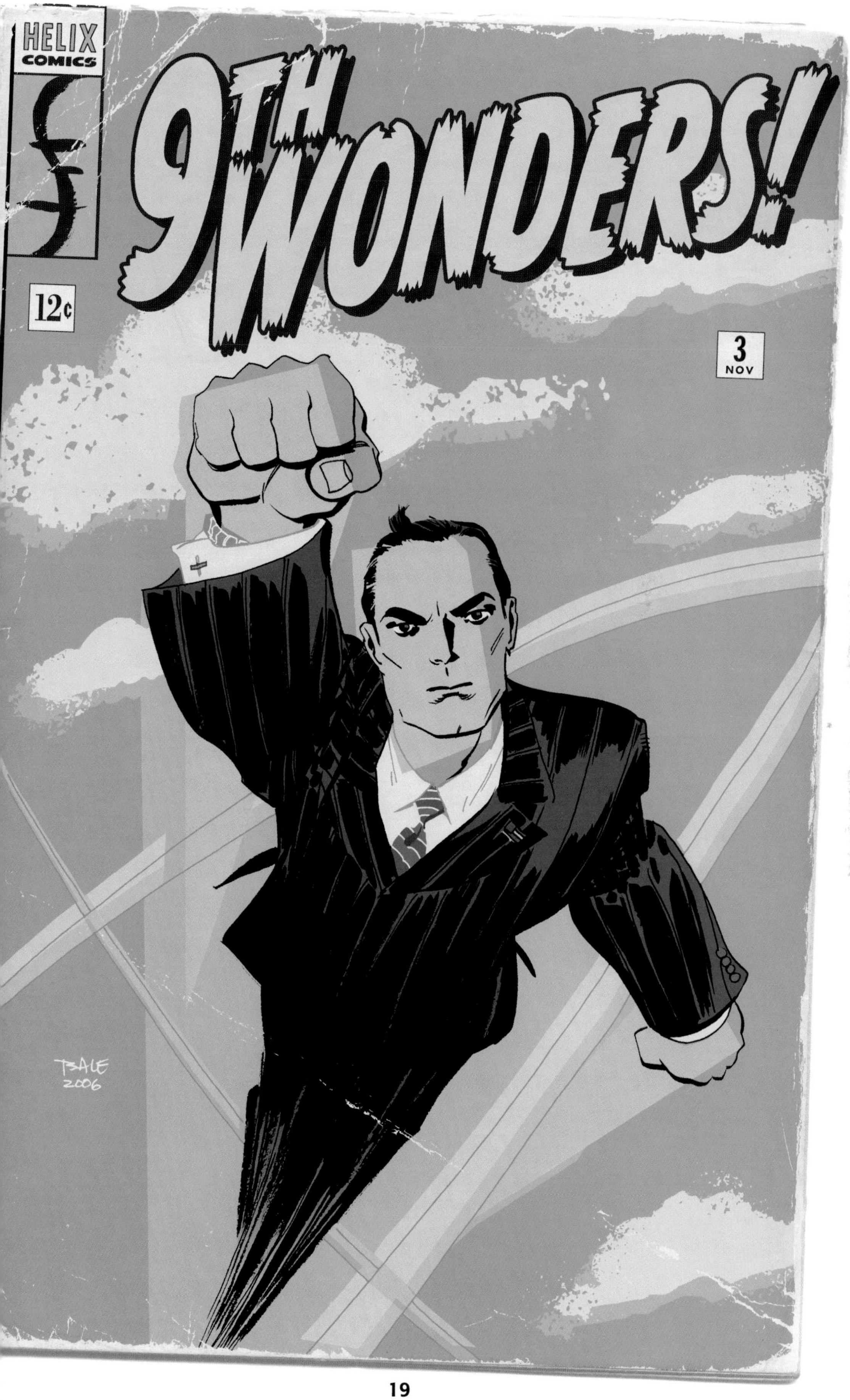
HELIX
COMICS
9TH WONDERS!
12¢
3
NOV
TSALE
2006

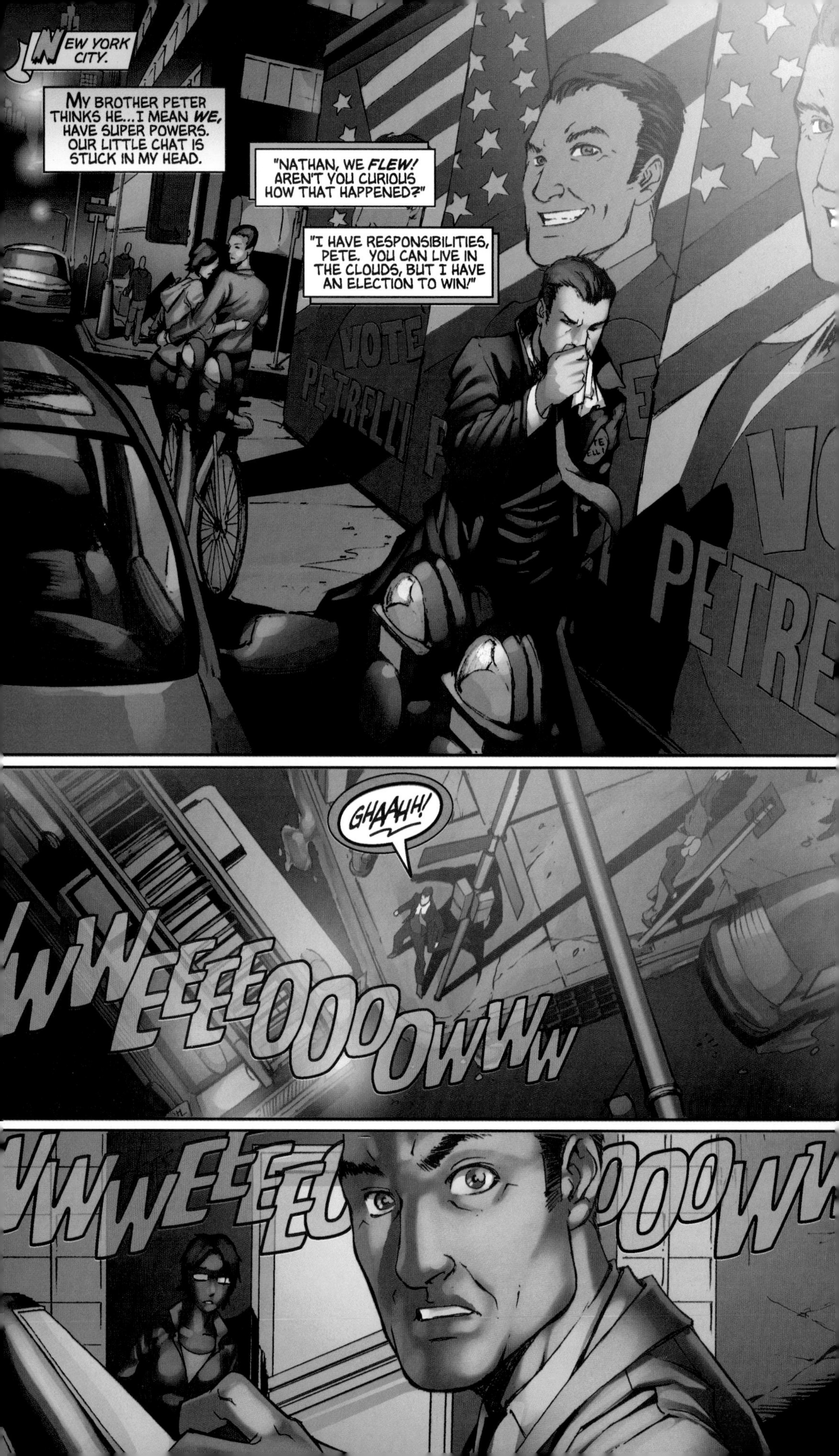
NEW YORK CITY.
MY BROTHER PETER THINKS HE...I MEAN WE, HAVE SUPER POWERS. OUR LITTLE CHAT IS STUCK IN MY HEAD.
"NATHAN, WE FLEW! AREN'T YOU CURIOUS HOW THAT HAPPENED?"
"I HAVE RESPONSIBILITIES, PETE. YOU CAN LIVE IN THE CLOUDS, BUT I HAVE AN ELECTION TO WIN!"
VOTE PETRELLI
GHAAHH!
WWEEEEOOOOWWW
WWWEEEE OOOOWW

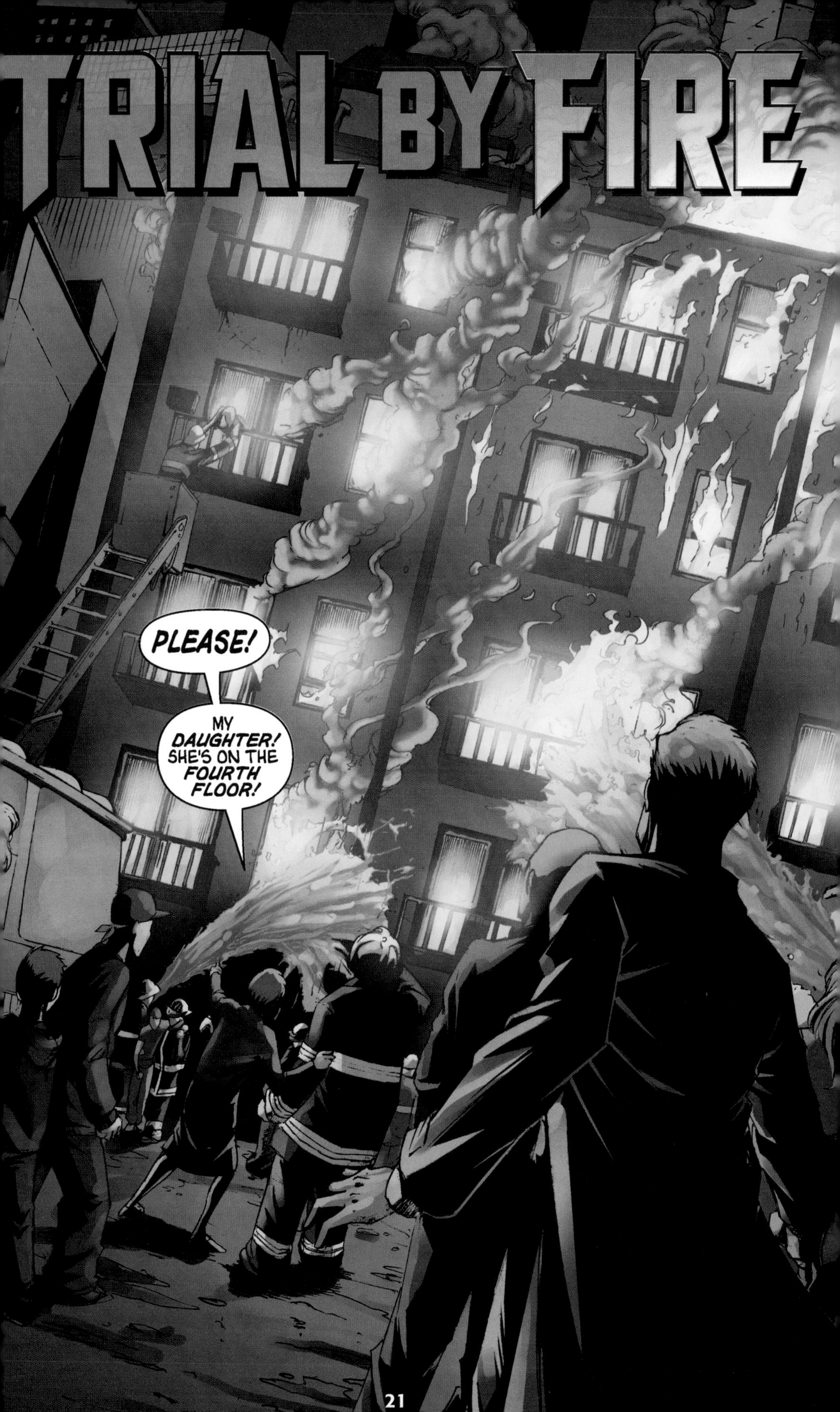
TRIAL BY FIRE
PLEASE!
MY DAUGHTER! SHE'S ON THE FOURTH FLOOR!

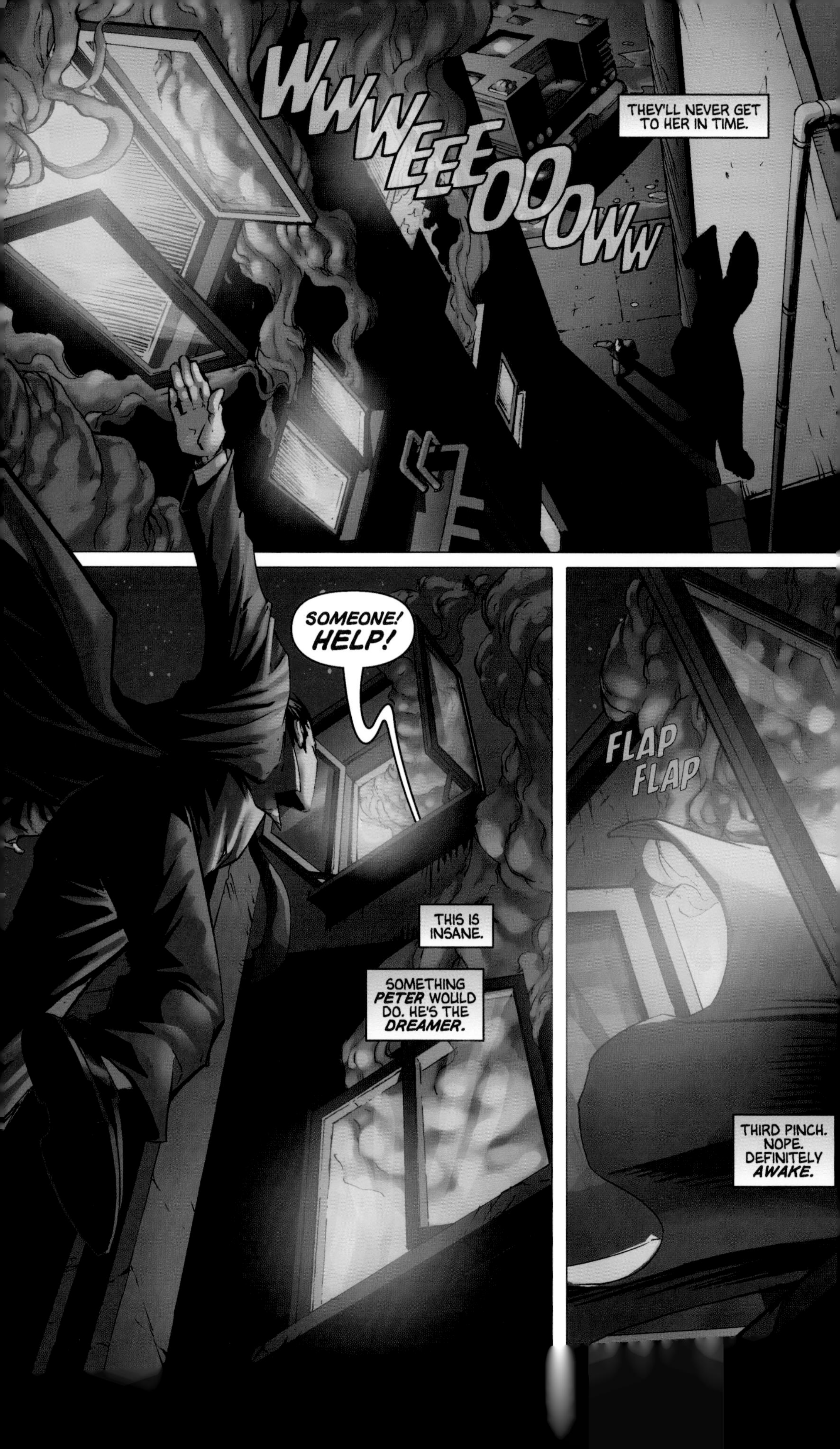
WWWEEEOOOWW
THEY'LL NEVER GET TO HER IN TIME.
SOMEONE! HELP!
THIS IS INSANE.
SOMETHING PETER WOULD DO. HE'S THE DREAMER.
FLAP FLAP
THIRD PINCH. NOPE. DEFINITELY AWAKE.

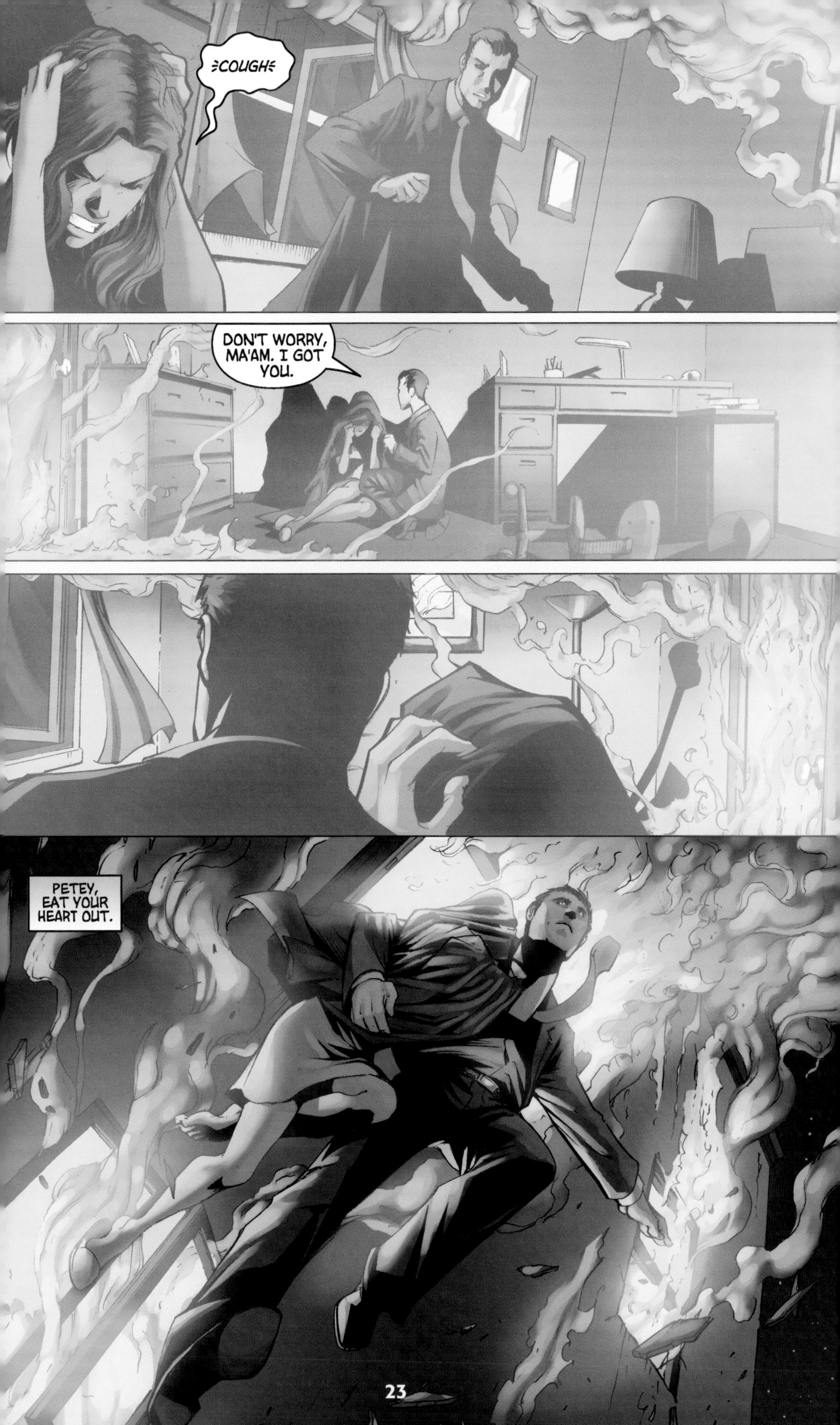
COUGH
DON'T WORRY, MA'AM. I GOT YOU.
PETEY, EAT YOUR HEART OUT.

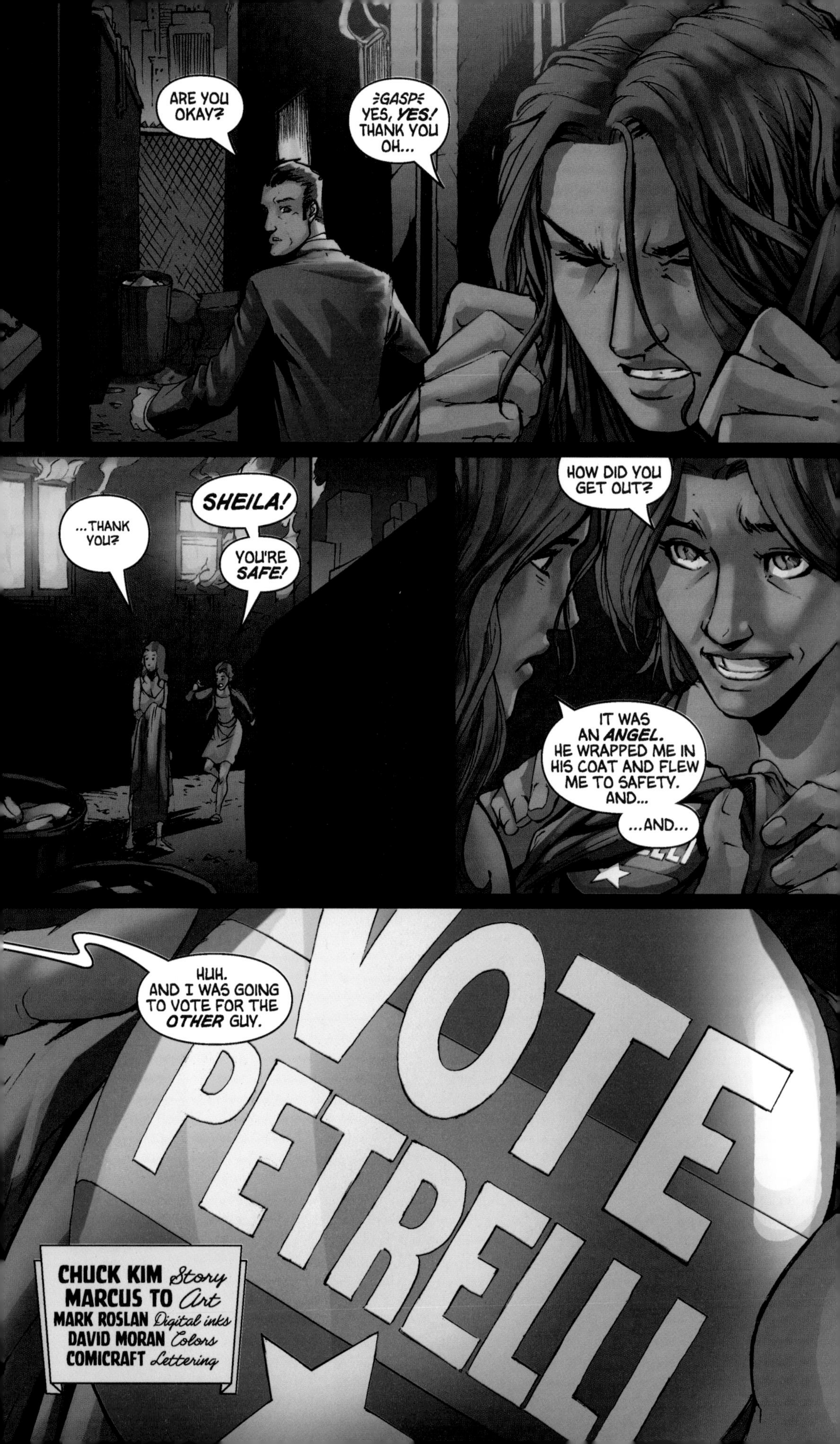
ARE YOU OKAY?
GASP YES, YES! THANK YOU OH...
...THANK YOU?
SHEILA!
YOU'RE SAFE!
HOW DID YOU GET OUT?
IT WAS AN ANGEL. HE WRAPPED ME IN HIS COAT AND FLEW ME TO SAFETY. AND...
...AND...
HUH. AND I WAS GOING TO VOTE FOR THE OTHER GUY.
VOTE PETRELLI
CHUCK KIM Story
MARCUS TO Art
MARK ROSLAN Digital inks
DAVID MORAN Colors
COMICRAFT Lettering

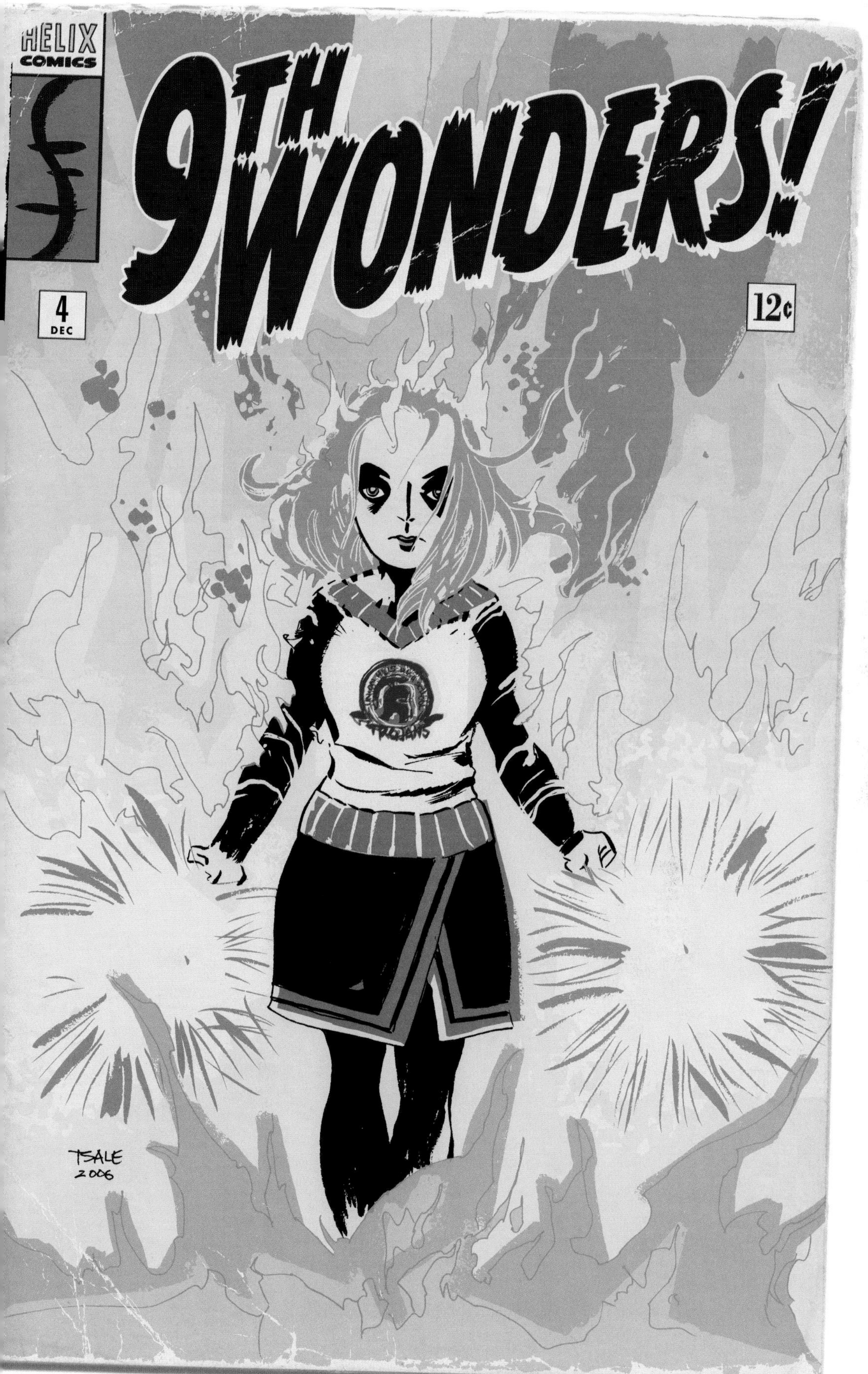
HELIX COMICS
9TH WONDERS!
4 DEC
12¢
TSALE 2006

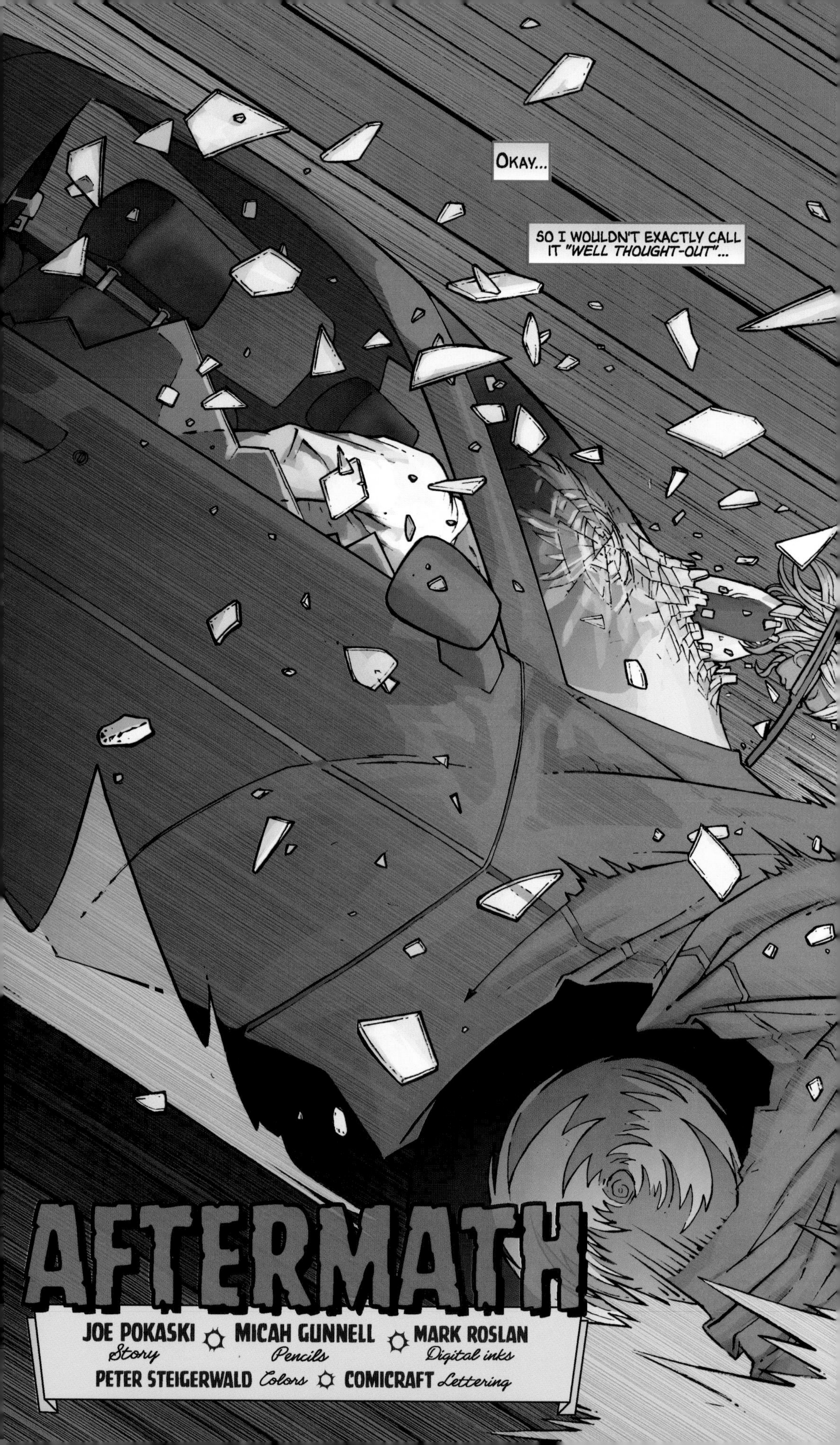
OKAY...
SO I WOULDN'T EXACTLY CALL IT "WELL THOUGHT-OUT"...
AFTERMATH
JOE POKASKI Story
MICAH GUNNELL Pencils
MARK ROSLAN Digital inks
PETER STEIGERWALD Colors
COMICRAFT Lettering

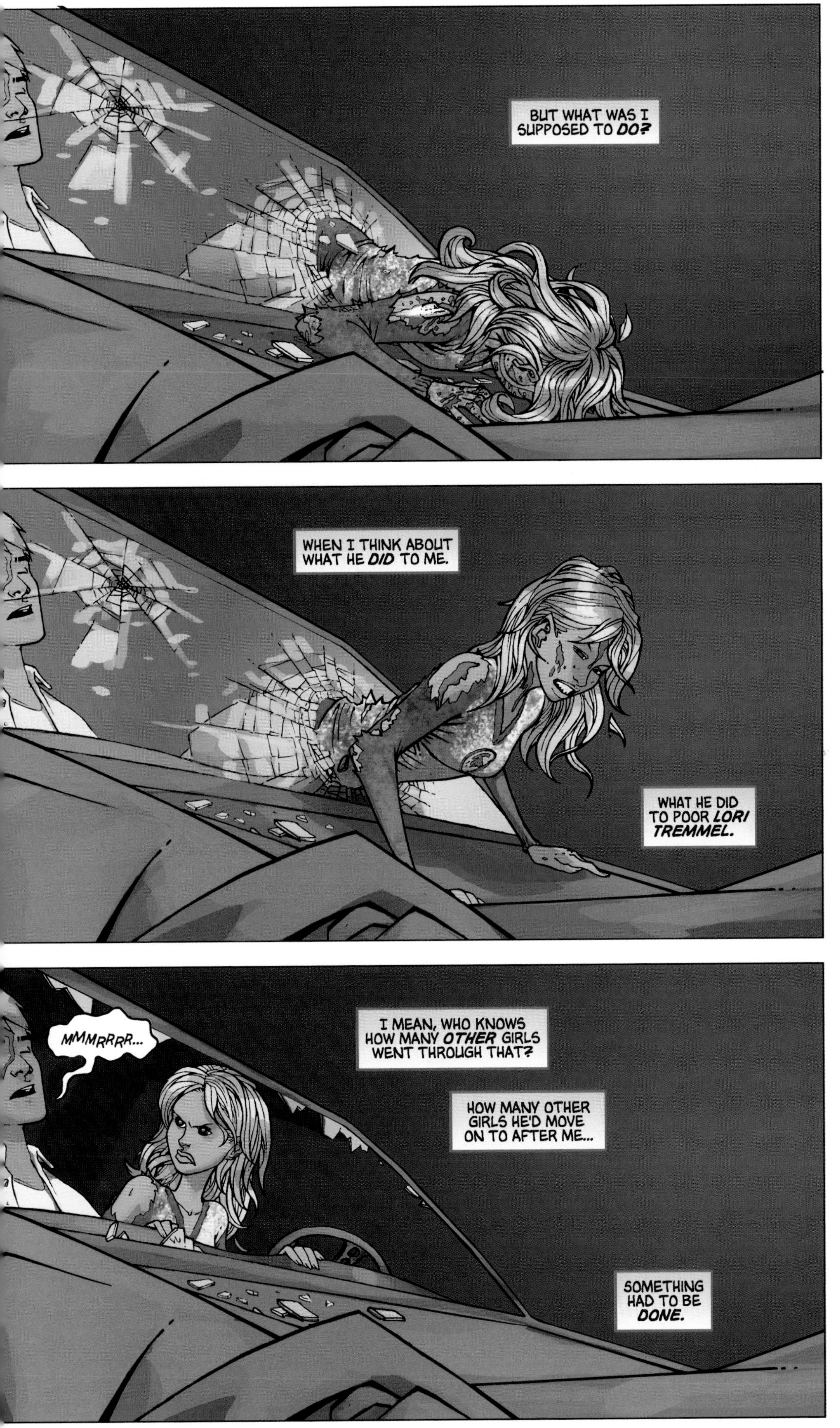
BUT WHAT WAS I SUPPOSED TO DO?
WHEN I THINK ABOUT WHAT HE DID TO ME.
WHAT HE DID TO POOR LORI TREMMEL.
MMMRRRR...
I MEAN, WHO KNOWS HOW MANY OTHER GIRLS WENT THROUGH THAT?
HOW MANY OTHER GIRLS HE'D MOVE ON TO AFTER ME...
SOMETHING HAD TO BE DONE.

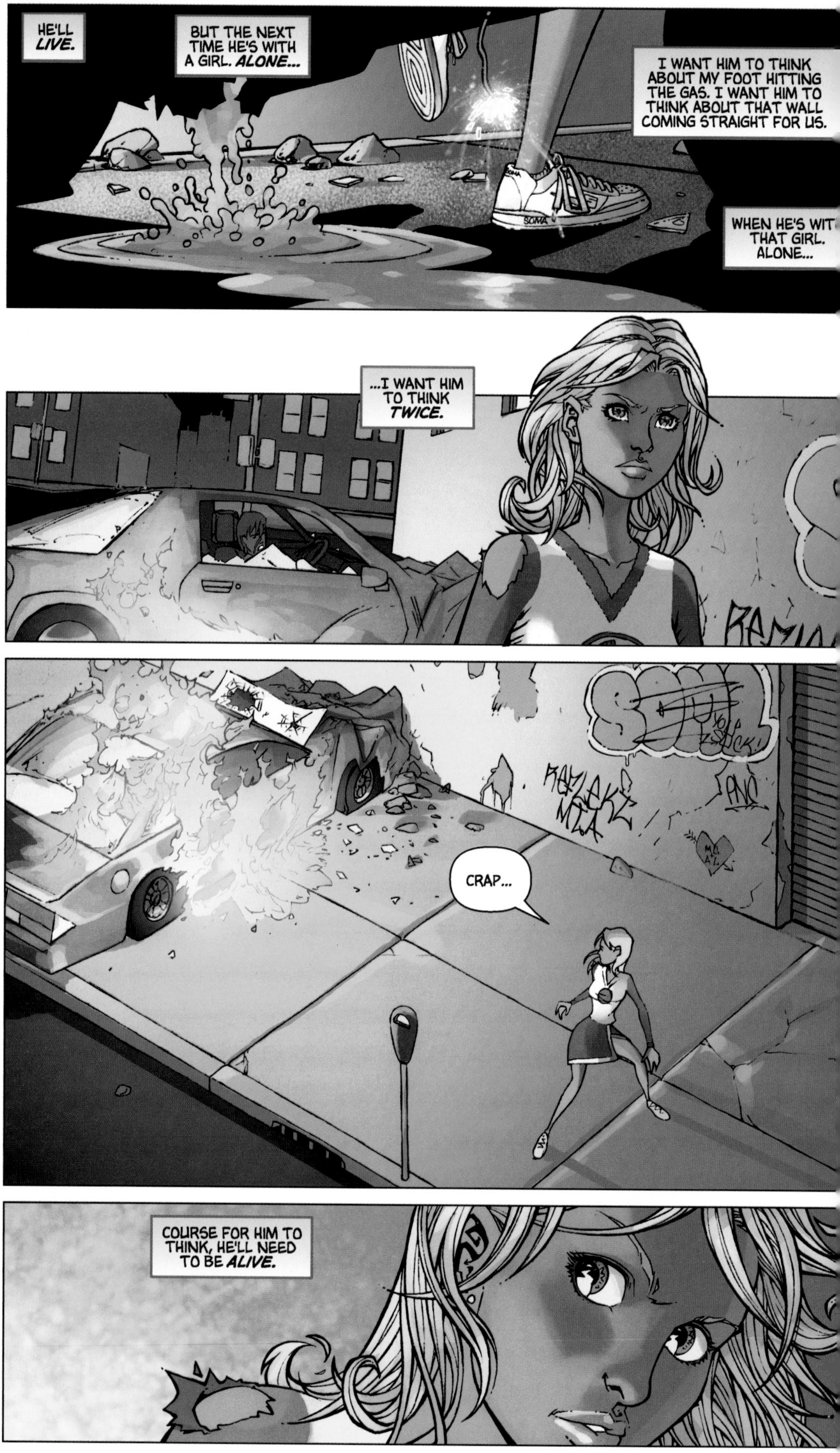
HE'LL *LIVE.*
BUT THE NEXT TIME HE'S WITH A GIRL. *ALONE...*
I WANT HIM TO THINK ABOUT MY FOOT HITTING THE GAS. I WANT HIM TO THINK ABOUT THAT WALL COMING STRAIGHT FOR US.
WHEN HE'S WIT THAT GIRL. ALONE...
...I WANT HIM TO THINK *TWICE.*
CRAP...
COURSE FOR HIM TO THINK, HE'LL NEED TO BE *ALIVE.*

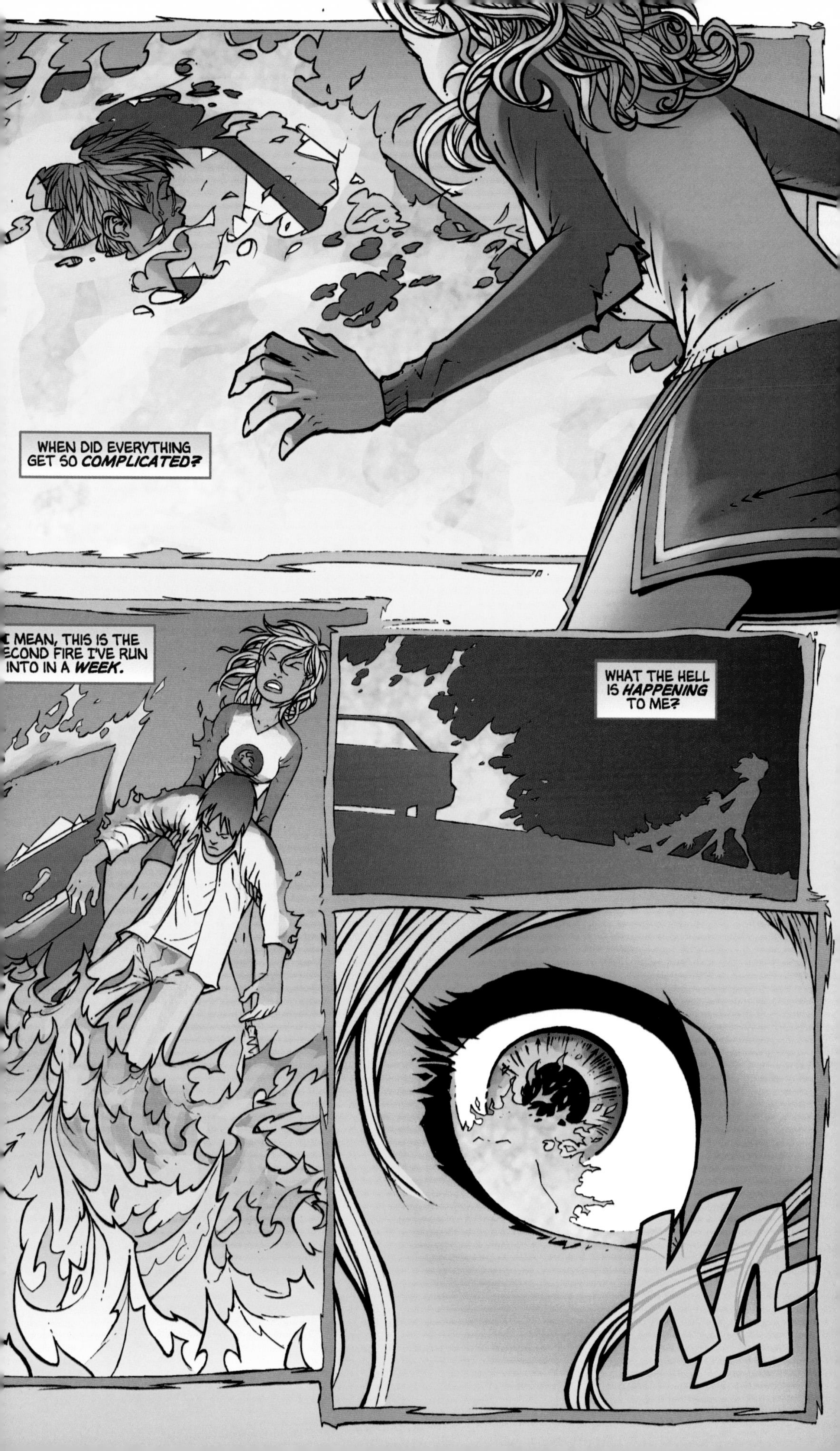
WHEN DID EVERYTHING GET SO *COMPLICATED?*
I MEAN, THIS IS THE SECOND FIRE I'VE RUN INTO IN A *WEEK.*
WHAT THE HELL IS *HAPPENING* TO ME?
KA-

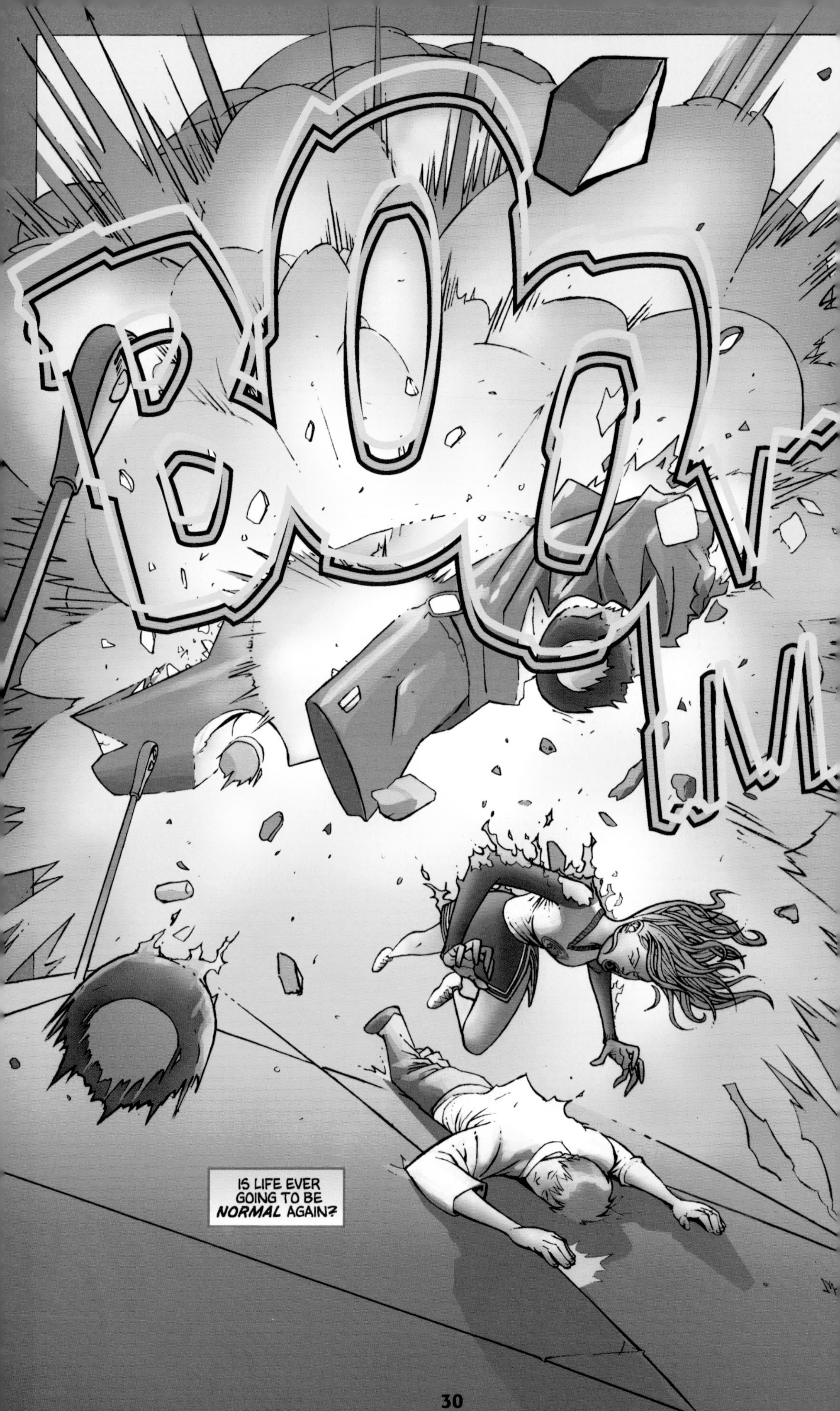
BOOOM
IS LIFE EVER GOING TO BE NORMAL AGAIN?

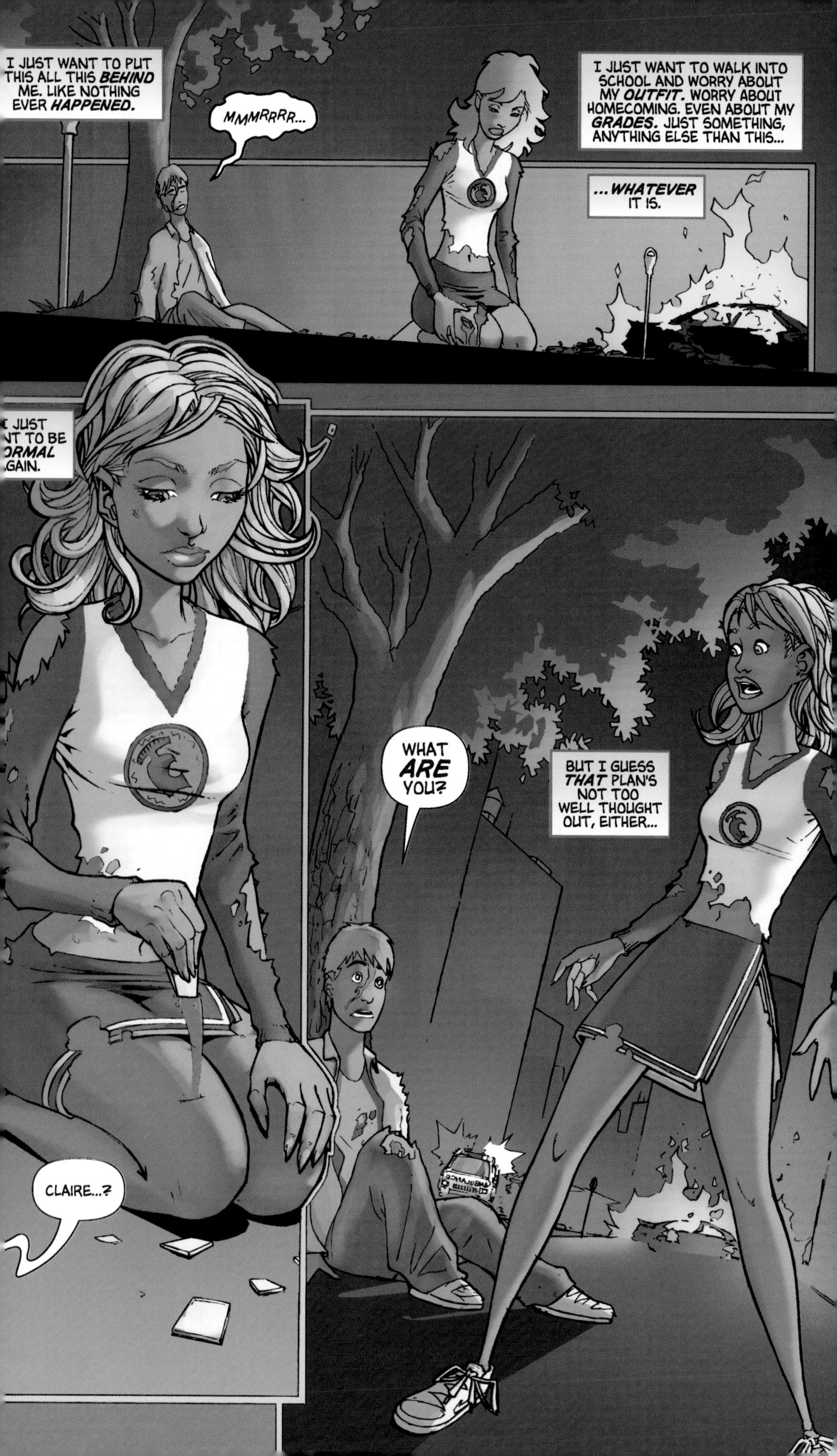
I JUST WANT TO PUT THIS ALL THIS *BEHIND* ME. LIKE NOTHING EVER *HAPPENED.*
MMMRRRR...
I JUST WANT TO WALK INTO SCHOOL AND WORRY ABOUT MY *OUTFIT.* WORRY ABOUT HOMECOMING. EVEN ABOUT MY *GRADES.* JUST SOMETHING, ANYTHING ELSE THAN THIS...
...*WHATEVER* IT IS.
I JUST NT TO BE ORMAL GAIN.
CLAIRE...?
WHAT *ARE* YOU?
BUT I GUESS *THAT* PLAN'S NOT TOO WELL THOUGHT OUT, EITHER...

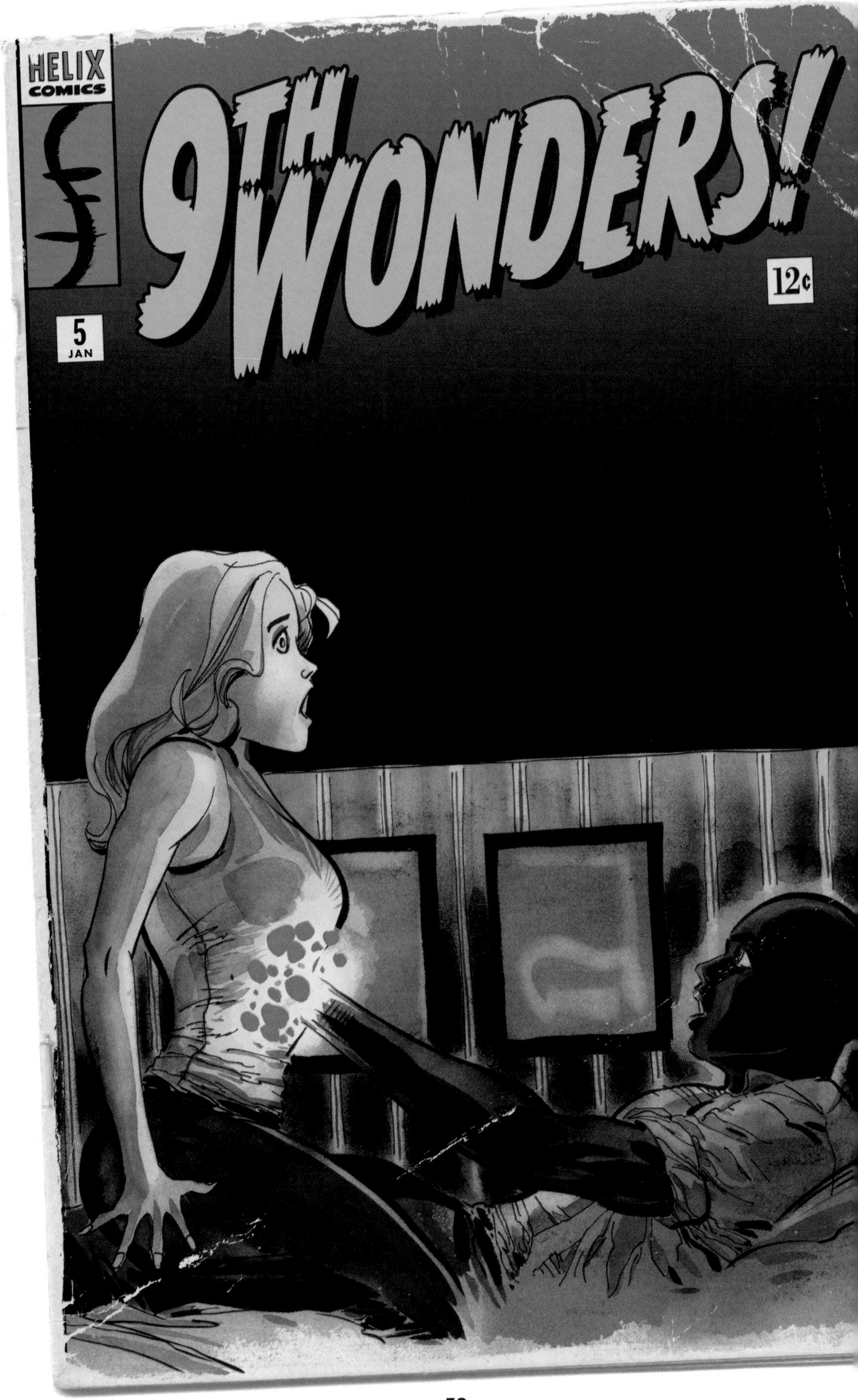
HELIX COMICS
9TH WONDERS!
12¢
5
JAN

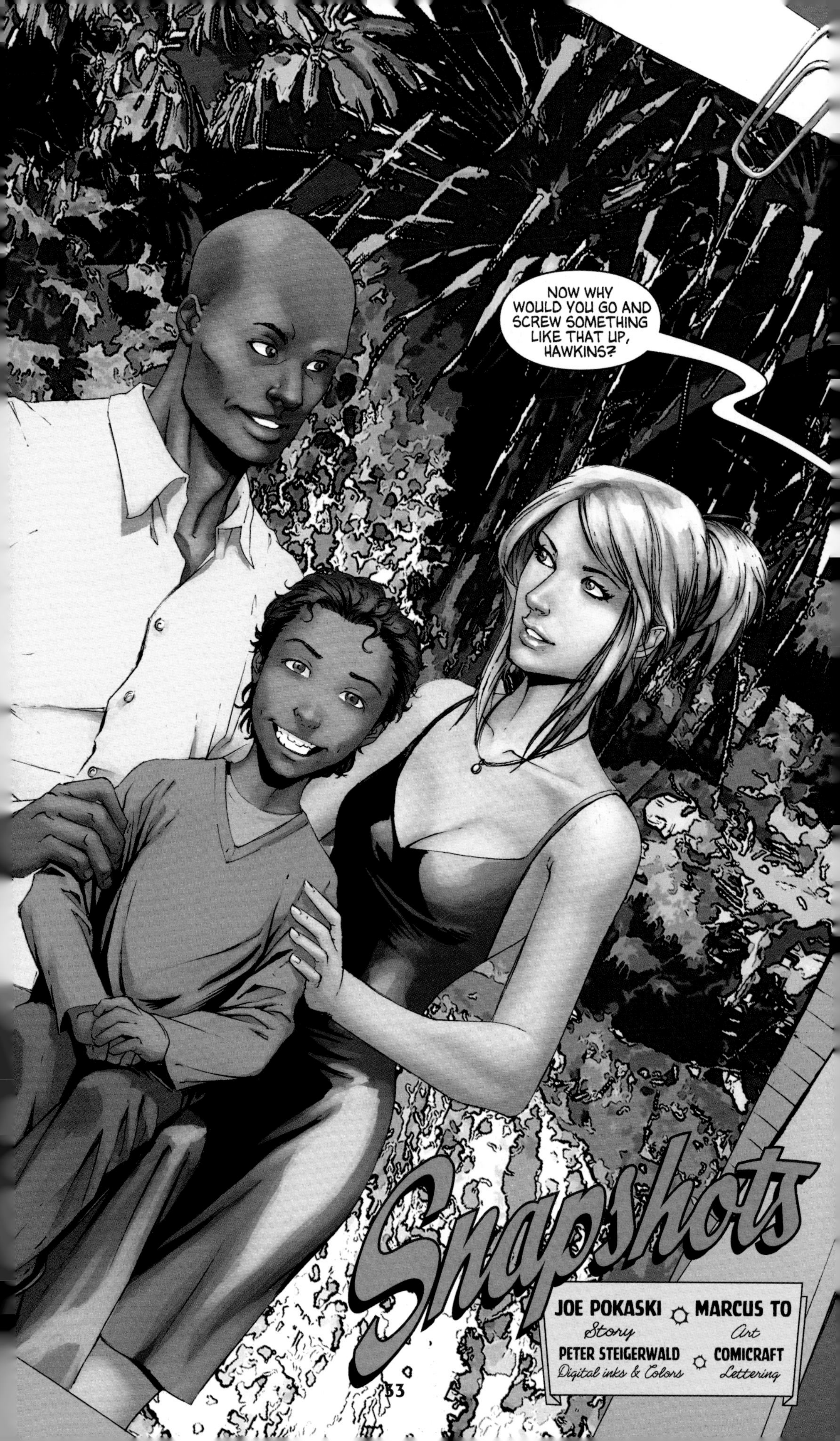
NOW WHY WOULD YOU GO AND SCREW SOMETHING LIKE THAT UP, HAWKINS?
Snapshots
JOE POKASKI Story
MARCUS TO Art
PETER STEIGERWALD Digital inks & Colors
COMICRAFT Lettering
33

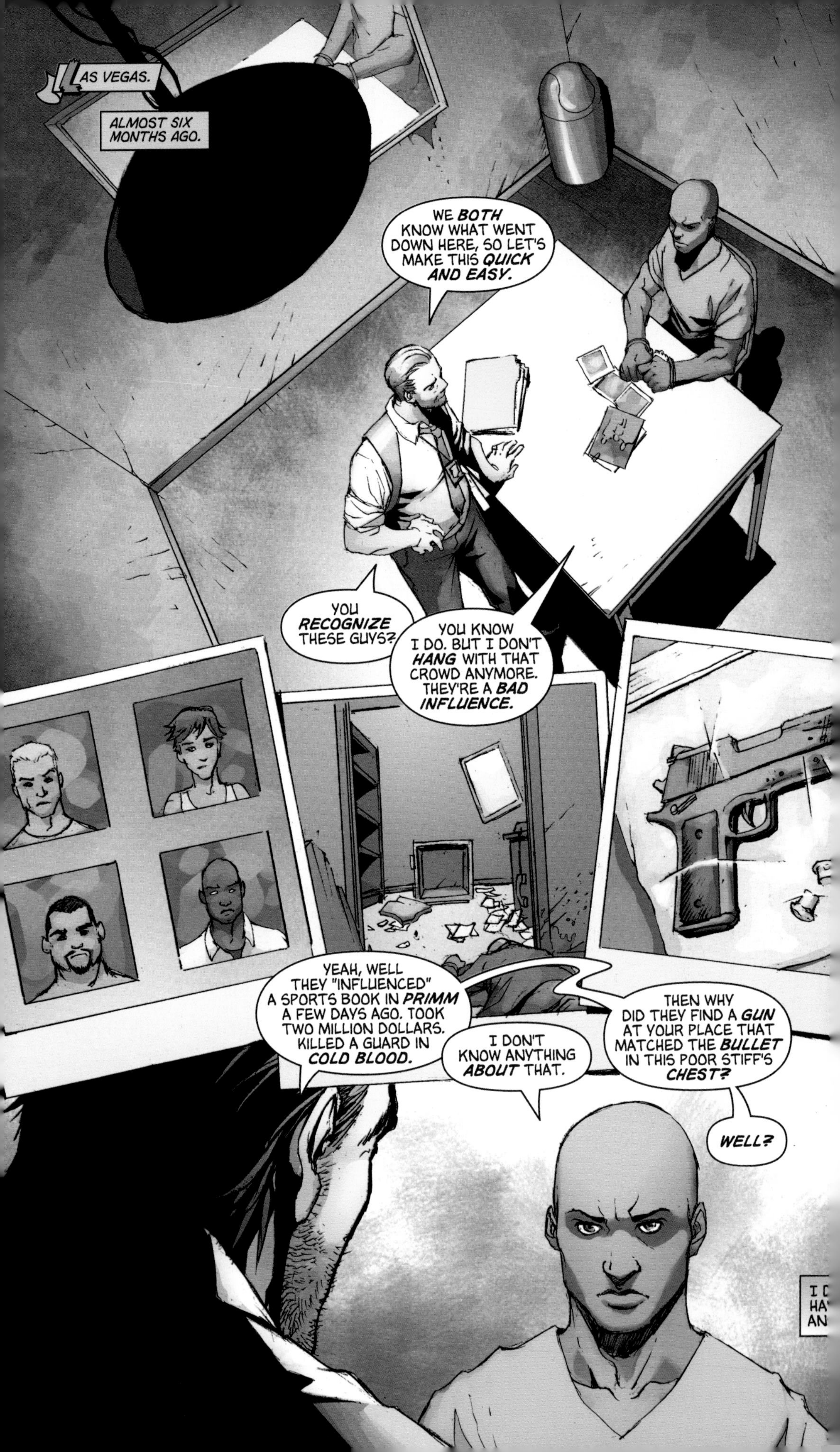
LAS VEGAS.
ALMOST SIX MONTHS AGO.
WE BOTH KNOW WHAT WENT DOWN HERE, SO LET'S MAKE THIS QUICK AND EASY.
YOU RECOGNIZE THESE GUYS?
YOU KNOW I DO. BUT I DON'T HANG WITH THAT CROWD ANYMORE. THEY'RE A BAD INFLUENCE.
YEAH, WELL THEY "INFLUENCED" A SPORTS BOOK IN PRIMM A FEW DAYS AGO. TOOK TWO MILLION DOLLARS. KILLED A GUARD IN COLD BLOOD.
I DON'T KNOW ANYTHING ABOUT THAT.
THEN WHY DID THEY FIND A GUN AT YOUR PLACE THAT MATCHED THE BULLET IN THIS POOR STIFF'S CHEST?
WELL?

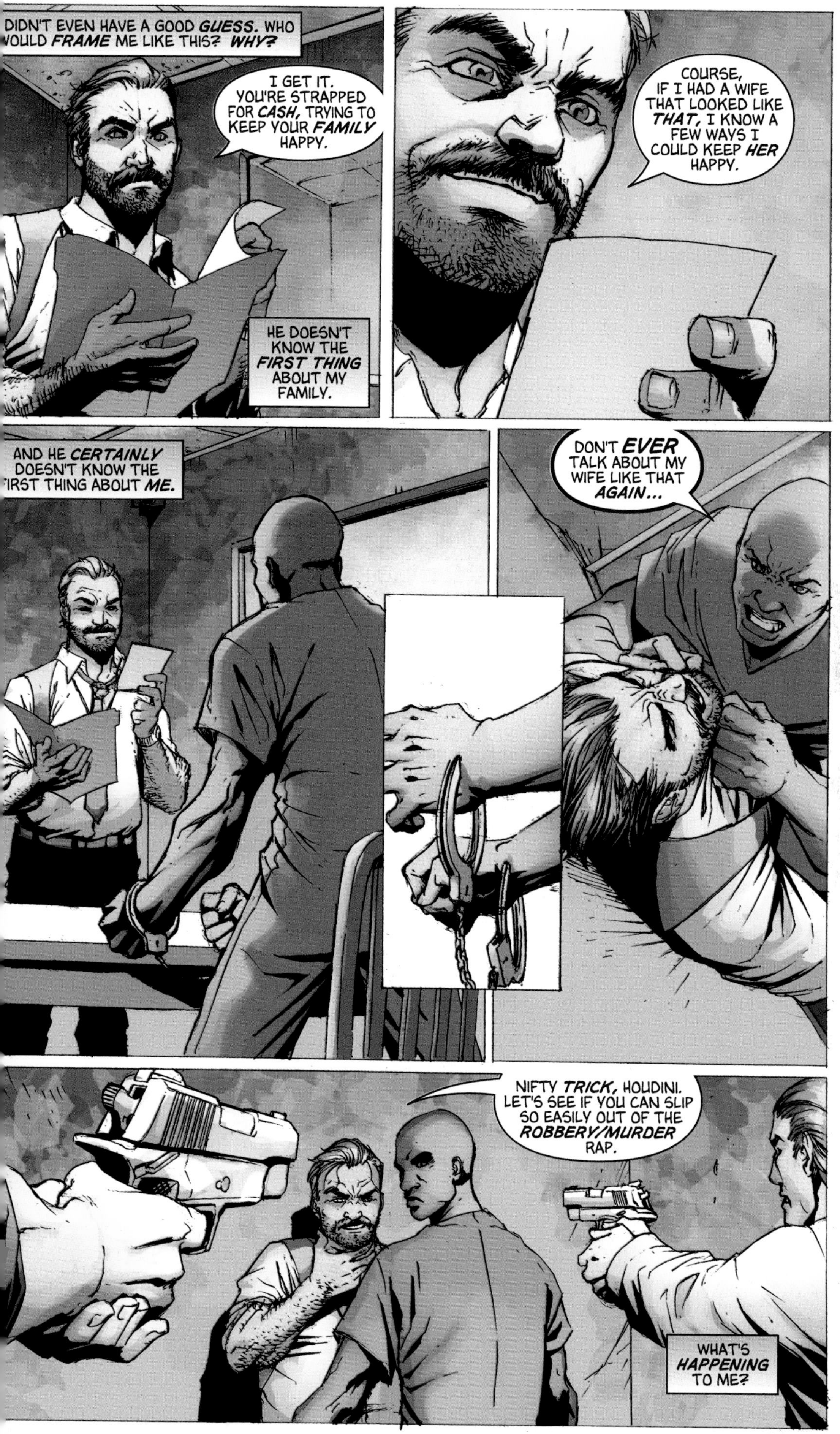
DIDN'T EVEN HAVE A GOOD GUESS. WHO WOULD FRAME ME LIKE THIS? WHY?
I GET IT. YOU'RE STRAPPED FOR CASH, TRYING TO KEEP YOUR FAMILY HAPPY.
HE DOESN'T KNOW THE FIRST THING ABOUT MY FAMILY.
COURSE, IF I HAD A WIFE THAT LOOKED LIKE THAT, I KNOW A FEW WAYS I COULD KEEP HER HAPPY.
AND HE CERTAINLY DOESN'T KNOW THE FIRST THING ABOUT ME.
DON'T EVER TALK ABOUT MY WIFE LIKE THAT AGAIN...
NIFTY TRICK, HOUDINI. LET'S SEE IF YOU CAN SLIP SO EASILY OUT OF THE ROBBERY/MURDER RAP.
WHAT'S HAPPENING TO ME?

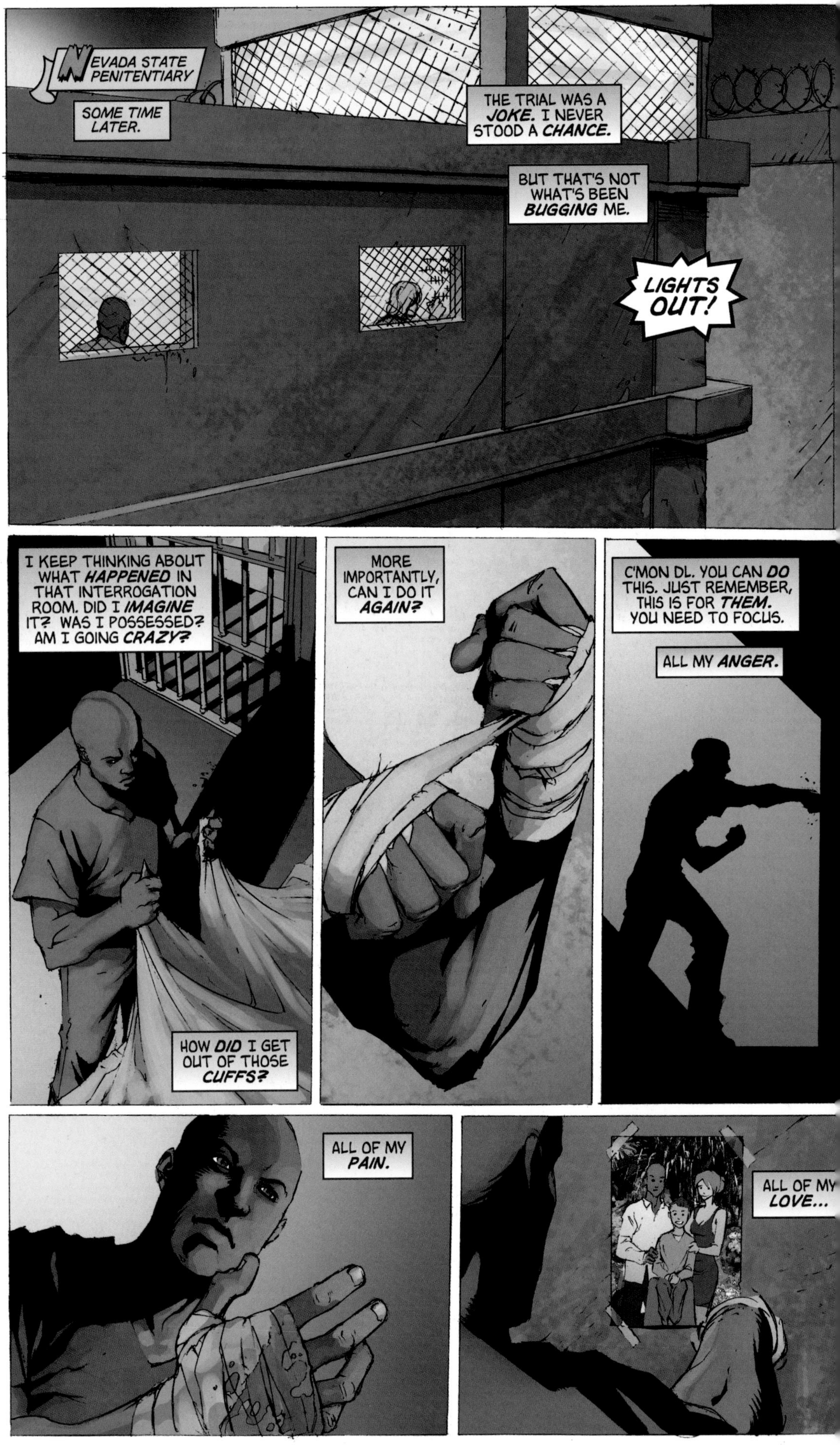
NEVADA STATE PENITENTIARY
SOME TIME LATER.
THE TRIAL WAS A JOKE. I NEVER STOOD A CHANCE.
BUT THAT'S NOT WHAT'S BEEN BUGGING ME.
LIGHTS OUT!
I KEEP THINKING ABOUT WHAT HAPPENED IN THAT INTERROGATION ROOM. DID I IMAGINE IT? WAS I POSSESSED? AM I GOING CRAZY?
HOW DID I GET OUT OF THOSE CUFFS?
MORE IMPORTANTLY, CAN I DO IT AGAIN?
C'MON DL. YOU CAN DO THIS. JUST REMEMBER, THIS IS FOR THEM. YOU NEED TO FOCUS.
ALL MY ANGER.
ALL OF MY PAIN.
ALL OF MY LOVE...

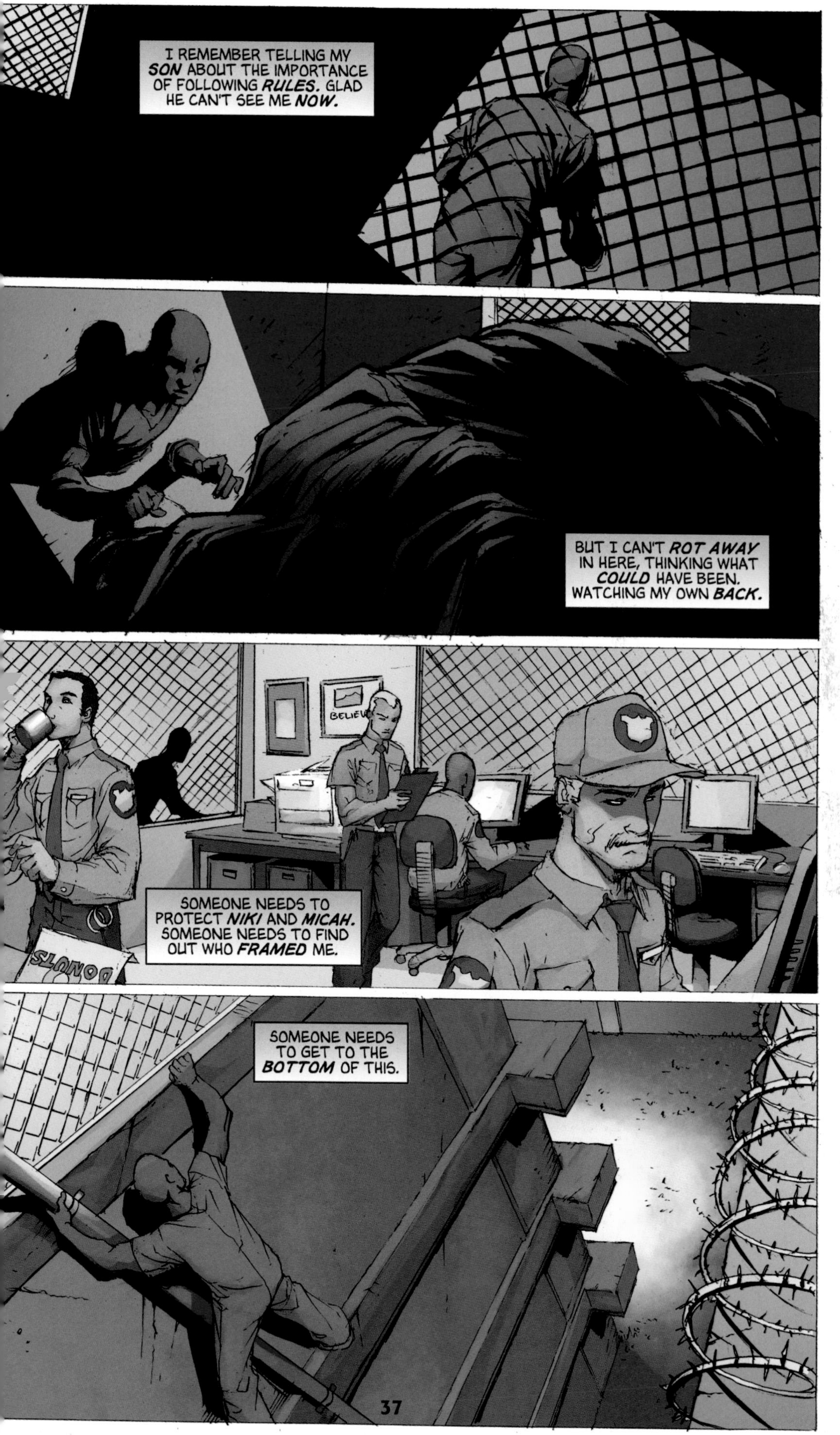
I REMEMBER TELLING MY SON ABOUT THE IMPORTANCE OF FOLLOWING RULES. GLAD HE CAN'T SEE ME NOW.
BUT I CAN'T ROT AWAY IN HERE, THINKING WHAT COULD HAVE BEEN. WATCHING MY OWN BACK.
SOMEONE NEEDS TO PROTECT NIKI AND MICAH. SOMEONE NEEDS TO FIND OUT WHO FRAMED ME.
SOMEONE NEEDS TO GET TO THE BOTTOM OF THIS.

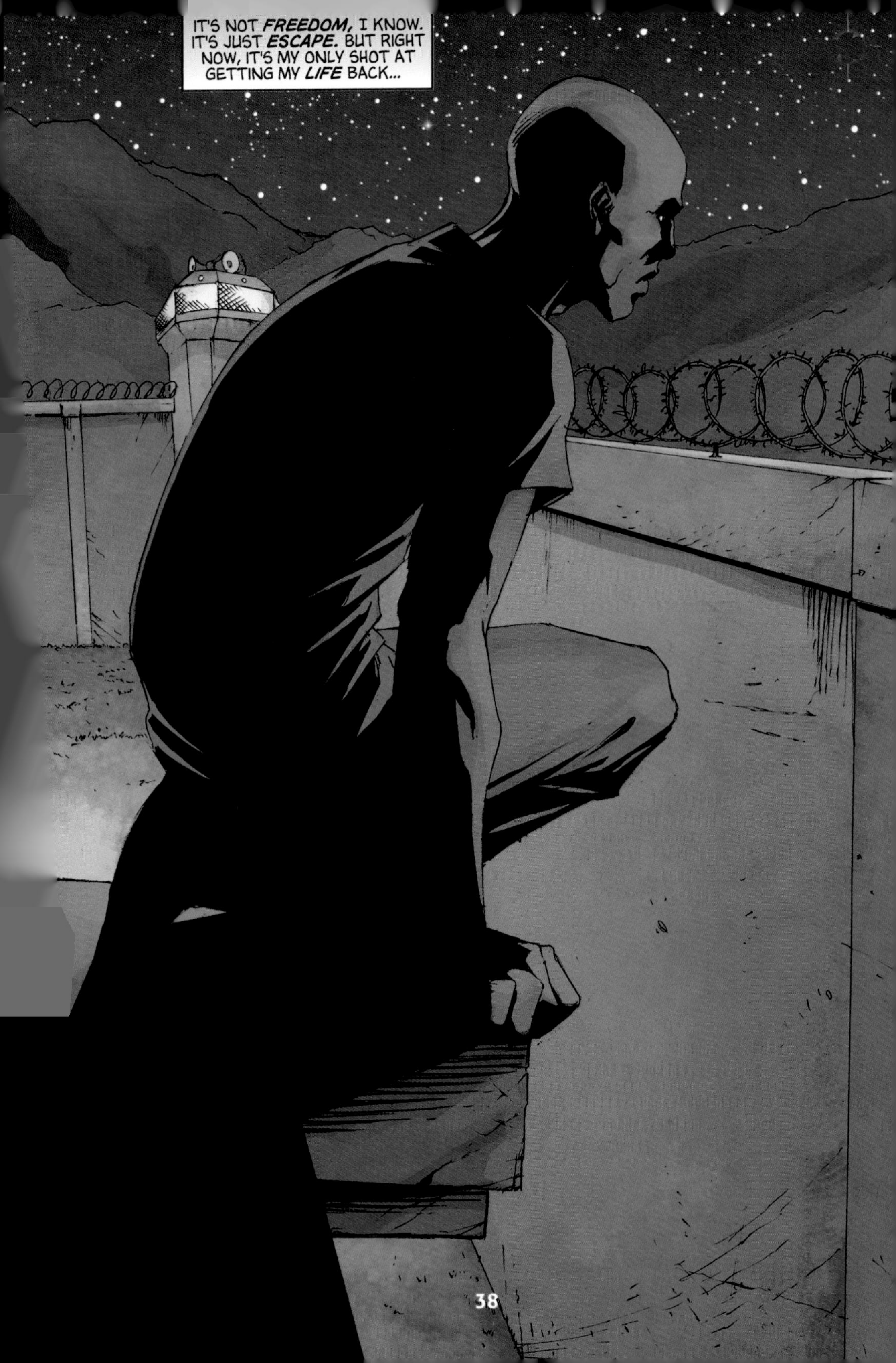
IT'S NOT FREEDOM, I KNOW. IT'S JUST ESCAPE. BUT RIGHT NOW, IT'S MY ONLY SHOT AT GETTING MY LIFE BACK...

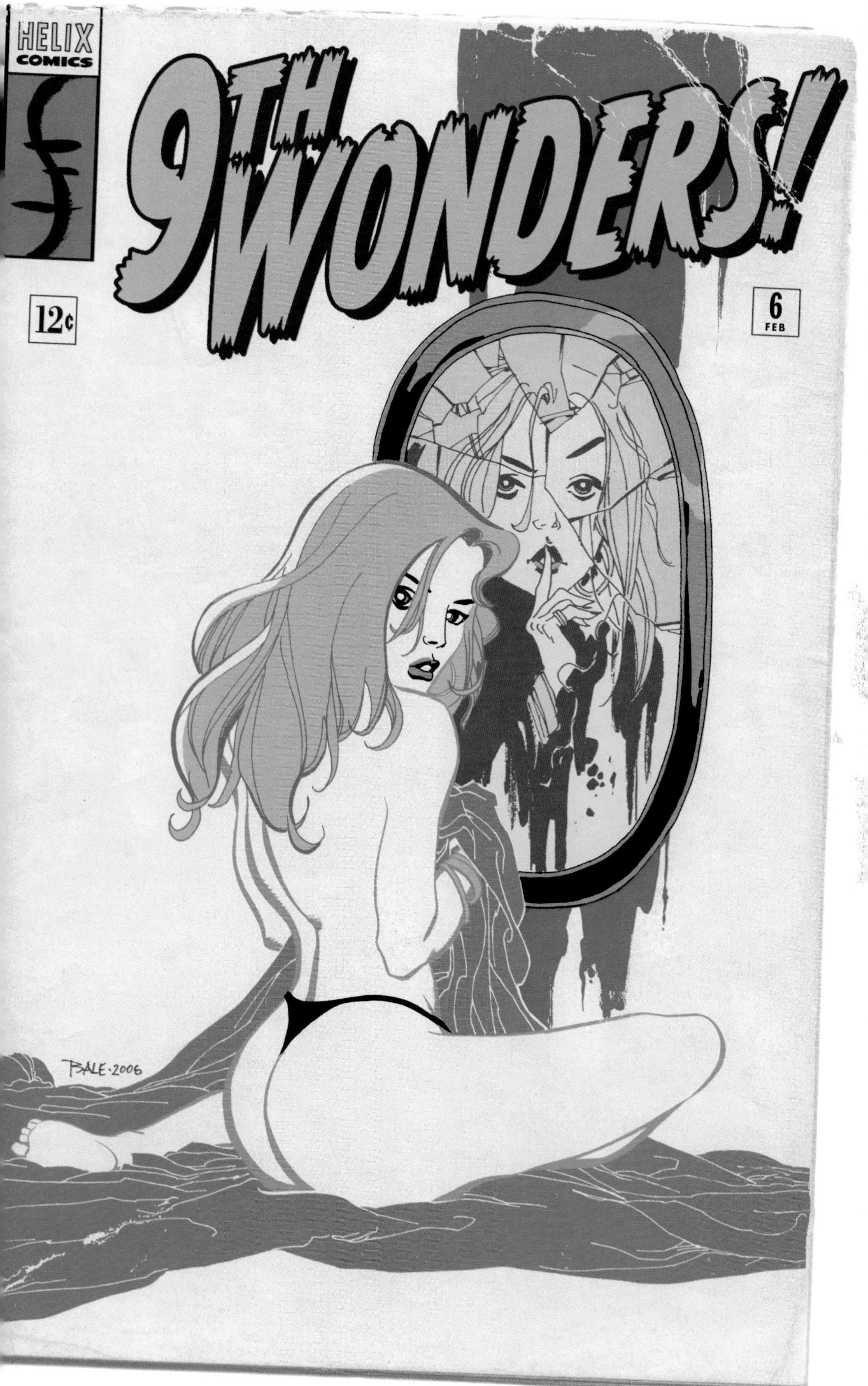
HELIX COMICS
9TH WONDERS!
12¢
6 FEB
BALE·2006

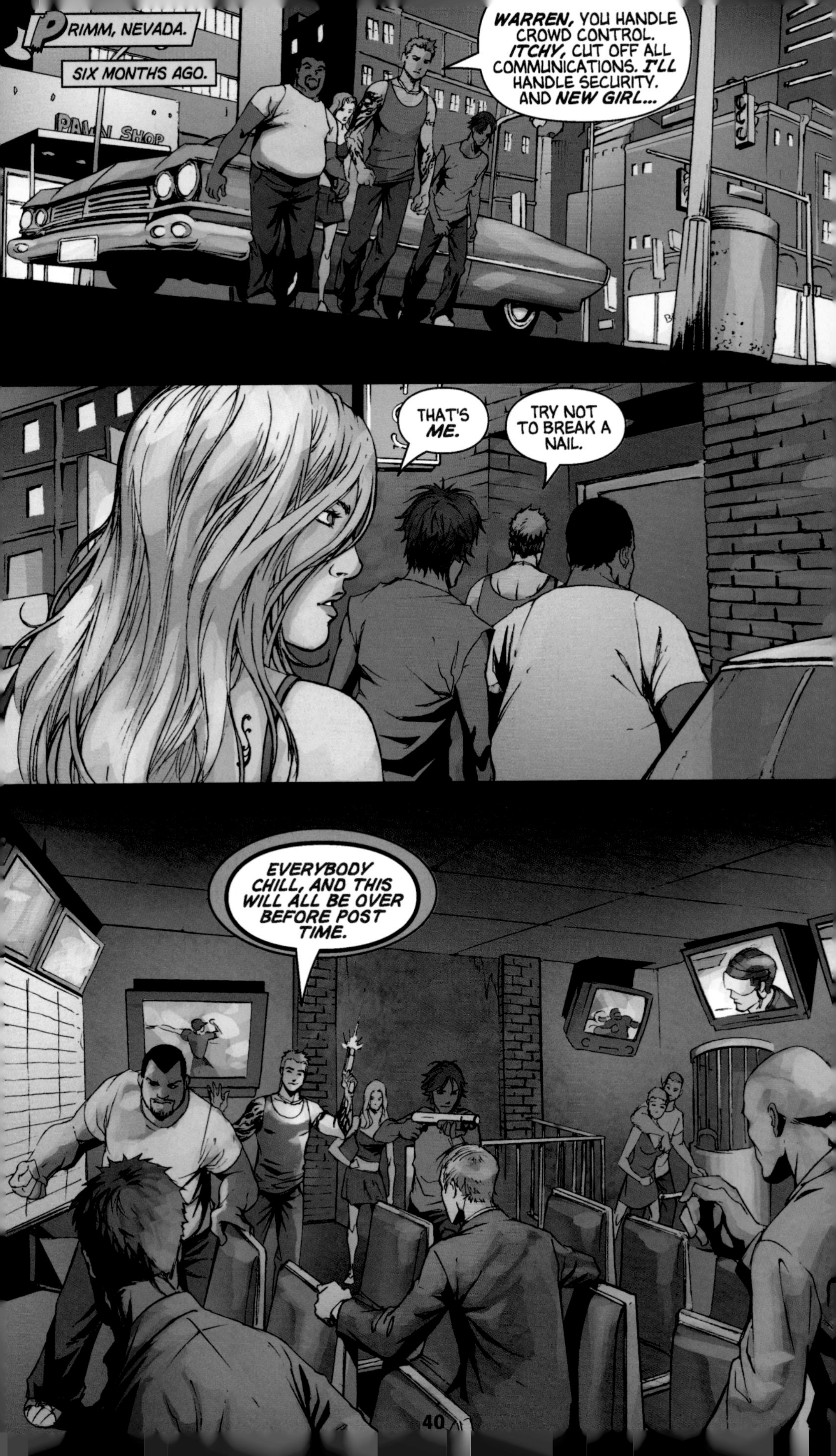
PRIMM, NEVADA.
SIX MONTHS AGO.
PAWN SHOP
WARREN, YOU HANDLE CROWD CONTROL. ITCHY, CUT OFF ALL COMMUNICATIONS. I'LL HANDLE SECURITY. AND NEW GIRL...
THAT'S ME.
TRY NOT TO BREAK A NAIL.
EVERYBODY CHILL, AND THIS WILL ALL BE OVER BEFORE POST TIME.

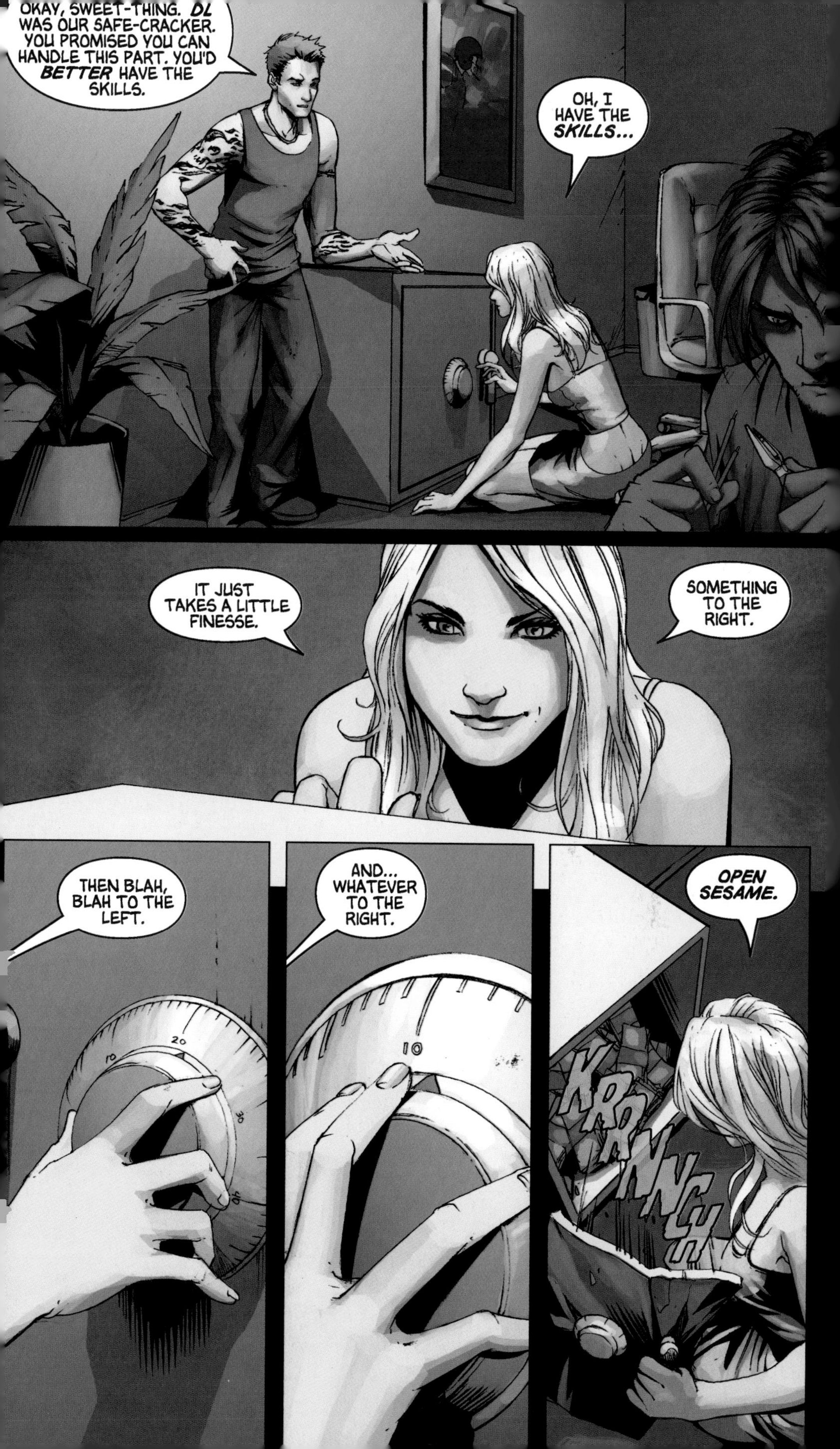
OKAY, SWEET-THING. DL WAS OUR SAFE-CRACKER. YOU PROMISED YOU CAN HANDLE THIS PART. YOU'D BETTER HAVE THE SKILLS.
OH, I HAVE THE SKILLS...
IT JUST TAKES A LITTLE FINESSE.
SOMETHING TO THE RIGHT.
THEN BLAH, BLAH TO THE LEFT.
AND... WHATEVER TO THE RIGHT.
OPEN SESAME.
KRANNCH

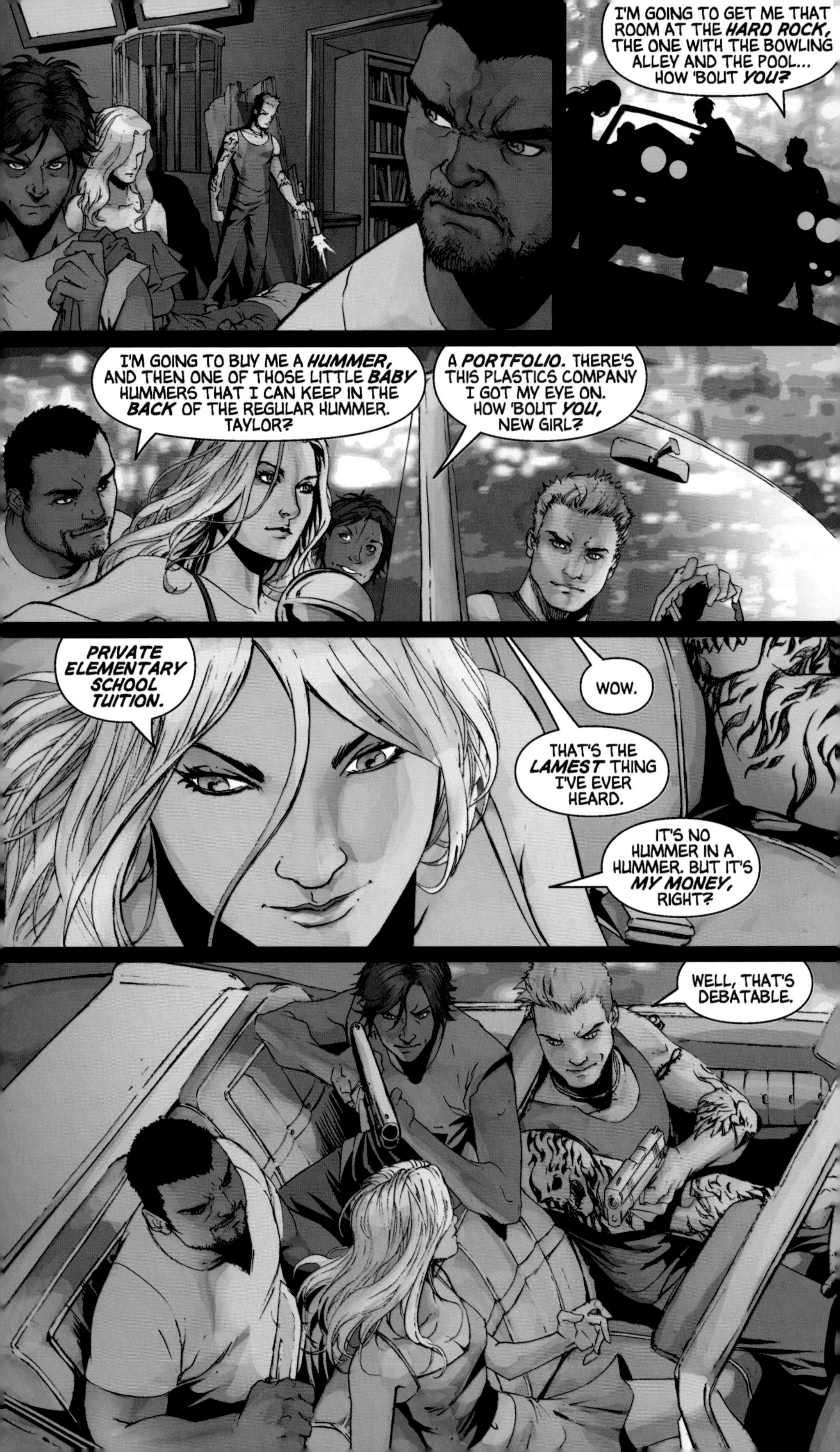
I'M GOING TO GET ME THAT ROOM AT THE HARD ROCK, THE ONE WITH THE BOWLING ALLEY AND THE POOL... HOW 'BOUT YOU?
I'M GOING TO BUY ME A HUMMER, AND THEN ONE OF THOSE LITTLE BABY HUMMERS THAT I CAN KEEP IN THE BACK OF THE REGULAR HUMMER. TAYLOR?
A PORTFOLIO. THERE'S THIS PLASTICS COMPANY I GOT MY EYE ON. HOW 'BOUT YOU, NEW GIRL?
PRIVATE ELEMENTARY SCHOOL TUITION.
WOW.
THAT'S THE LAMEST THING I'VE EVER HEARD.
IT'S NO HUMMER IN A HUMMER. BUT IT'S MY MONEY, RIGHT?
WELL, THAT'S DEBATABLE.

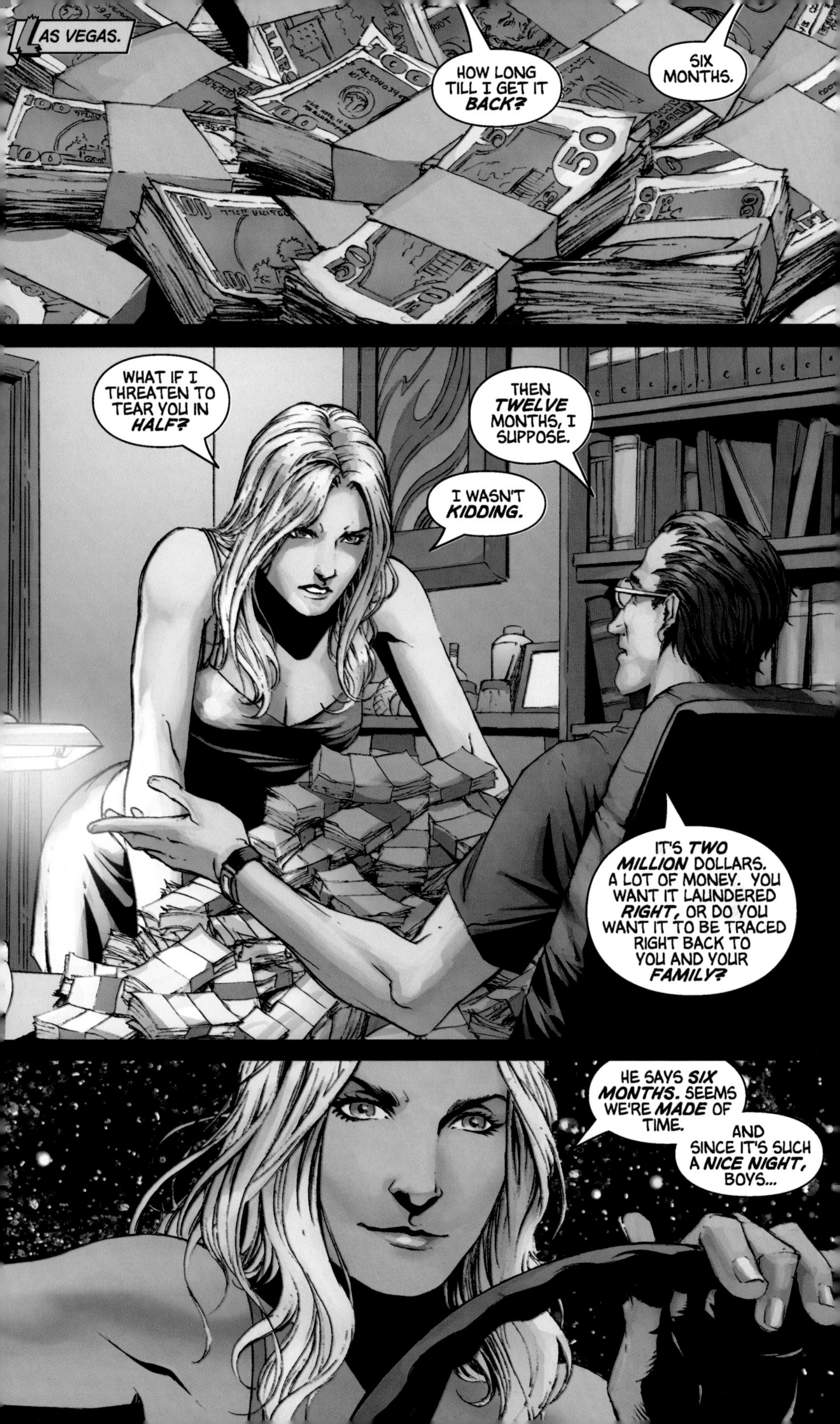
LAS VEGAS.
HOW LONG TILL I GET IT BACK?
SIX MONTHS.
WHAT IF I THREATEN TO TEAR YOU IN HALF?
THEN TWELVE MONTHS, I SUPPOSE.
I WASN'T KIDDING.
IT'S TWO MILLION DOLLARS. A LOT OF MONEY. YOU WANT IT LAUNDERED RIGHT, OR DO YOU WANT IT TO BE TRACED RIGHT BACK TO YOU AND YOUR FAMILY?
HE SAYS SIX MONTHS. SEEMS WE'RE MADE OF TIME.
AND SINCE IT'S SUCH A NICE NIGHT, BOYS...

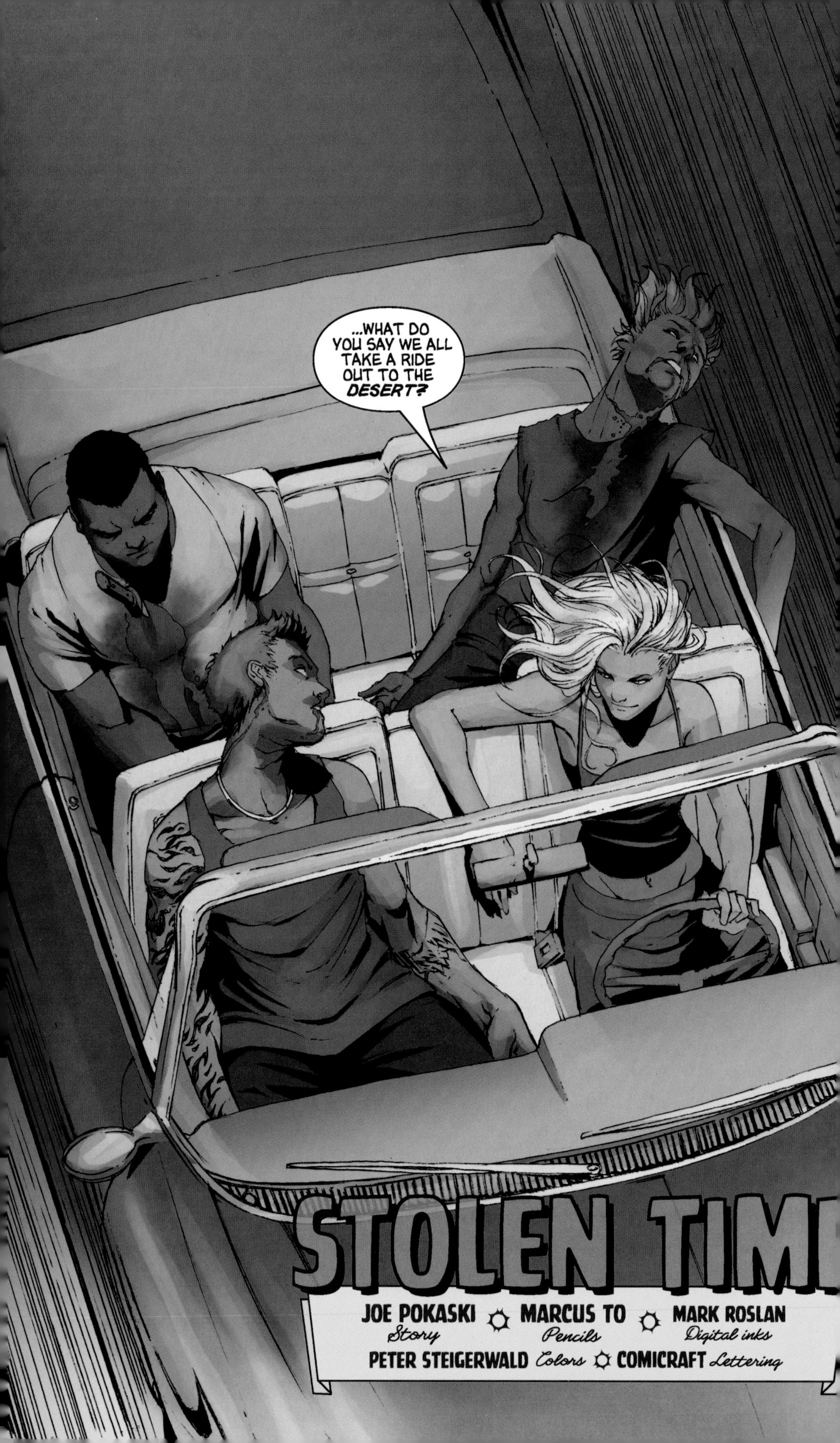
...WHAT DO YOU SAY WE ALL TAKE A RIDE OUT TO THE DESERT?
STOLEN TIM
JOE POKASKI Story
MARCUS TO Pencils
MARK ROSLAN Digital inks
PETER STEIGERWALD Colors
COMICRAFT Lettering

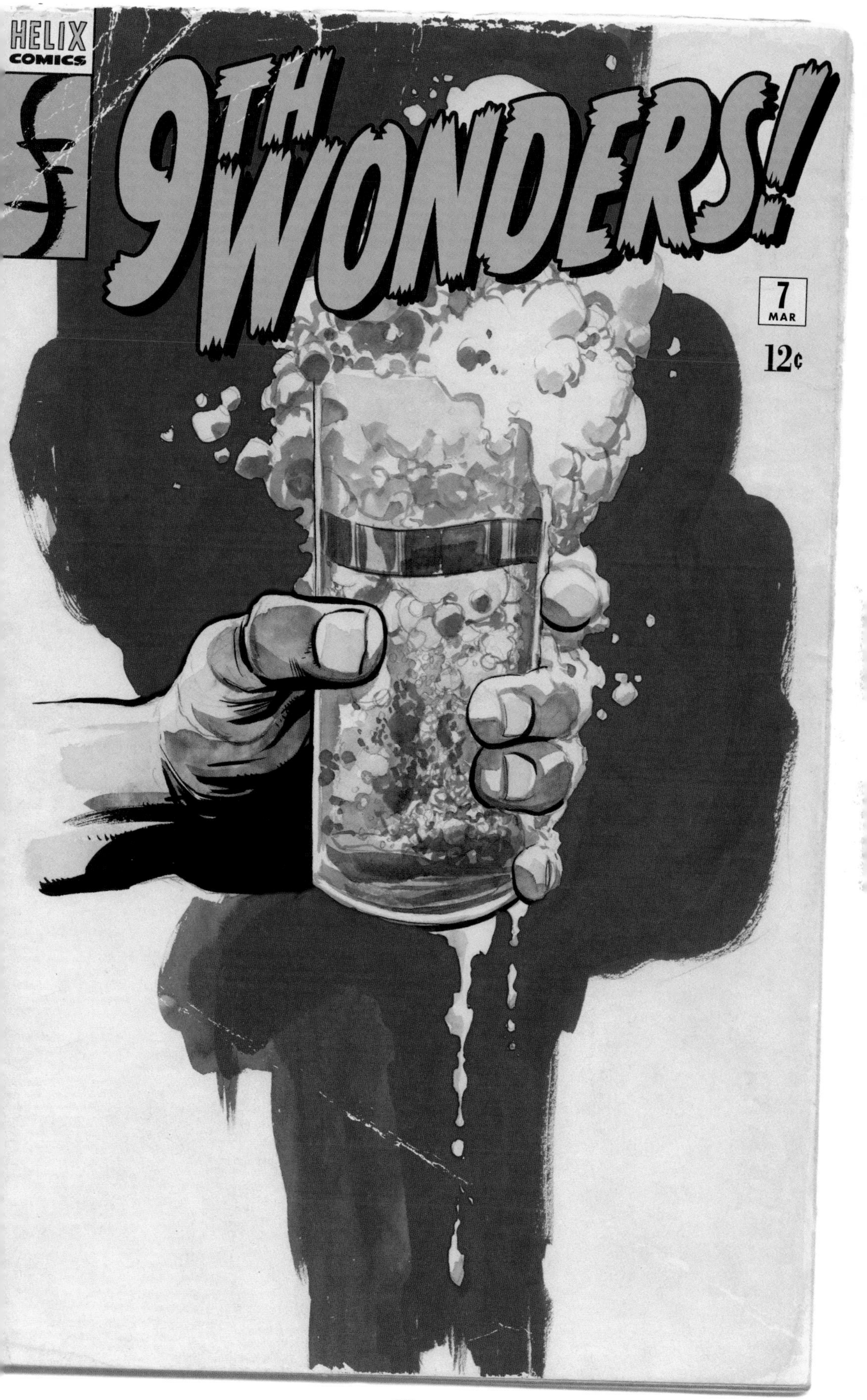
HELIX
COMICS
9TH WONDERS!
7
MAR
12¢

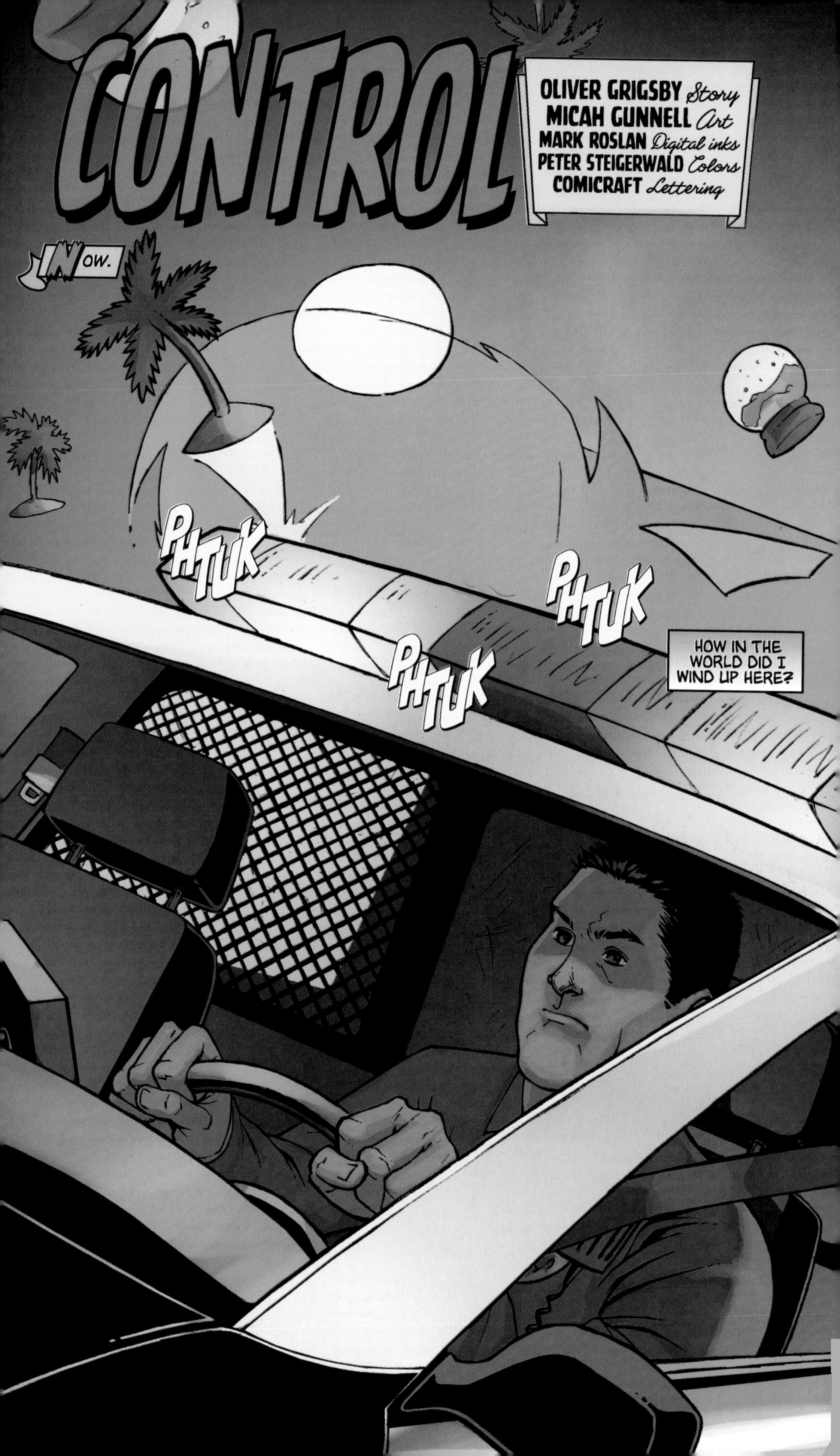
CONTROL
OLIVER GRIGSBY Story
MICAH GUNNELL Art
MARK ROSLAN Digital inks
PETER STEIGERWALD Colors
COMICRAFT Lettering
NOW.
PHTUK
PHTUK
PHTUK
HOW IN THE WORLD DID I WIND UP HERE?

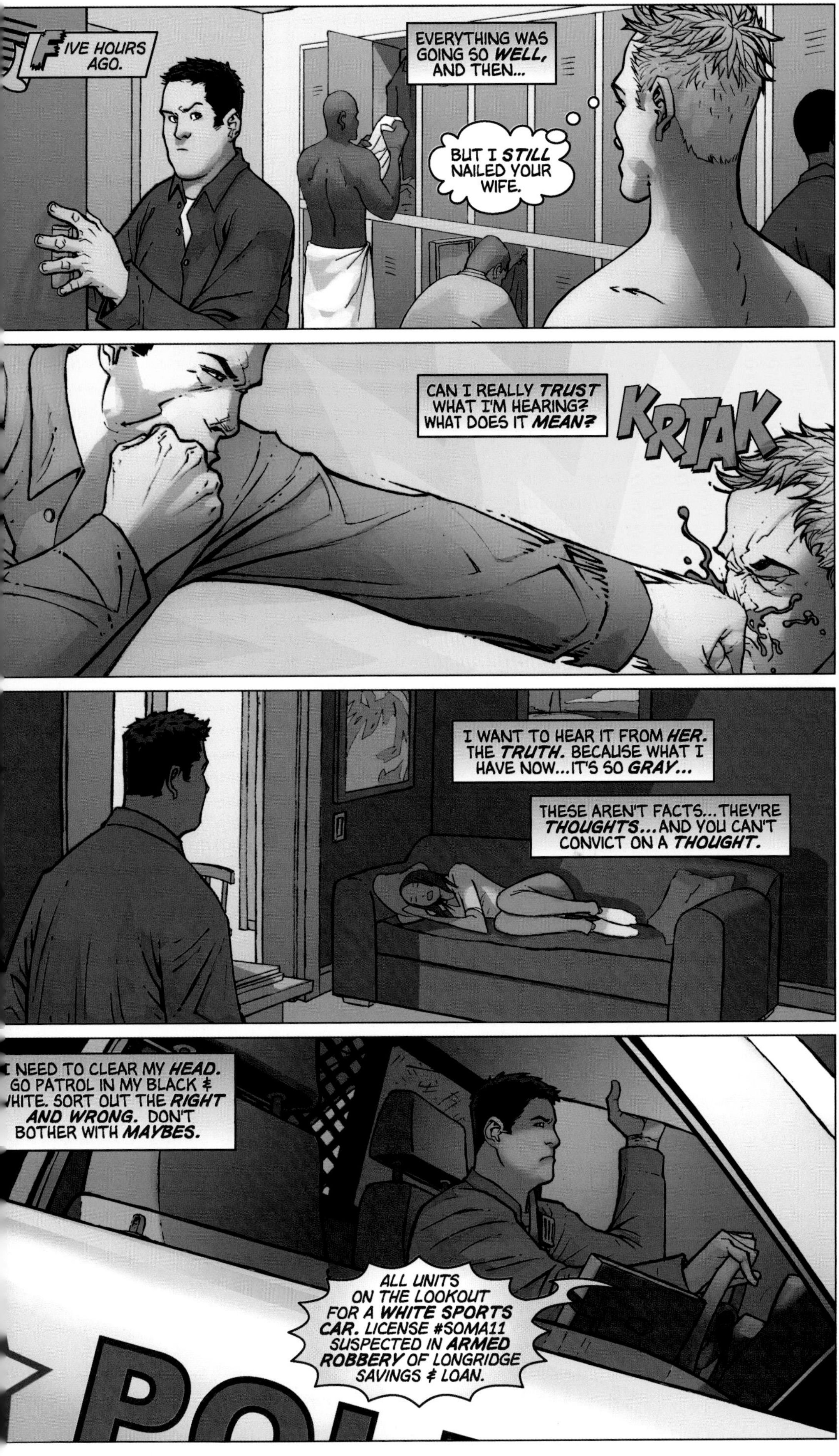
FIVE HOURS AGO.
EVERYTHING WAS GOING SO WELL, AND THEN...
BUT I STILL NAILED YOUR WIFE.
CAN I REALLY TRUST WHAT I'M HEARING? WHAT DOES IT MEAN?
KRTAK
I WANT TO HEAR IT FROM HER. THE TRUTH. BECAUSE WHAT I HAVE NOW...IT'S SO GRAY...
THESE AREN'T FACTS...THEY'RE THOUGHTS...AND YOU CAN'T CONVICT ON A THOUGHT.
I NEED TO CLEAR MY HEAD. GO PATROL IN MY BLACK & WHITE. SORT OUT THE RIGHT AND WRONG. DON'T BOTHER WITH MAYBES.
ALL UNITS ON THE LOOKOUT FOR A WHITE SPORTS CAR. LICENSE #SOMA11 SUSPECTED IN ARMED ROBBERY OF LONGRIDGE SAVINGS & LOAN.

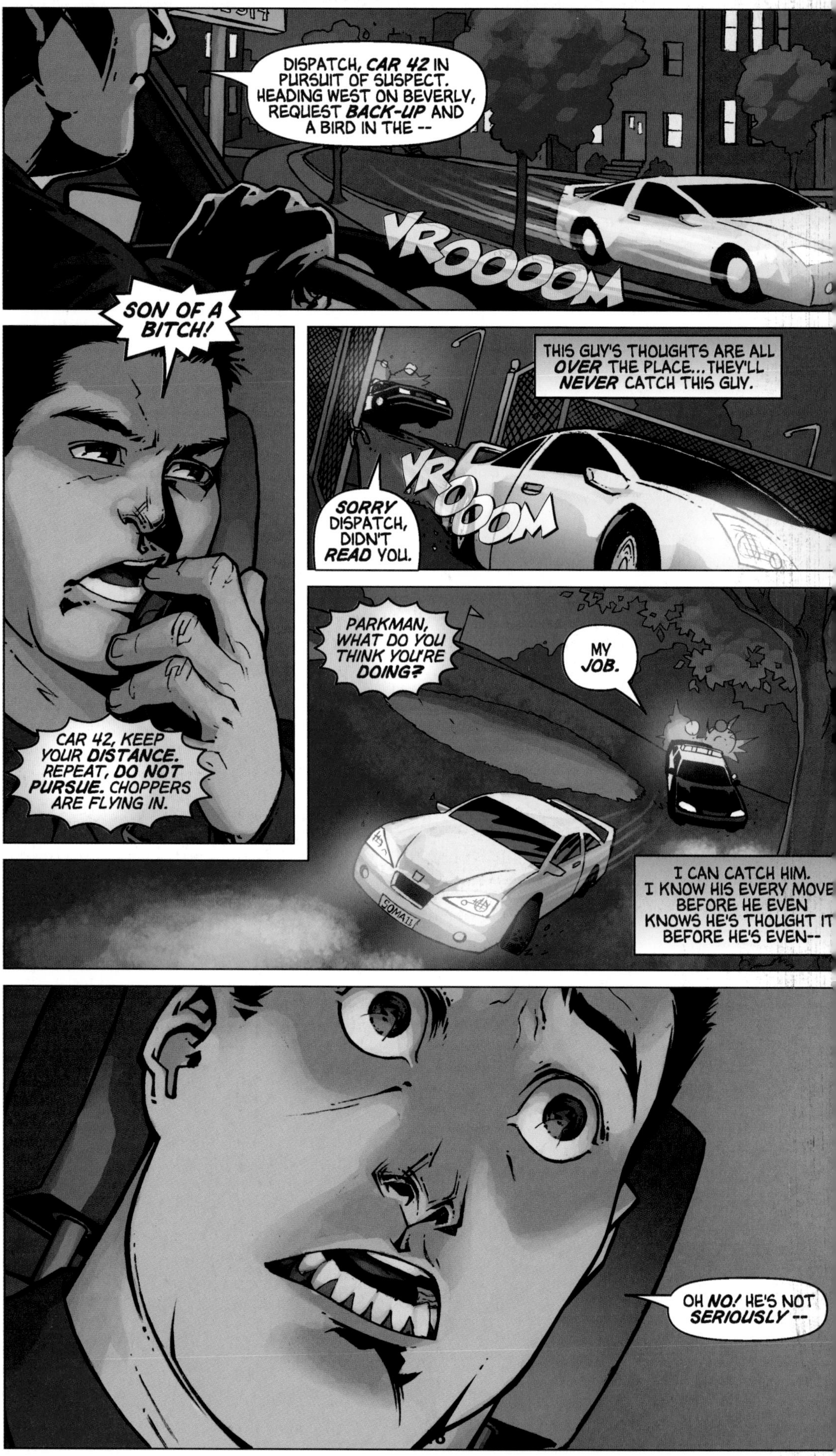
DISPATCH, CAR 42 IN PURSUIT OF SUSPECT. HEADING WEST ON BEVERLY, REQUEST BACK-UP AND A BIRD IN THE --
VROOOOM
SON OF A BITCH!
THIS GUY'S THOUGHTS ARE ALL OVER THE PLACE...THEY'LL NEVER CATCH THIS GUY.
VROOOM
SORRY DISPATCH, DIDN'T READ YOU.
CAR 42, KEEP YOUR DISTANCE. REPEAT, DO NOT PURSUE. CHOPPERS ARE FLYING IN.
PARKMAN, WHAT DO YOU THINK YOU'RE DOING?
MY JOB.
I CAN CATCH HIM. I KNOW HIS EVERY MOVE BEFORE HE EVEN KNOWS HE'S THOUGHT IT BEFORE HE'S EVEN--
OH NO! HE'S NOT SERIOUSLY --

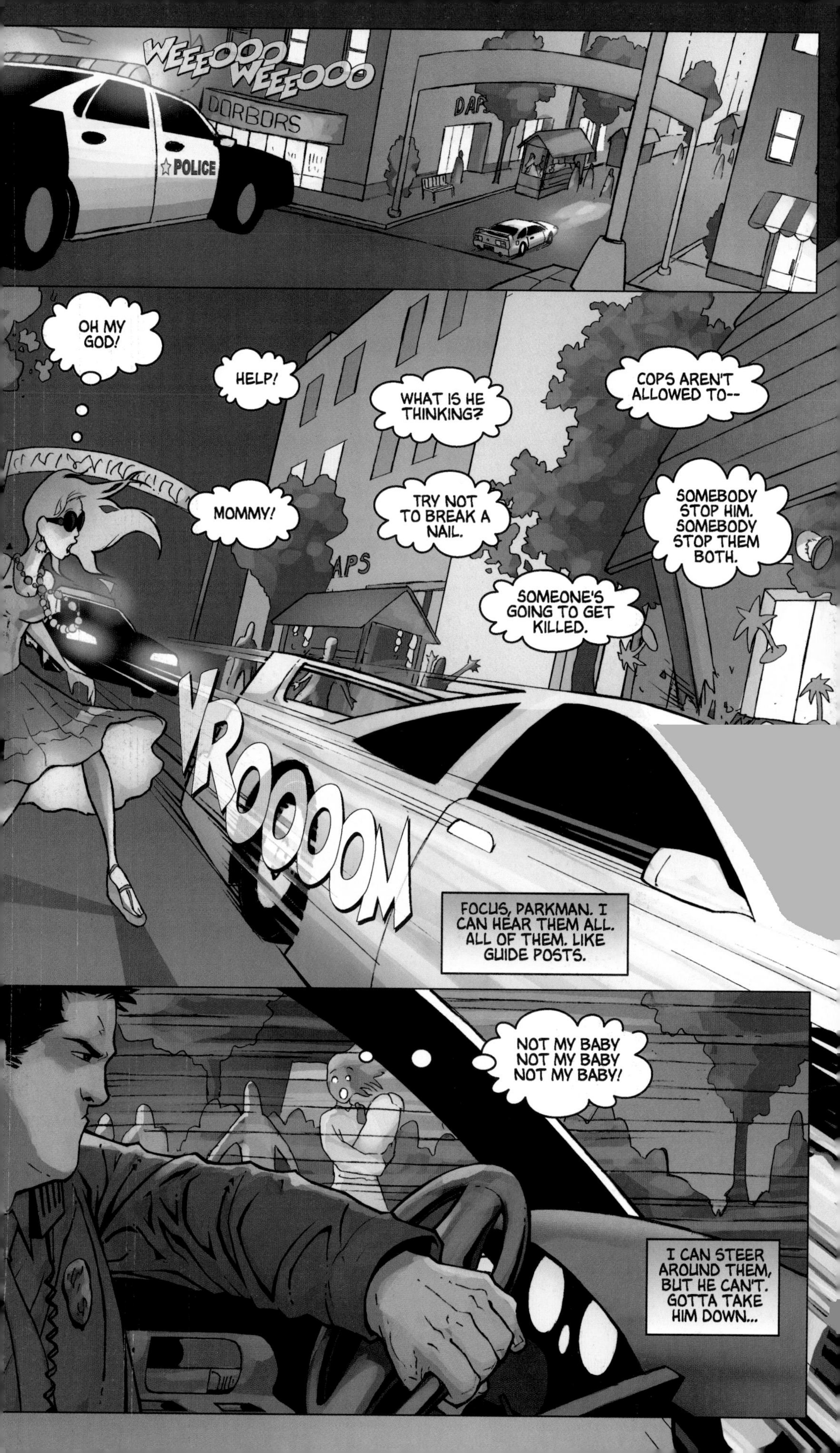

WEEEOOO WEEEOOO
POLICE
DORBORS
DAPS
OH MY GOD!
HELP!
WHAT IS HE THINKING?
COPS AREN'T ALLOWED TO--
MOMMY!
TRY NOT TO BREAK A NAIL.
SOMEBODY STOP HIM. SOMEBODY STOP THEM BOTH.
APS
SOMEONE'S GOING TO GET KILLED.
VROOOOM
FOCUS, PARKMAN. I CAN HEAR THEM ALL. ALL OF THEM. LIKE GUIDE POSTS.
NOT MY BABY NOT MY BABY NOT MY BABY!
I CAN STEER AROUND THEM, BUT HE CAN'T. GOTTA TAKE HIM DOWN...

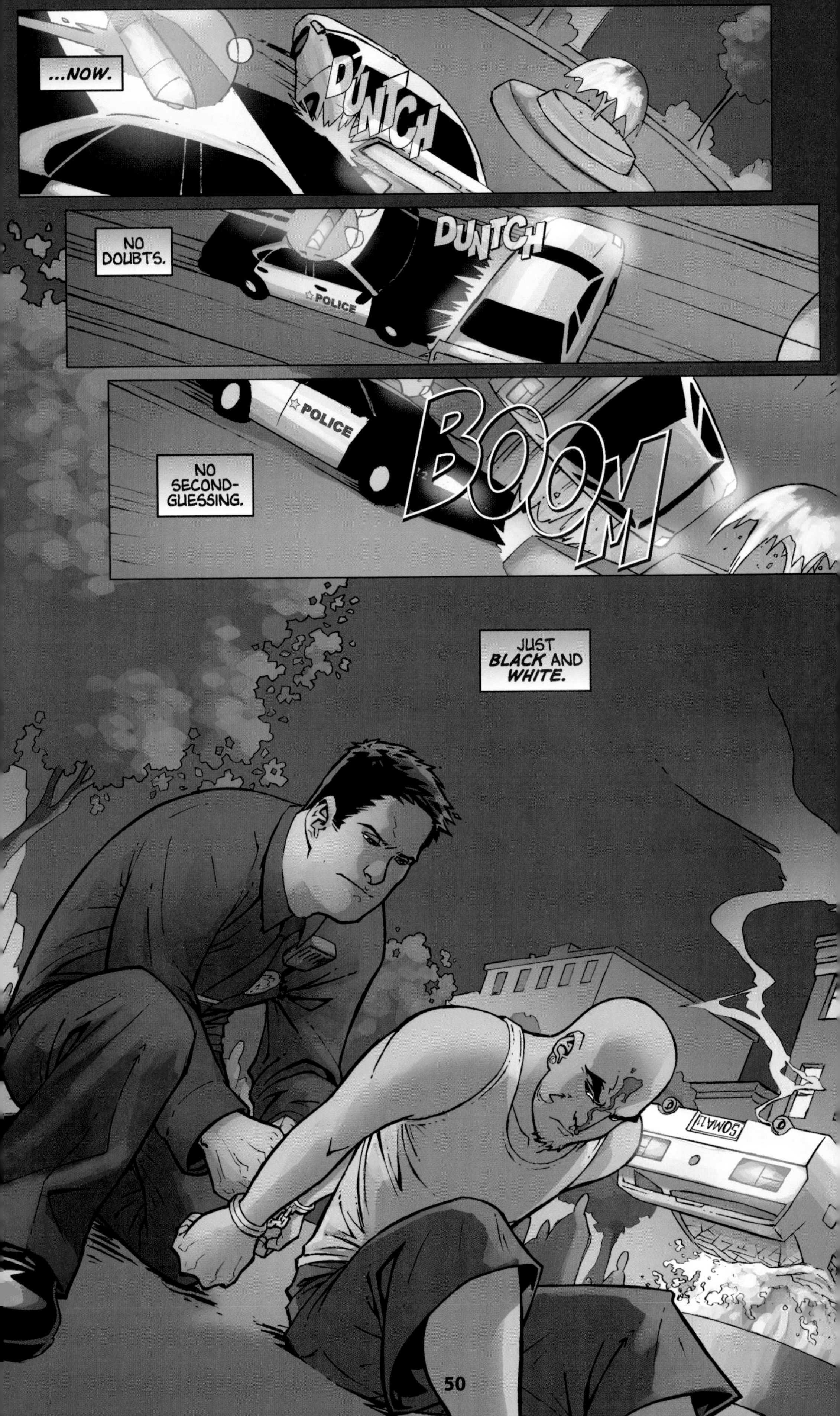
...NOW.
DUNTCH
NO DOUBTS.
DUNTCH
POLICE
POLICE
BOOM
NO SECOND-GUESSING.
JUST BLACK AND WHITE.

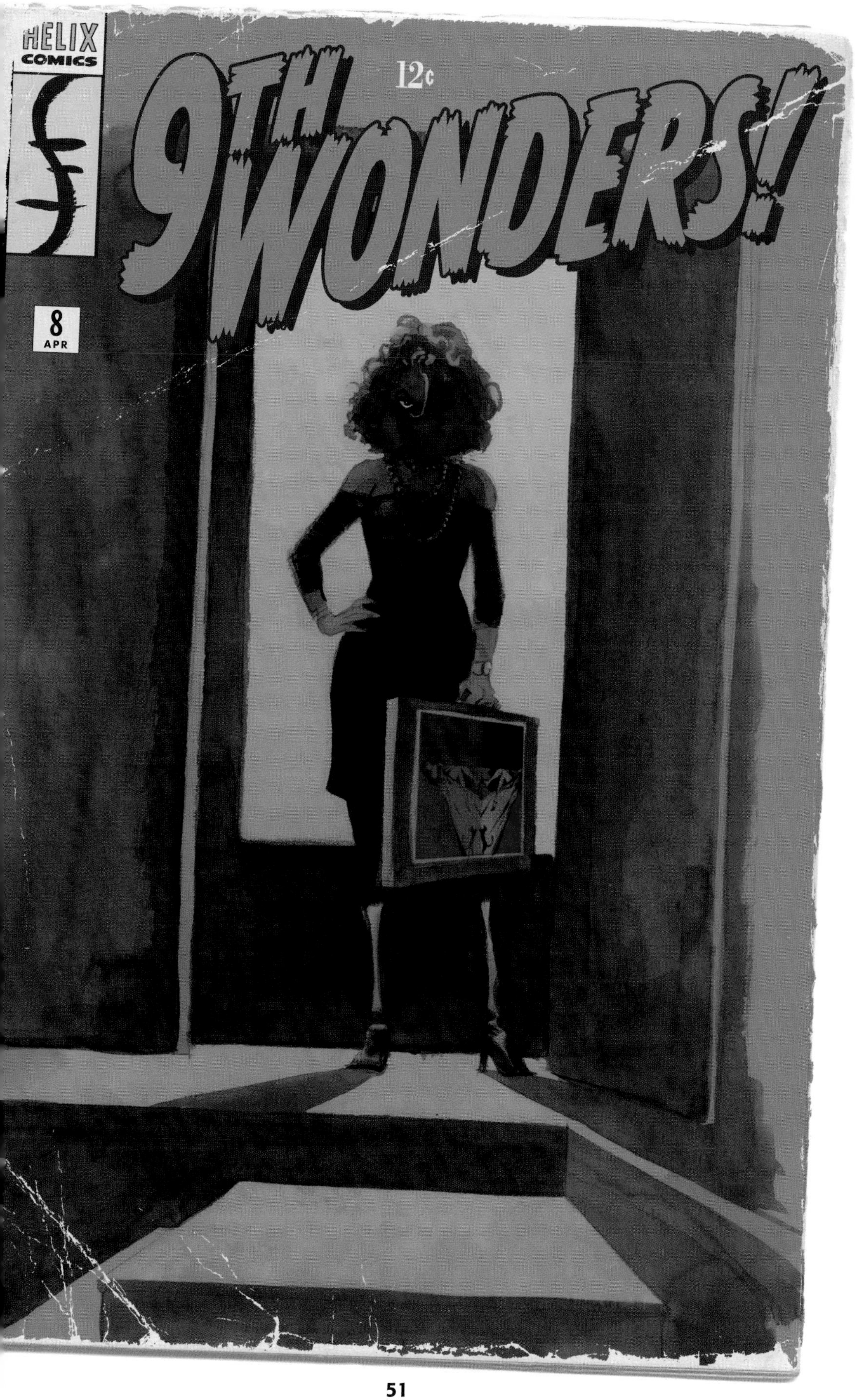

HELIX
COMICS
12¢
9TH WONDERS!
8
APR

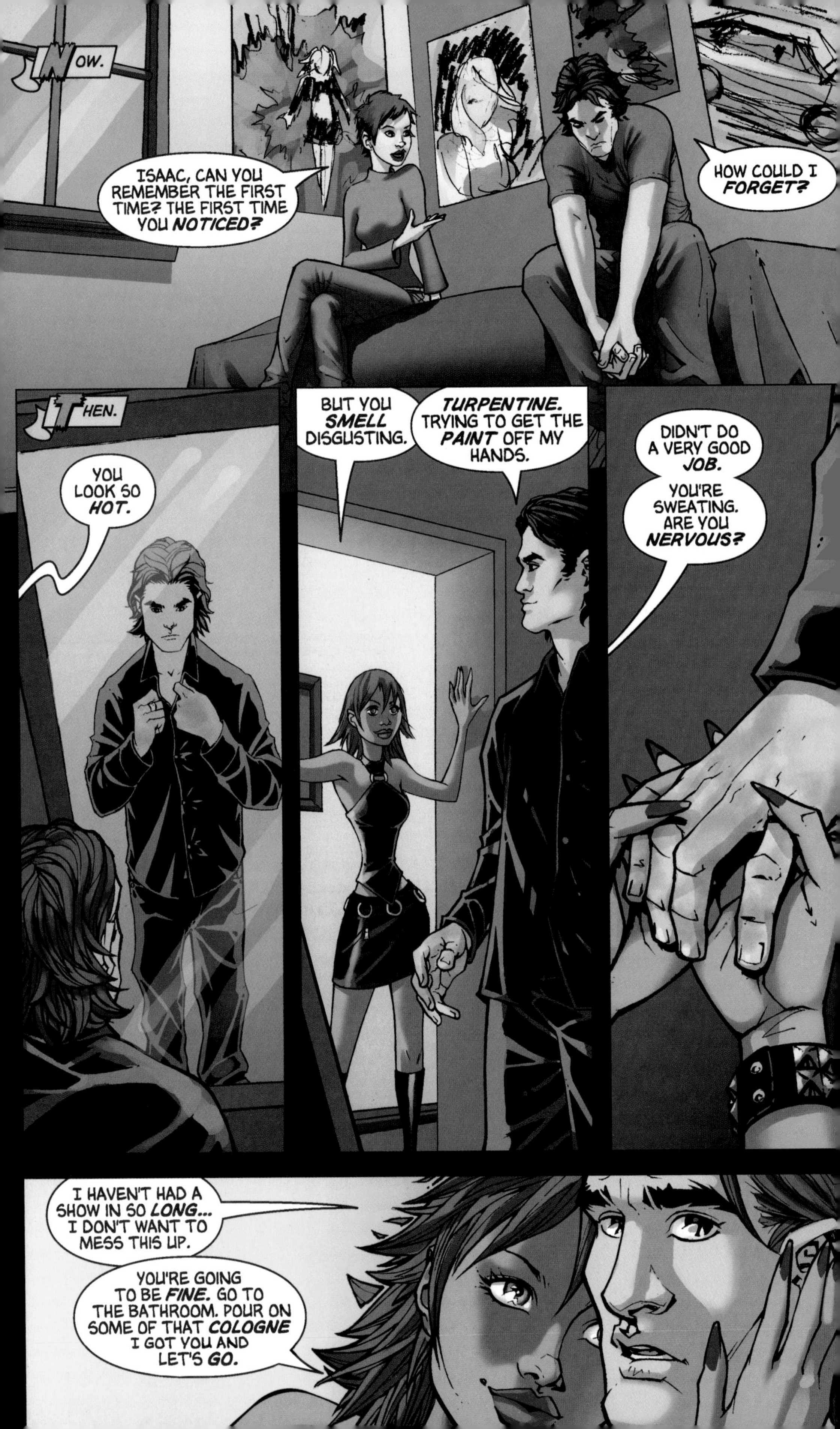
NOW.
ISAAC, CAN YOU REMEMBER THE FIRST TIME? THE FIRST TIME YOU **NOTICED?**
HOW COULD I **FORGET?**
THEN.
YOU LOOK SO **HOT.**
BUT YOU **SMELL** DISGUSTING.
TURPENTINE. TRYING TO GET THE **PAINT** OFF MY HANDS.
DIDN'T DO A VERY GOOD **JOB.**
YOU'RE SWEATING. ARE YOU **NERVOUS?**
I HAVEN'T HAD A SHOW IN SO **LONG...** I DON'T WANT TO MESS THIS UP.
YOU'RE GOING TO BE **FINE.** GO TO THE BATHROOM. POUR ON SOME OF THAT **COLOGNE** I GOT YOU AND LET'S **GO.**

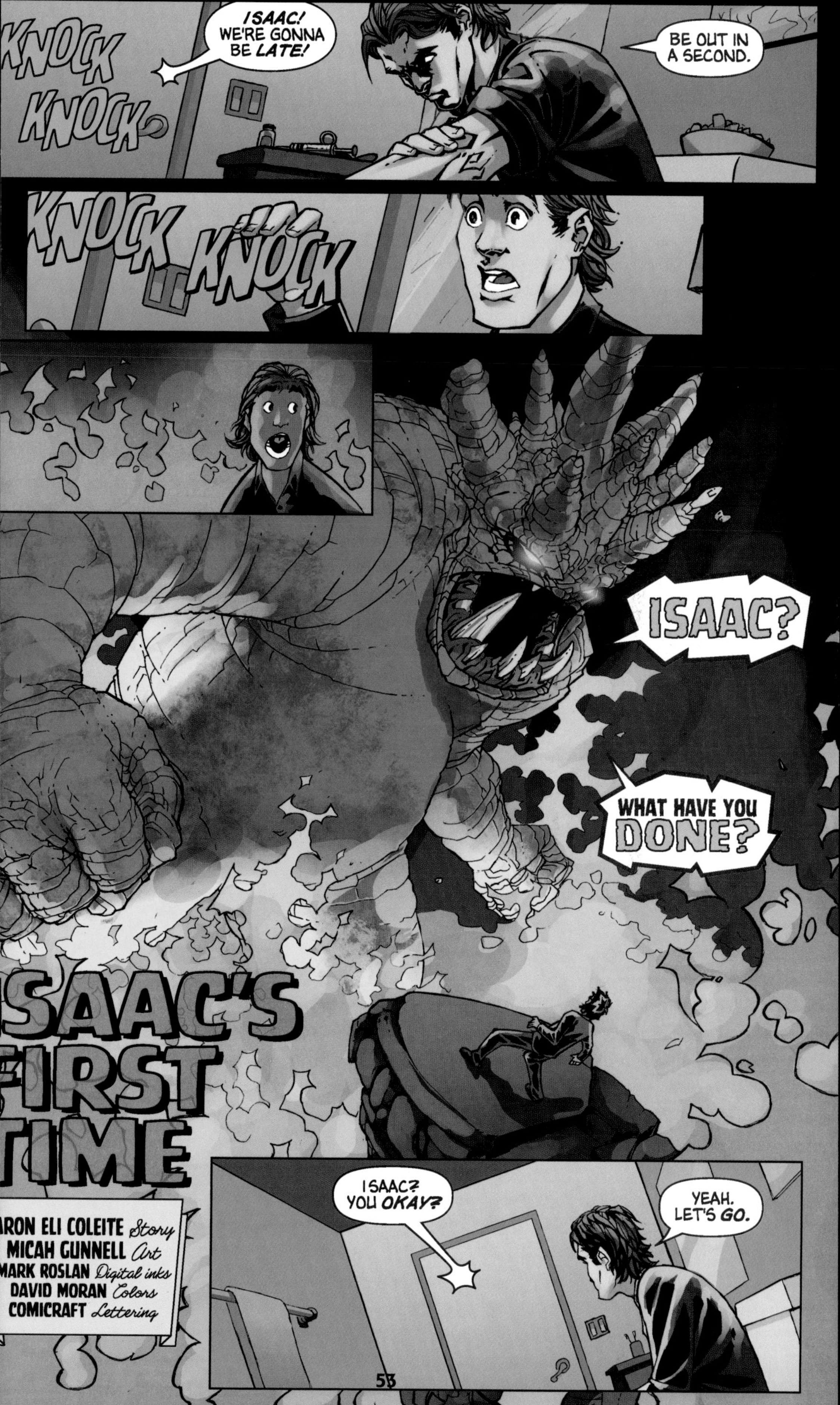
KNOCK KNOCK
ISAAC! WE'RE GONNA BE LATE!
BE OUT IN A SECOND.
KNOCK KNOCK
ISAAC?
WHAT HAVE YOU DONE?
SAAC'S FIRST TIME
ARON ELI COLEITE Story
MICAH GUNNELL Art
MARK ROSLAN Digital inks
DAVID MORAN Colors
COMICRAFT Lettering
ISAAC? YOU OKAY?
YEAH. LET'S GO.

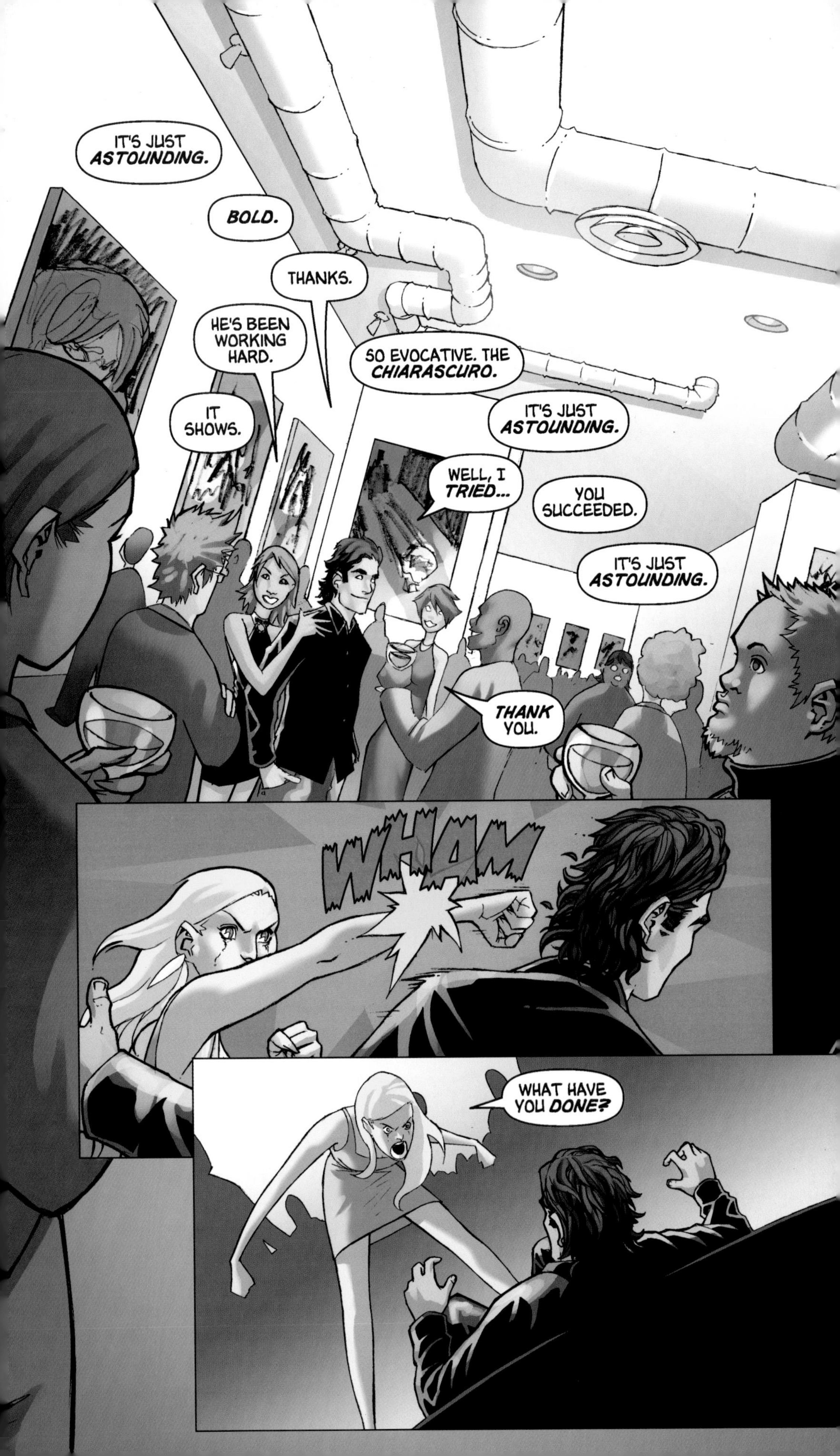
IT'S JUST ASTOUNDING.
BOLD.
THANKS.
HE'S BEEN WORKING HARD.
IT SHOWS.
SO EVOCATIVE. THE CHIARASCURO.
IT'S JUST ASTOUNDING.
WELL, I TRIED...
YOU SUCCEEDED.
IT'S JUST ASTOUNDING.
THANK YOU.
WHAM
WHAT HAVE YOU DONE?

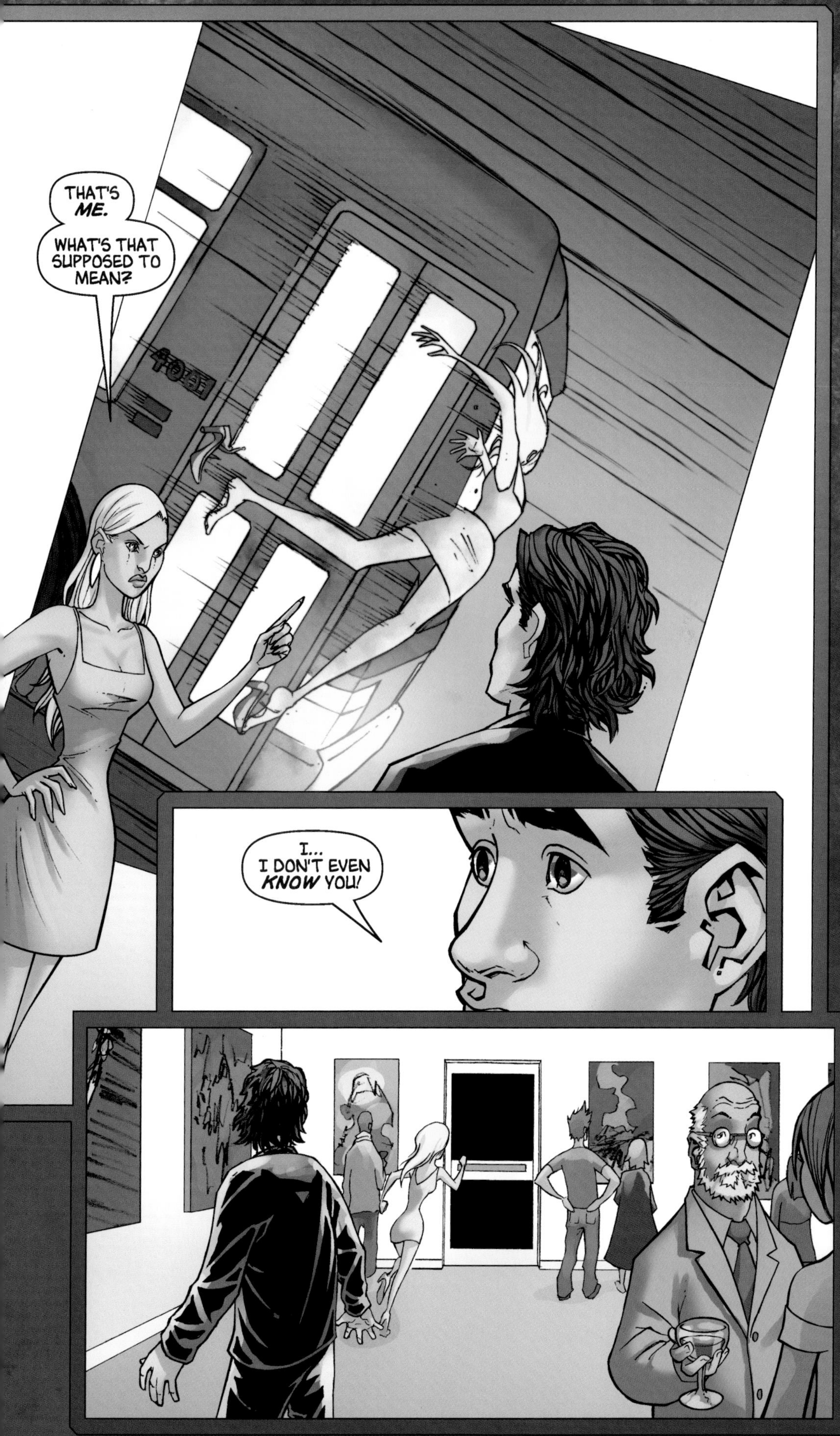
THAT'S *ME.*
WHAT'S THAT SUPPOSED TO MEAN?
I... I DON'T EVEN *KNOW* YOU!

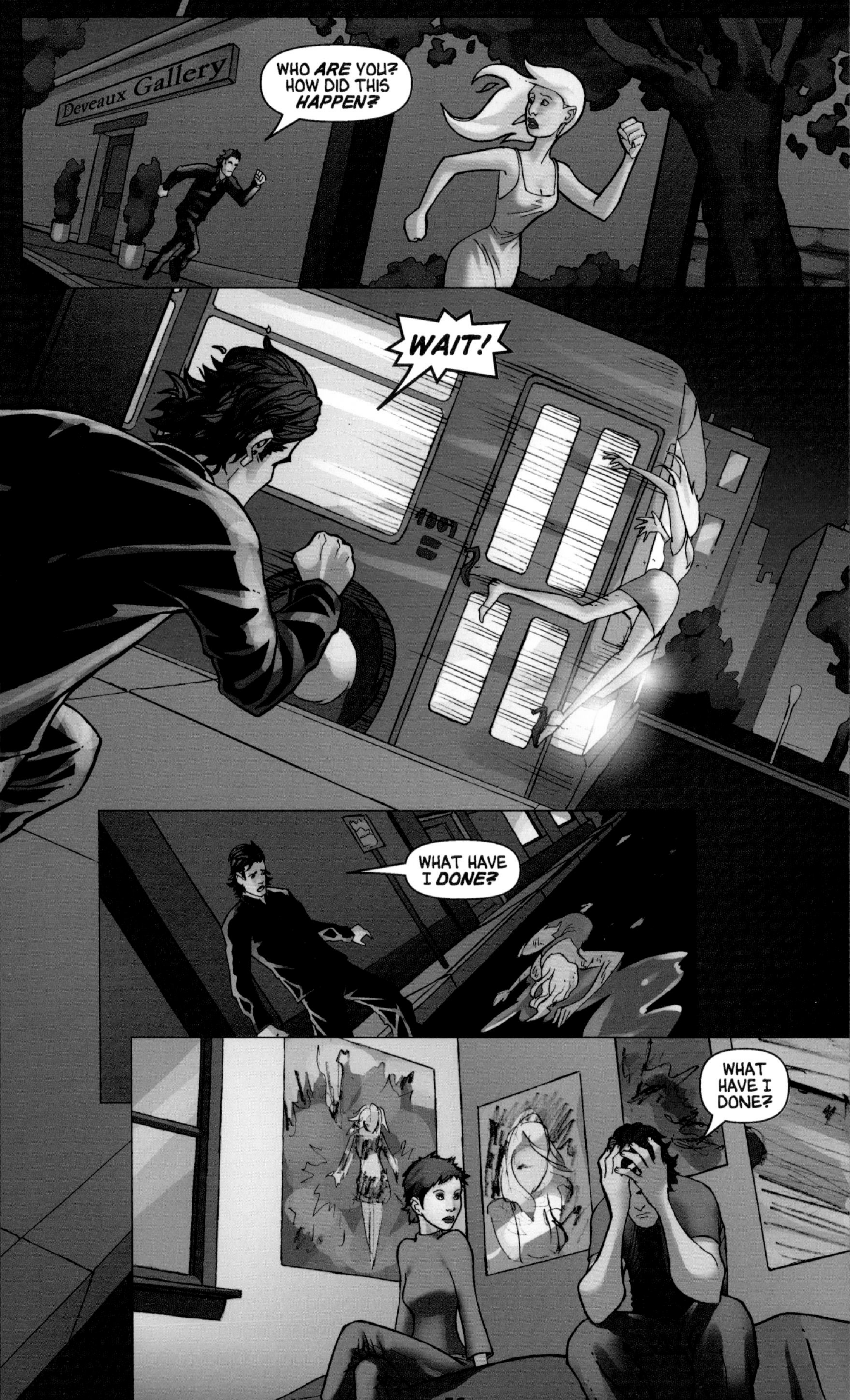
Deveaux Gallery
WHO ARE YOU? HOW DID THIS HAPPEN?
WAIT!
WHAT HAVE I DONE?
WHAT HAVE I DONE?

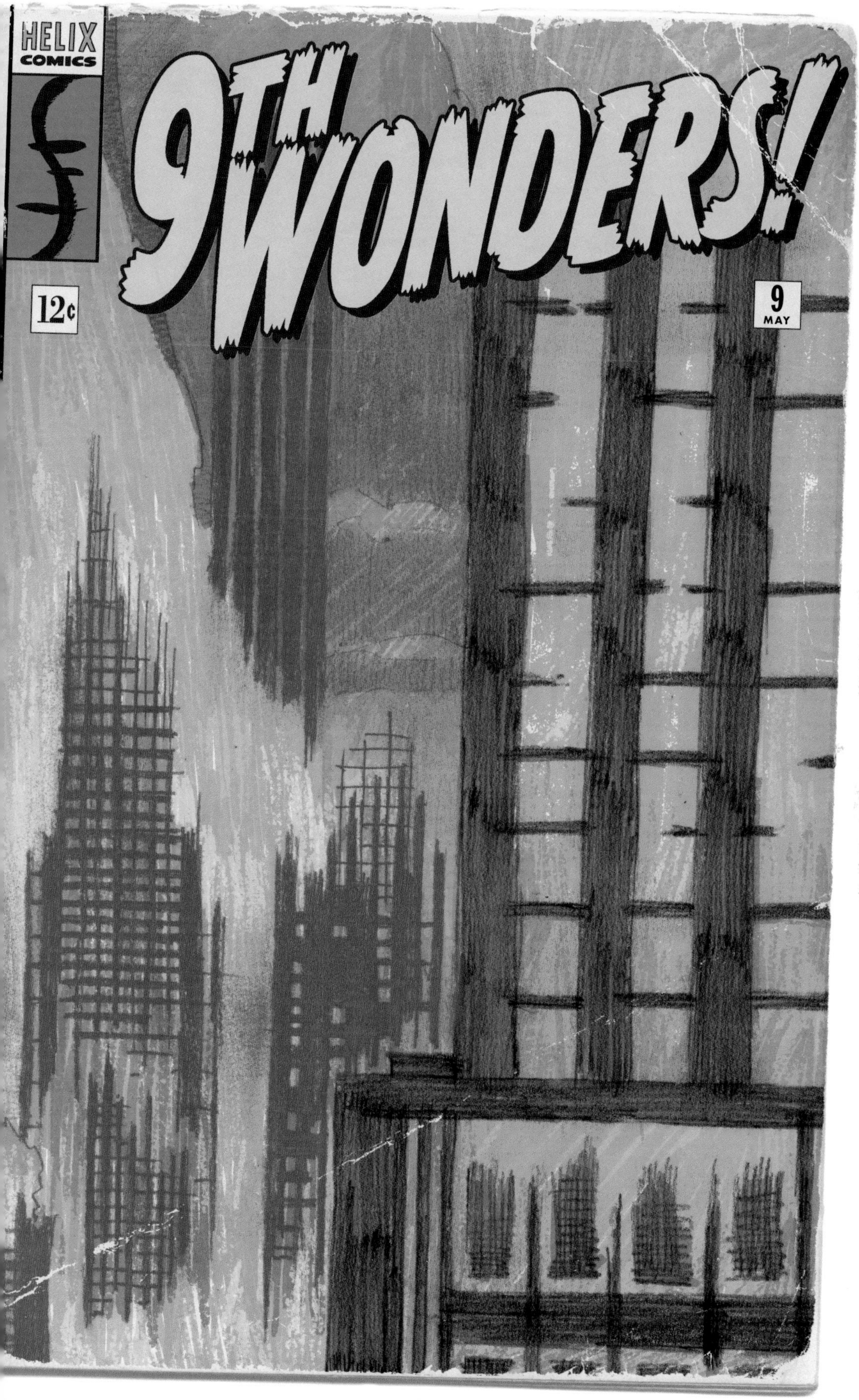
HELIX COMICS
9TH WONDERS!
12¢
9
MAY

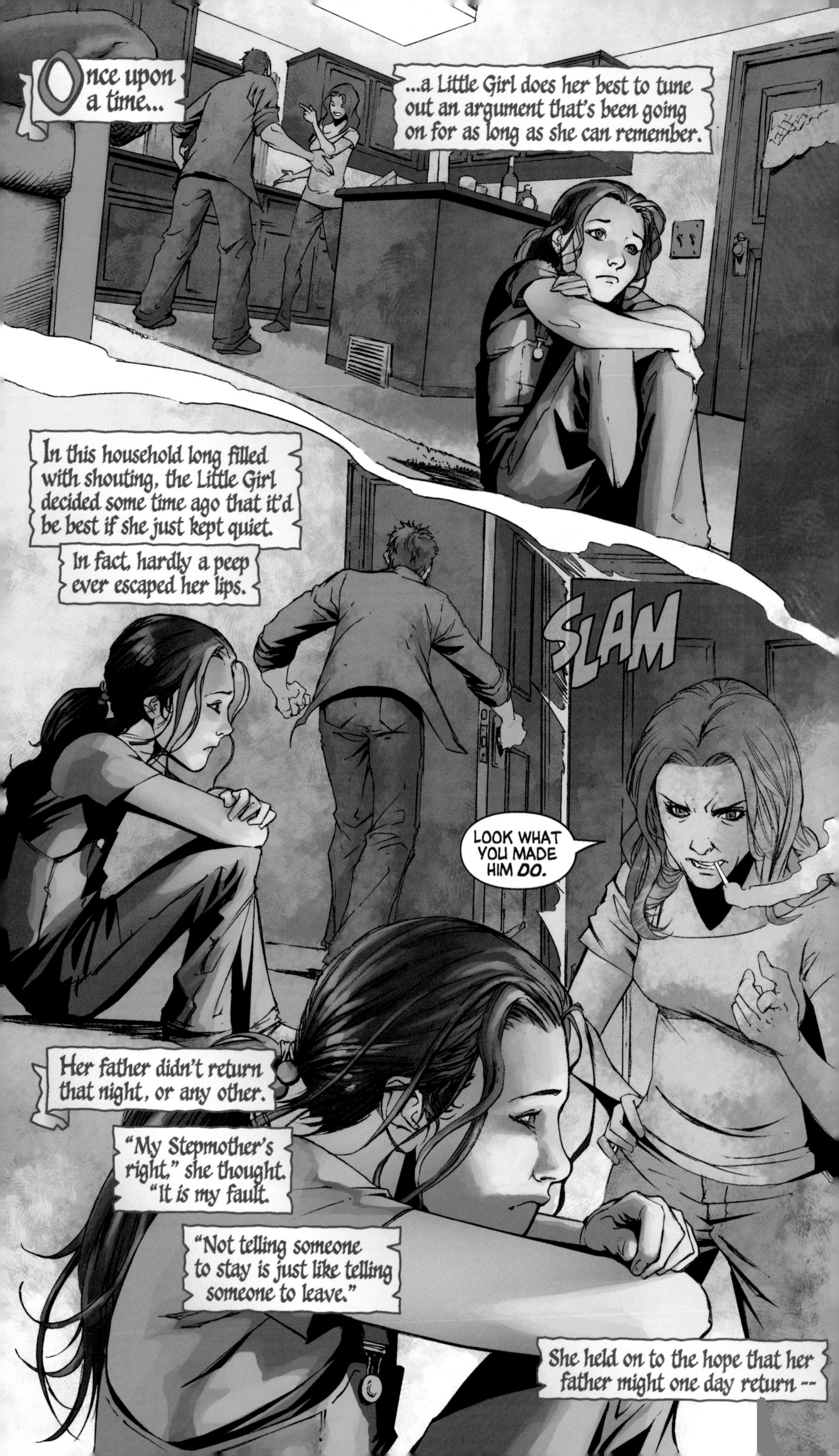
Once upon a time...
...a Little Girl does her best to tune out an argument that's been going on for as long as she can remember.
In this household long filled with shouting, the Little Girl decided some time ago that it'd be best if she just kept quiet.
In fact, hardly a peep ever escaped her lips.
SLAM
LOOK WHAT YOU MADE HIM DO.
Her father didn't return that night, or any other.
"My Stepmother's right," she thought. "It is my fault.
"Not telling someone to stay is just like telling someone to leave."
She held on to the hope that her father might one day return --

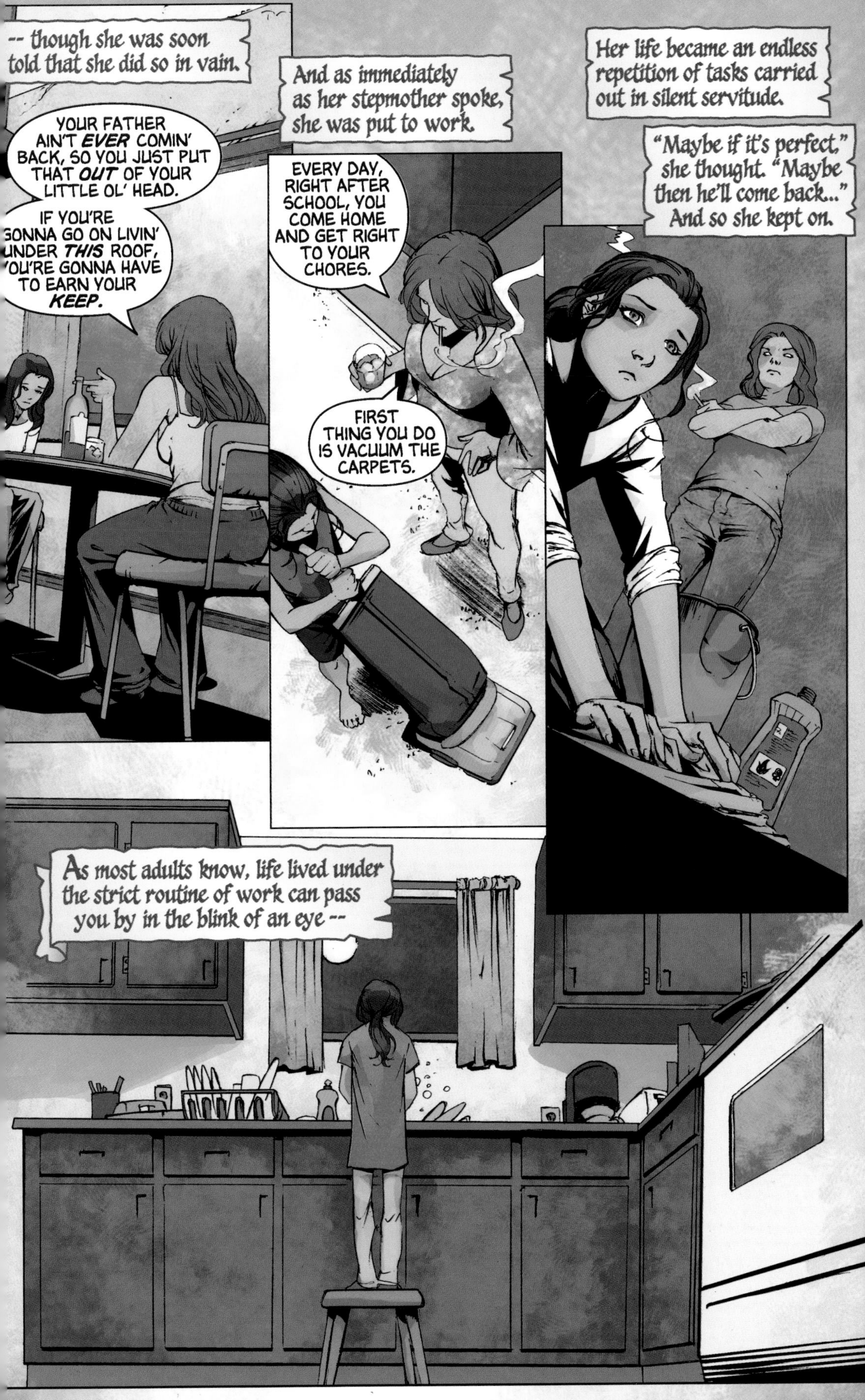

-- though she was soon told that she did so in vain.
YOUR FATHER AIN'T EVER COMIN' BACK, SO YOU JUST PUT THAT OUT OF YOUR LITTLE OL' HEAD.
IF YOU'RE GONNA GO ON LIVIN' UNDER THIS ROOF, YOU'RE GONNA HAVE TO EARN YOUR KEEP.
And as immediately as her stepmother spoke, she was put to work.
EVERY DAY, RIGHT AFTER SCHOOL, YOU COME HOME AND GET RIGHT TO YOUR CHORES.
FIRST THING YOU DO IS VACUUM THE CARPETS.
Her life became an endless repetition of tasks carried out in silent servitude.
"Maybe if it's perfect," she thought. "Maybe then he'll come back..." And so she kept on.
As most adults know, life lived under the strict routine of work can pass you by in the blink of an eye --

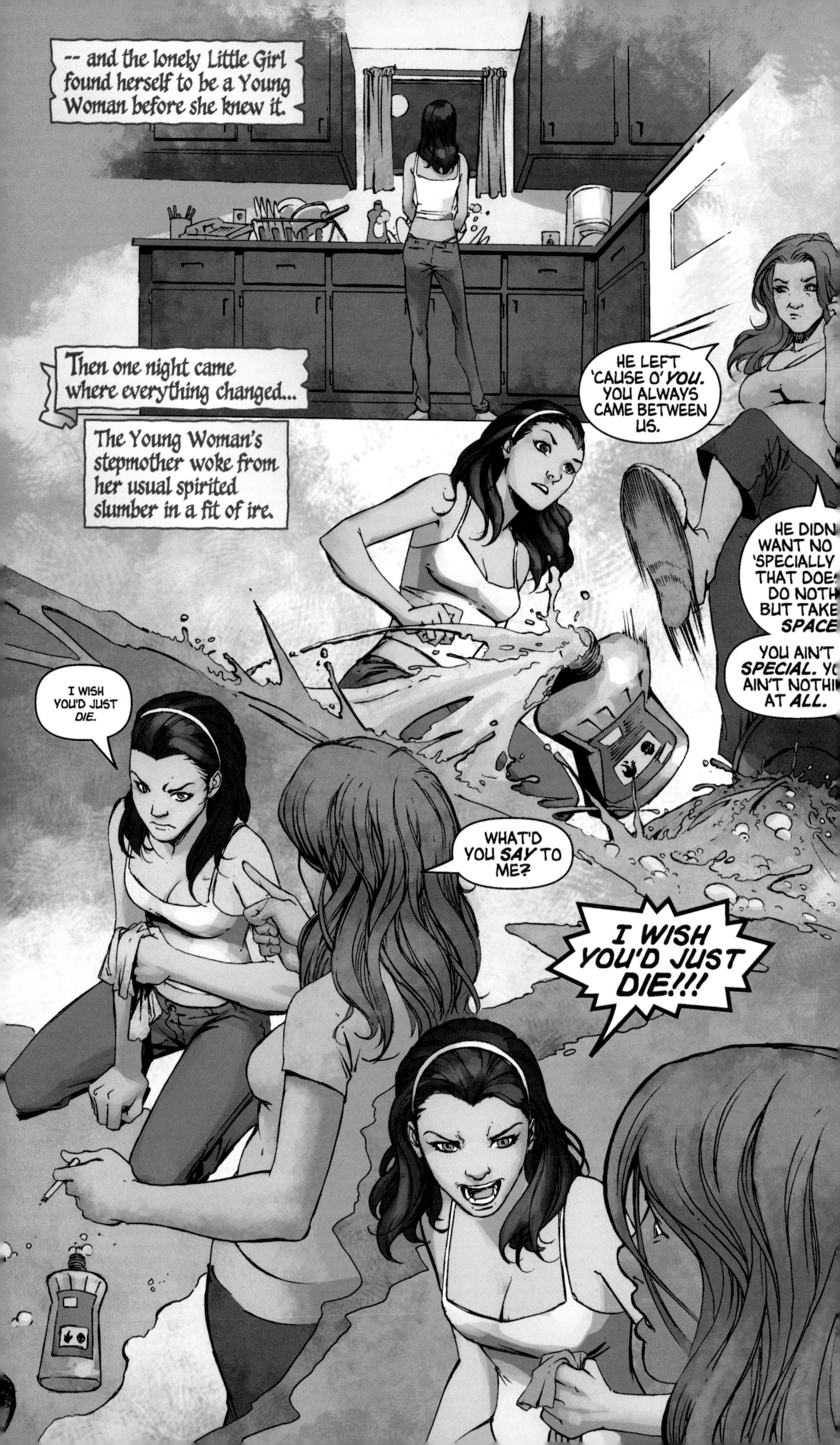

-- and the lonely Little Girl found herself to be a Young Woman before she knew it.
Then one night came where everything changed...
The Young Woman's stepmother woke from her usual spirited slumber in a fit of ire.
HE LEFT 'CAUSE O' YOU. YOU ALWAYS CAME BETWEEN US.
HE DIDN WANT NO 'SPECIALLY THAT DOES DO NOTH BUT TAKE SPACE
YOU AIN'T SPECIAL. YO AIN'T NOTHI AT ALL.
I WISH YOU'D JUST DIE.
WHAT'D YOU SAY TO ME?
I WISH YOU'D JUST DIE!!!

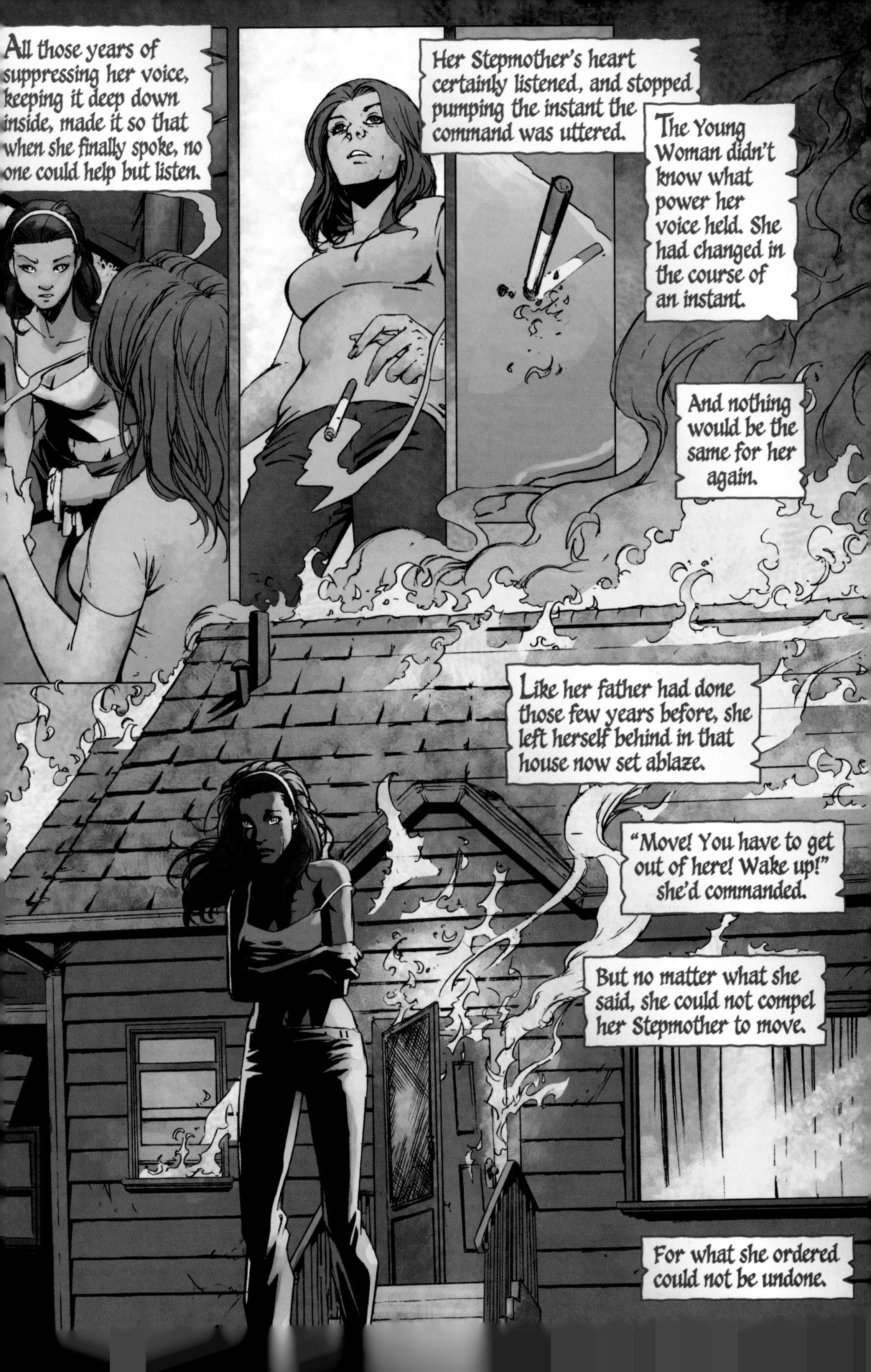
All those years of suppressing her voice, keeping it deep down inside, made it so that when she finally spoke, no one could help but listen.
Her Stepmother's heart certainly listened, and stopped pumping the instant the command was uttered.
The Young Woman didn't know what power her voice held. She had changed in the course of an instant.
And nothing would be the same for her again.
Like her father had done those few years before, she left herself behind in that house now set ablaze.
"Move! You have to get out of here! Wake up!" she'd commanded.
But no matter what she said, she could not compel her Stepmother to move.
For what she ordered could not be undone.

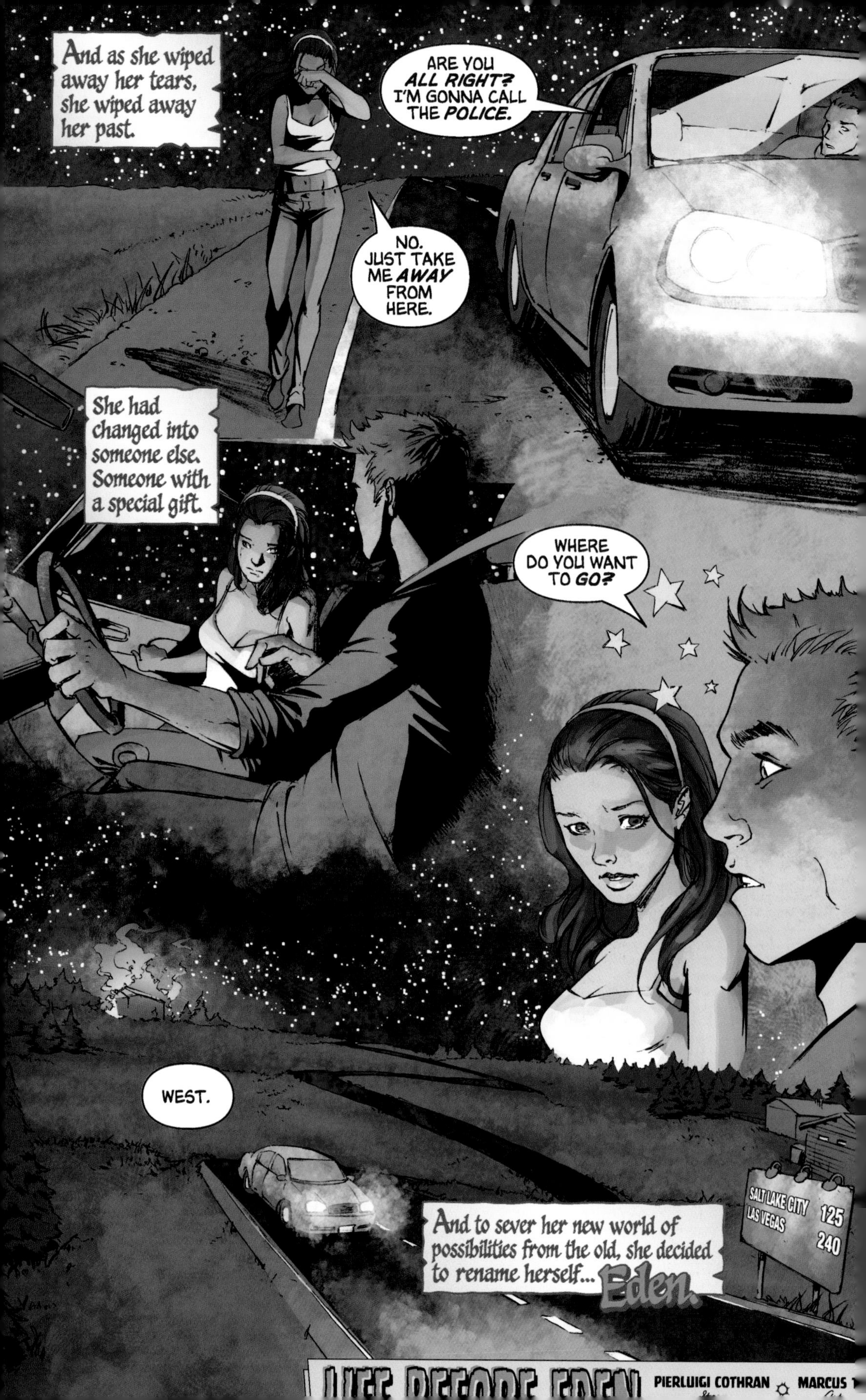
And as she wiped away her tears, she wiped away her past.
ARE YOU ALL RIGHT? I'M GONNA CALL THE POLICE.
NO. JUST TAKE ME AWAY FROM HERE.
She had changed into someone else. Someone with a special gift.
WHERE DO YOU WANT TO GO?
WEST.
SALT LAKE CITY 125
LAS VEGAS 240
And to sever her new world of possibilities from the old, she decided to rename herself... Eden.
PIERLUIGI COTHRAN
MARCUS

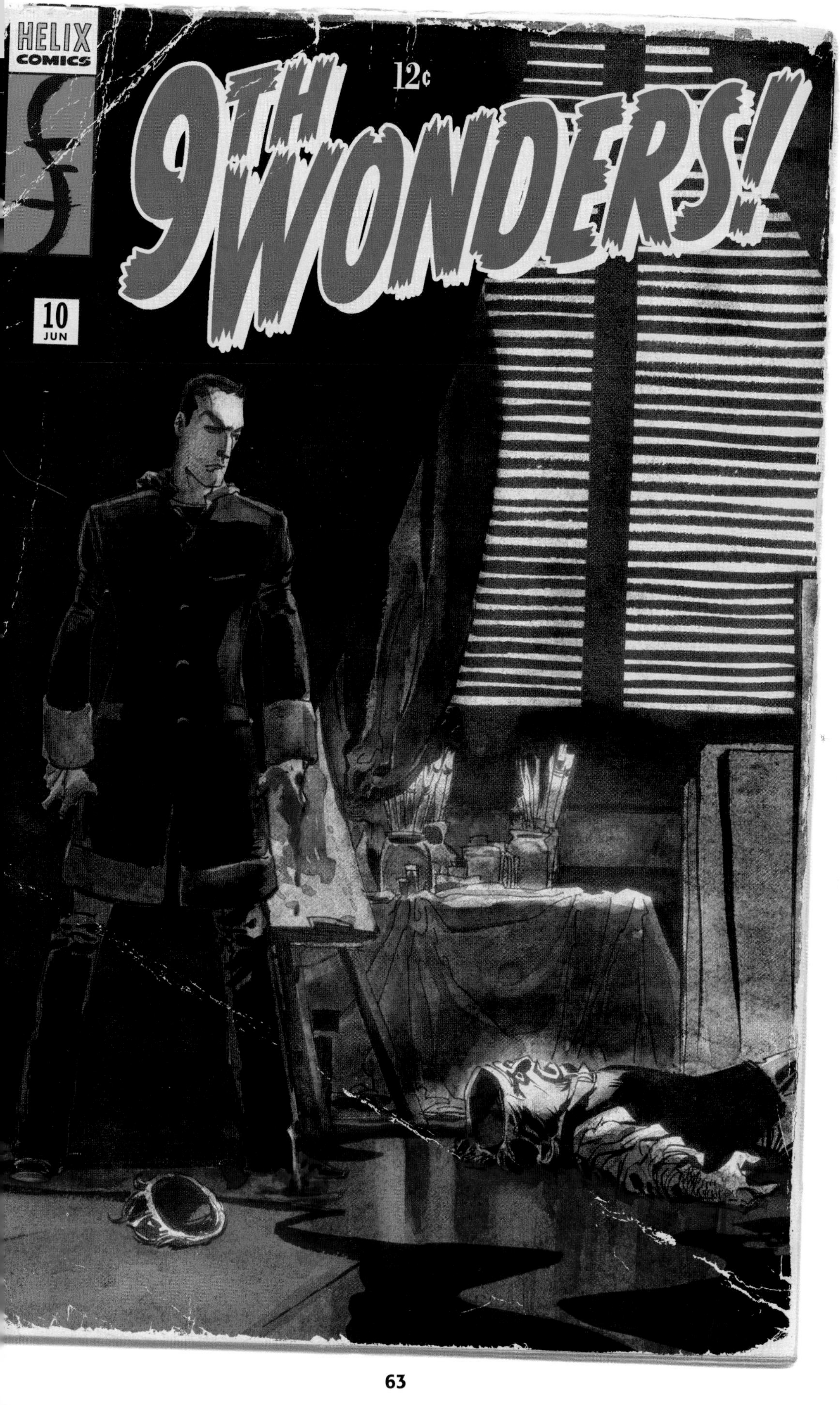
HELIX
COMICS
12¢
9TH WONDERS!
10
JUN

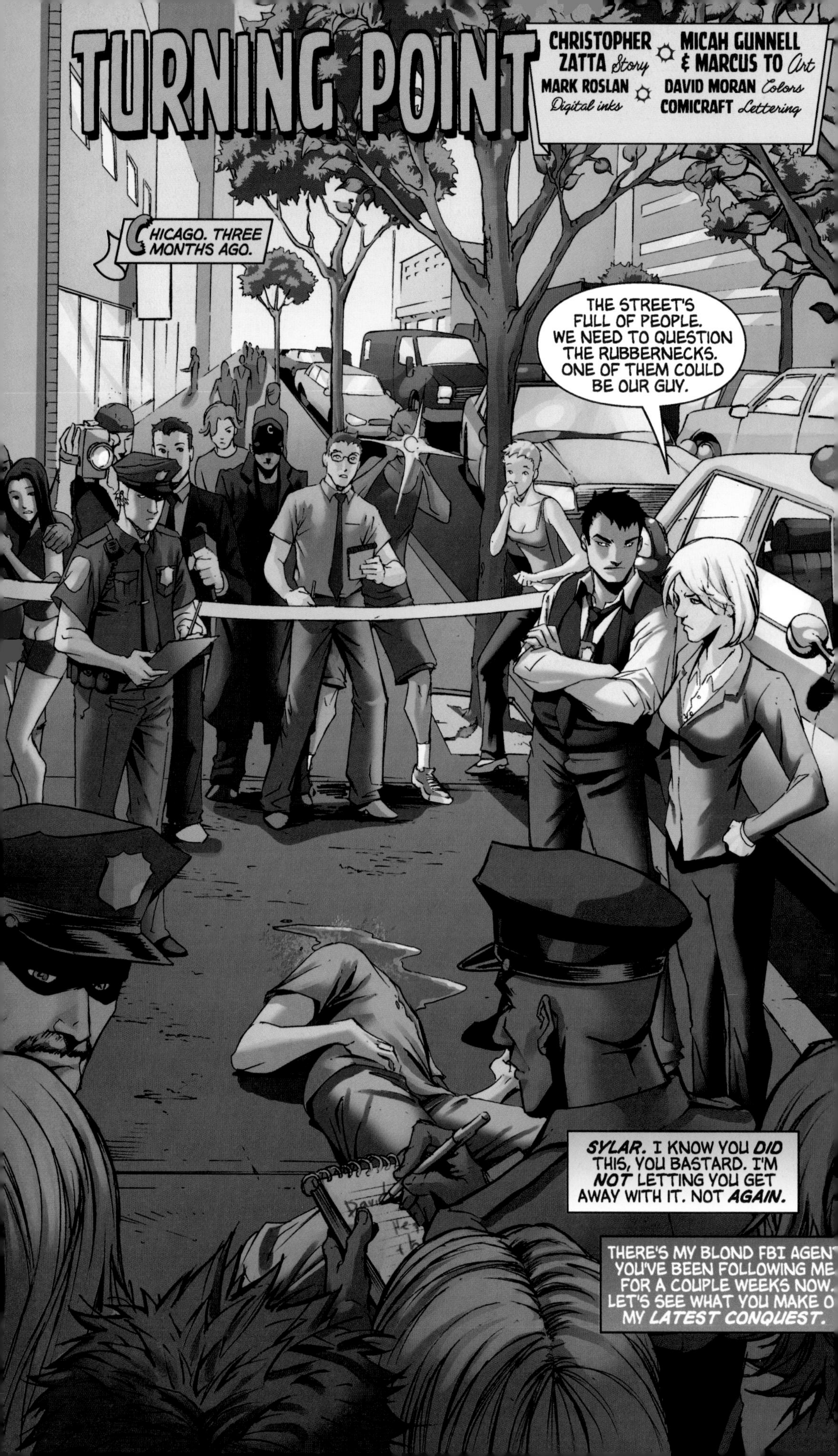
TURNING POINT
CHRISTOPHER ZATTA Story
MICAH GUNNELL & MARCUS TO Art
MARK ROSLAN Digital inks
DAVID MORAN Colors
COMICRAFT Lettering
CHICAGO. THREE MONTHS AGO.
THE STREET'S FULL OF PEOPLE. WE NEED TO QUESTION THE RUBBERNECKS. ONE OF THEM COULD BE OUR GUY.
SYLAR. I KNOW YOU DID THIS, YOU BASTARD. I'M NOT LETTING YOU GET AWAY WITH IT. NOT AGAIN.
THERE'S MY BLOND FBI AGEN
YOU'VE BEEN FOLLOWING ME
FOR A COUPLE WEEKS NOW.
LET'S SEE WHAT YOU MAKE O
MY LATEST CONQUEST.

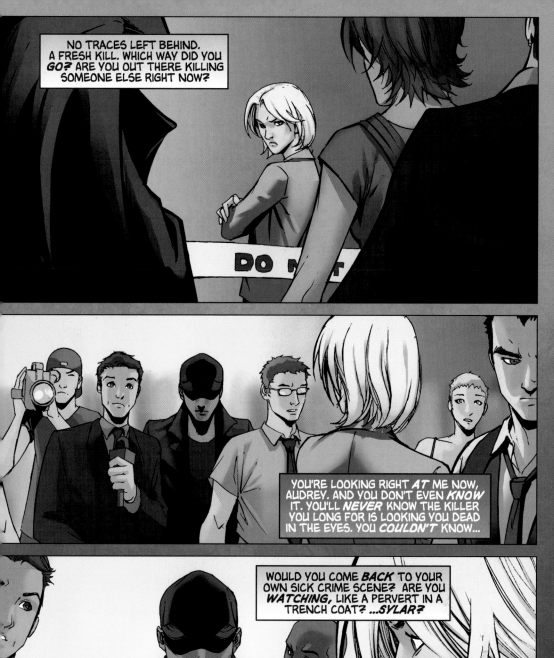

NO TRACES LEFT BEHIND. A FRESH KILL. WHICH WAY DID YOU *GO*? ARE YOU OUT THERE KILLING SOMEONE ELSE RIGHT NOW?

DO N T

YOU'RE LOOKING RIGHT *AT* ME NOW, AUDREY. AND YOU DON'T EVEN *KNOW* IT. YOU'LL *NEVER* KNOW THE KILLER YOU LONG FOR IS LOOKING YOU DEAD IN THE EYES. YOU *COULDN'T* KNOW...

WOULD YOU COME *BACK* TO YOUR OWN SICK CRIME SCENE? ARE YOU *WATCHING*, LIKE A PERVERT IN A TRENCH COAT? ...*SYLAR?*

SYLAR!

CAUGHT. *IMPRESSIVE.* LET'S TURN IT *UP* A NOTCH.

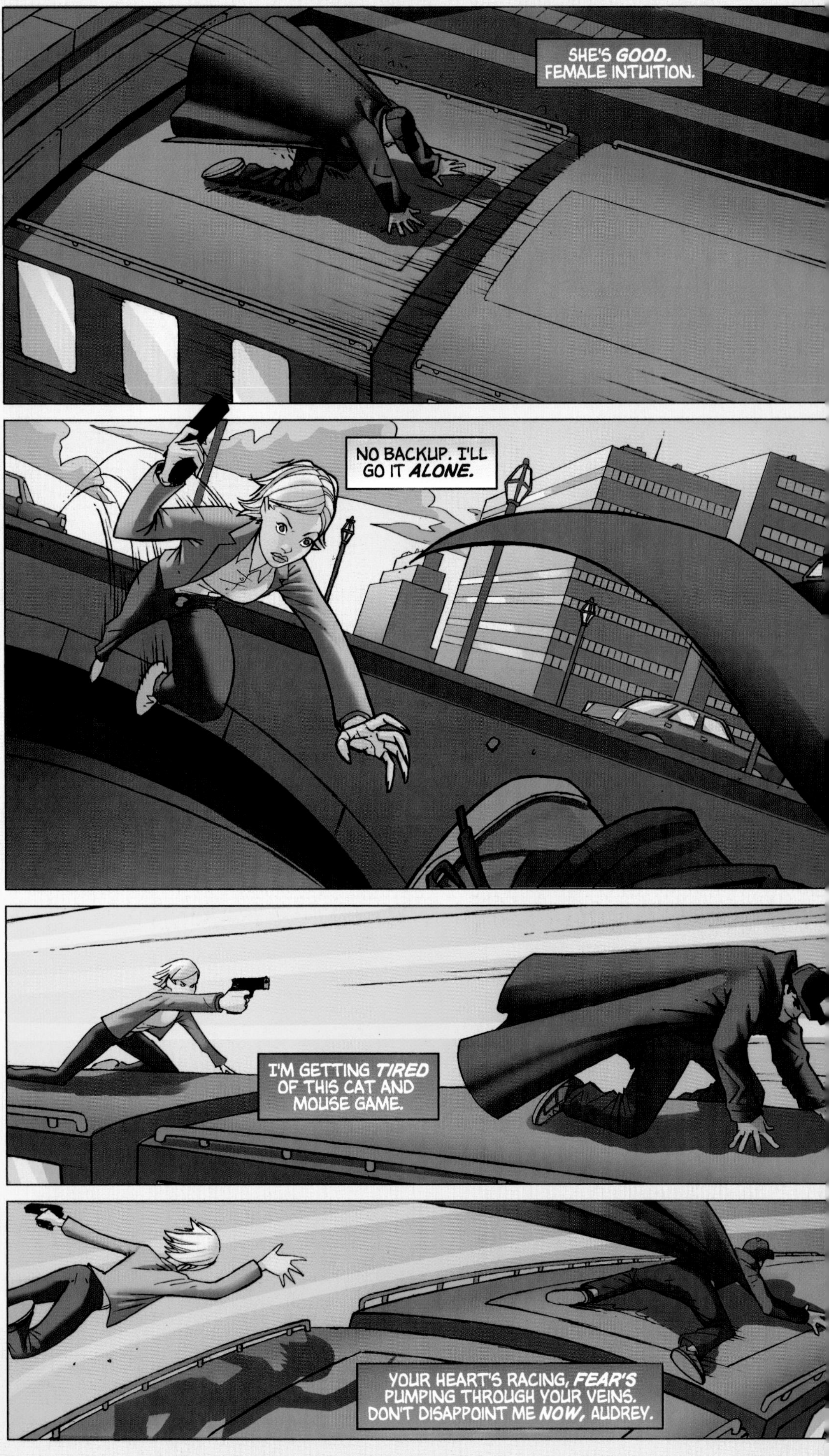
SHE'S GOOD. FEMALE INTUITION.
NO BACKUP. I'LL GO IT ALONE.
I'M GETTING TIRED OF THIS CAT AND MOUSE GAME.
YOUR HEART'S RACING, FEAR'S PUMPING THROUGH YOUR VEINS. DON'T DISAPPOINT ME NOW, AUDREY.

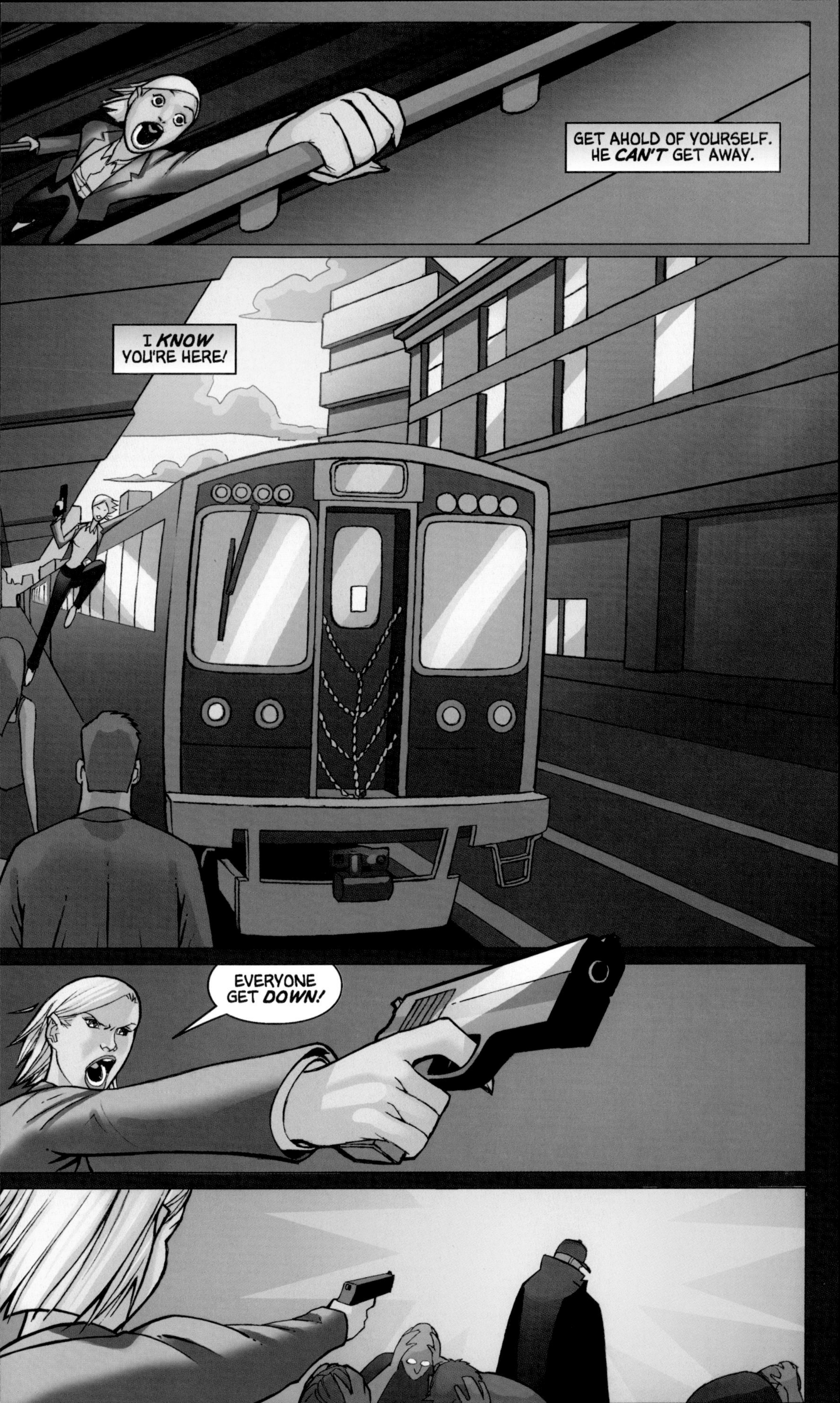
GET AHOLD OF YOURSELF. HE *CAN'T* GET AWAY.
I *KNOW* YOU'RE HERE!
EVERYONE GET *DOWN!*

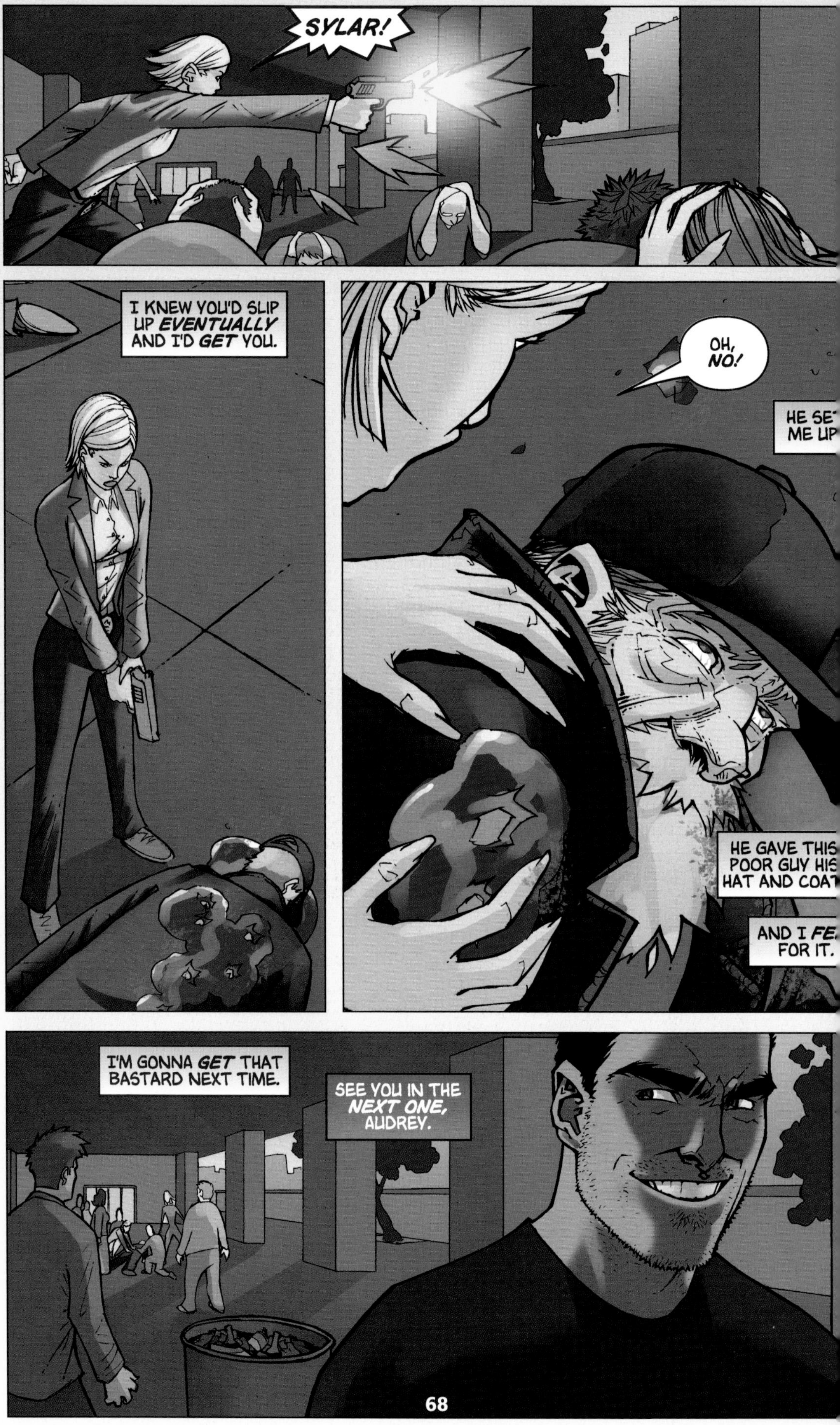
SYLAR!
I KNEW YOU'D SLIP UP EVENTUALLY AND I'D GET YOU.
OH, NO!
HE SE
ME UP
HE GAVE THIS POOR GUY HIS HAT AND COA
AND I FE
FOR IT.
I'M GONNA GET THAT BASTARD NEXT TIME.
SEE YOU IN THE NEXT ONE, AUDREY.

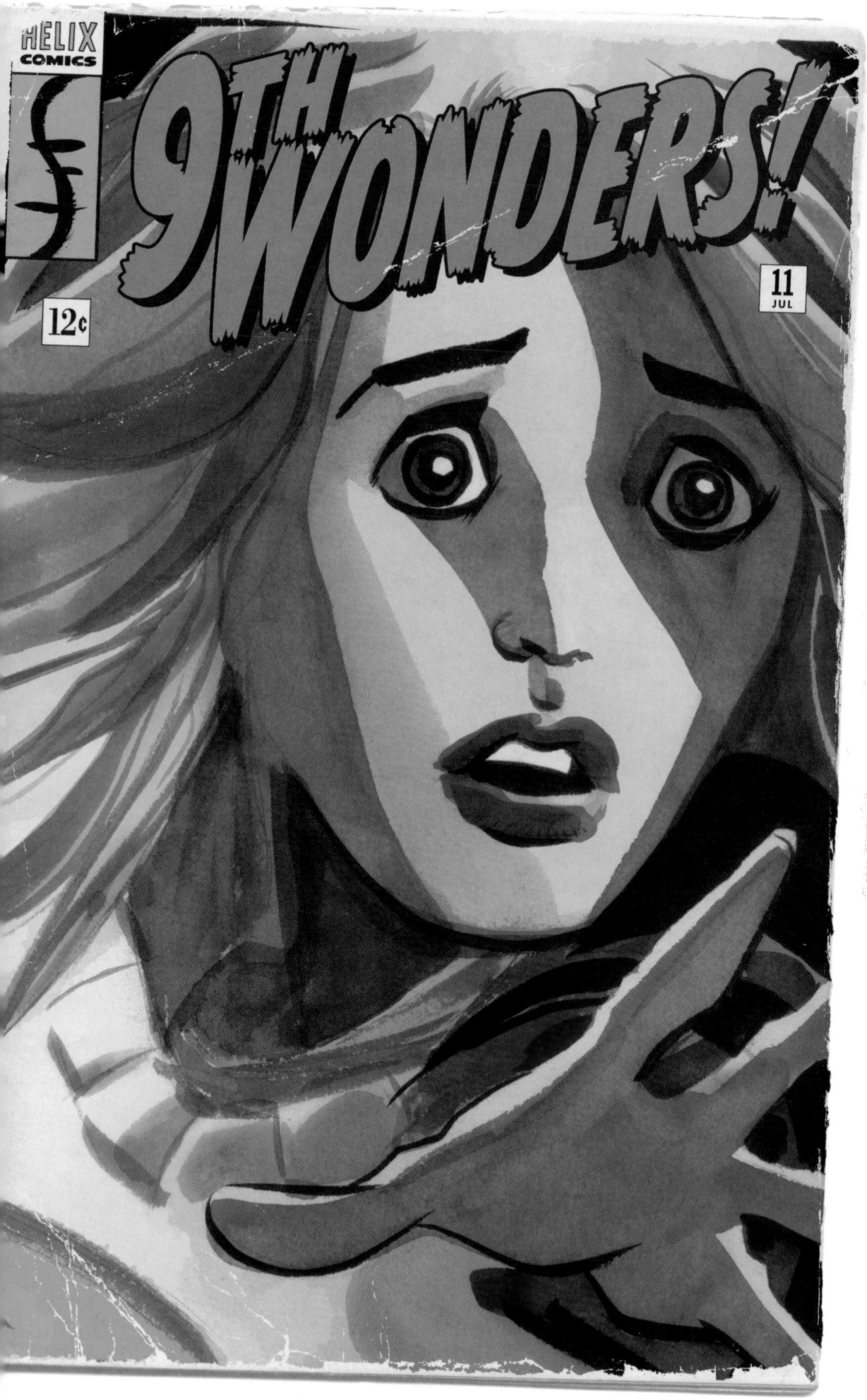
HELIX
COMICS
9TH WONDERS!
12¢
11
JUL

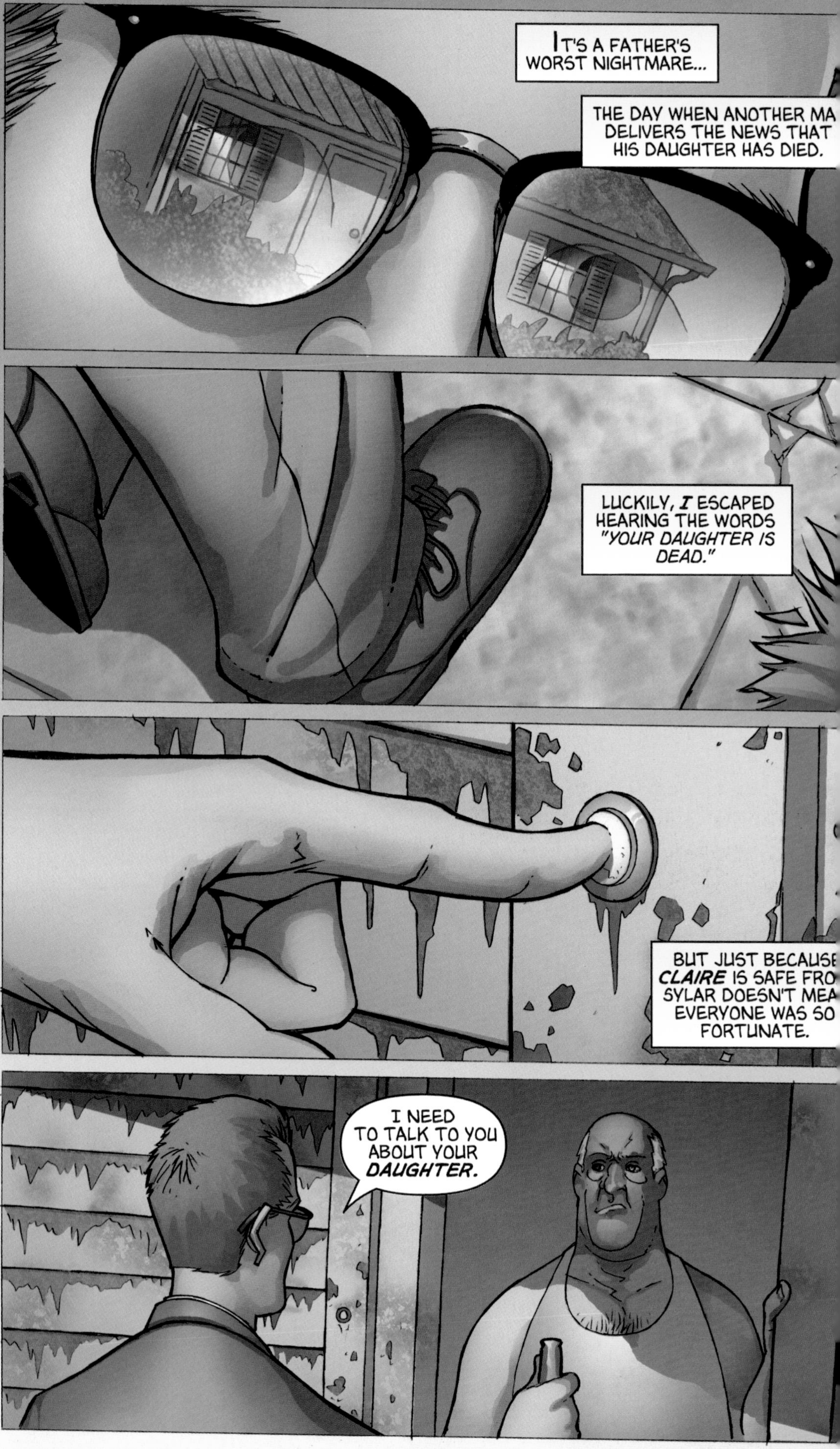
IT'S A FATHER'S WORST NIGHTMARE...
THE DAY WHEN ANOTHER MA DELIVERS THE NEWS THAT HIS DAUGHTER HAS DIED.
LUCKILY, I ESCAPED HEARING THE WORDS "YOUR DAUGHTER IS DEAD."
BUT JUST BECAUSE CLAIRE IS SAFE FRO SYLAR DOESN'T MEA EVERYONE WAS SO FORTUNATE.
I NEED TO TALK TO YOU ABOUT YOUR DAUGHTER.

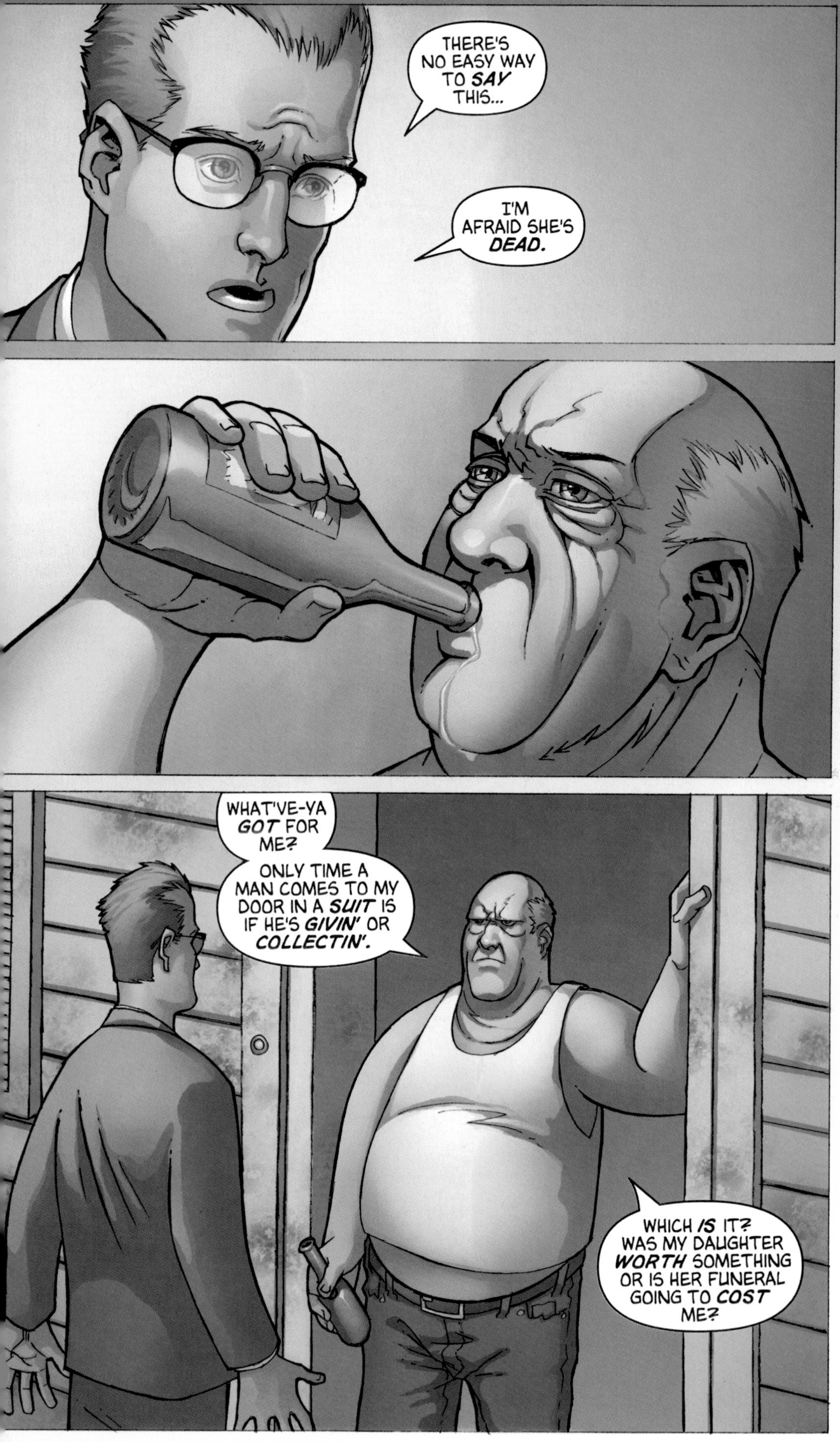
THERE'S NO EASY WAY TO SAY THIS...
I'M AFRAID SHE'S DEAD.
WHAT'VE-YA GOT FOR ME?
ONLY TIME A MAN COMES TO MY DOOR IN A SUIT IS IF HE'S GIVIN' OR COLLECTIN'.
WHICH IS IT? WAS MY DAUGHTER WORTH SOMETHING OR IS HER FUNERAL GOING TO COST ME?

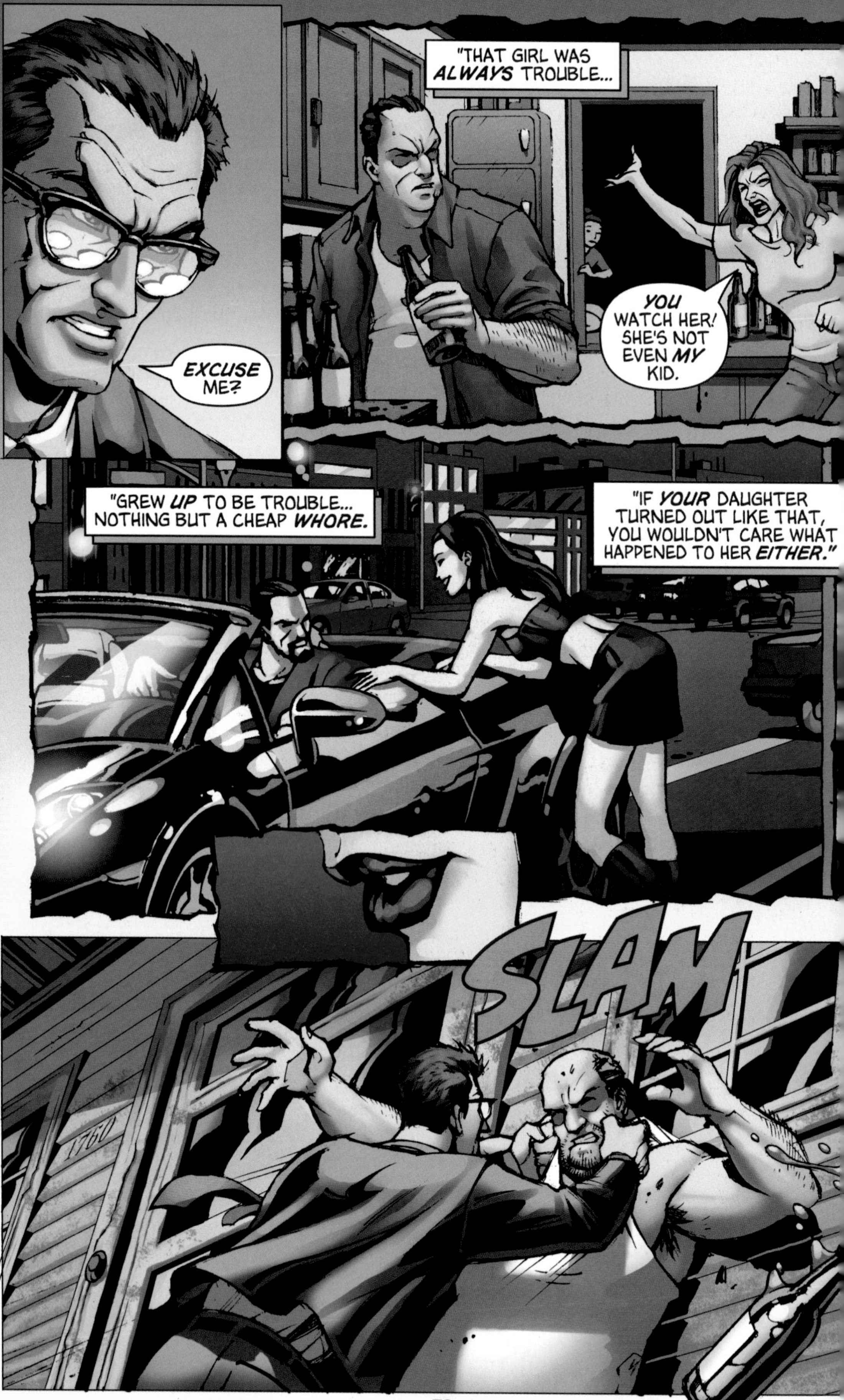

EXCUSE ME?
"THAT GIRL WAS ALWAYS TROUBLE...
YOU WATCH HER! SHE'S NOT EVEN MY KID.
"GREW UP TO BE TROUBLE... NOTHING BUT A CHEAP WHORE.
"IF YOUR DAUGHTER TURNED OUT LIKE THAT, YOU WOULDN'T CARE WHAT HAPPENED TO HER EITHER."
SLAM

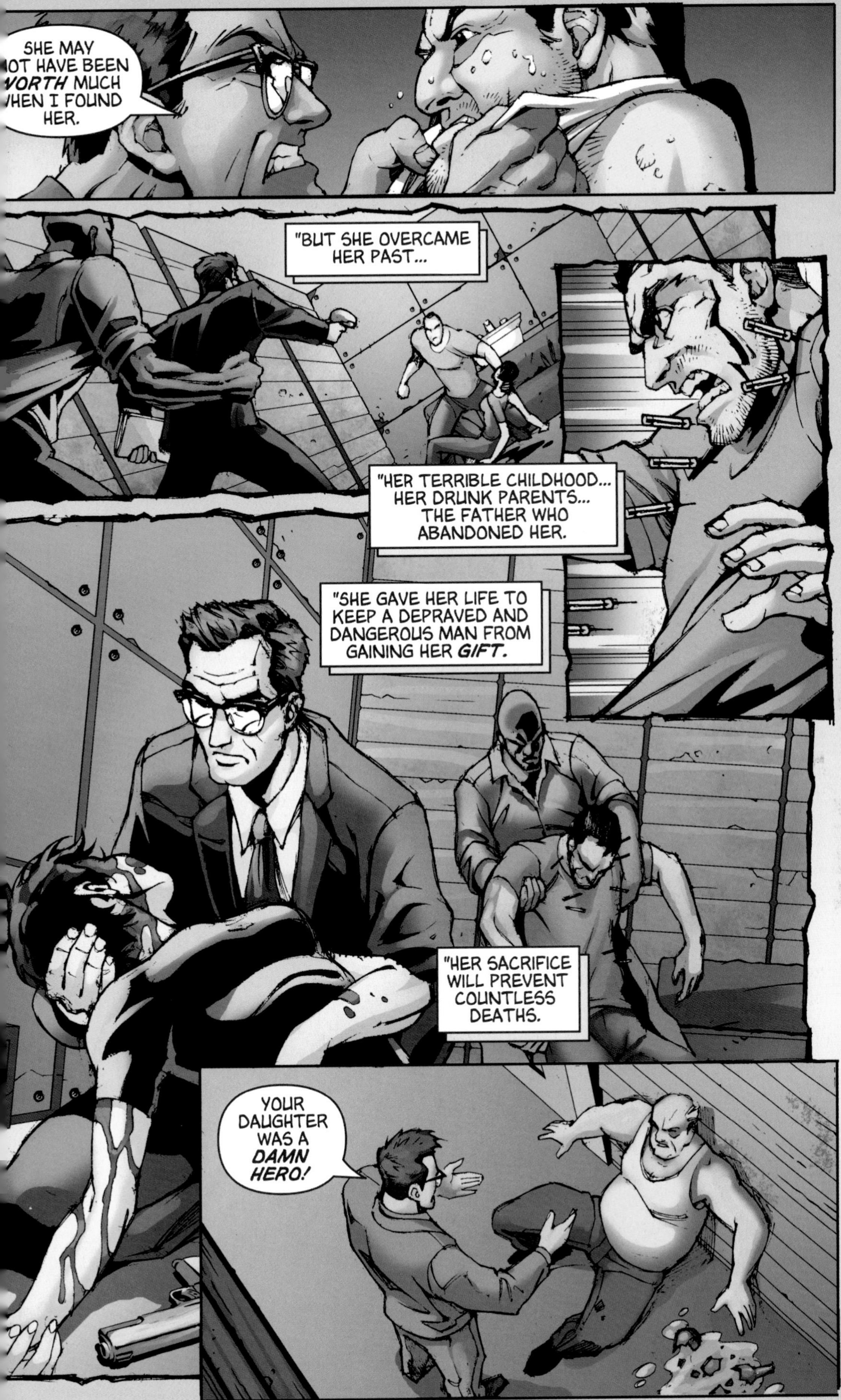
SHE MAY NOT HAVE BEEN WORTH MUCH WHEN I FOUND HER.
"BUT SHE OVERCAME HER PAST...
"HER TERRIBLE CHILDHOOD... HER DRUNK PARENTS... THE FATHER WHO ABANDONED HER.
"SHE GAVE HER LIFE TO KEEP A DEPRAVED AND DANGEROUS MAN FROM GAINING HER GIFT.
"HER SACRIFICE WILL PREVENT COUNTLESS DEATHS.
YOUR DAUGHTER WAS A DAMN HERO!

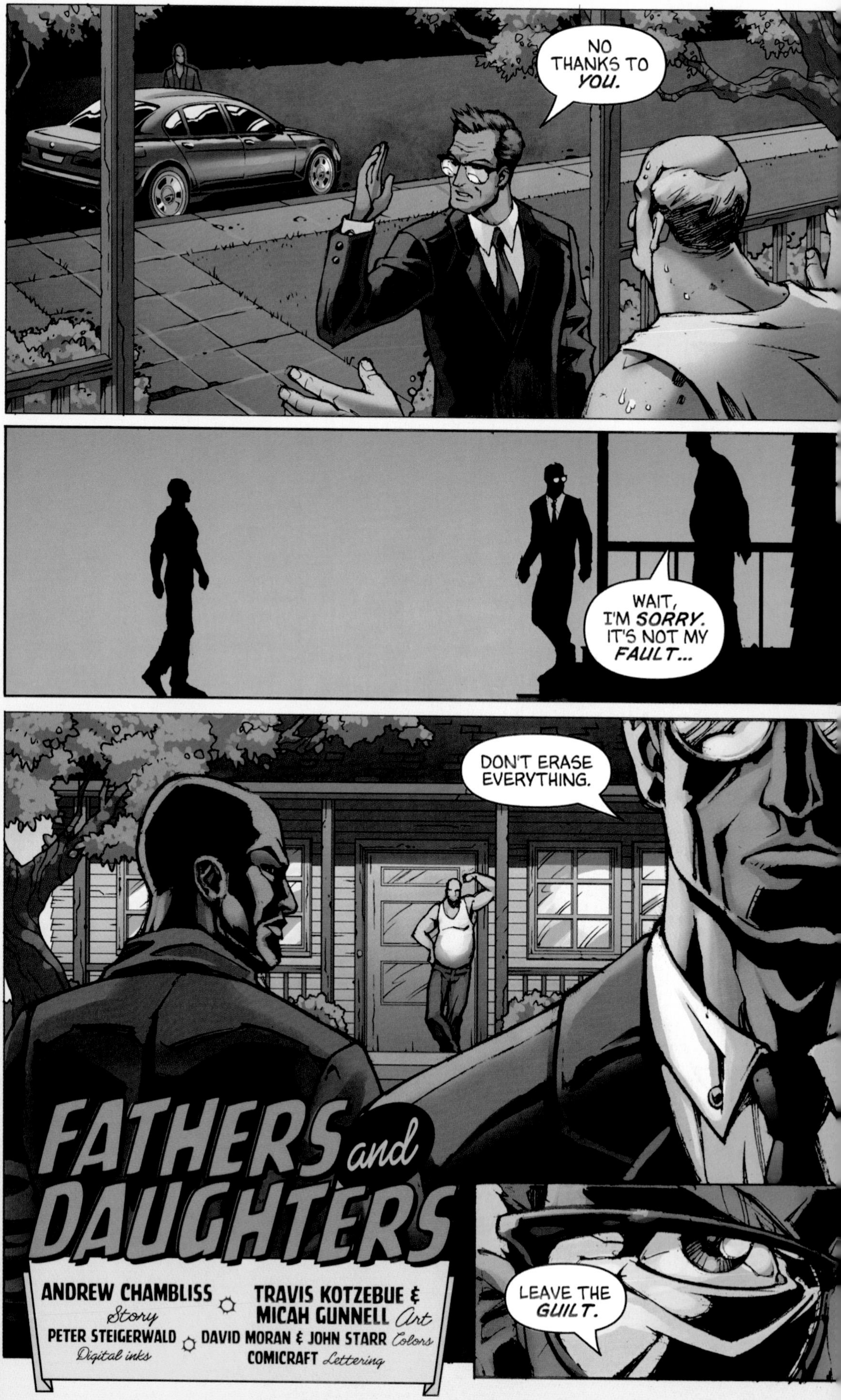
NO THANKS TO YOU.
WAIT, I'M SORRY. IT'S NOT MY FAULT...
DON'T ERASE EVERYTHING.
FATHERS and DAUGHTERS
ANDREW CHAMBLISS Story
TRAVIS KOTZEBUE & MICAH GUNNELL Art
PETER STEIGERWALD Digital inks
DAVID MORAN & JOHN STARR Colors
COMICRAFT Lettering
LEAVE THE GUILT.

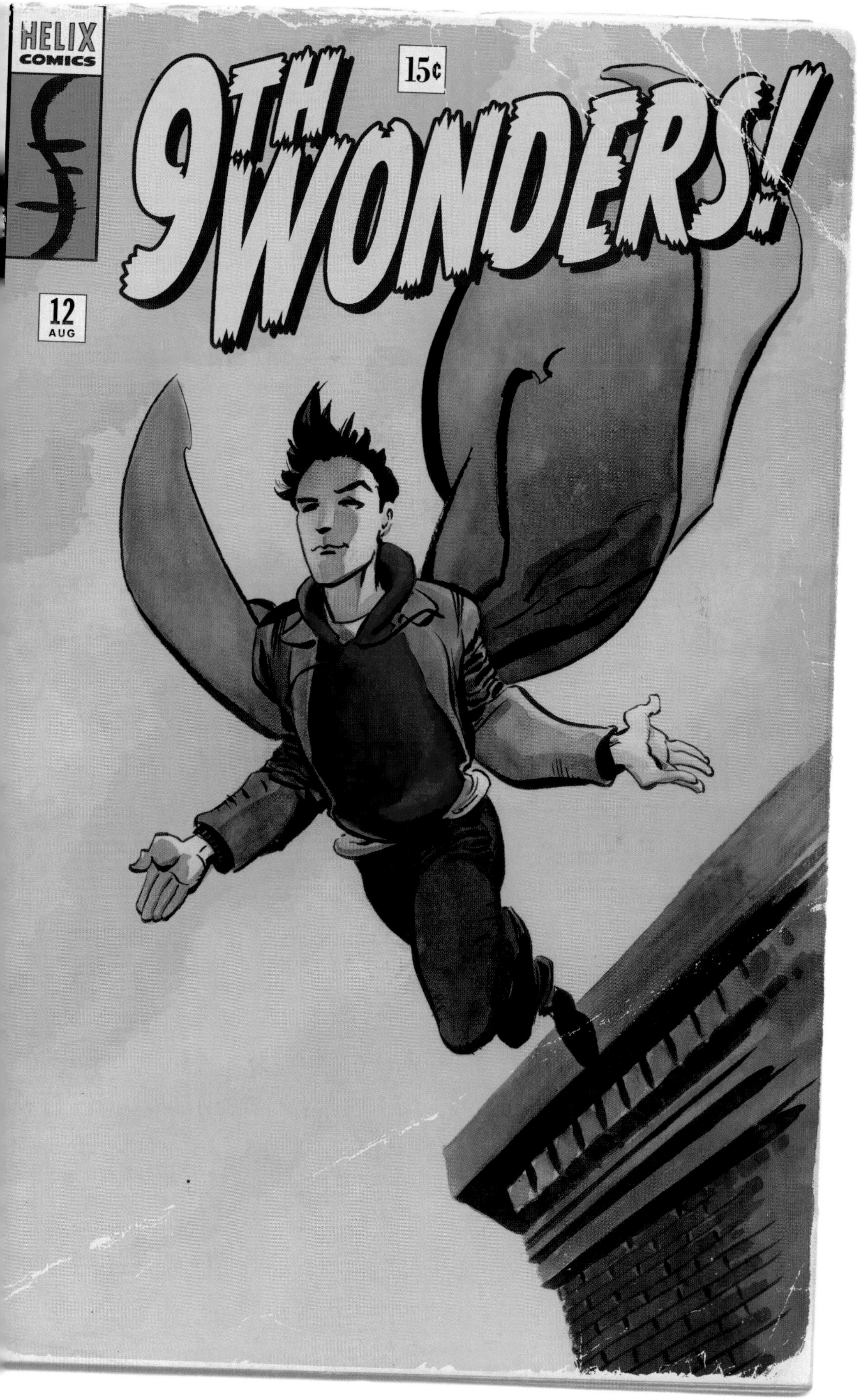

HELIX
COMICS
15¢
9TH WONDERS!
12
AUG

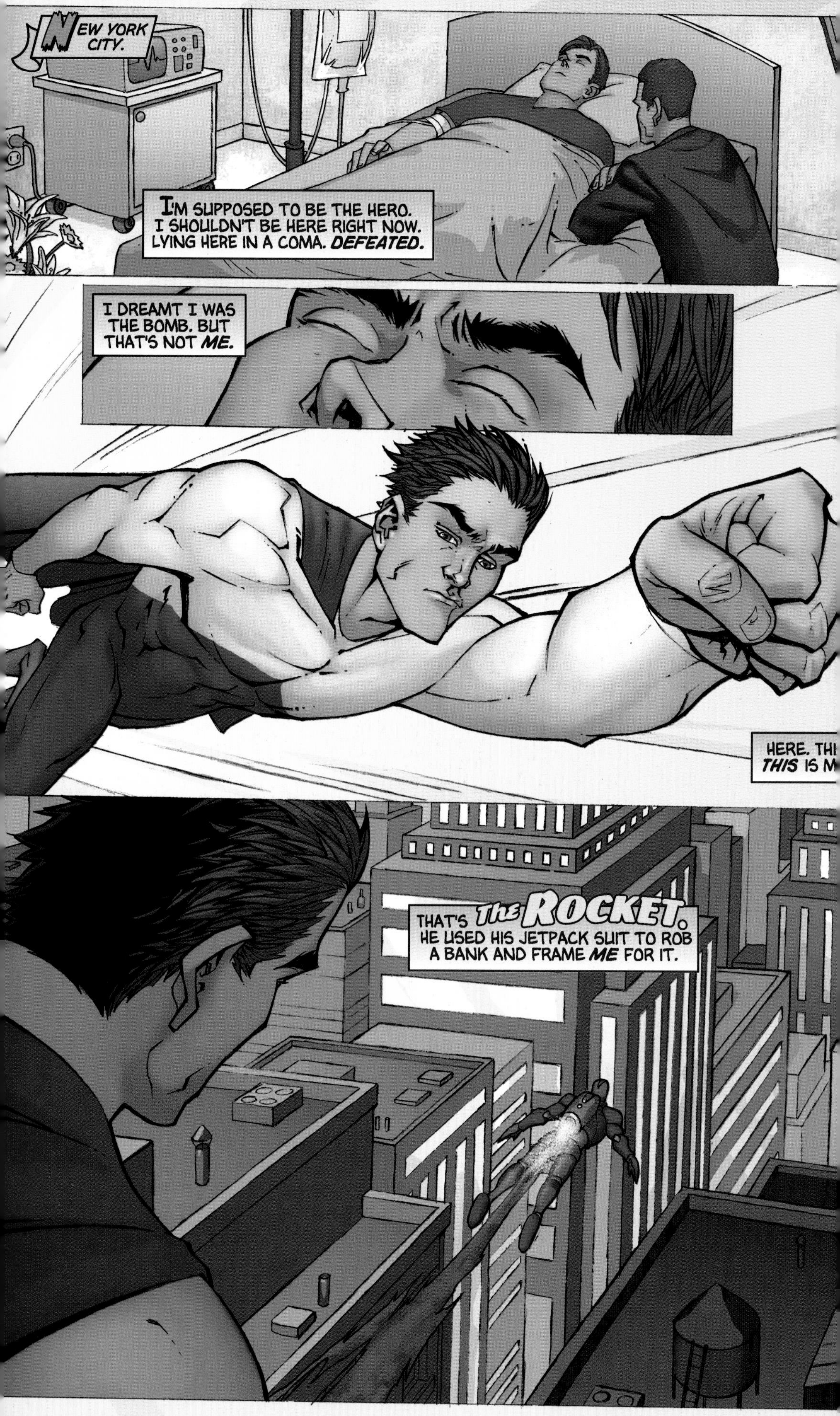
NEW YORK CITY.
I'M SUPPOSED TO BE THE HERO. I SHOULDN'T BE HERE RIGHT NOW. LYING HERE IN A COMA. DEFEATED.
I DREAMT I WAS THE BOMB. BUT THAT'S NOT ME.
HERE. THI
THIS IS M
THAT'S The ROCKET. HE USED HIS JETPACK SUIT TO ROB A BANK AND FRAME ME FOR IT.

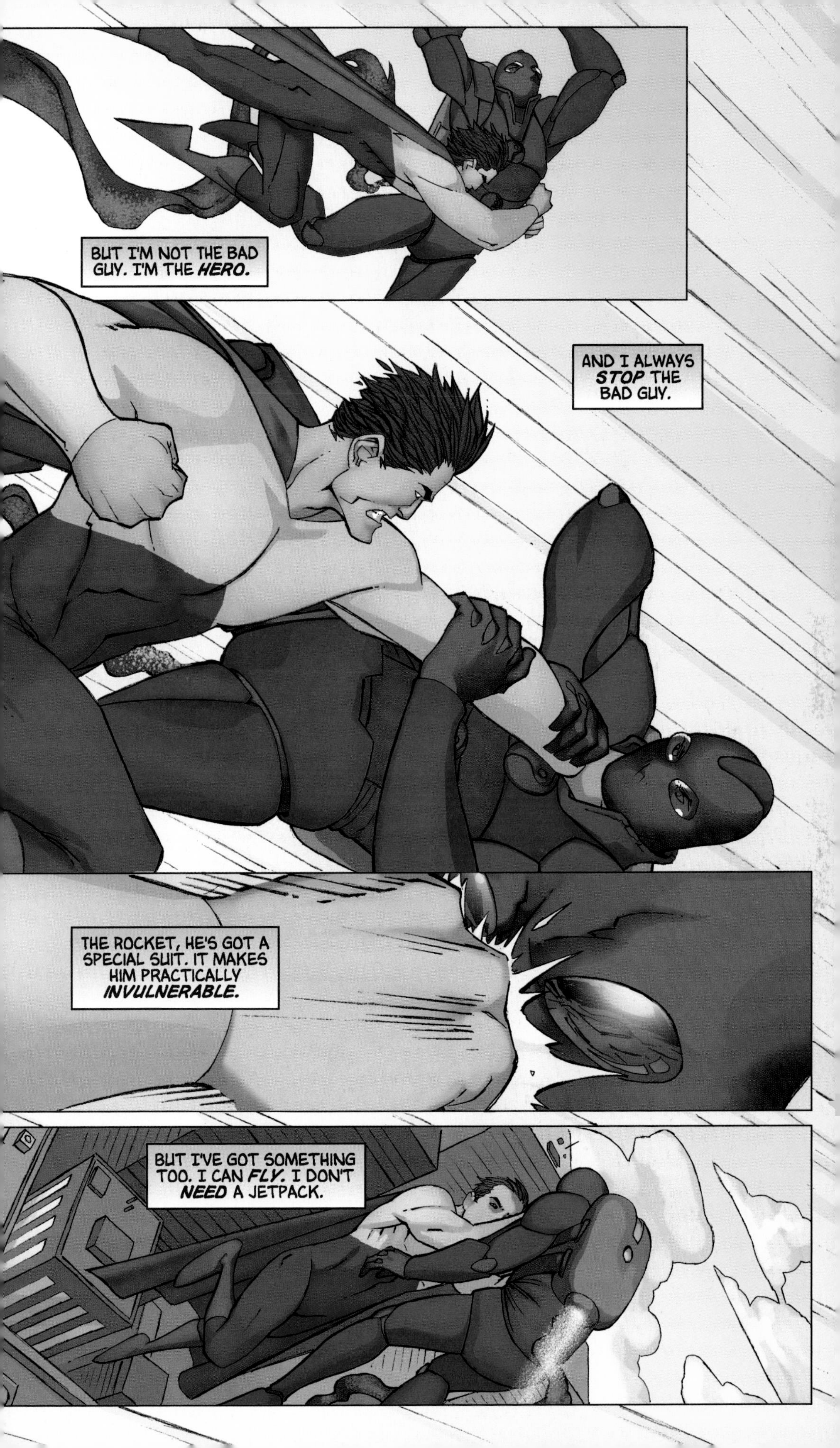

BUT I'M NOT THE BAD GUY. I'M THE HERO.
AND I ALWAYS STOP THE BAD GUY.
THE ROCKET, HE'S GOT A SPECIAL SUIT. IT MAKES HIM PRACTICALLY INVULNERABLE.
BUT I'VE GOT SOMETHING TOO. I CAN FLY. I DON'T NEED A JETPACK.

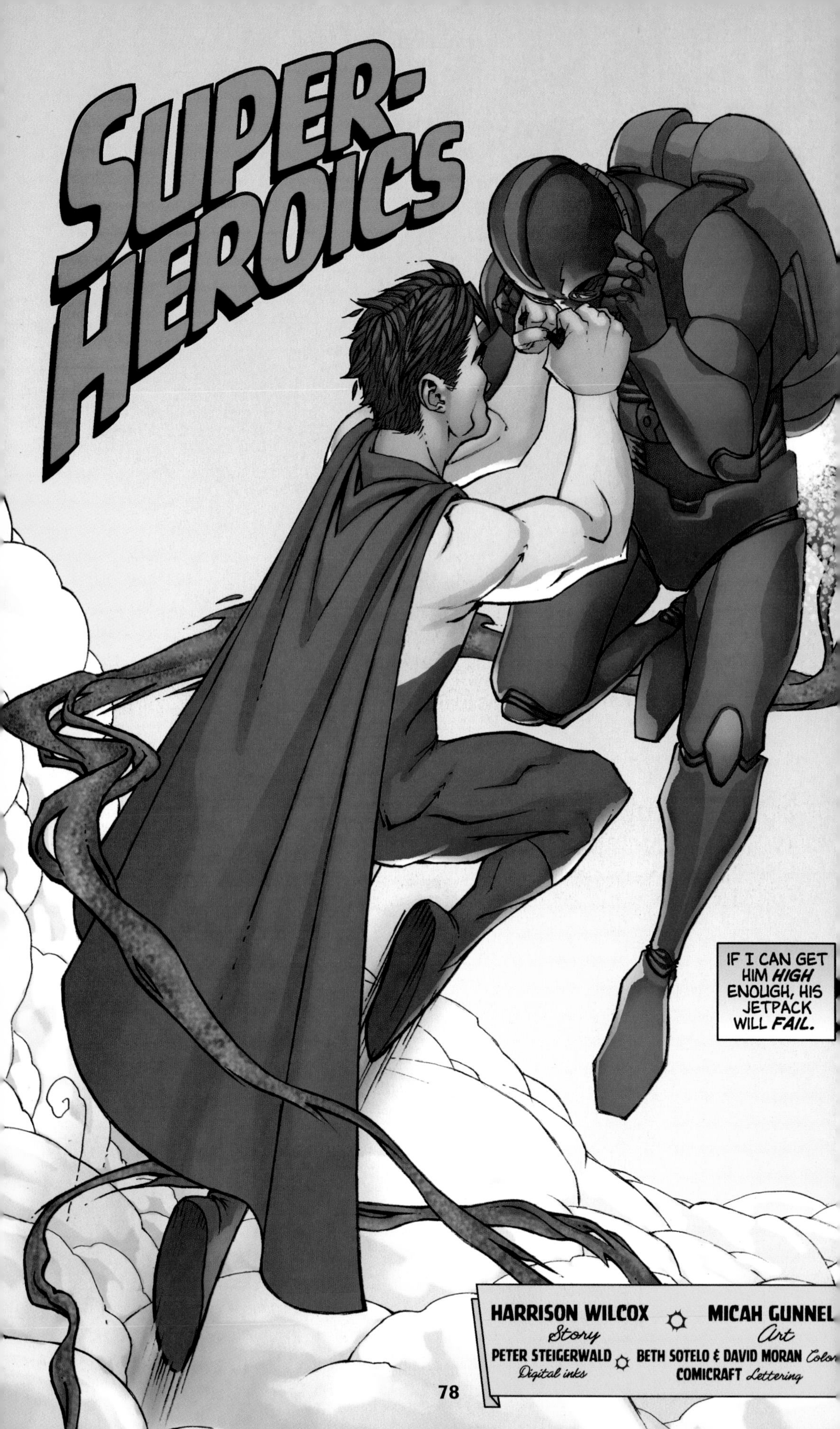
SUPER-HEROICS
IF I CAN GET HIM HIGH ENOUGH, HIS JETPACK WILL FAIL.
HARRISON WILCOX Story
MICAH GUNNEL Art
PETER STEIGERWALD Digital inks
BETH SOTELO & DAVID MORAN Colors
COMICRAFT Lettering

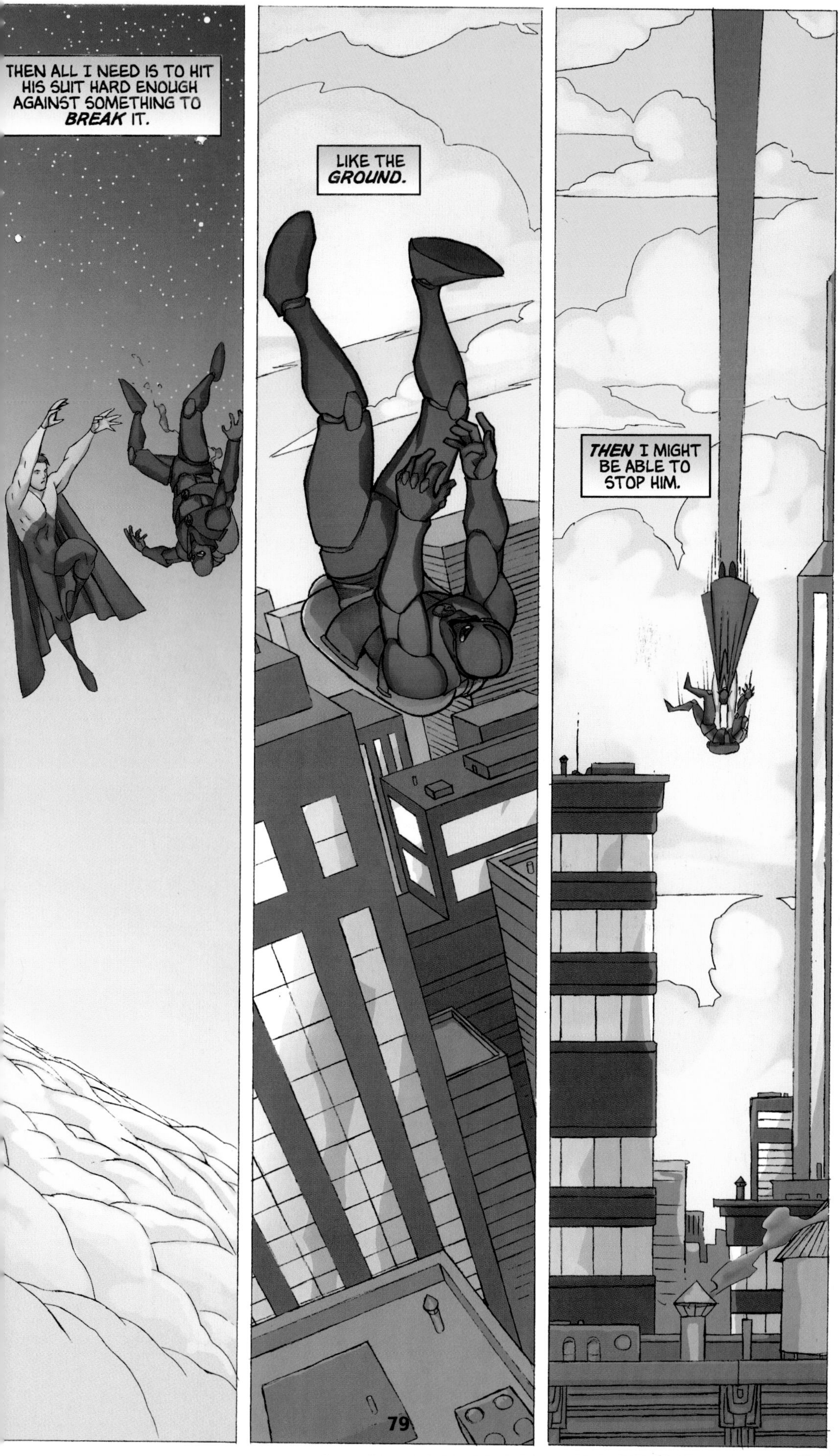
THEN ALL I NEED IS TO HIT HIS SUIT HARD ENOUGH AGAINST SOMETHING TO *BREAK* IT.
LIKE THE *GROUND.*
THEN I MIGHT BE ABLE TO STOP HIM.

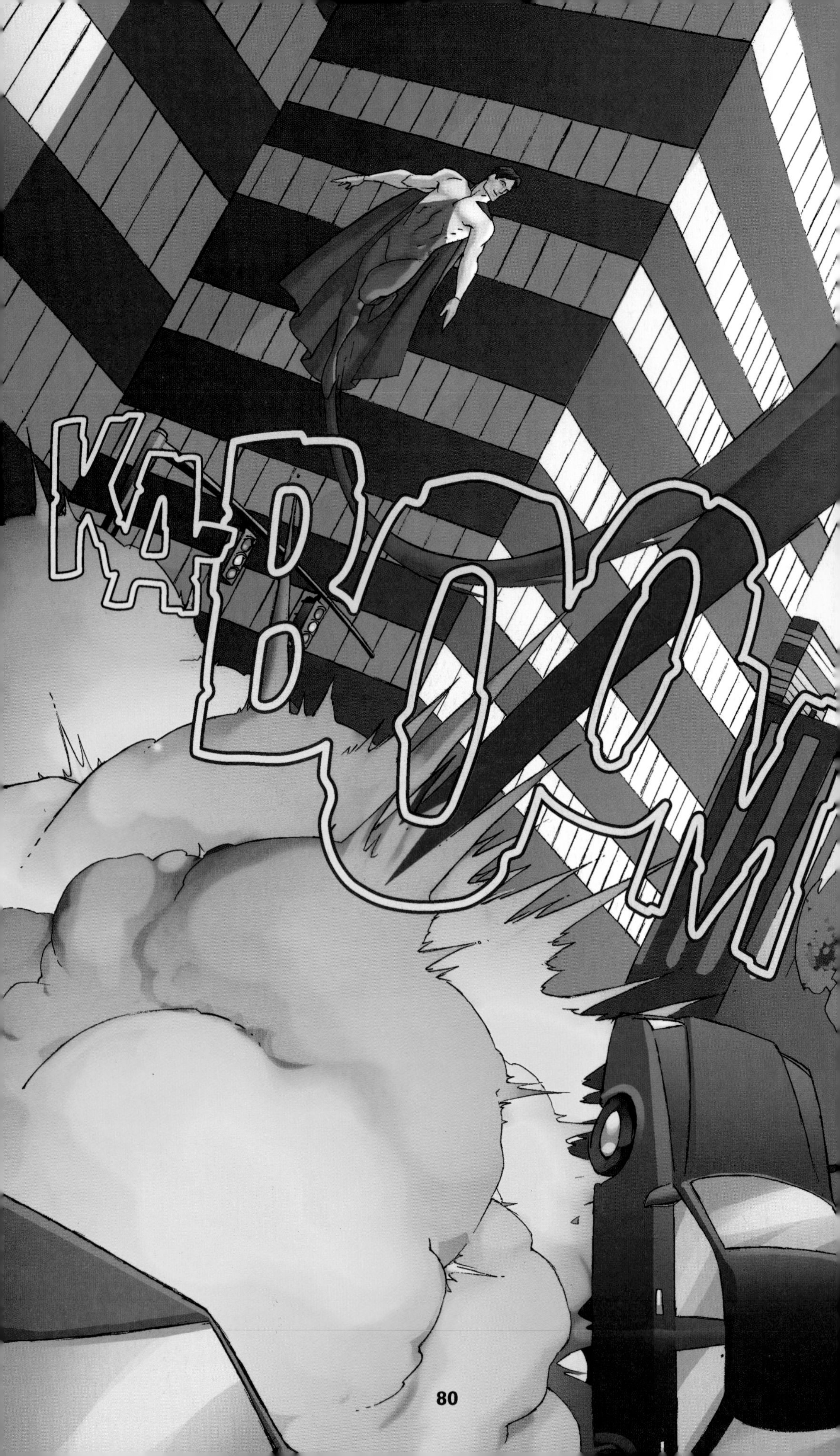
KABOOM

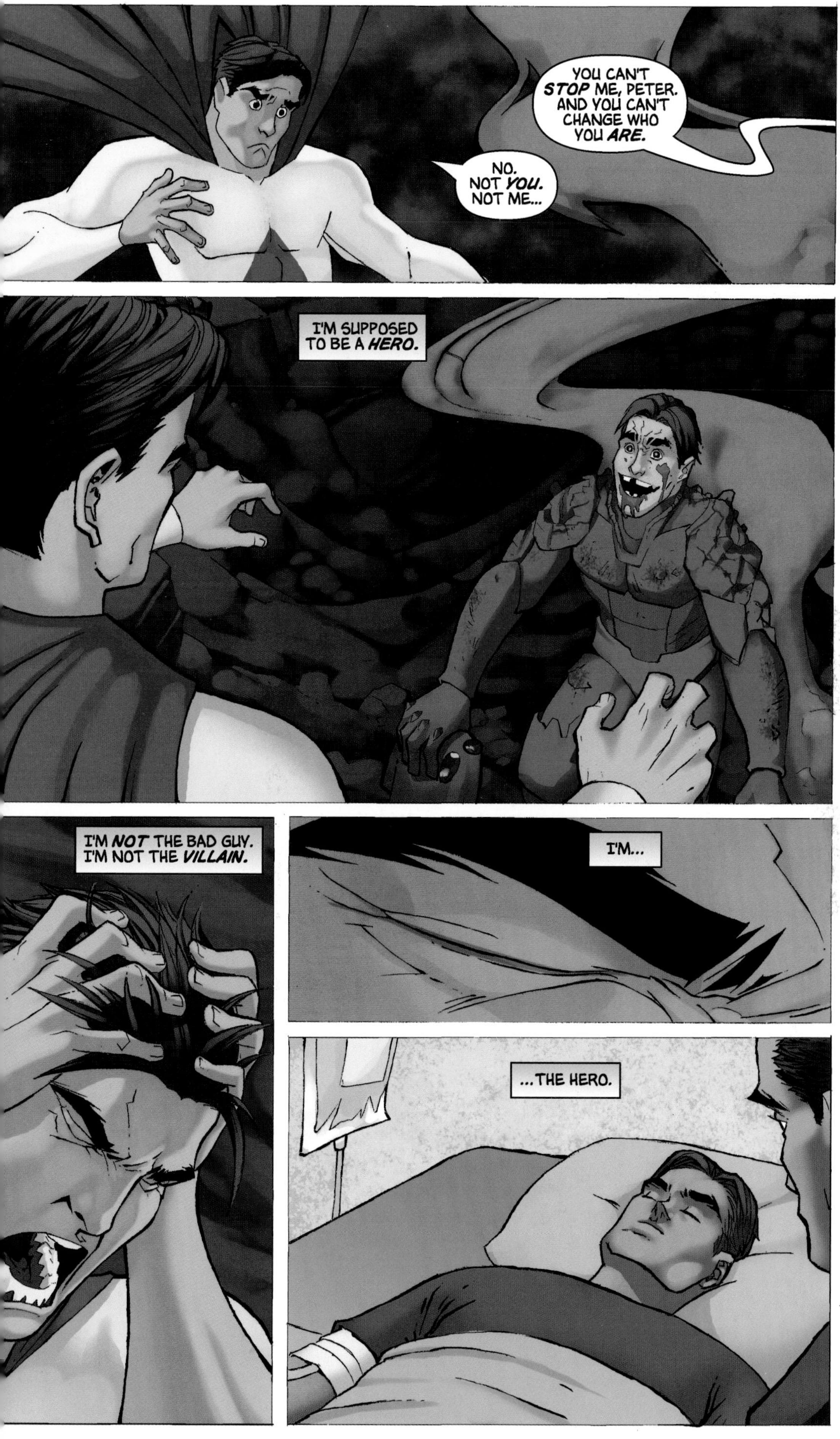
YOU CAN'T STOP ME, PETER. AND YOU CAN'T CHANGE WHO YOU ARE.
NO. NOT YOU. NOT ME...
I'M SUPPOSED TO BE A HERO.
I'M NOT THE BAD GUY. I'M NOT THE VILLAIN.
I'M...
...THE HERO.

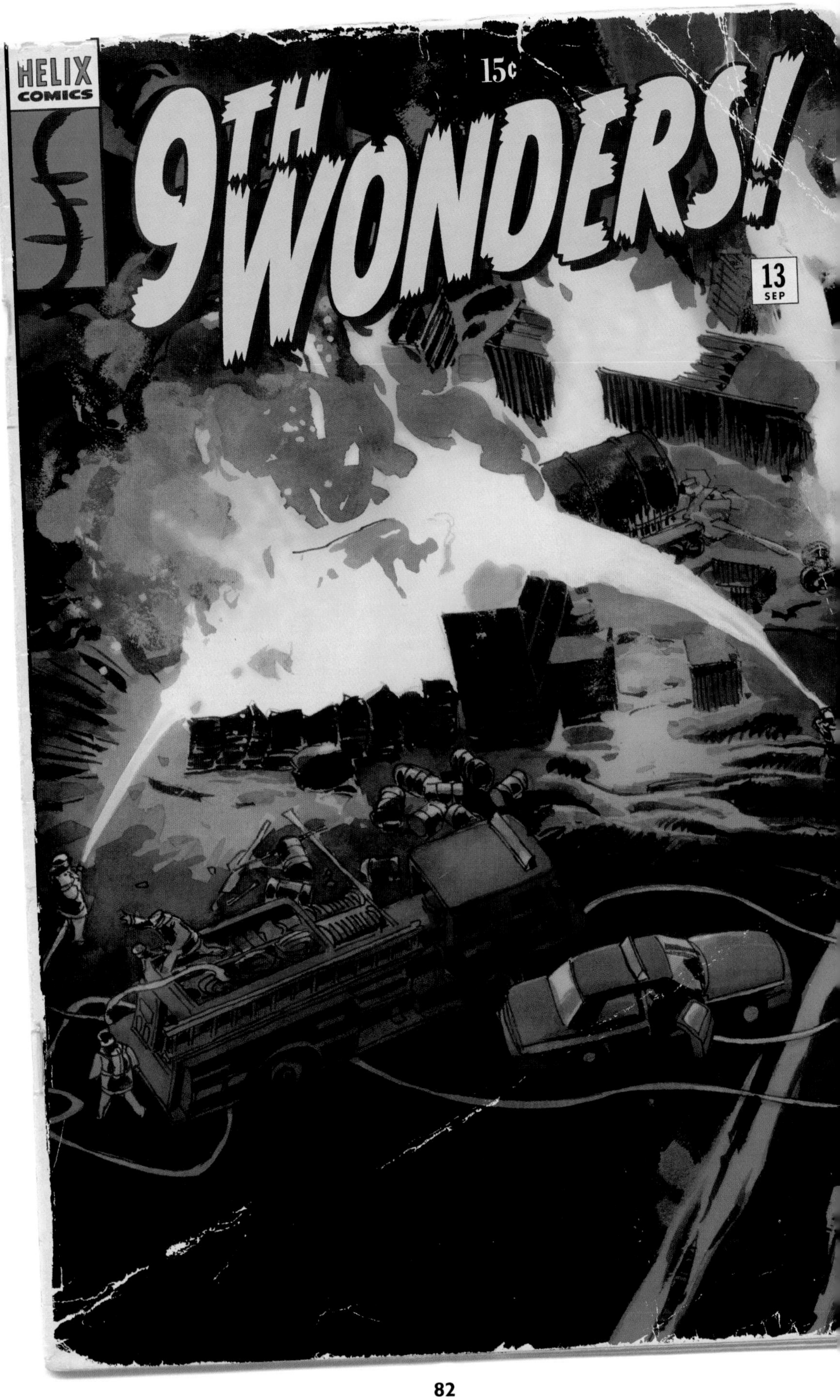
HELIX
COMICS
15¢
9TH WONDERS!
13
SEP

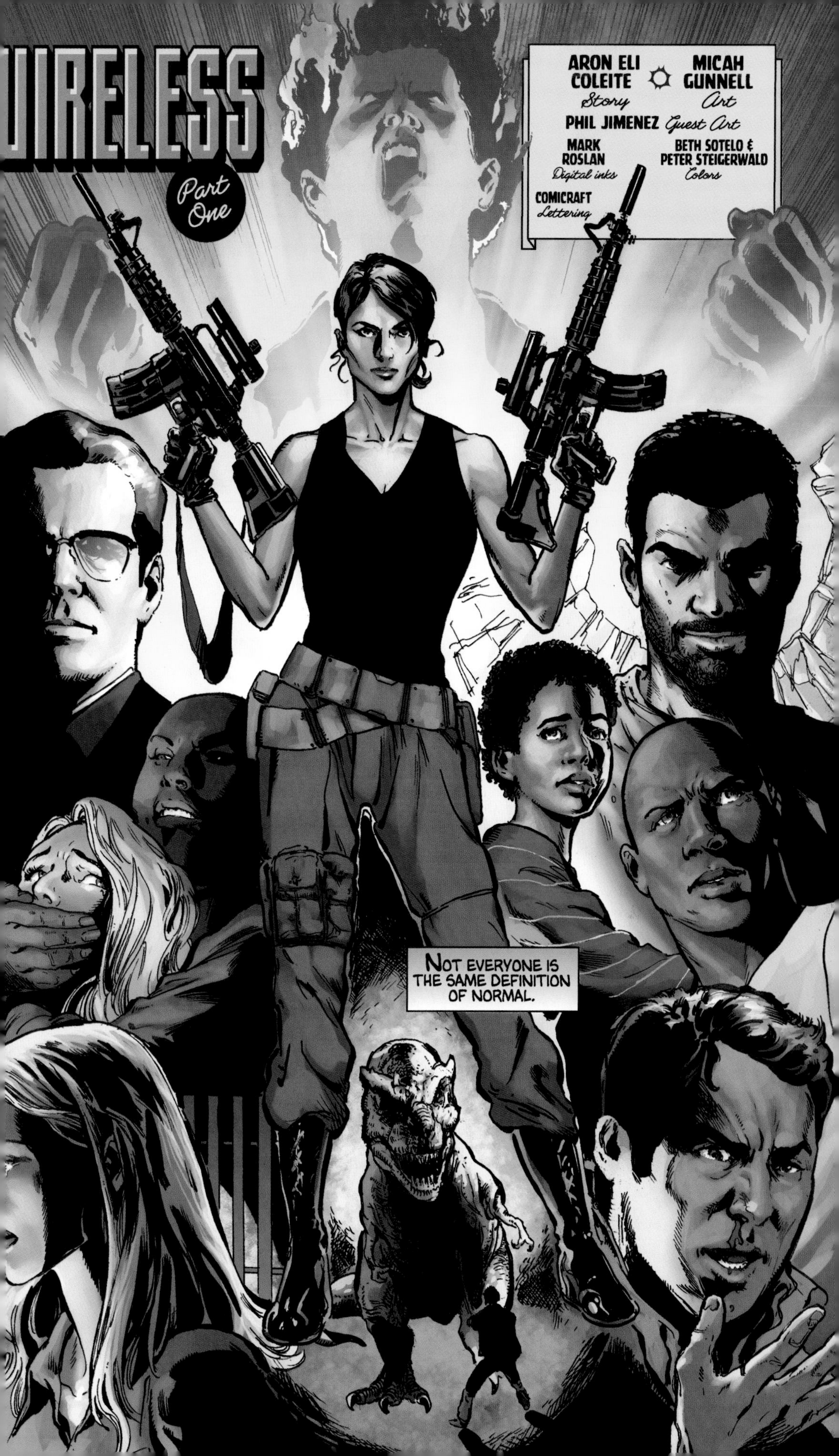
IRELESS
Part One
ARON ELI COLEITE Story
MICAH GUNNELL Art
PHIL JIMENEZ Guest Art
MARK ROSLAN Digital inks
BETH SOTELO & PETER STEIGERWALD Colors
COMICRAFT Lettering
NOT EVERYONE IS THE SAME DEFINITION OF NORMAL.

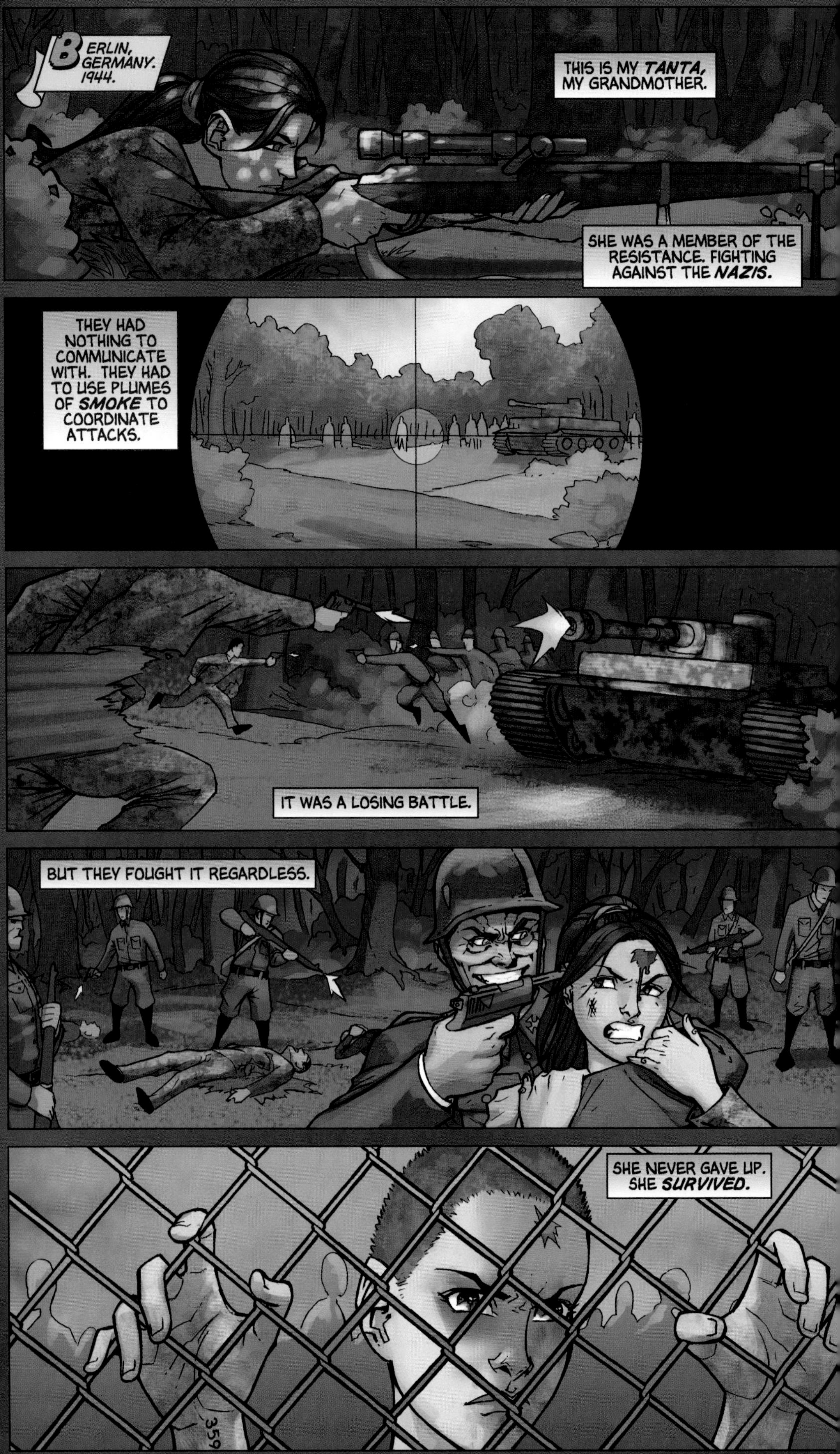
BERLIN, GERMANY. 1944.
THIS IS MY TANTA, MY GRANDMOTHER.
SHE WAS A MEMBER OF THE RESISTANCE. FIGHTING AGAINST THE NAZIS.
THEY HAD NOTHING TO COMMUNICATE WITH. THEY HAD TO USE PLUMES OF SMOKE TO COORDINATE ATTACKS.
IT WAS A LOSING BATTLE.
BUT THEY FOUGHT IT REGARDLESS.
SHE NEVER GAVE UP. SHE SURVIVED.
359

JERUSALEM, ISRAEL. 1967.

THAT'S MY MOTHER. *ZAHAVA.* YOU CAN'T TELL UNDERNEATH THAT FLIGHT HELMET, BUT SHE'S QUITE BEAUTIFUL.

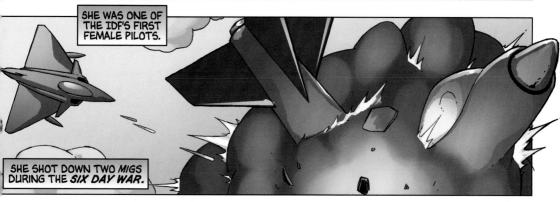

SHE WAS ONE OF THE IDF'S FIRST FEMALE PILOTS.

SHE SHOT DOWN TWO *MIGS* DURING THE *SIX DAY WAR.*

I'M THE GAP TOOTHED GIRL IN THE MIDDLE. *HANA.*

A FAR CRY FROM MY MOTHER AND GRANDMOTHER'S LEGACY.

THE WARS WERE OVER. THE MAJOR BATTLES FINISHED. OR AT LEAST, THAT'S WHAT WE WANTED TO *BELIEVE.*

BUS

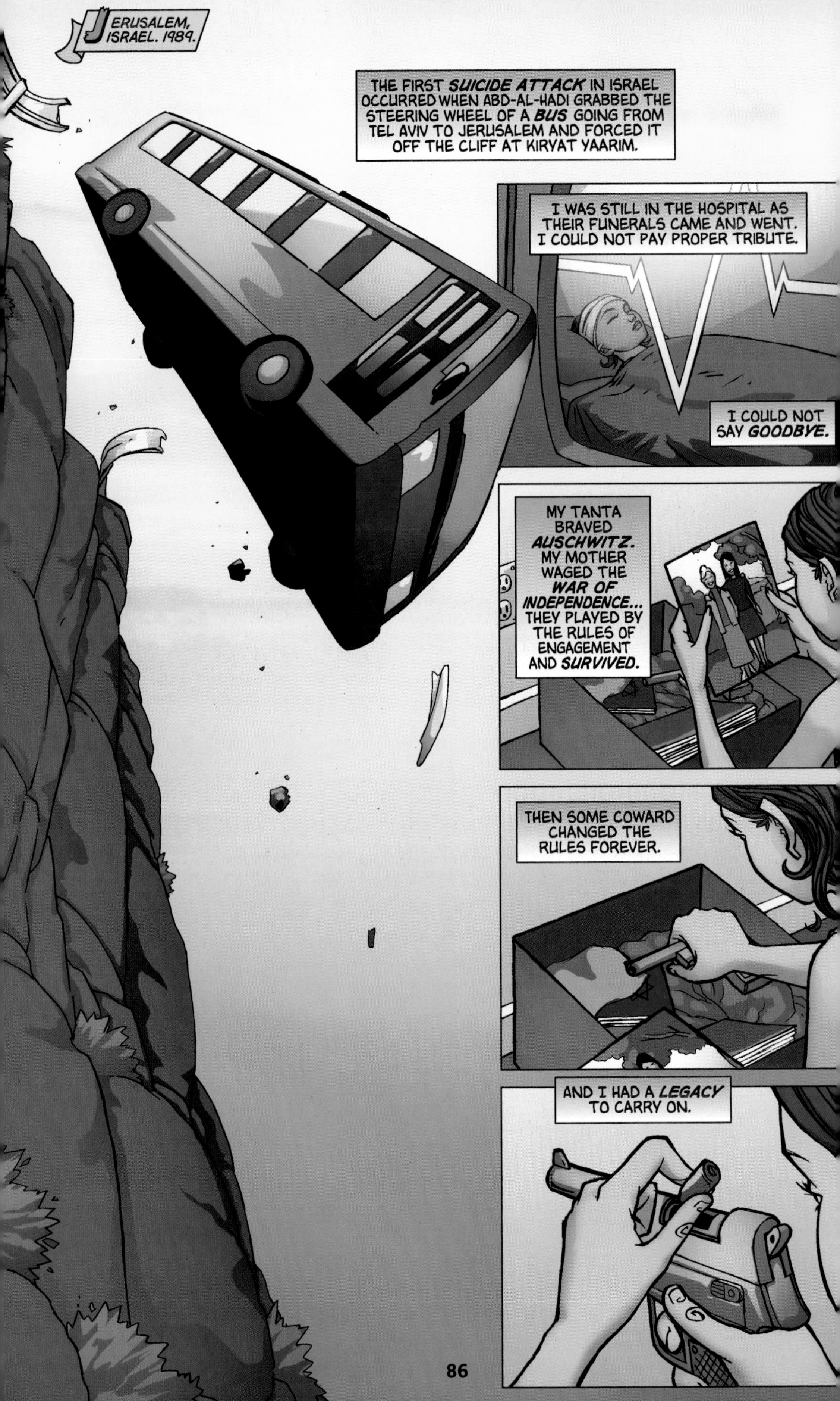
JERUSALEM, ISRAEL. 1989.
THE FIRST SUICIDE ATTACK IN ISRAEL OCCURRED WHEN ABD-AL-HADI GRABBED THE STEERING WHEEL OF A BUS GOING FROM TEL AVIV TO JERUSALEM AND FORCED IT OFF THE CLIFF AT KIRYAT YAARIM.
I WAS STILL IN THE HOSPITAL AS THEIR FUNERALS CAME AND WENT. I COULD NOT PAY PROPER TRIBUTE.
I COULD NOT SAY GOODBYE.
MY TANTA BRAVED AUSCHWITZ. MY MOTHER WAGED THE WAR OF INDEPENDENCE... THEY PLAYED BY THE RULES OF ENGAGEMENT AND SURVIVED.
THEN SOME COWARD CHANGED THE RULES FOREVER.
AND I HAD A LEGACY TO CARRY ON.

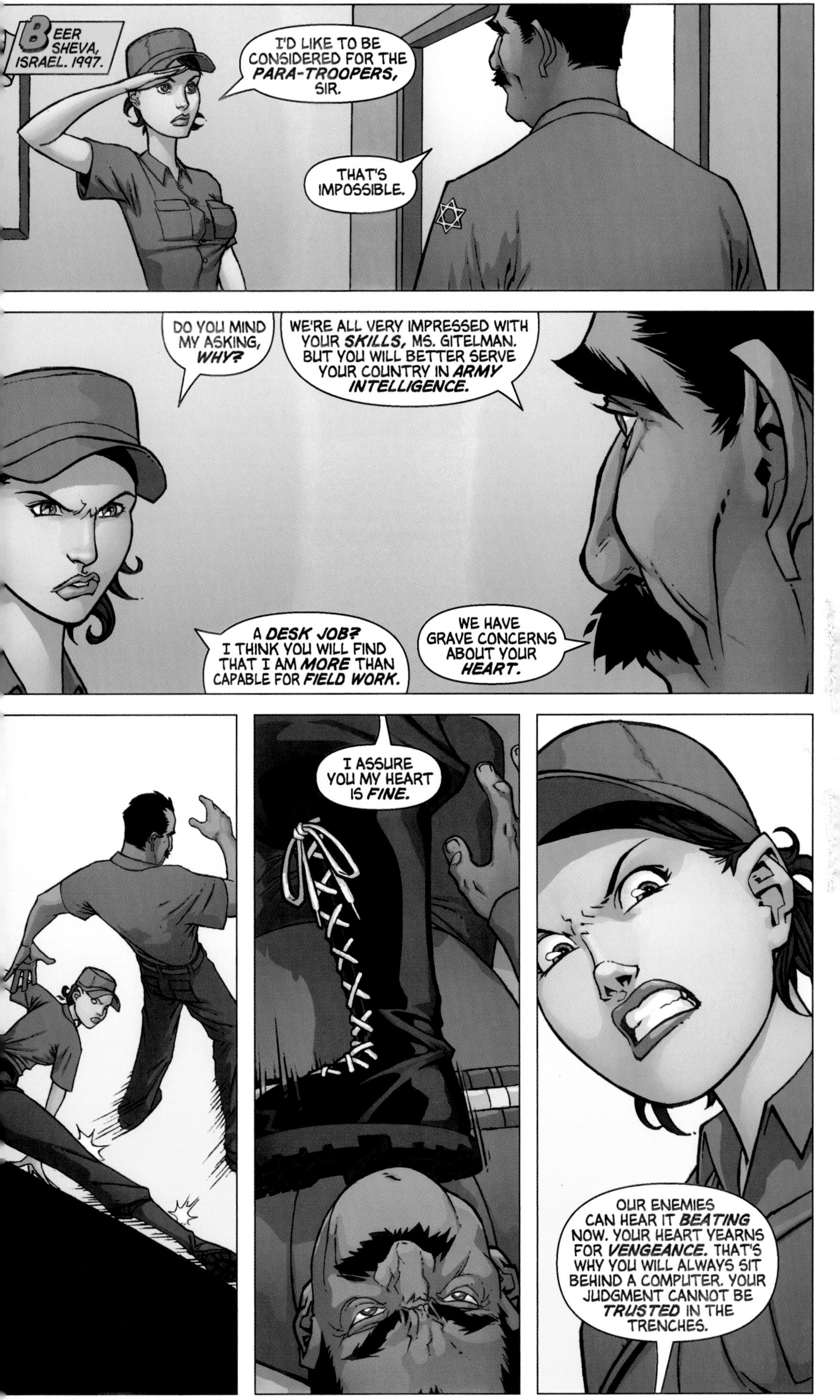
BEER SHEVA, ISRAEL. 1997.
I'D LIKE TO BE CONSIDERED FOR THE PARA-TROOPERS, SIR.
THAT'S IMPOSSIBLE.
DO YOU MIND MY ASKING, WHY?
WE'RE ALL VERY IMPRESSED WITH YOUR SKILLS, MS. GITELMAN. BUT YOU WILL BETTER SERVE YOUR COUNTRY IN ARMY INTELLIGENCE.
A DESK JOB? I THINK YOU WILL FIND THAT I AM MORE THAN CAPABLE FOR FIELD WORK.
WE HAVE GRAVE CONCERNS ABOUT YOUR HEART.
I ASSURE YOU MY HEART IS FINE.
OUR ENEMIES CAN HEAR IT BEATING NOW. YOUR HEART YEARNS FOR VENGEANCE. THAT'S WHY YOU WILL ALWAYS SIT BEHIND A COMPUTER. YOUR JUDGMENT CANNOT BE TRUSTED IN THE TRENCHES.

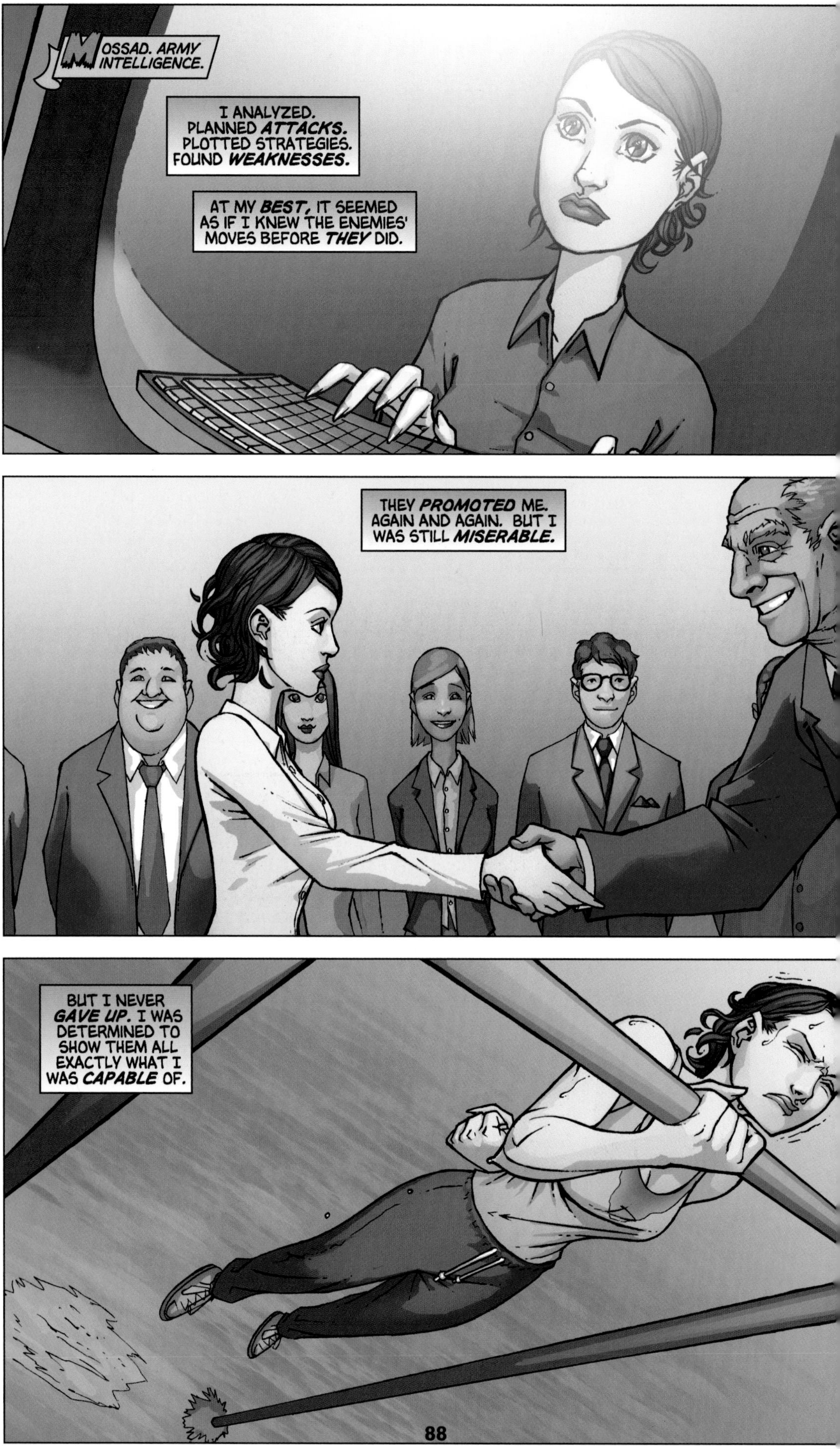
MOSSAD. ARMY INTELLIGENCE.
I ANALYZED. PLANNED ATTACKS. PLOTTED STRATEGIES. FOUND WEAKNESSES.
AT MY BEST, IT SEEMED AS IF I KNEW THE ENEMIES' MOVES BEFORE THEY DID.
THEY PROMOTED ME. AGAIN AND AGAIN. BUT I WAS STILL MISERABLE.
BUT I NEVER GAVE UP. I WAS DETERMINED TO SHOW THEM ALL EXACTLY WHAT I WAS CAPABLE OF.

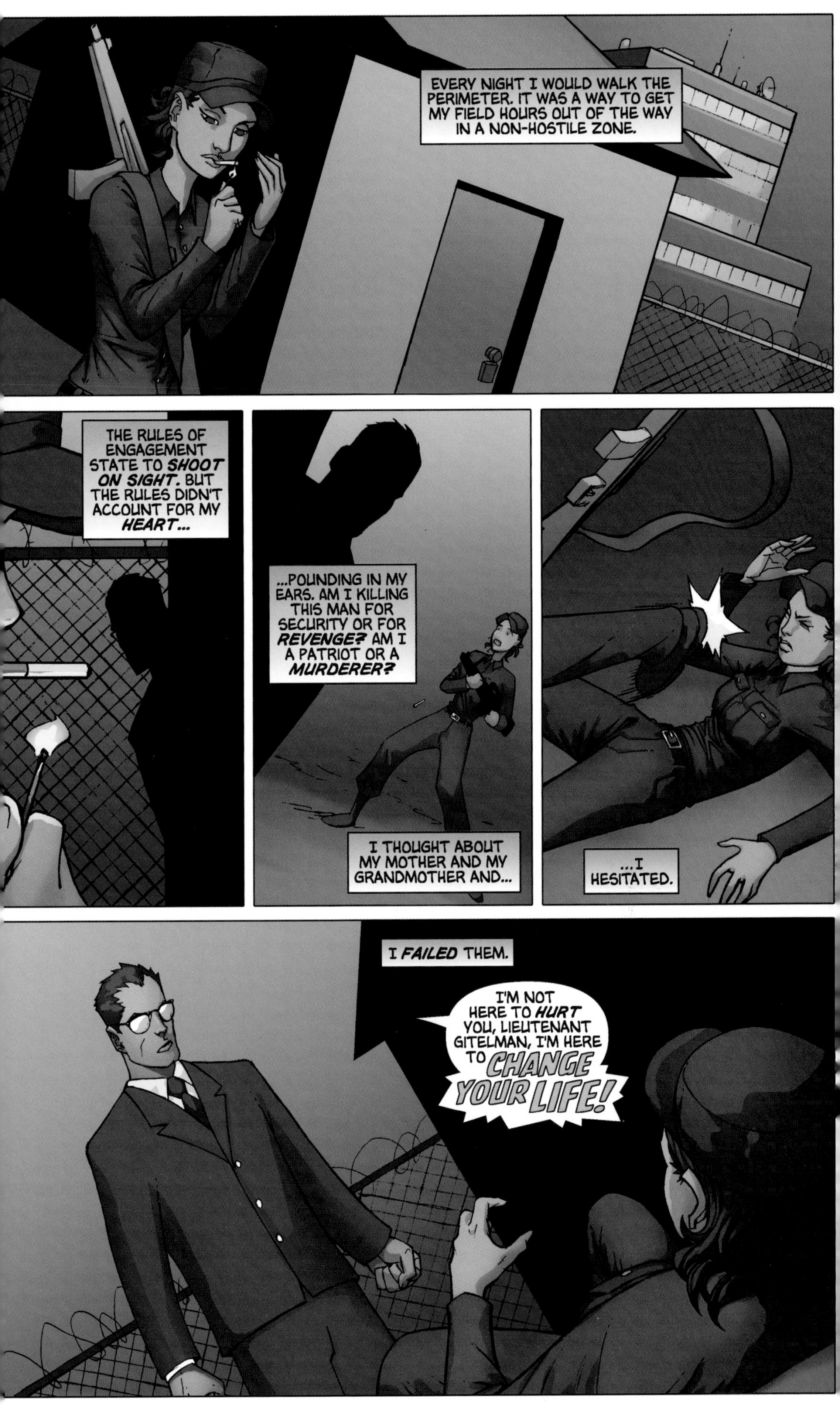
EVERY NIGHT I WOULD WALK THE PERIMETER. IT WAS A WAY TO GET MY FIELD HOURS OUT OF THE WAY IN A NON-HOSTILE ZONE.
THE RULES OF ENGAGEMENT STATE TO *SHOOT ON SIGHT*. BUT THE RULES DIDN'T ACCOUNT FOR MY *HEART*...
...POUNDING IN MY EARS. AM I KILLING THIS MAN FOR SECURITY OR FOR *REVENGE?* AM I A PATRIOT OR A *MURDERER?*
I THOUGHT ABOUT MY MOTHER AND MY GRANDMOTHER AND...
...I HESITATED.
I *FAILED* THEM.
I'M NOT HERE TO *HURT* YOU, LIEUTENANT GITELMAN, I'M HERE TO *CHANGE YOUR LIFE!*

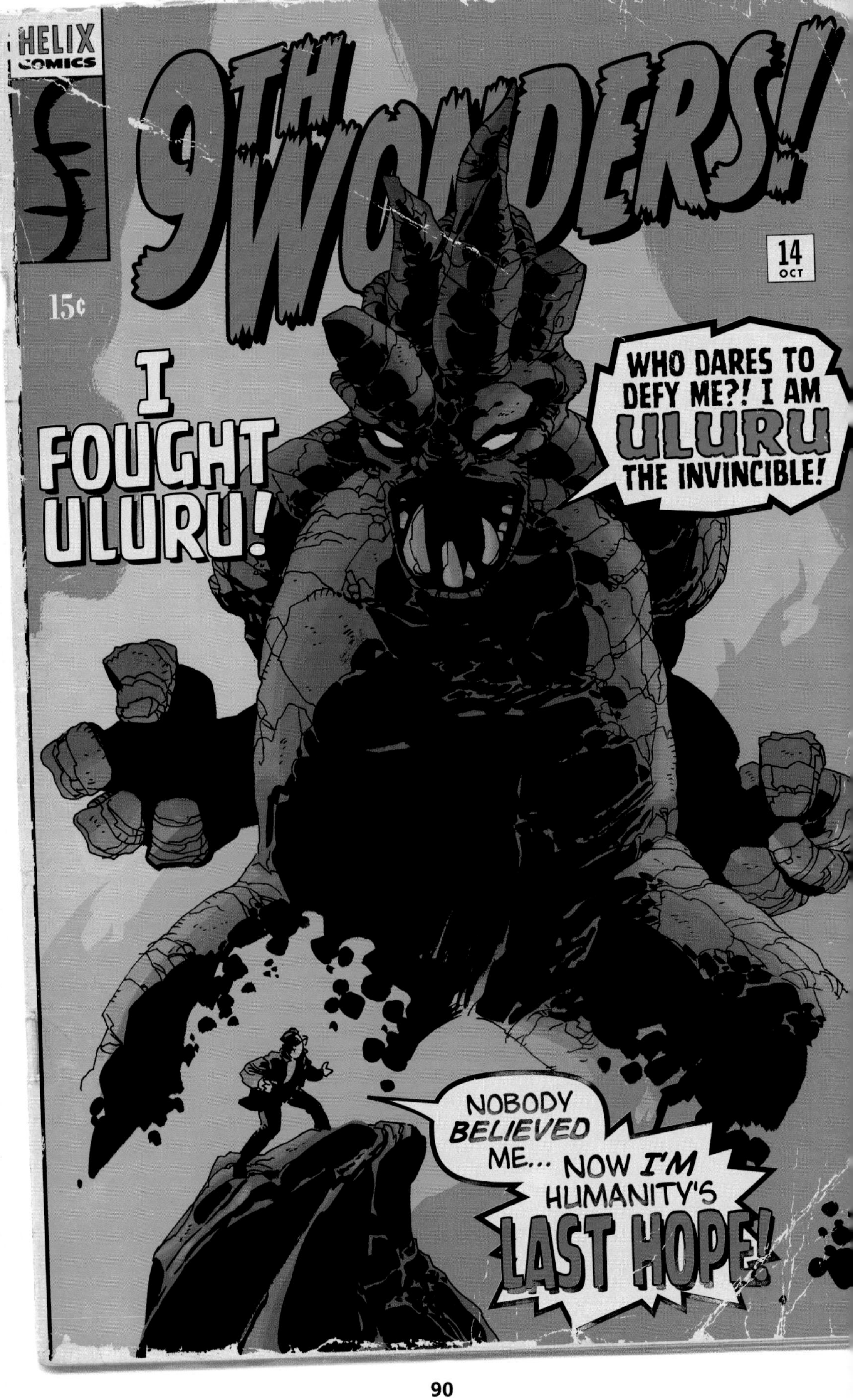
HELIX COMICS
9TH WONDERS!
15¢
14 OCT
I FOUGHT ULURU!
WHO DARES TO DEFY ME?! I AM ULURU THE INVINCIBLE!
NOBODY BELIEVED ME... NOW I'M HUMANITY'S LAST HOPE!

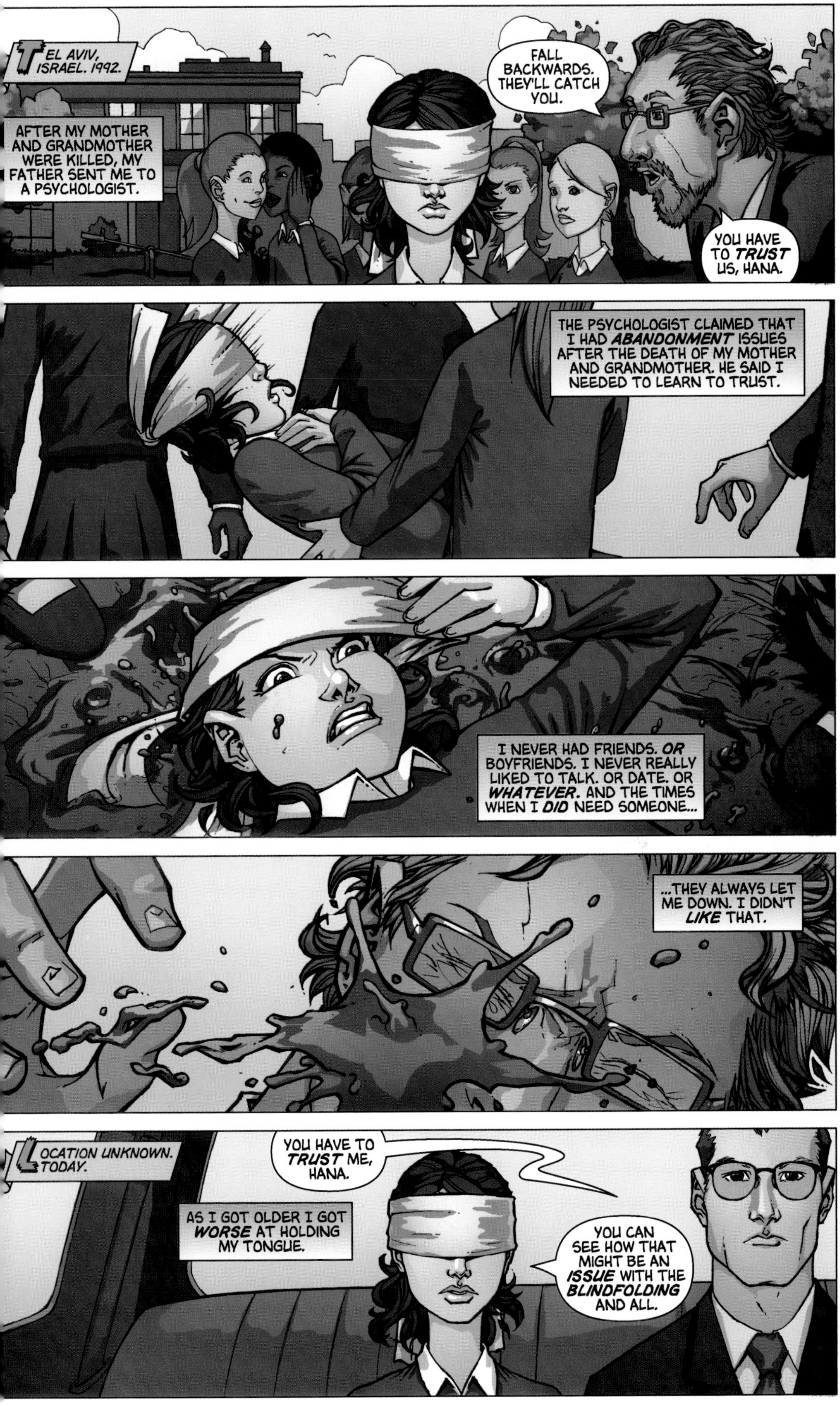
TEL AVIV, ISRAEL. 1992.
AFTER MY MOTHER AND GRANDMOTHER WERE KILLED, MY FATHER SENT ME TO A PSYCHOLOGIST.
FALL BACKWARDS. THEY'LL CATCH YOU.
YOU HAVE TO TRUST US, HANA.
THE PSYCHOLOGIST CLAIMED THAT I HAD ABANDONMENT ISSUES AFTER THE DEATH OF MY MOTHER AND GRANDMOTHER. HE SAID I NEEDED TO LEARN TO TRUST.
I NEVER HAD FRIENDS. OR BOYFRIENDS. I NEVER REALLY LIKED TO TALK. OR DATE. OR WHATEVER. AND THE TIMES WHEN I DID NEED SOMEONE...
...THEY ALWAYS LET ME DOWN. I DIDN'T LIKE THAT.
LOCATION UNKNOWN. TODAY.
YOU HAVE TO TRUST ME, HANA.
AS I GOT OLDER I GOT WORSE AT HOLDING MY TONGUE.
YOU CAN SEE HOW THAT MIGHT BE AN ISSUE WITH THE BLINDFOLDING AND ALL.

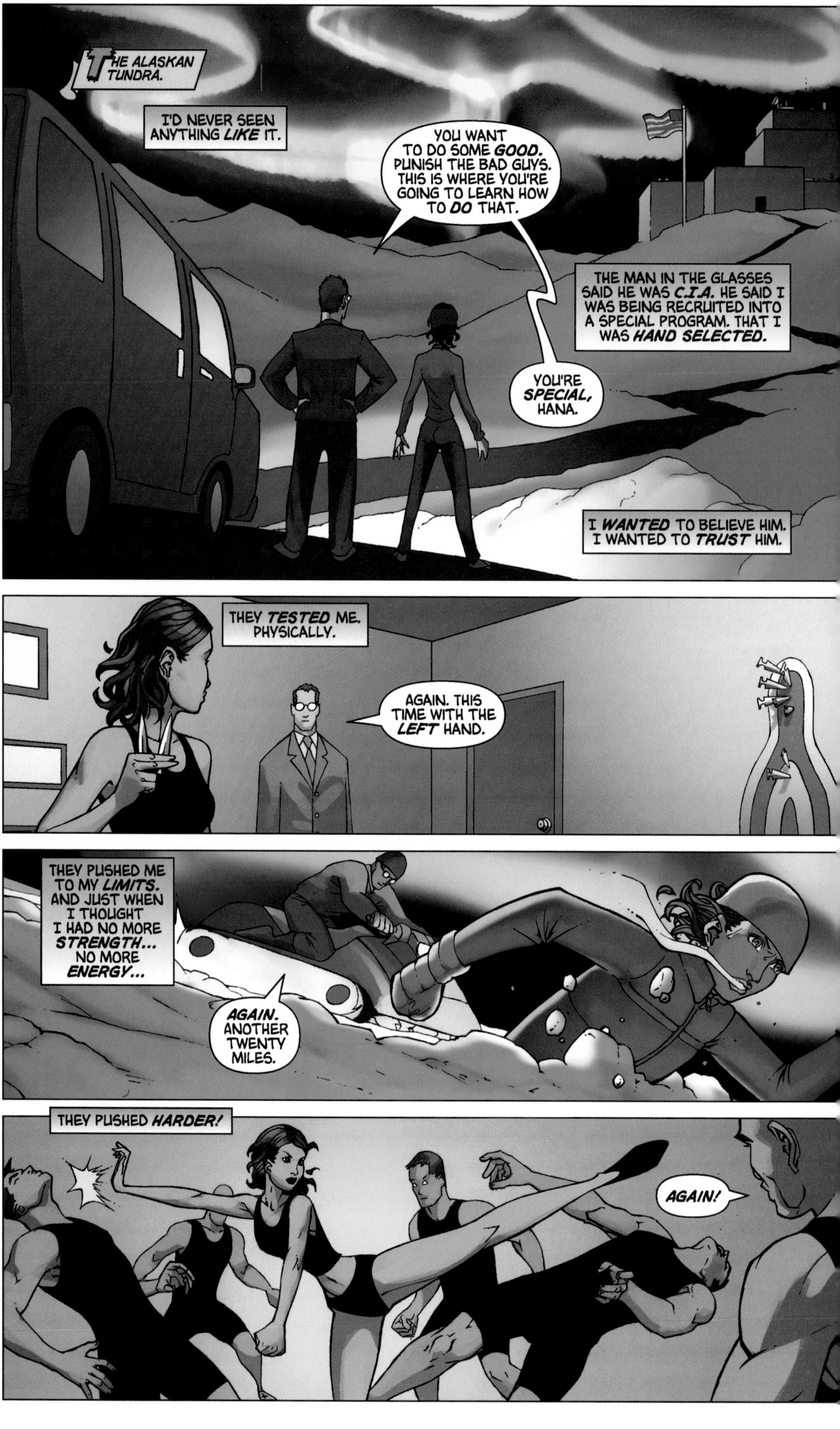
THE ALASKAN TUNDRA.
I'D NEVER SEEN ANYTHING LIKE IT.
YOU WANT TO DO SOME GOOD. PUNISH THE BAD GUYS. THIS IS WHERE YOU'RE GOING TO LEARN HOW TO DO THAT.
THE MAN IN THE GLASSES SAID HE WAS C.I.A. HE SAID I WAS BEING RECRUITED INTO A SPECIAL PROGRAM. THAT I WAS HAND SELECTED.
YOU'RE SPECIAL, HANA.
I WANTED TO BELIEVE HIM. I WANTED TO TRUST HIM.
THEY TESTED ME. PHYSICALLY.
AGAIN. THIS TIME WITH THE LEFT HAND.
THEY PUSHED ME TO MY LIMITS. AND JUST WHEN I THOUGHT I HAD NO MORE STRENGTH... NO MORE ENERGY...
AGAIN. ANOTHER TWENTY MILES.
THEY PUSHED HARDER!
AGAIN!

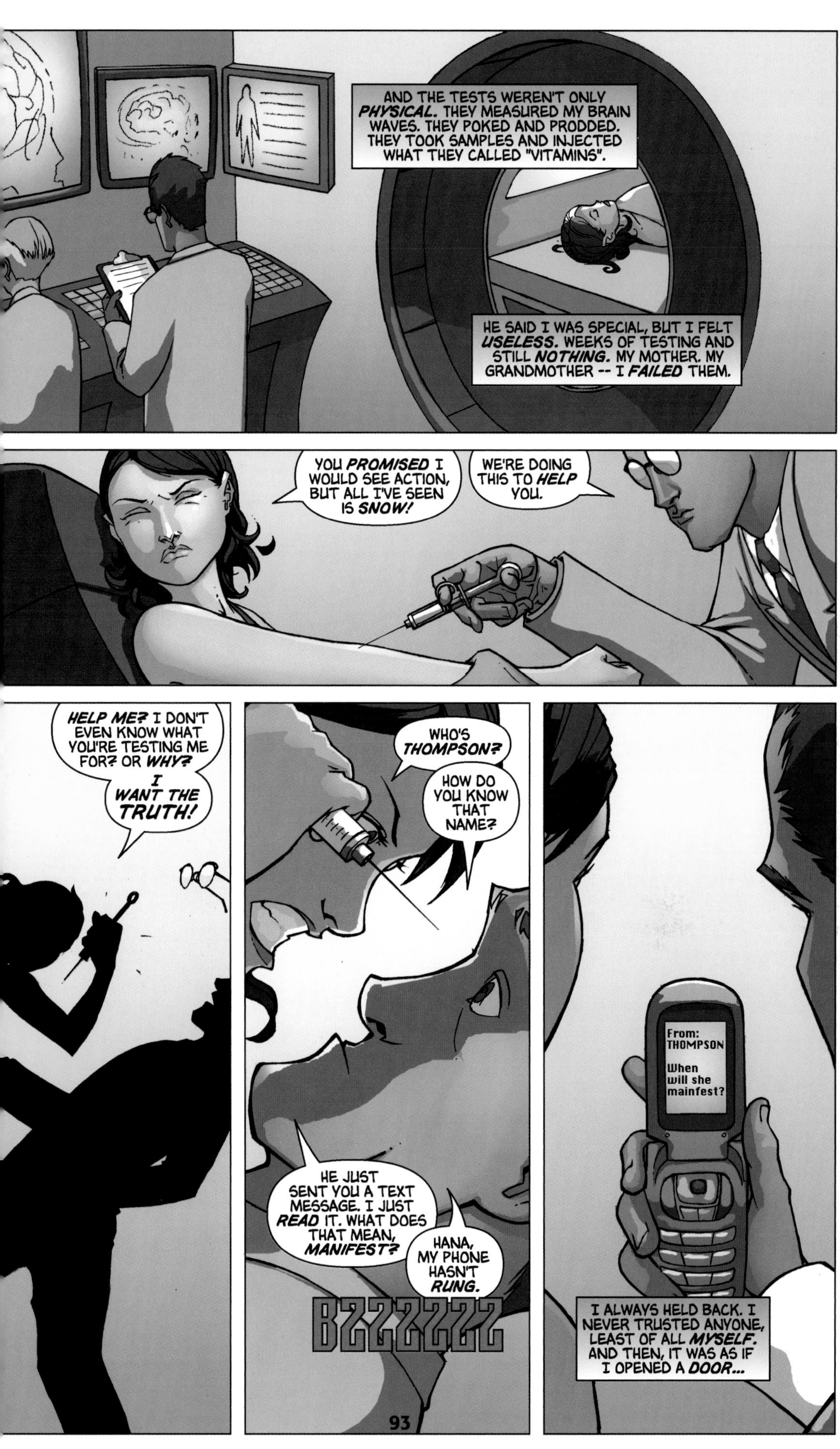
AND THE TESTS WEREN'T ONLY PHYSICAL. THEY MEASURED MY BRAIN WAVES. THEY POKED AND PRODDED. THEY TOOK SAMPLES AND INJECTED WHAT THEY CALLED "VITAMINS".
HE SAID I WAS SPECIAL, BUT I FELT USELESS. WEEKS OF TESTING AND STILL NOTHING. MY MOTHER. MY GRANDMOTHER -- I FAILED THEM.
YOU PROMISED I WOULD SEE ACTION, BUT ALL I'VE SEEN IS SNOW!
WE'RE DOING THIS TO HELP YOU.
HELP ME? I DON'T EVEN KNOW WHAT YOU'RE TESTING ME FOR? OR WHY?
I WANT THE TRUTH!
WHO'S THOMPSON?
HOW DO YOU KNOW THAT NAME?
HE JUST SENT YOU A TEXT MESSAGE. I JUST READ IT. WHAT DOES THAT MEAN, MANIFEST?
HANA, MY PHONE HASN'T RUNG.
BZZZZZZ
From: THOMPSON
When will she mainfest?
I ALWAYS HELD BACK. I NEVER TRUSTED ANYONE, LEAST OF ALL MYSELF. AND THEN, IT WAS AS IF I OPENED A DOOR...

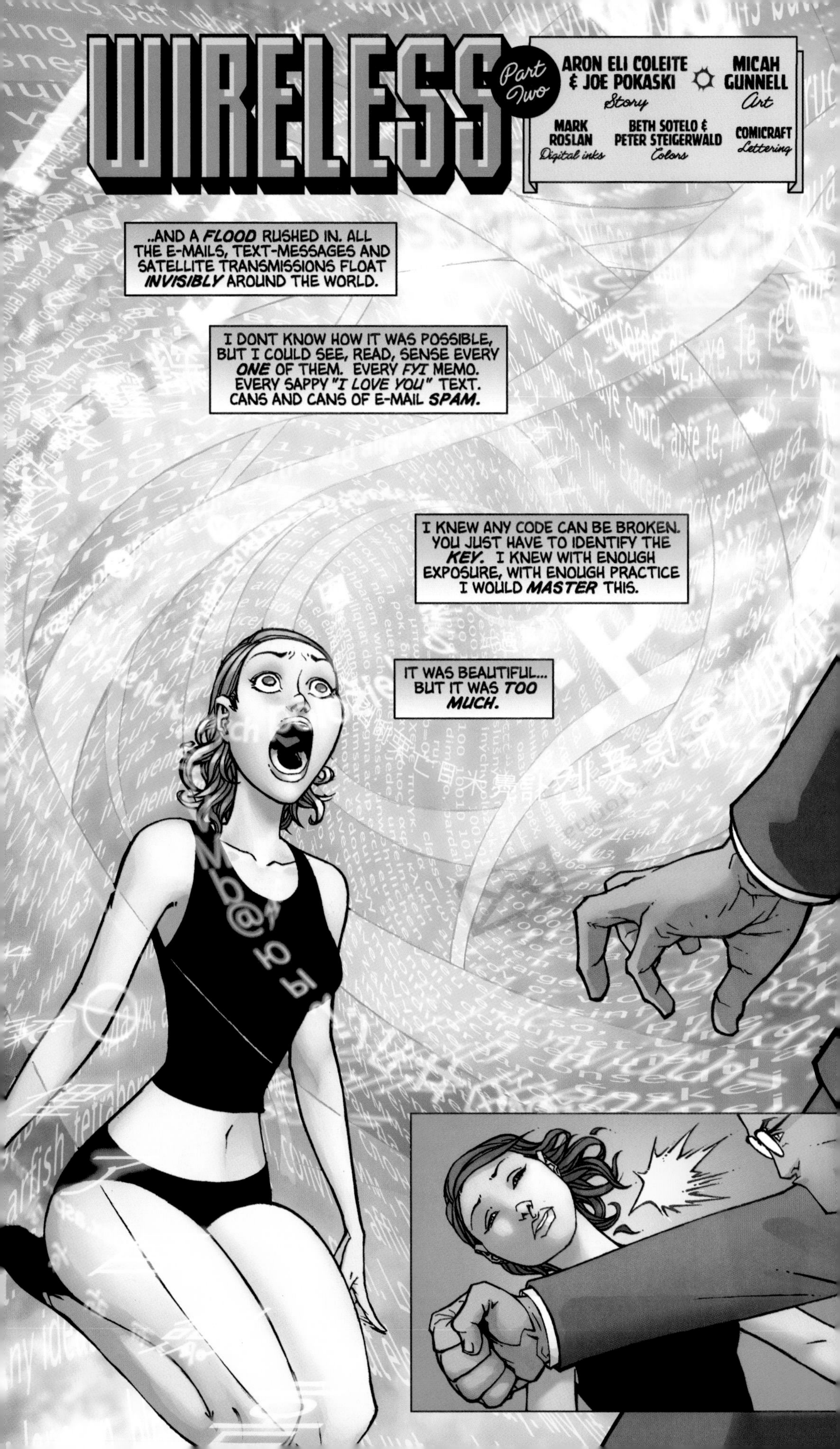
WIRELESS
Part Two
ARON ELI COLEITE & JOE POKASKI Story
MICAH GUNNELL Art
MARK ROSLAN Digital inks
BETH SOTELO & PETER STEIGERWALD Colors
COMICRAFT Lettering
..AND A FLOOD RUSHED IN. ALL THE E-MAILS, TEXT-MESSAGES AND SATELLITE TRANSMISSIONS FLOAT INVISIBLY AROUND THE WORLD.
I DONT KNOW HOW IT WAS POSSIBLE, BUT I COULD SEE, READ, SENSE EVERY ONE OF THEM. EVERY FYI MEMO. EVERY SAPPY "I LOVE YOU" TEXT. CANS AND CANS OF E-MAIL SPAM.
I KNEW ANY CODE CAN BE BROKEN. YOU JUST HAVE TO IDENTIFY THE KEY. I KNEW WITH ENOUGH EXPOSURE, WITH ENOUGH PRACTICE I WOULD MASTER THIS.
IT WAS BEAUTIFUL... BUT IT WAS TOO MUCH.

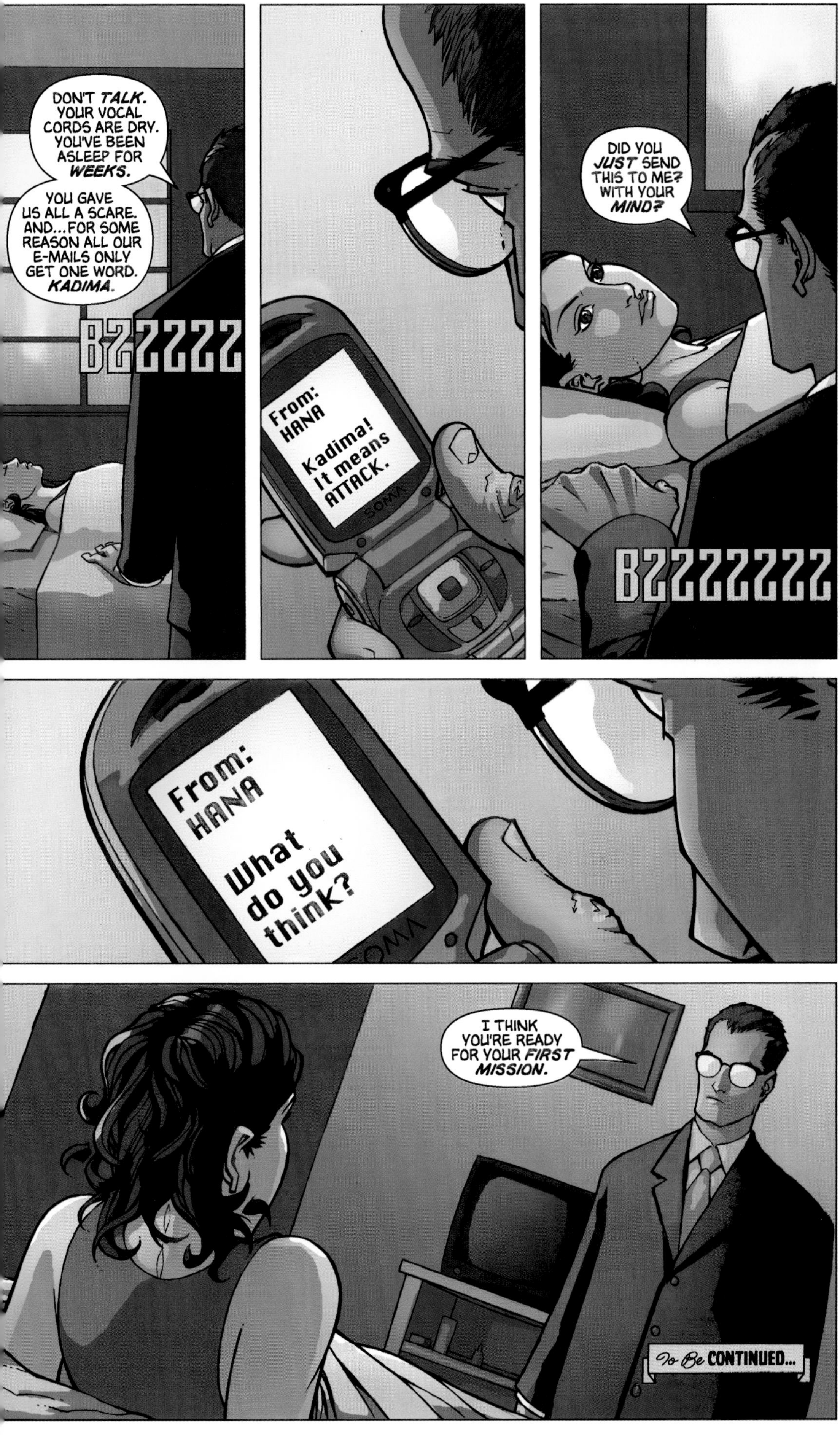
DON'T *TALK.* YOUR VOCAL CORDS ARE DRY. YOU'VE BEEN ASLEEP FOR *WEEKS.*
YOU GAVE US ALL A SCARE. AND...FOR SOME REASON ALL OUR E-MAILS ONLY GET ONE WORD. *KADIMA.*
BZZZZZ
From: HANA Kadima! It means ATTACK.
SOMA
DID YOU *JUST* SEND THIS TO ME? WITH YOUR *MIND?*
BZZZZZZZ
From: HANA What do you think?
SOMA
I THINK YOU'RE READY FOR YOUR *FIRST MISSION.*
To Be CONTINUED...

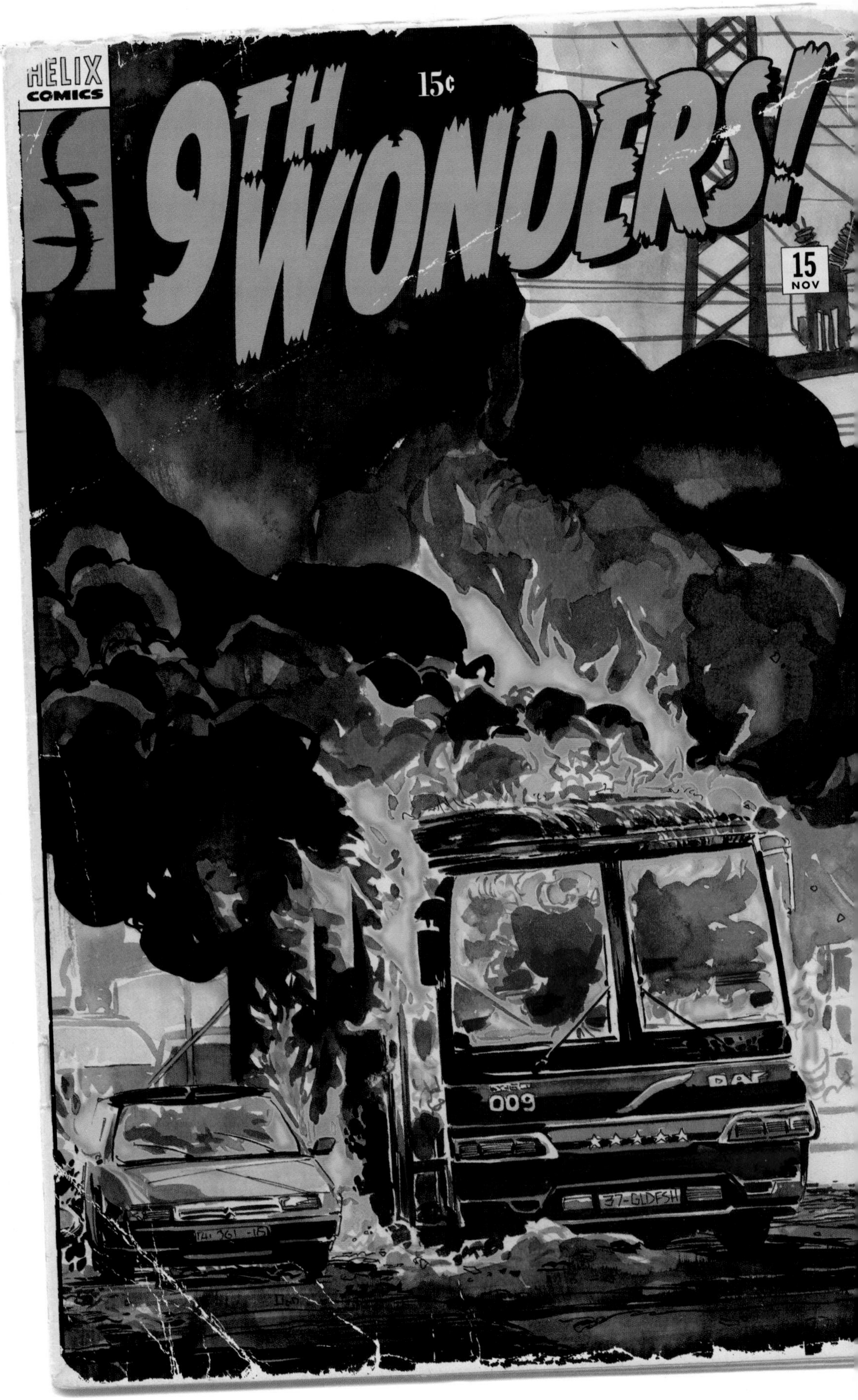
HELIX
COMICS
15¢
9TH WONDERS!
15
NOV
009
DAF
37-GLDFSH

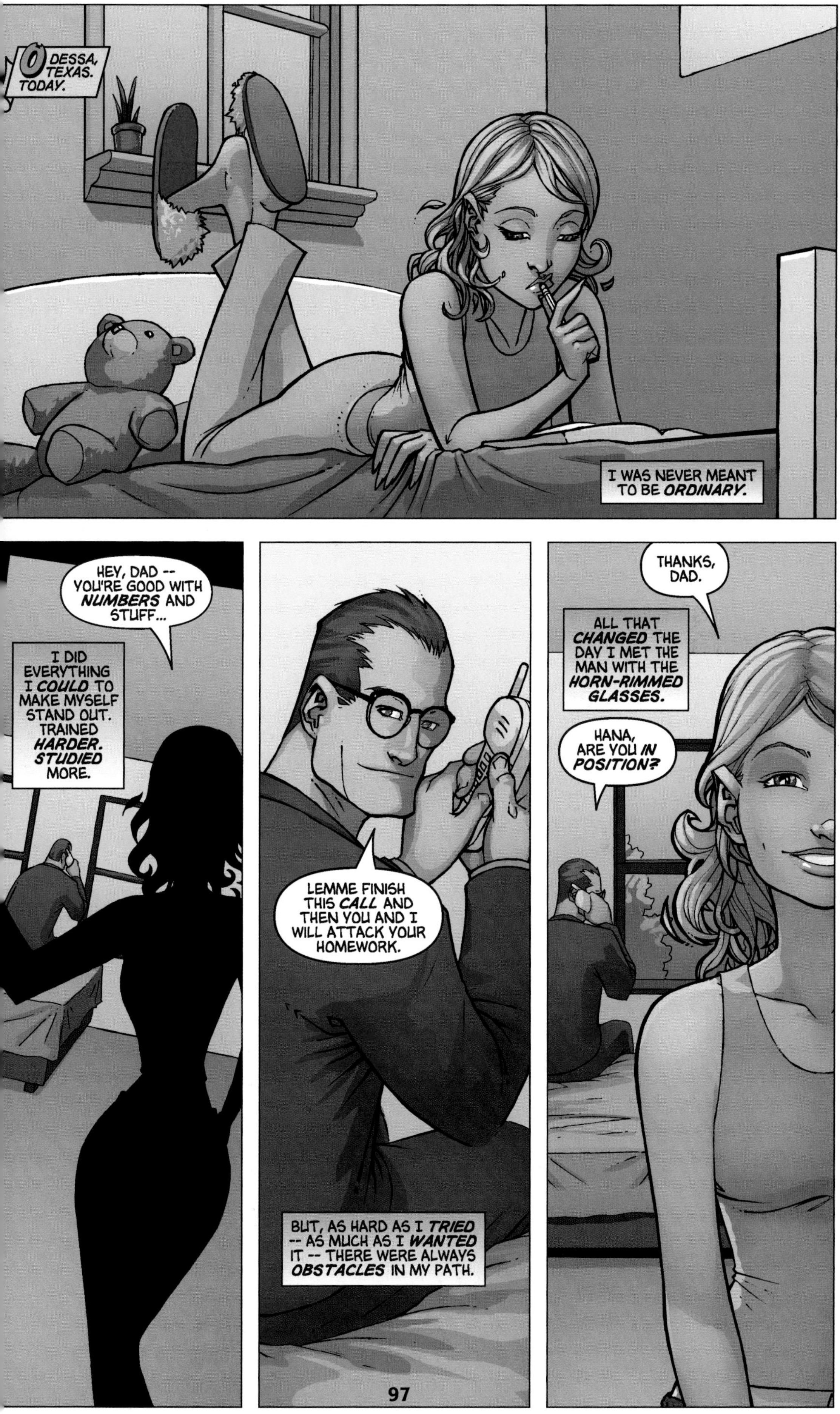
ODESSA, TEXAS. TODAY.
I WAS NEVER MEANT TO BE ORDINARY.
HEY, DAD -- YOU'RE GOOD WITH NUMBERS AND STUFF...
I DID EVERYTHING I COULD TO MAKE MYSELF STAND OUT. TRAINED HARDER. STUDIED MORE.
LEMME FINISH THIS CALL AND THEN YOU AND I WILL ATTACK YOUR HOMEWORK.
BUT, AS HARD AS I TRIED -- AS MUCH AS I WANTED IT -- THERE WERE ALWAYS OBSTACLES IN MY PATH.
THANKS, DAD.
ALL THAT CHANGED THE DAY I MET THE MAN WITH THE HORN-RIMMED GLASSES.
HANA, ARE YOU IN POSITION?

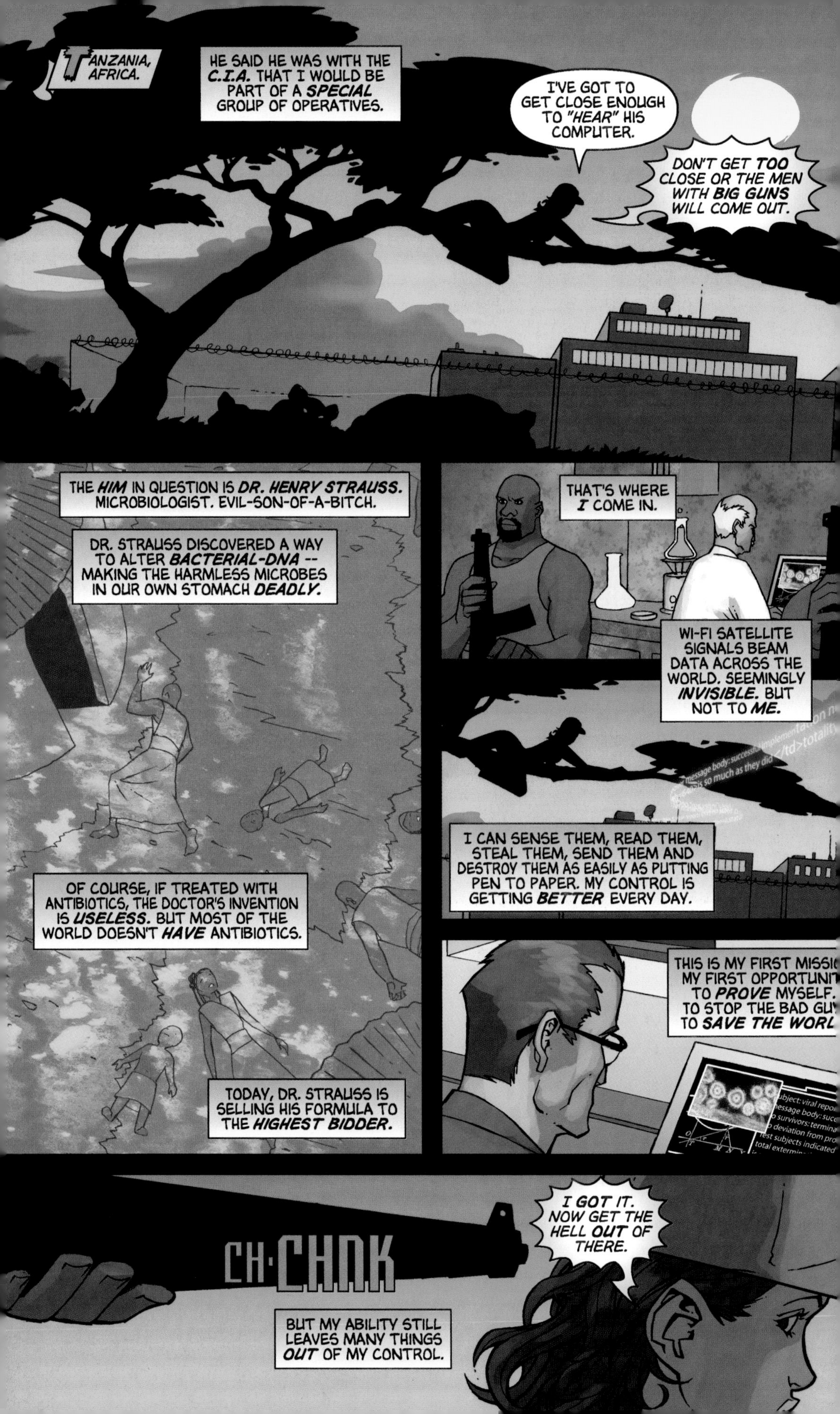
TANZANIA, AFRICA.
HE SAID HE WAS WITH THE C.I.A. THAT I WOULD BE PART OF A SPECIAL GROUP OF OPERATIVES.
I'VE GOT TO GET CLOSE ENOUGH TO "HEAR" HIS COMPUTER.
DON'T GET TOO CLOSE OR THE MEN WITH BIG GUNS WILL COME OUT.
THE HIM IN QUESTION IS DR. HENRY STRAUSS. MICROBIOLOGIST. EVIL-SON-OF-A-BITCH.
DR. STRAUSS DISCOVERED A WAY TO ALTER BACTERIAL-DNA -- MAKING THE HARMLESS MICROBES IN OUR OWN STOMACH DEADLY.
OF COURSE, IF TREATED WITH ANTIBIOTICS, THE DOCTOR'S INVENTION IS USELESS. BUT MOST OF THE WORLD DOESN'T HAVE ANTIBIOTICS.
TODAY, DR. STRAUSS IS SELLING HIS FORMULA TO THE HIGHEST BIDDER.
THAT'S WHERE I COME IN.
WI-FI SATELLITE SIGNALS BEAM DATA ACROSS THE WORLD. SEEMINGLY INVISIBLE. BUT NOT TO ME.
I CAN SENSE THEM, READ THEM, STEAL THEM, SEND THEM AND DESTROY THEM AS EASILY AS PUTTING PEN TO PAPER. MY CONTROL IS GETTING BETTER EVERY DAY.
THIS IS MY FIRST MISSI
MY FIRST OPPORTUNIT
TO PROVE MYSELF.
TO STOP THE BAD GU
TO SAVE THE WORL
CH-CHNK
I GOT IT. NOW GET THE HELL OUT OF THERE.
BUT MY ABILITY STILL LEAVES MANY THINGS OUT OF MY CONTROL.

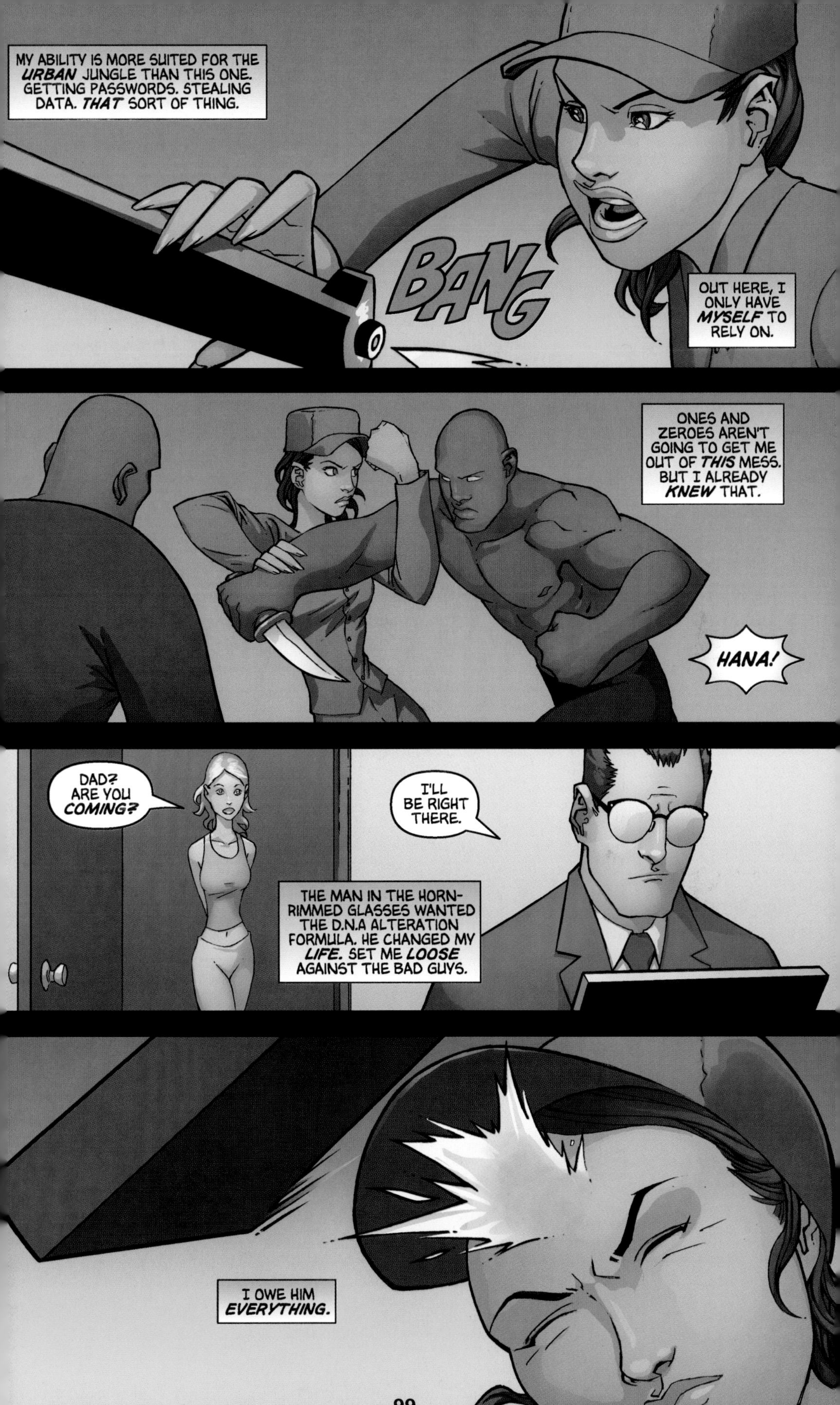
MY ABILITY IS MORE SUITED FOR THE *URBAN* JUNGLE THAN THIS ONE. GETTING PASSWORDS. STEALING DATA. *THAT* SORT OF THING.
BANG
OUT HERE, I ONLY HAVE *MYSELF* TO RELY ON.
ONES AND ZEROES AREN'T GOING TO GET ME OUT OF *THIS* MESS. BUT I ALREADY *KNEW* THAT.
HANA!
DAD? ARE YOU *COMING?*
I'LL BE RIGHT THERE.
THE MAN IN THE HORN-RIMMED GLASSES WANTED THE D.N.A ALTERATION FORMULA. HE CHANGED MY *LIFE.* SET ME *LOOSE* AGAINST THE BAD GUYS.
I OWE HIM *EVERYTHING.*

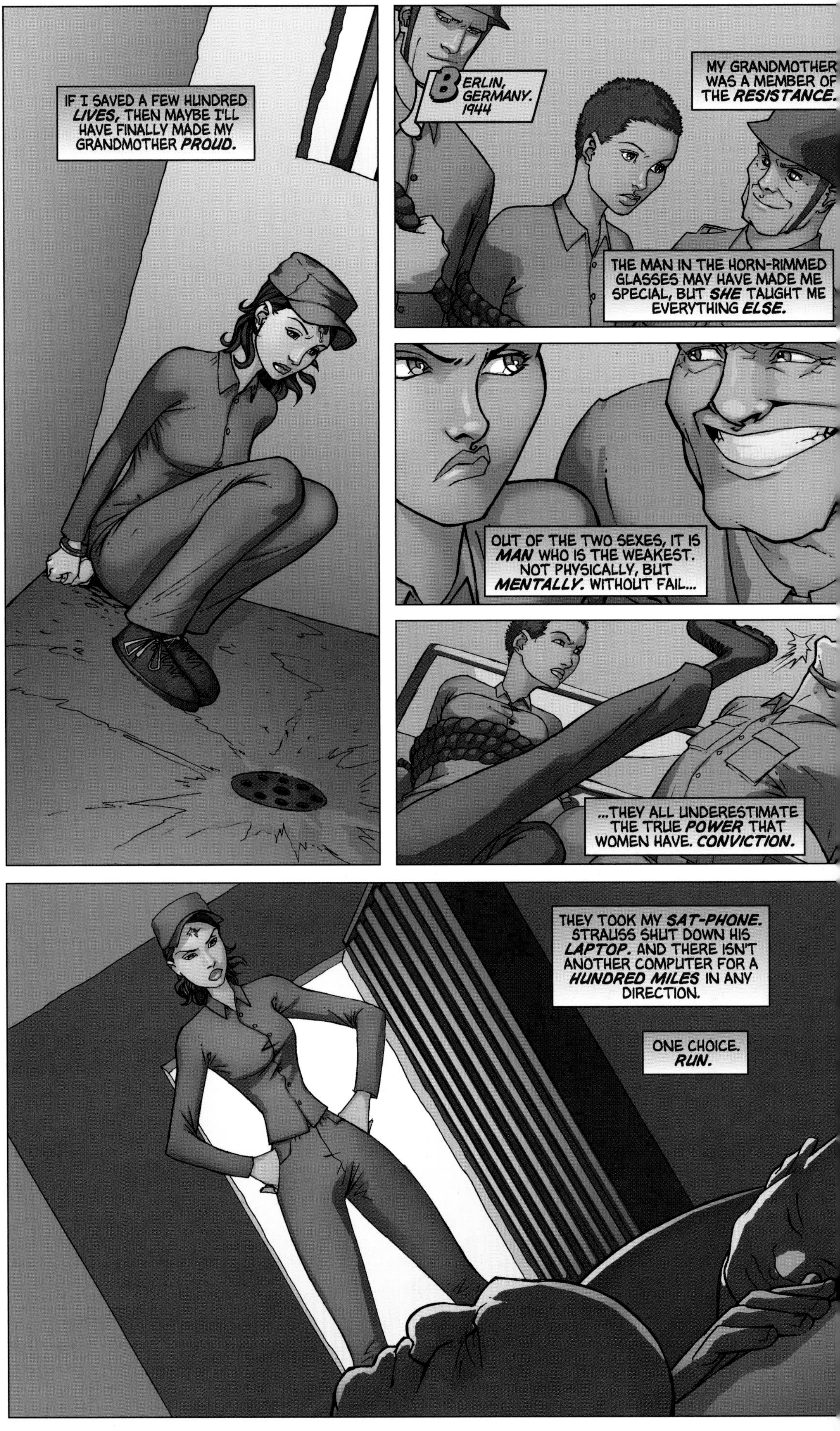
IF I SAVED A FEW HUNDRED LIVES, THEN MAYBE I'LL HAVE FINALLY MADE MY GRANDMOTHER PROUD.
BERLIN, GERMANY. 1944
MY GRANDMOTHER WAS A MEMBER OF THE RESISTANCE.
THE MAN IN THE HORN-RIMMED GLASSES MAY HAVE MADE ME SPECIAL, BUT SHE TAUGHT ME EVERYTHING ELSE.
OUT OF THE TWO SEXES, IT IS MAN WHO IS THE WEAKEST. NOT PHYSICALLY, BUT MENTALLY. WITHOUT FAIL...
...THEY ALL UNDERESTIMATE THE TRUE POWER THAT WOMEN HAVE. CONVICTION.
THEY TOOK MY SAT-PHONE. STRAUSS SHUT DOWN HIS LAPTOP. AND THERE ISN'T ANOTHER COMPUTER FOR A HUNDRED MILES IN ANY DIRECTION.
ONE CHOICE. RUN.

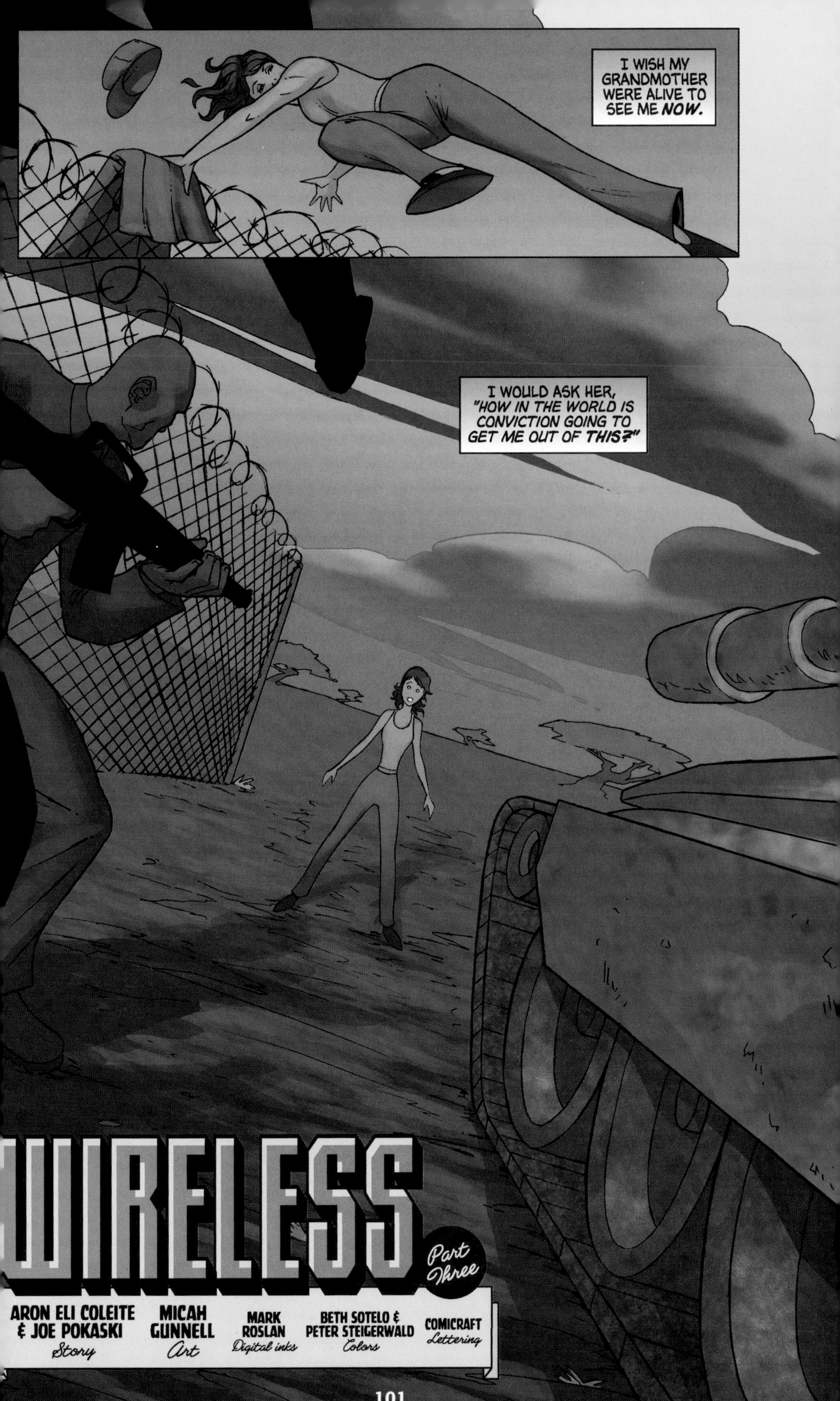
I WISH MY GRANDMOTHER WERE ALIVE TO SEE ME *NOW.*
I WOULD ASK HER, *"HOW IN THE WORLD IS CONVICTION GOING TO GET ME OUT OF THIS?"*
WIRELESS
Part Three
ARON ELI COLEITE & JOE POKASKI Story
MICAH GUNNELL Art
MARK ROSLAN Digital inks
BETH SOTELO & PETER STEIGERWALD Colors
COMICRAFT Lettering

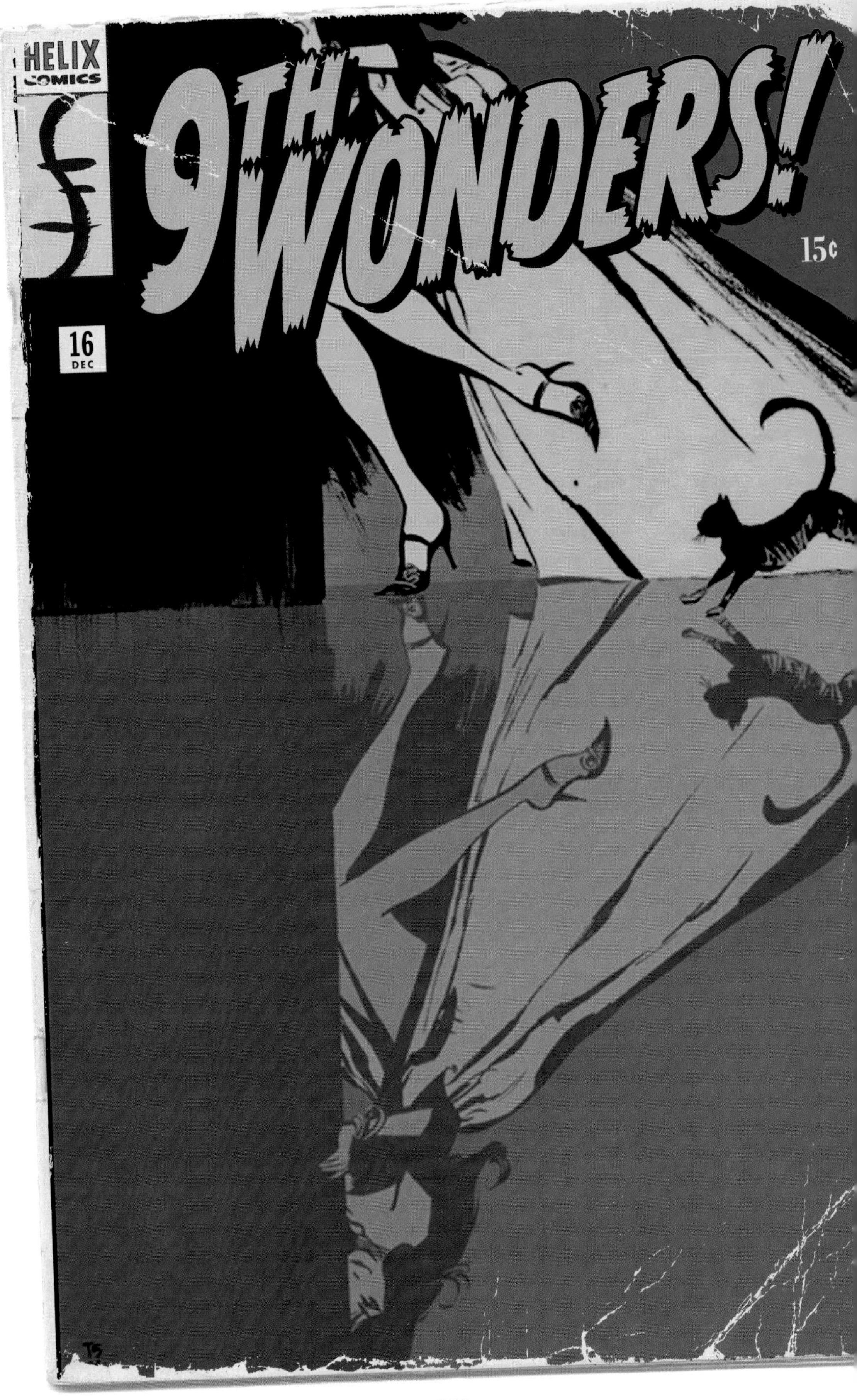
HELIX
COMICS
9TH WONDERS!
15¢
16
DEC
TS

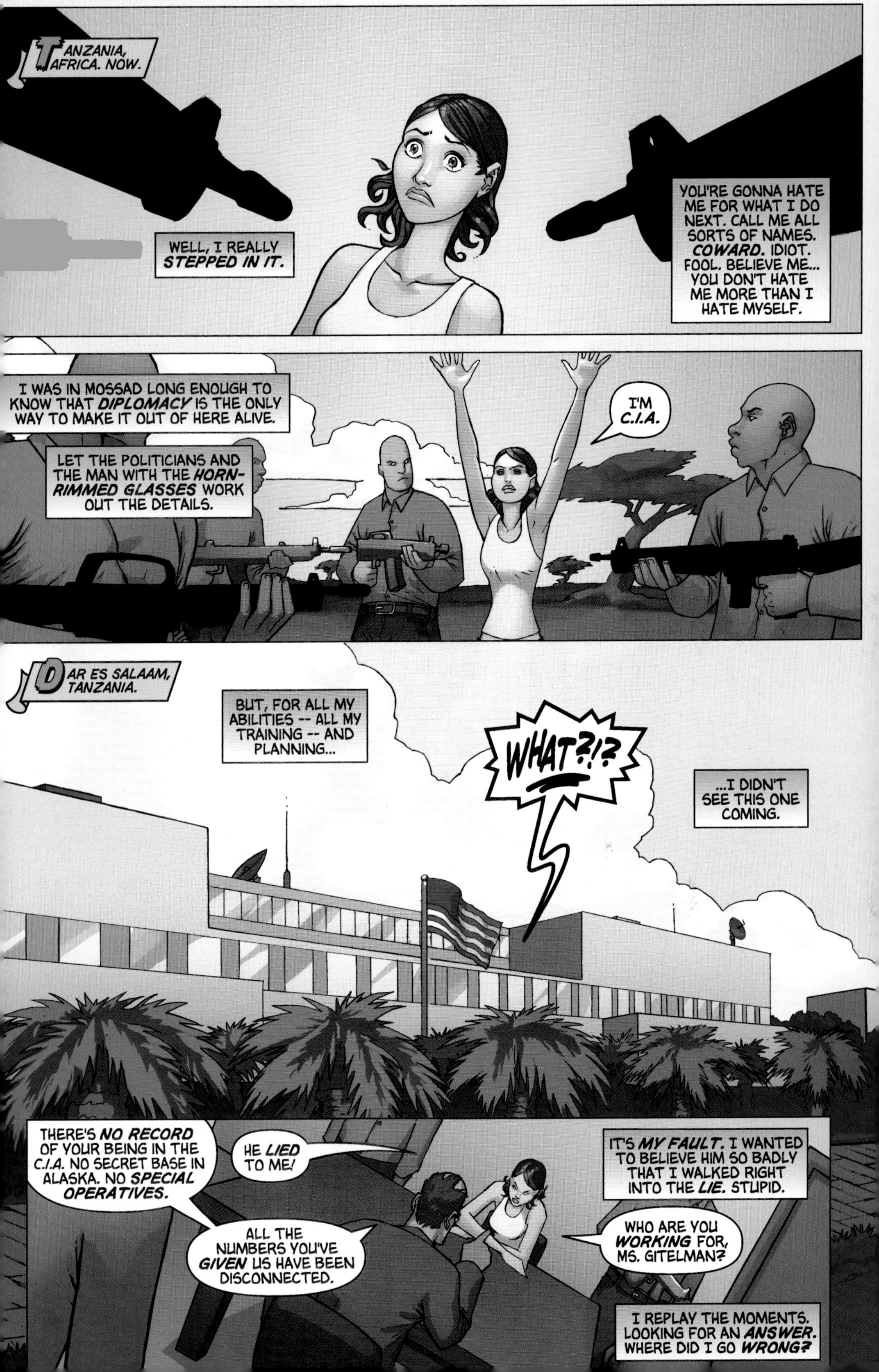
TANZANIA, AFRICA. NOW.
WELL, I REALLY STEPPED IN IT.
YOU'RE GONNA HATE ME FOR WHAT I DO NEXT. CALL ME ALL SORTS OF NAMES. COWARD. IDIOT. FOOL. BELIEVE ME... YOU DON'T HATE ME MORE THAN I HATE MYSELF.
I WAS IN MOSSAD LONG ENOUGH TO KNOW THAT DIPLOMACY IS THE ONLY WAY TO MAKE IT OUT OF HERE ALIVE.
LET THE POLITICIANS AND THE MAN WITH THE HORN-RIMMED GLASSES WORK OUT THE DETAILS.
I'M C.I.A.
DAR ES SALAAM, TANZANIA.
BUT, FOR ALL MY ABILITIES -- ALL MY TRAINING -- AND PLANNING...
WHAT?!?
...I DIDN'T SEE THIS ONE COMING.
THERE'S NO RECORD OF YOUR BEING IN THE C.I.A. NO SECRET BASE IN ALASKA. NO SPECIAL OPERATIVES.
HE LIED TO ME!
ALL THE NUMBERS YOU'VE GIVEN US HAVE BEEN DISCONNECTED.
IT'S MY FAULT. I WANTED TO BELIEVE HIM SO BADLY THAT I WALKED RIGHT INTO THE LIE. STUPID.
WHO ARE YOU WORKING FOR, MS. GITELMAN?
I REPLAY THE MOMENTS. LOOKING FOR AN ANSWER. WHERE DID I GO WRONG?

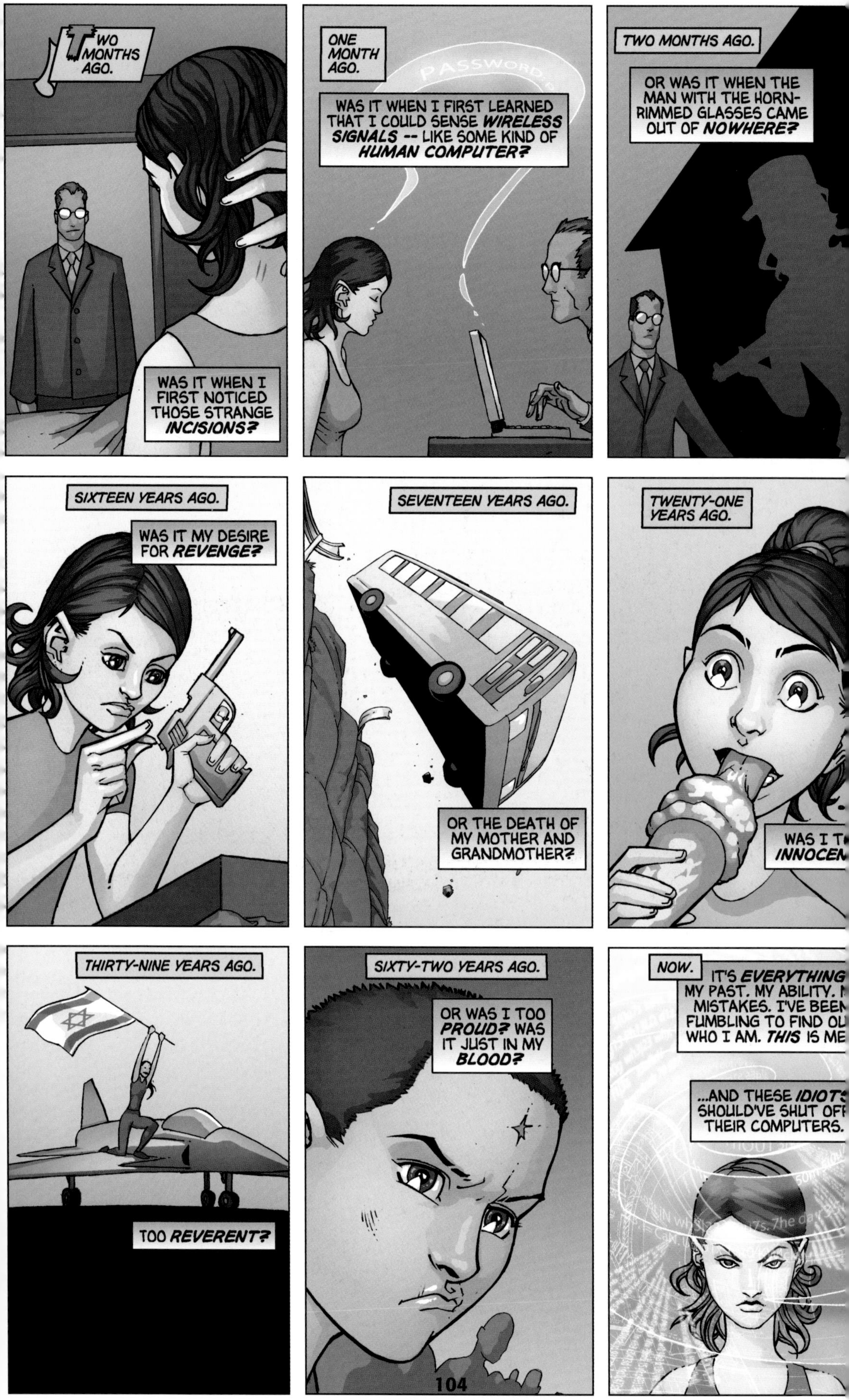
TWO MONTHS AGO.
WAS IT WHEN I FIRST NOTICED THOSE STRANGE INCISIONS?
ONE MONTH AGO.
WAS IT WHEN I FIRST LEARNED THAT I COULD SENSE WIRELESS SIGNALS -- LIKE SOME KIND OF HUMAN COMPUTER?
TWO MONTHS AGO.
OR WAS IT WHEN THE MAN WITH THE HORN-RIMMED GLASSES CAME OUT OF NOWHERE?
SIXTEEN YEARS AGO.
WAS IT MY DESIRE FOR REVENGE?
SEVENTEEN YEARS AGO.
OR THE DEATH OF MY MOTHER AND GRANDMOTHER?
TWENTY-ONE YEARS AGO.
WAS I T
INNOCEN
THIRTY-NINE YEARS AGO.
TOO REVERENT?
SIXTY-TWO YEARS AGO.
OR WAS I TOO PROUD? WAS IT JUST IN MY BLOOD?
NOW.
IT'S EVERYTHING
MY PAST. MY ABILITY.
MISTAKES. I'VE BEEN
FUMBLING TO FIND OU
WHO I AM. THIS IS ME
...AND THESE IDIOTS
SHOULD'VE SHUT OFF
THEIR COMPUTERS.

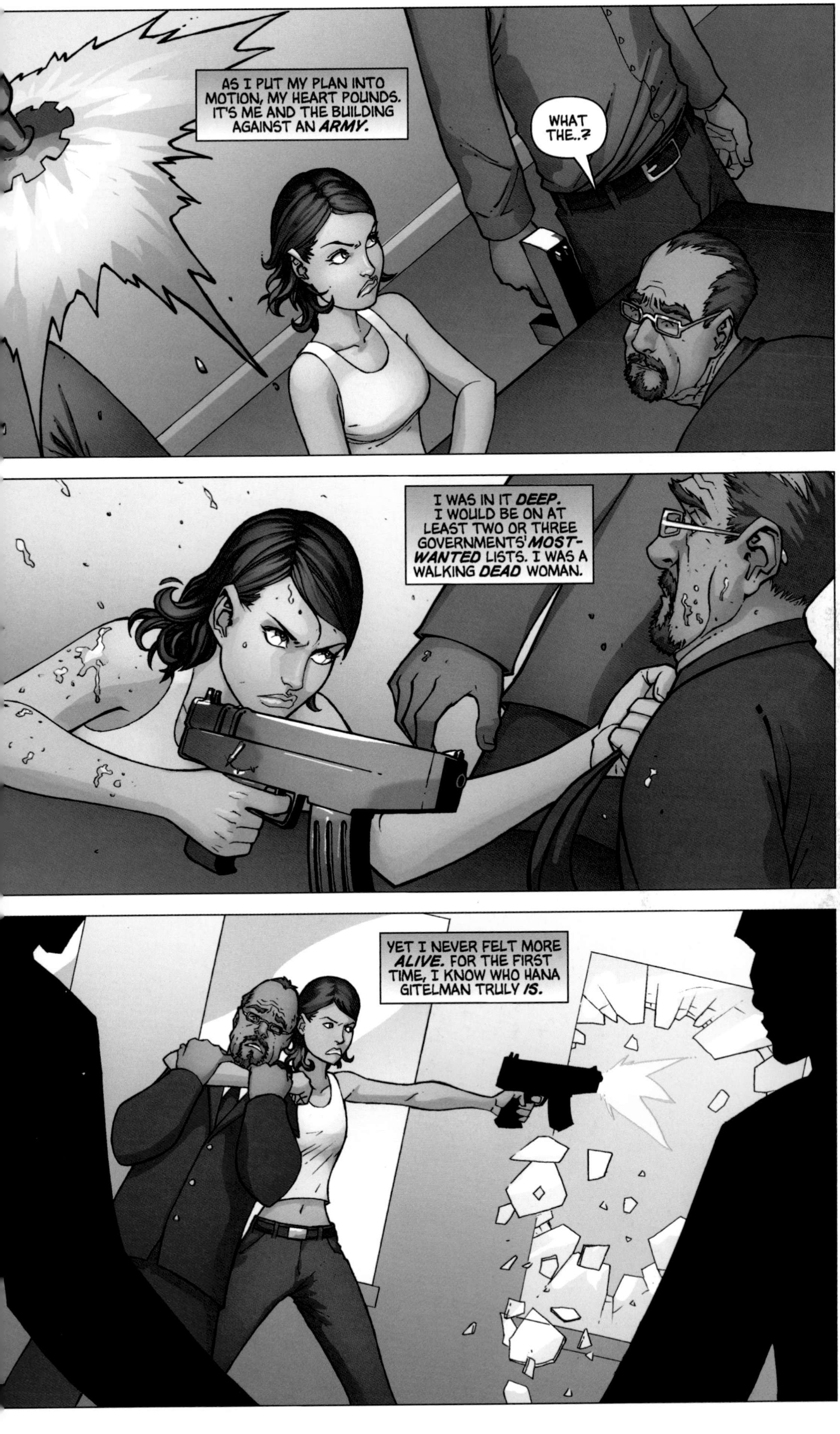

AS I PUT MY PLAN INTO MOTION, MY HEART POUNDS. IT'S ME AND THE BUILDING AGAINST AN *ARMY*.
WHAT THE..?
I WAS IN IT *DEEP*. I WOULD BE ON AT LEAST TWO OR THREE GOVERNMENTS' *MOST-WANTED* LISTS. I WAS A WALKING *DEAD* WOMAN.
YET I NEVER FELT MORE *ALIVE*. FOR THE FIRST TIME, I KNOW WHO HANA GITELMAN TRULY *IS*.

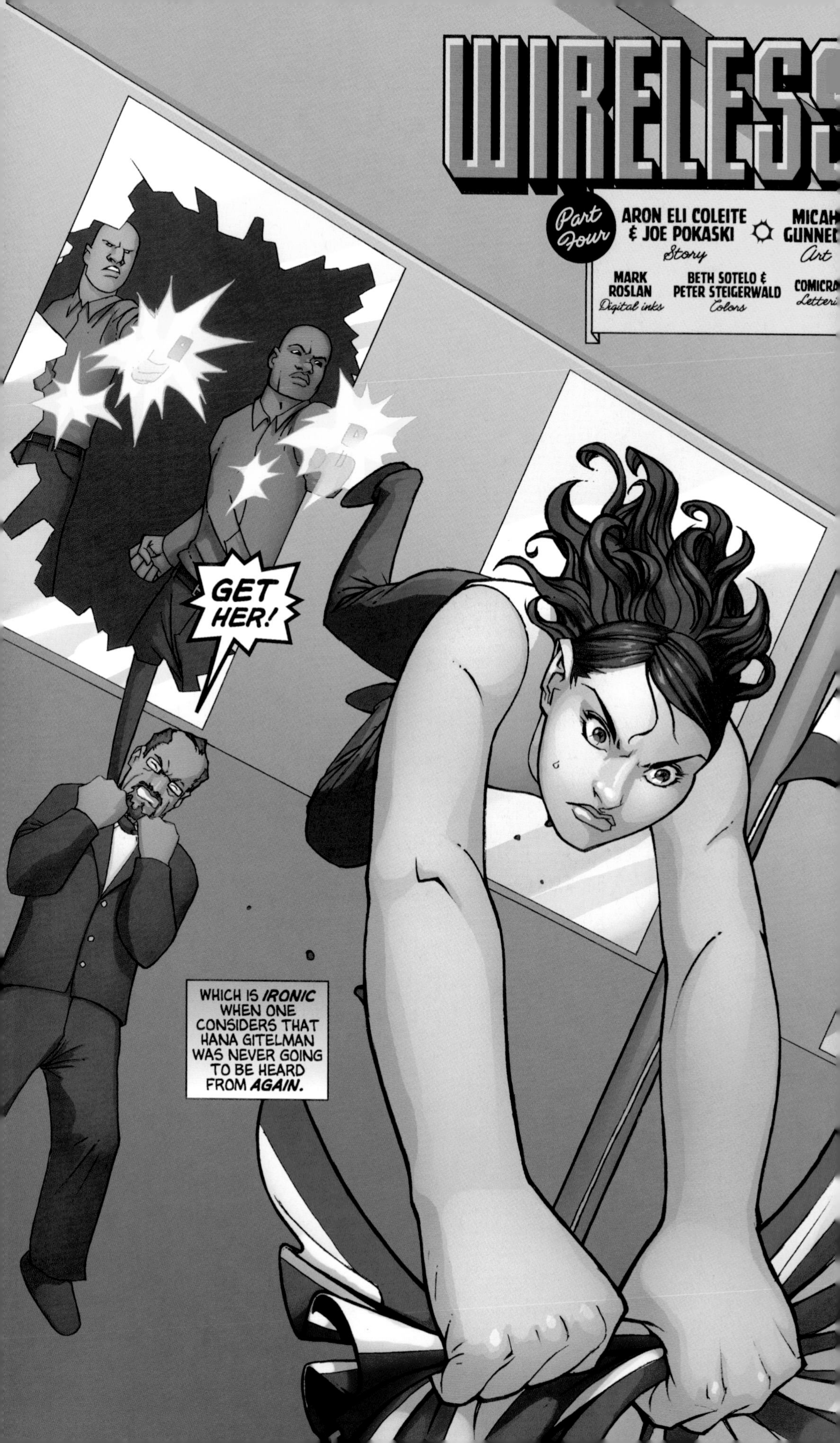
WIRELESS
Part Four
ARON ELI COLEITE & JOE POKASKI Story
MICAH GUNNE[...] Art
MARK ROSLAN Digital inks
BETH SOTELO & PETER STEIGERWALD Colors
COMICRA[...] Letteri[...]
GET HER!
WHICH IS IRONIC WHEN ONE CONSIDERS THAT HANA GITELMAN WAS NEVER GOING TO BE HEARD FROM AGAIN.

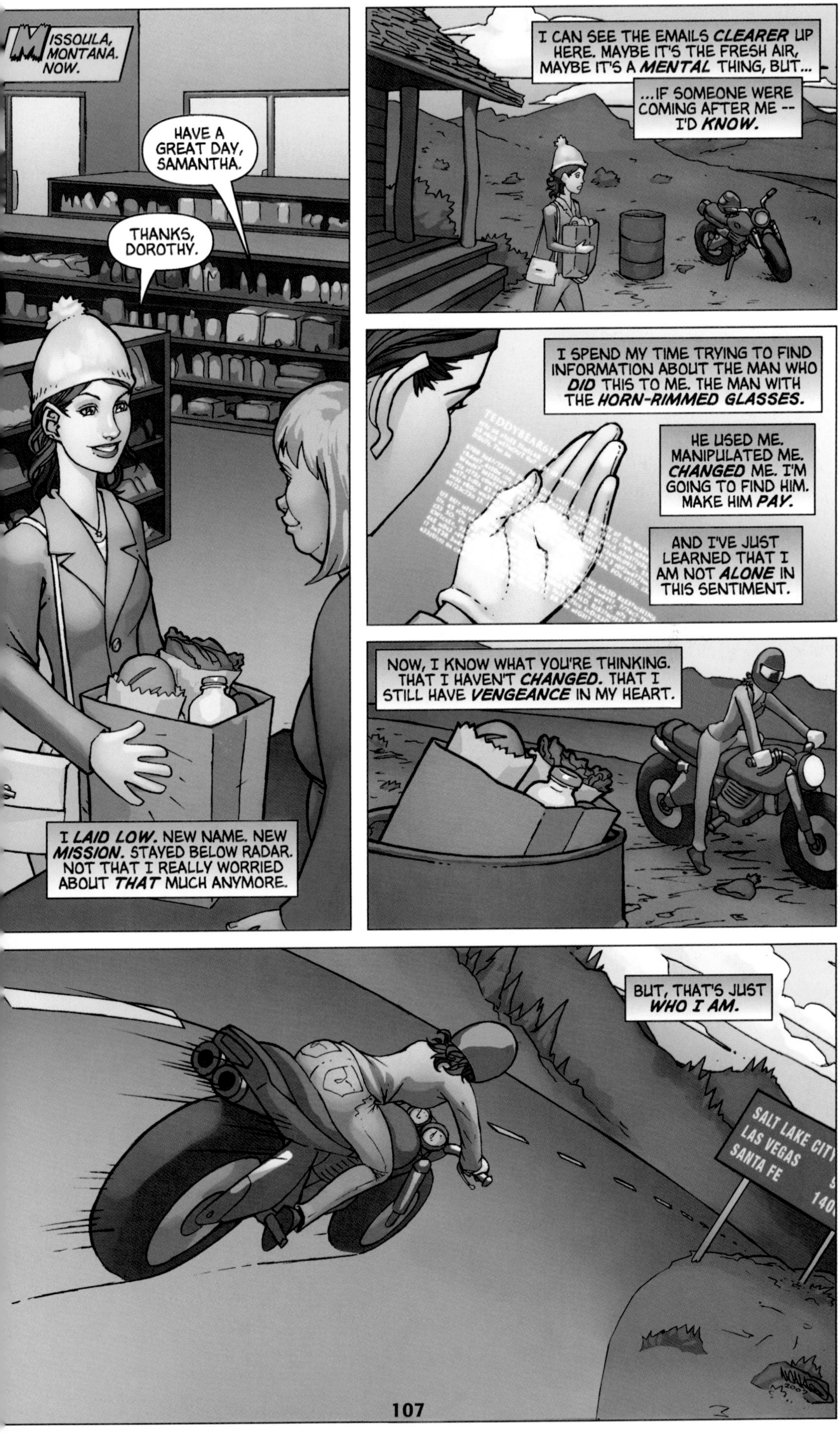
MISSOULA, MONTANA. NOW.
HAVE A GREAT DAY, SAMANTHA.
THANKS, DOROTHY.
I LAID LOW. NEW NAME. NEW MISSION. STAYED BELOW RADAR. NOT THAT I REALLY WORRIED ABOUT THAT MUCH ANYMORE.
I CAN SEE THE EMAILS CLEARER UP HERE. MAYBE IT'S THE FRESH AIR, MAYBE IT'S A MENTAL THING, BUT...
...IF SOMEONE WERE COMING AFTER ME -- I'D KNOW.
I SPEND MY TIME TRYING TO FIND INFORMATION ABOUT THE MAN WHO DID THIS TO ME. THE MAN WITH THE HORN-RIMMED GLASSES.
HE USED ME. MANIPULATED ME. CHANGED ME. I'M GOING TO FIND HIM. MAKE HIM PAY.
AND I'VE JUST LEARNED THAT I AM NOT ALONE IN THIS SENTIMENT.
NOW, I KNOW WHAT YOU'RE THINKING. THAT I HAVEN'T CHANGED. THAT I STILL HAVE VENGEANCE IN MY HEART.
BUT, THAT'S JUST WHO I AM.
SALT LAKE CITY
LAS VEGAS
SANTA FE

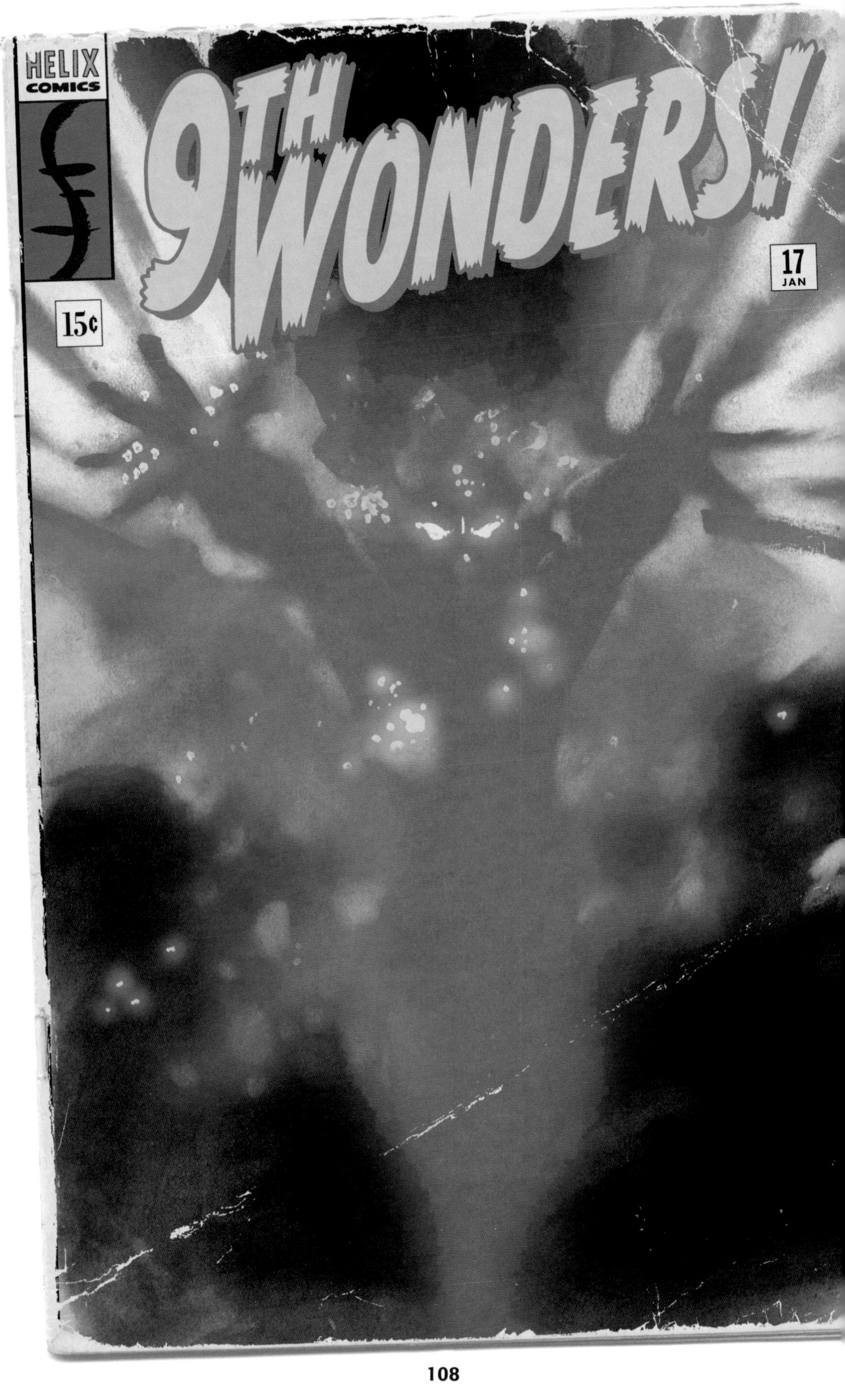
HELIX COMICS
9TH WONDERS!
17 JAN
15¢

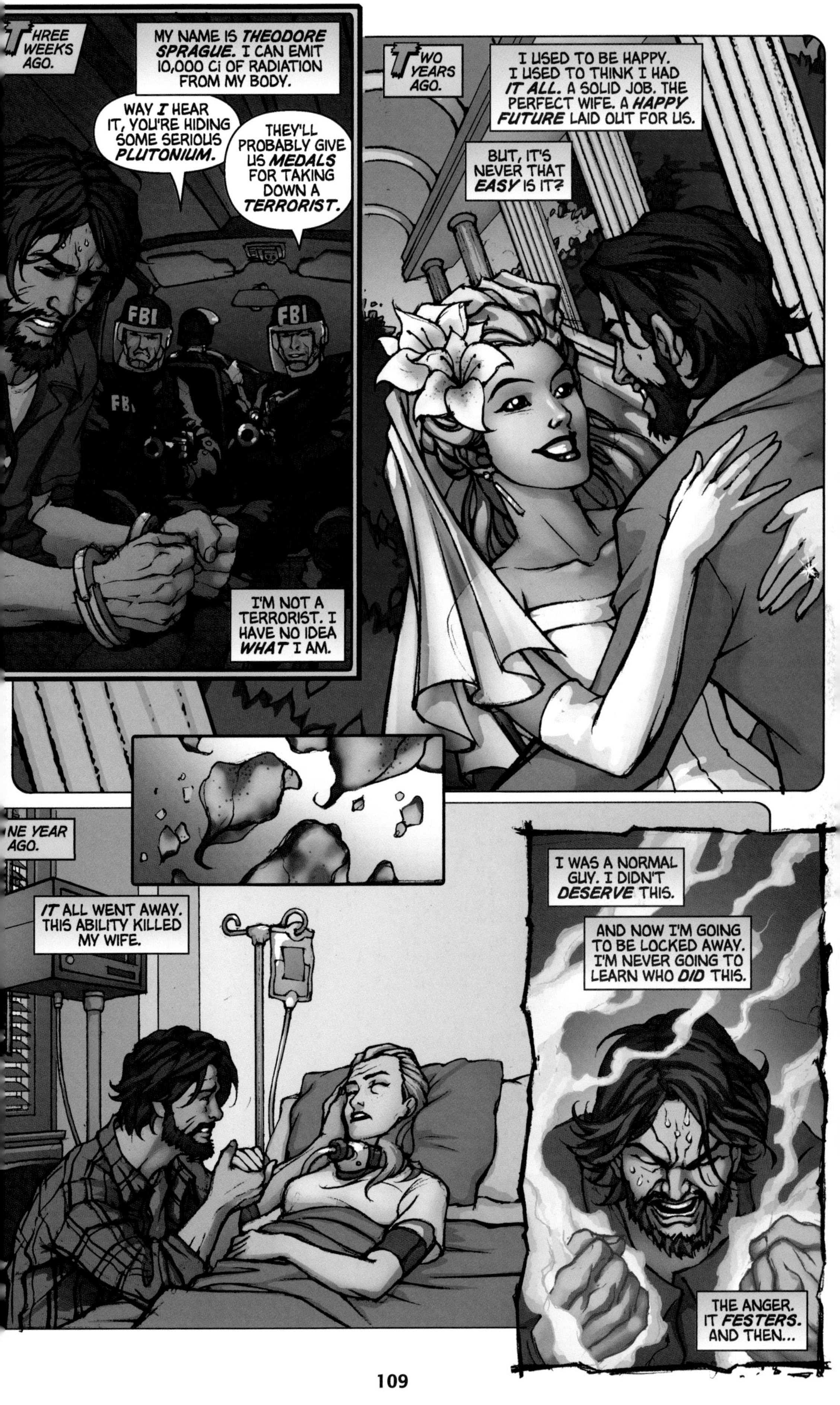
THREE WEEKS AGO.
MY NAME IS THEODORE SPRAGUE. I CAN EMIT 10,000 Ci OF RADIATION FROM MY BODY.
WAY I HEAR IT, YOU'RE HIDING SOME SERIOUS PLUTONIUM.
THEY'LL PROBABLY GIVE US MEDALS FOR TAKING DOWN A TERRORIST.
FBI
FBI
FBI
I'M NOT A TERRORIST. I HAVE NO IDEA WHAT I AM.
TWO YEARS AGO.
I USED TO BE HAPPY. I USED TO THINK I HAD IT ALL. A SOLID JOB. THE PERFECT WIFE. A HAPPY FUTURE LAID OUT FOR US.
BUT, IT'S NEVER THAT EASY IS IT?
NE YEAR AGO.
IT ALL WENT AWAY. THIS ABILITY KILLED MY WIFE.
I WAS A NORMAL GUY. I DIDN'T DESERVE THIS.
AND NOW I'M GOING TO BE LOCKED AWAY. I'M NEVER GOING TO LEARN WHO DID THIS.
THE ANGER. IT FESTERS. AND THEN...

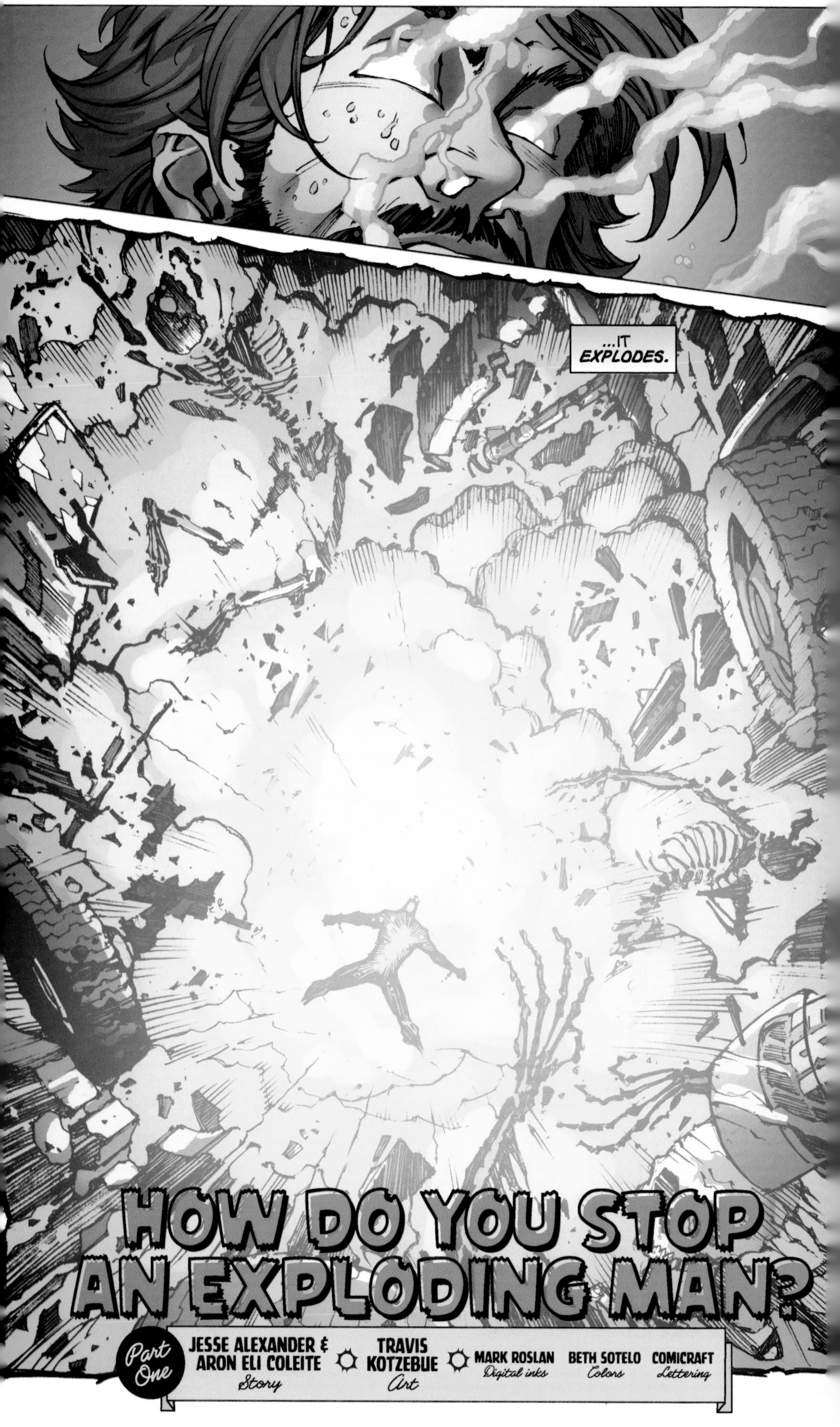

...IT EXPLODES.
HOW DO YOU STOP AN EXPLODING MAN?
Part One
JESSE ALEXANDER & ARON ELI COLEITE Story
TRAVIS KOTZEBUE Art
MARK ROSLAN Digital inks
BETH SOTELO Colors
COMICRAFT Lettering

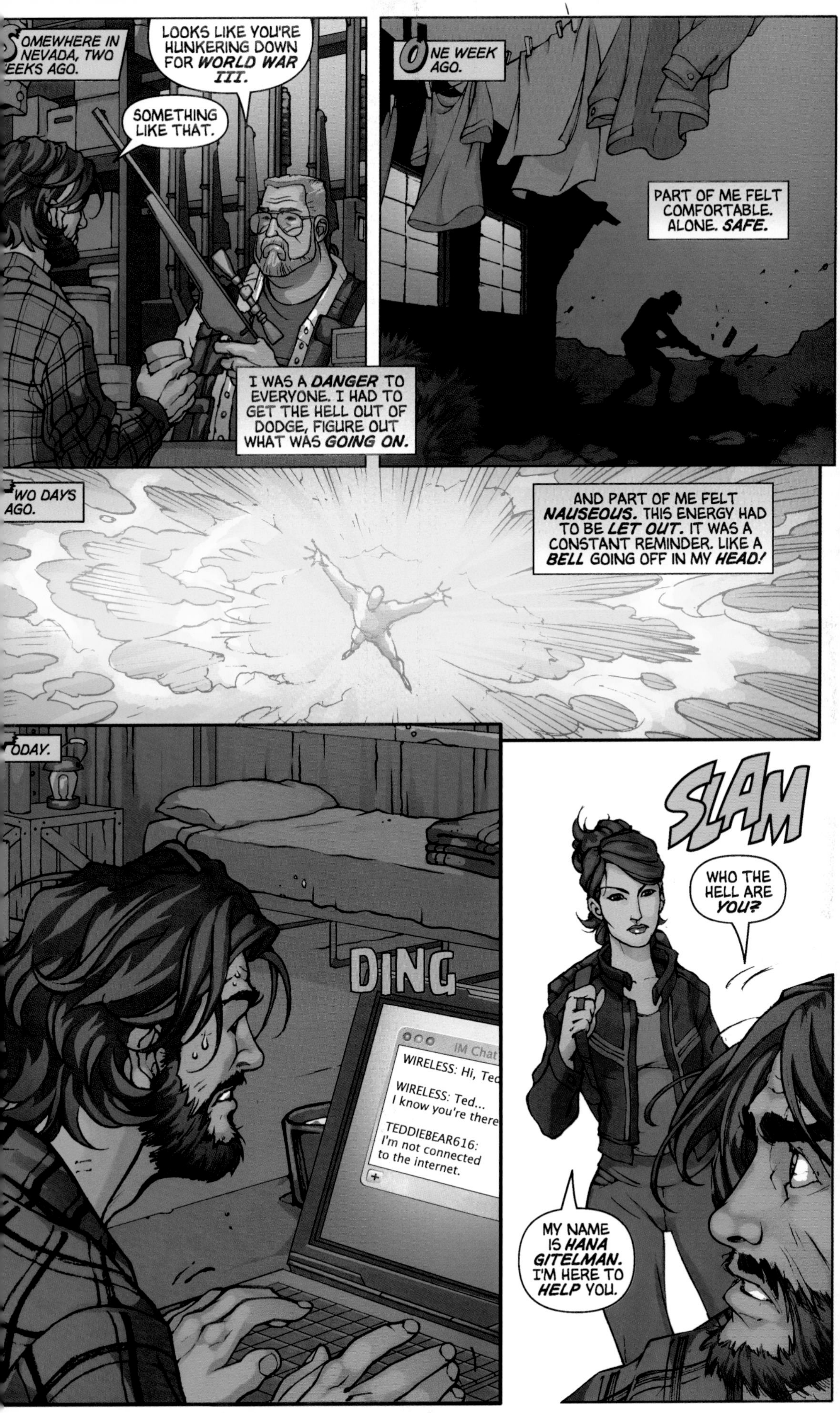
SOMEWHERE IN NEVADA, TWO WEEKS AGO.
LOOKS LIKE YOU'RE HUNKERING DOWN FOR WORLD WAR III.
SOMETHING LIKE THAT.
I WAS A DANGER TO EVERYONE. I HAD TO GET THE HELL OUT OF DODGE, FIGURE OUT WHAT WAS GOING ON.
ONE WEEK AGO.
PART OF ME FELT COMFORTABLE. ALONE. SAFE.
TWO DAYS AGO.
AND PART OF ME FELT NAUSEOUS. THIS ENERGY HAD TO BE LET OUT. IT WAS A CONSTANT REMINDER. LIKE A BELL GOING OFF IN MY HEAD!
TODAY.
DING
IM Chat
WIRELESS: Hi, Ted
WIRELESS: Ted... I know you're there
TEDDIEBEAR616: I'm not connected to the internet.
SLAM
WHO THE HELL ARE YOU?
MY NAME IS HANA GITELMAN. I'M HERE TO HELP YOU.

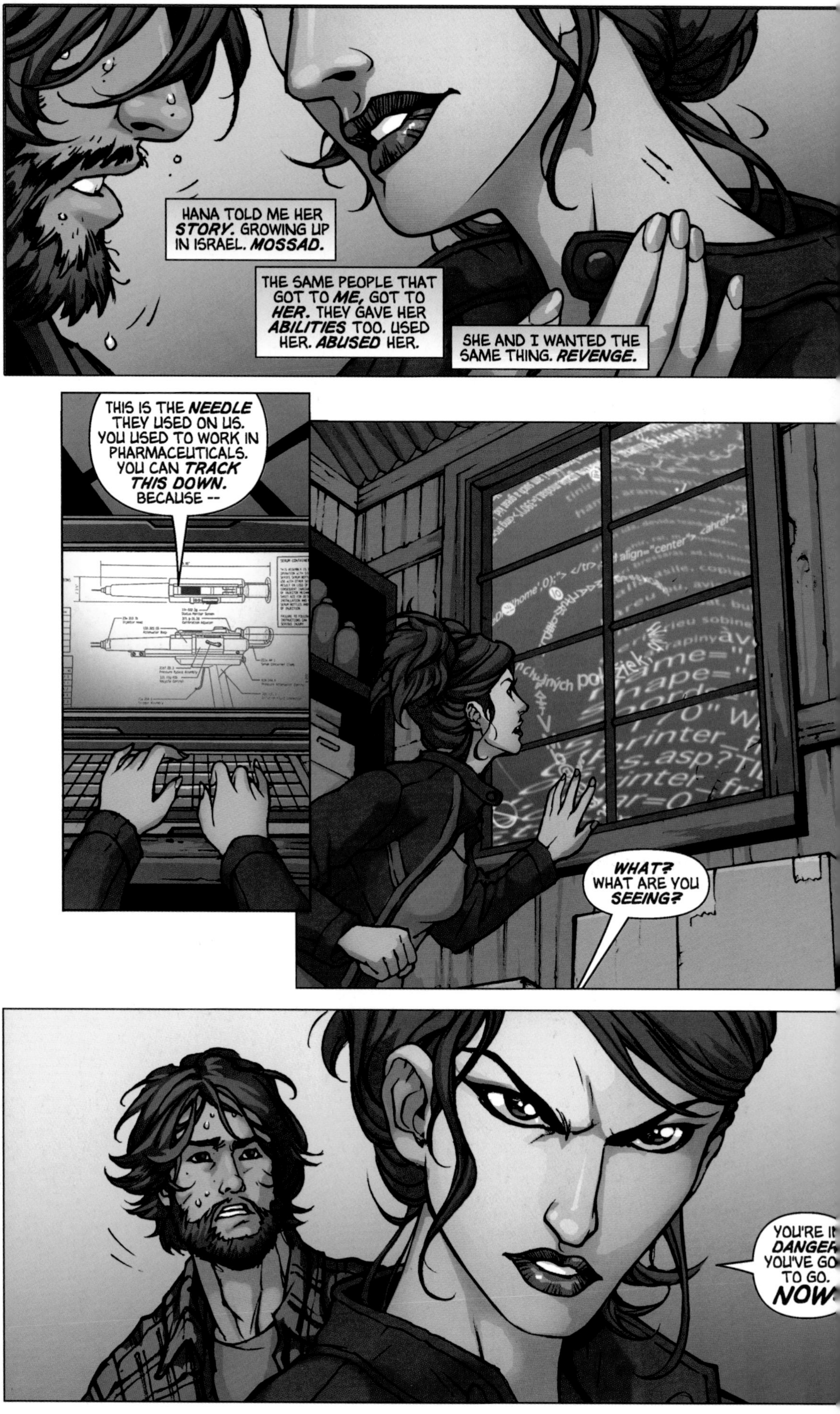
HANA TOLD ME HER *STORY.* GROWING UP IN ISRAEL. *MOSSAD.*
THE SAME PEOPLE THAT GOT TO *ME,* GOT TO *HER.* THEY GAVE HER *ABILITIES* TOO. USED HER. *ABUSED* HER.
SHE AND I WANTED THE SAME THING. *REVENGE.*
THIS IS THE *NEEDLE* THEY USED ON US. YOU USED TO WORK IN PHARMACEUTICALS. YOU CAN *TRACK THIS DOWN.* BECAUSE --
WHAT? WHAT ARE YOU *SEEING?*
YOU'RE I *DANGE* YOU'VE GO TO GO. *NOW*

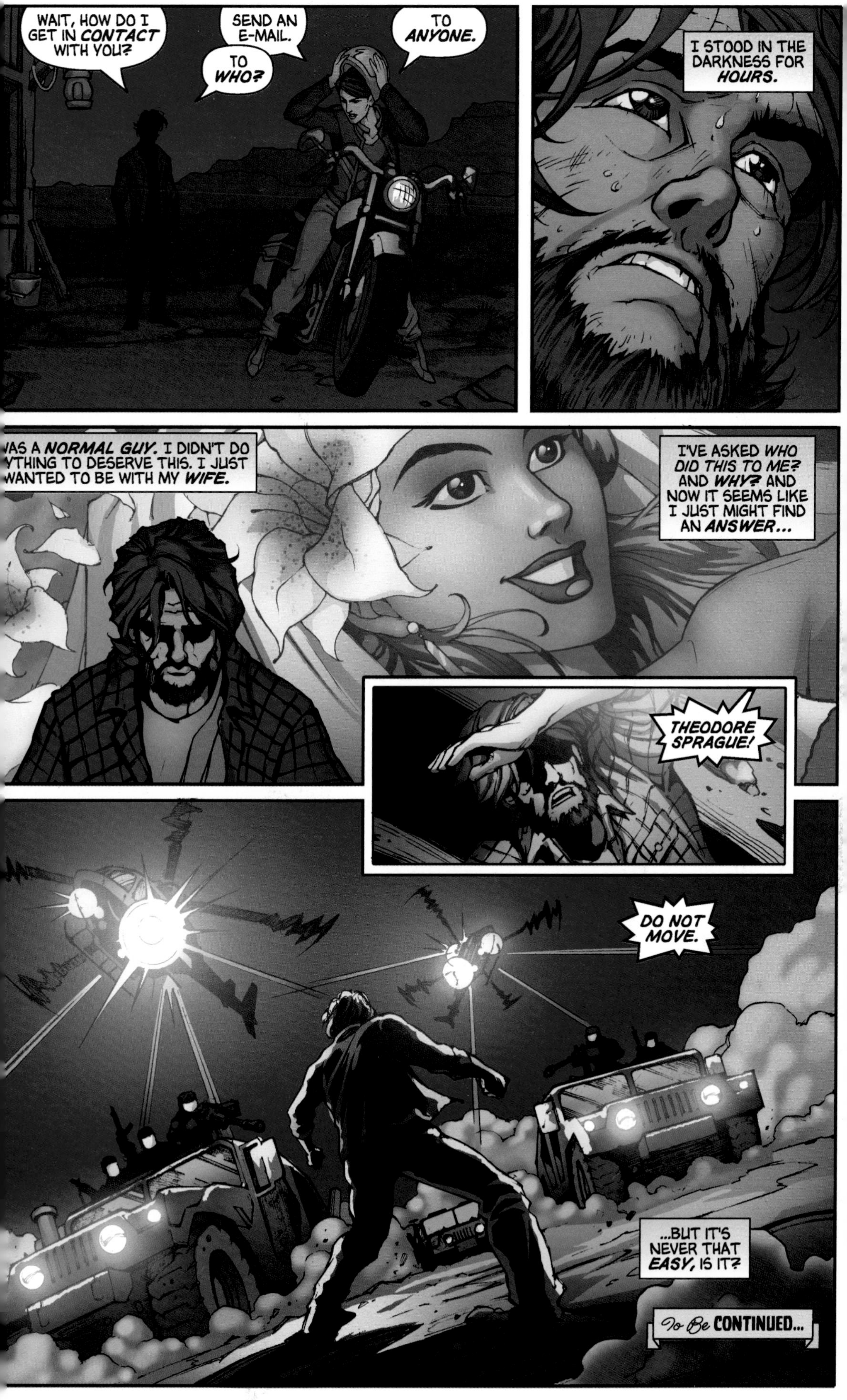
WAIT, HOW DO I GET IN CONTACT WITH YOU?
SEND AN E-MAIL.
TO WHO?
TO ANYONE.
I STOOD IN THE DARKNESS FOR HOURS.
WAS A NORMAL GUY. I DIDN'T DO YTHING TO DESERVE THIS. I JUST WANTED TO BE WITH MY WIFE.
I'VE ASKED WHO DID THIS TO ME? AND WHY? AND NOW IT SEEMS LIKE I JUST MIGHT FIND AN ANSWER...
THEODORE SPRAGUE!
DO NOT MOVE.
...BUT IT'S NEVER THAT EASY, IS IT?
To Be CONTINUED...

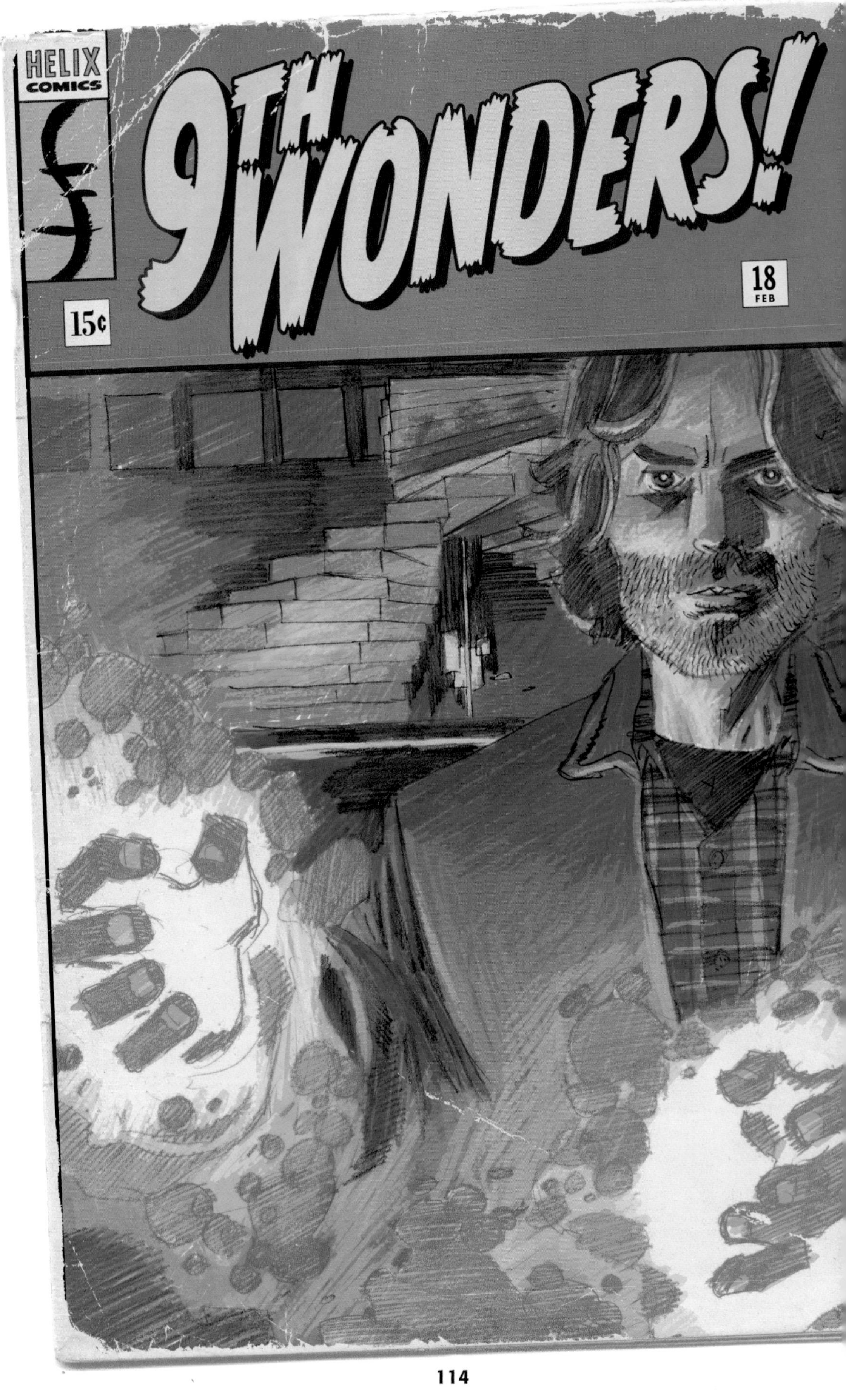
HELIX COMICS
9TH WONDERS!
15¢
18
FEB

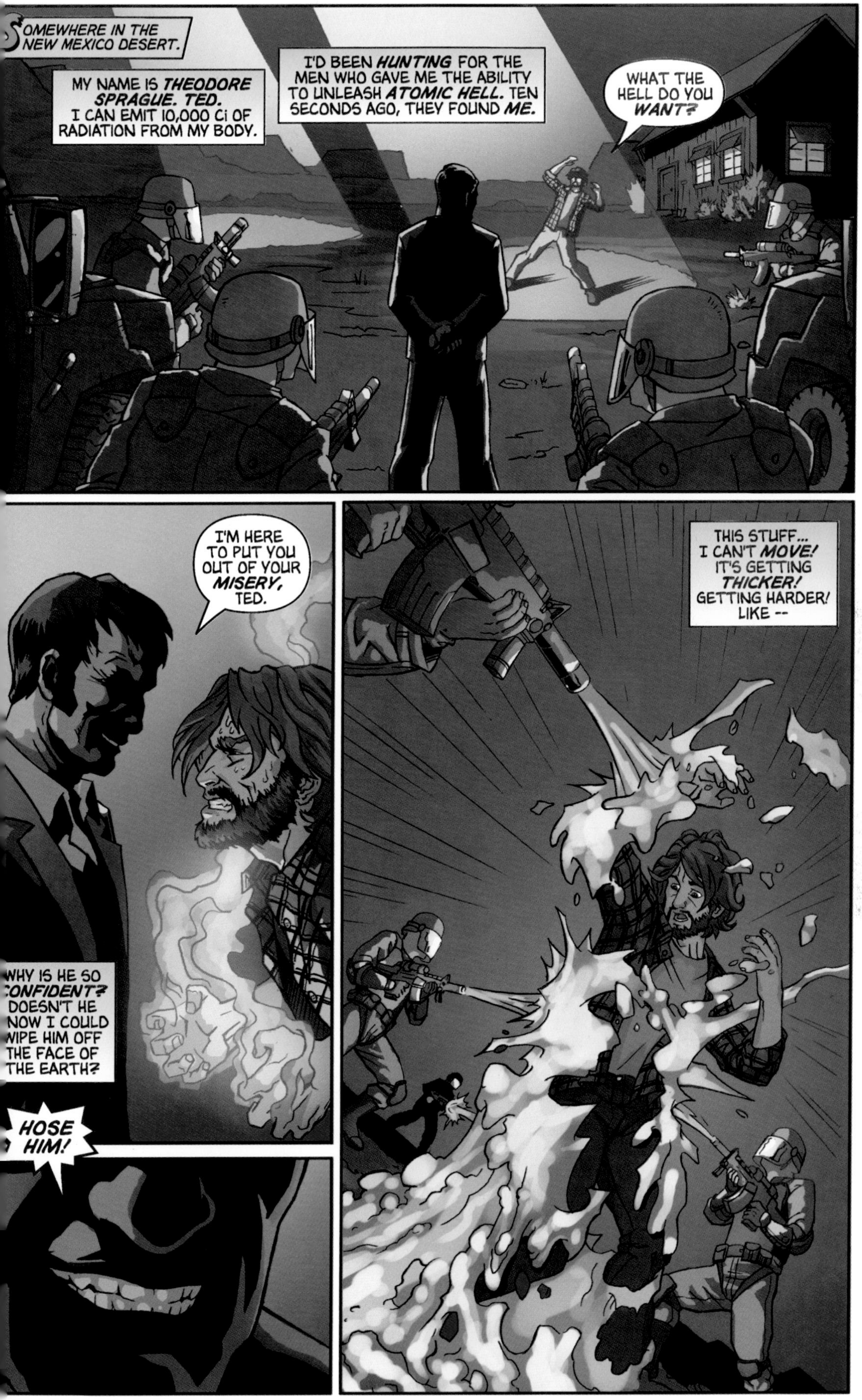
SOMEWHERE IN THE NEW MEXICO DESERT.
MY NAME IS THEODORE SPRAGUE. TED. I CAN EMIT 10,000 Ci OF RADIATION FROM MY BODY.
I'D BEEN HUNTING FOR THE MEN WHO GAVE ME THE ABILITY TO UNLEASH ATOMIC HELL. TEN SECONDS AGO, THEY FOUND ME.
WHAT THE HELL DO YOU WANT?
I'M HERE TO PUT YOU OUT OF YOUR MISERY, TED.
WHY IS HE SO CONFIDENT? DOESN'T HE NOW I COULD WIPE HIM OFF THE FACE OF THE EARTH?
HOSE HIM!
THIS STUFF... I CAN'T MOVE! IT'S GETTING THICKER! GETTING HARDER! LIKE --

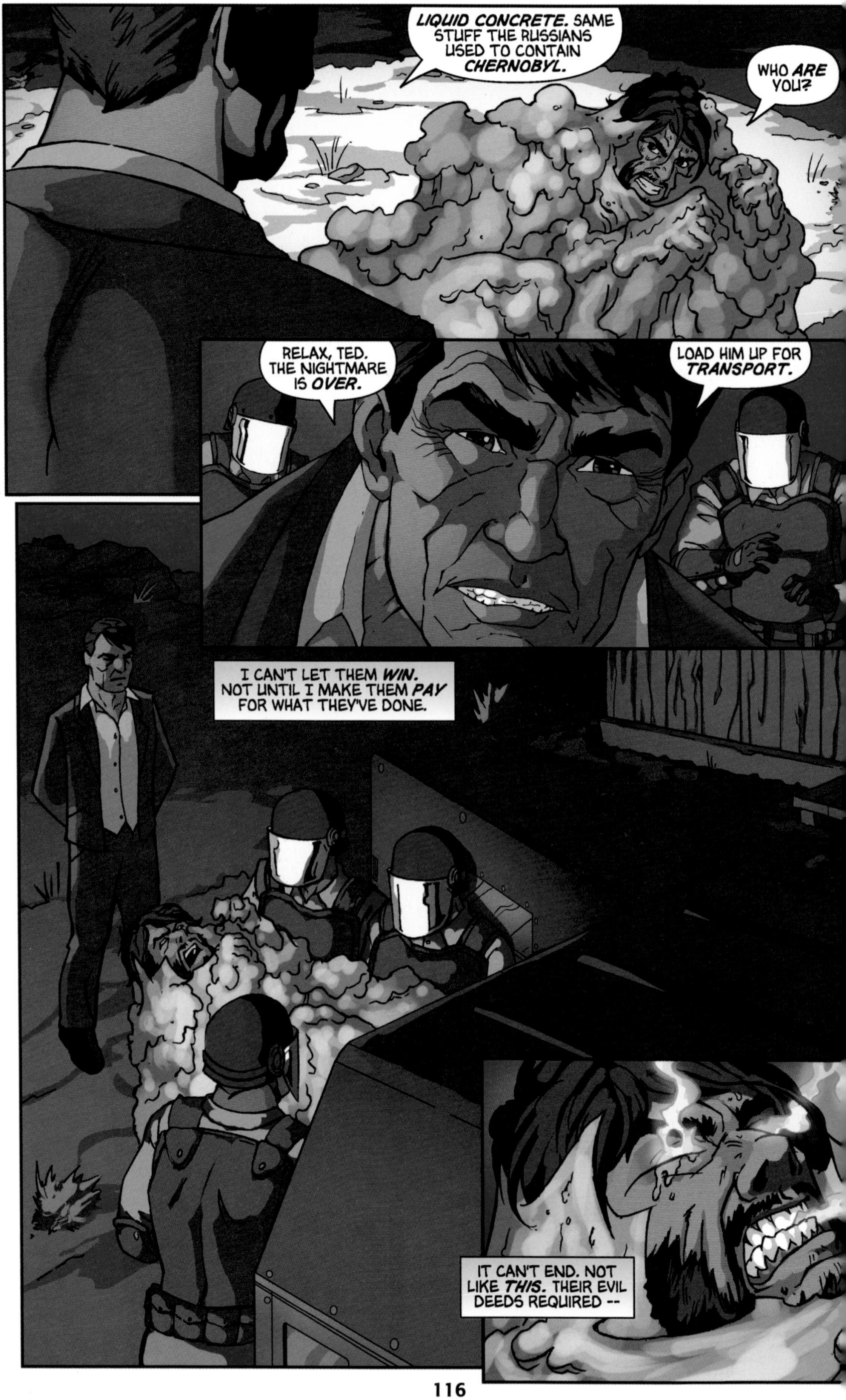
LIQUID CONCRETE. SAME STUFF THE RUSSIANS USED TO CONTAIN CHERNOBYL.
WHO ARE YOU?
RELAX, TED. THE NIGHTMARE IS OVER.
LOAD HIM UP FOR TRANSPORT.
I CAN'T LET THEM WIN. NOT UNTIL I MAKE THEM PAY FOR WHAT THEY'VE DONE.
IT CAN'T END. NOT LIKE THIS. THEIR EVIL DEEDS REQUIRED --

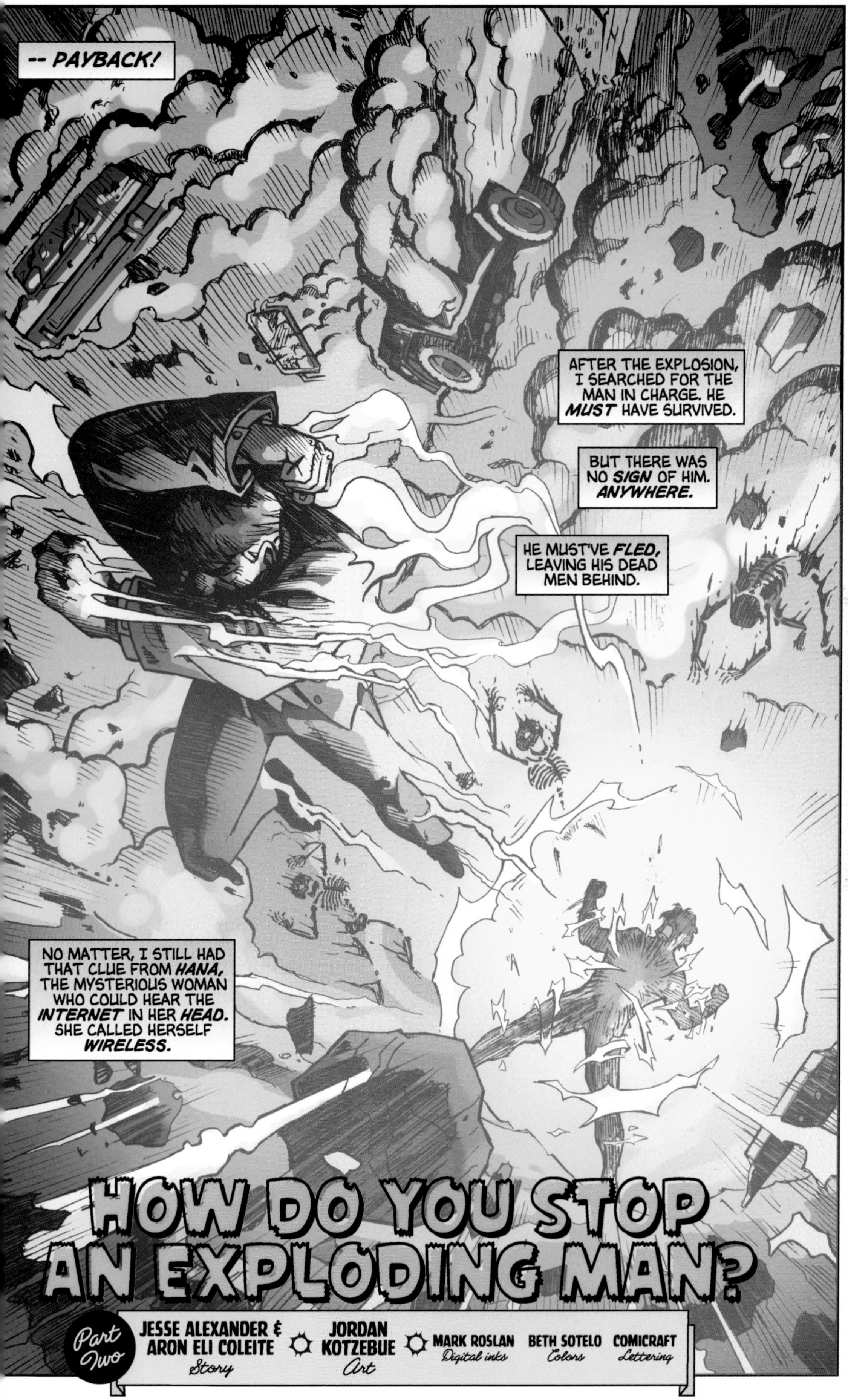

-- PAYBACK!
AFTER THE EXPLOSION, I SEARCHED FOR THE MAN IN CHARGE. HE MUST HAVE SURVIVED.
BUT THERE WAS NO SIGN OF HIM. ANYWHERE.
HE MUST'VE FLED, LEAVING HIS DEAD MEN BEHIND.
NO MATTER, I STILL HAD THAT CLUE FROM HANA, THE MYSTERIOUS WOMAN WHO COULD HEAR THE INTERNET IN HER HEAD. SHE CALLED HERSELF WIRELESS.
HOW DO YOU STOP AN EXPLODING MAN?
Part Two
JESSE ALEXANDER & ARON ELI COLEITE Story
JORDAN KOTZEBUE Art
MARK ROSLAN Digital inks
BETH SOTELO Colors
COMICRAFT Lettering

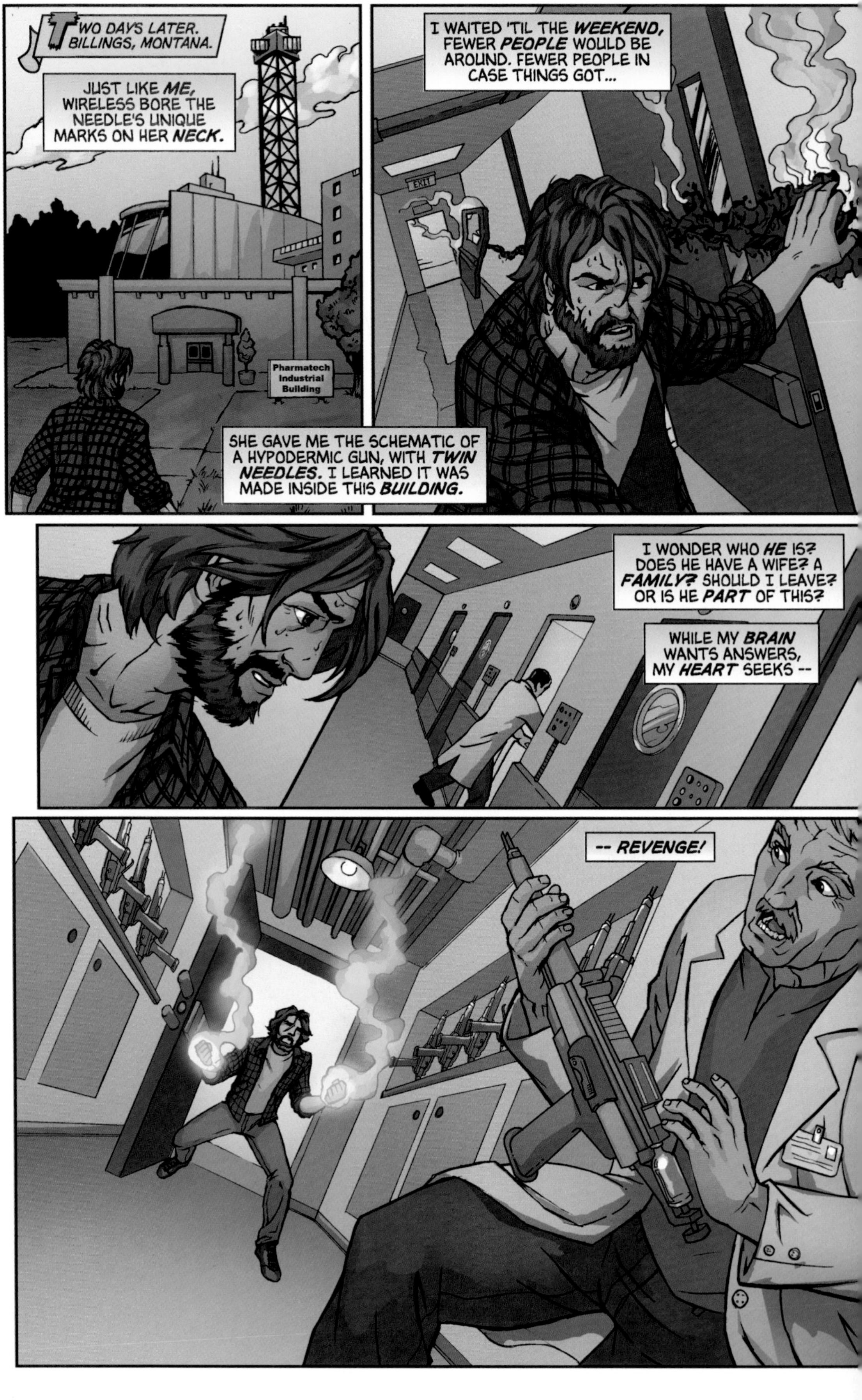
TWO DAYS LATER. BILLINGS, MONTANA.
JUST LIKE ME, WIRELESS BORE THE NEEDLE'S UNIQUE MARKS ON HER NECK.
Pharmatech Industrial Building
I WAITED 'TIL THE WEEKEND, FEWER PEOPLE WOULD BE AROUND. FEWER PEOPLE IN CASE THINGS GOT...
EXIT
SHE GAVE ME THE SCHEMATIC OF A HYPODERMIC GUN, WITH TWIN NEEDLES. I LEARNED IT WAS MADE INSIDE THIS BUILDING.
I WONDER WHO HE IS? DOES HE HAVE A WIFE? A FAMILY? SHOULD I LEAVE? OR IS HE PART OF THIS?
WHILE MY BRAIN WANTS ANSWERS, MY HEART SEEKS --
-- REVENGE!

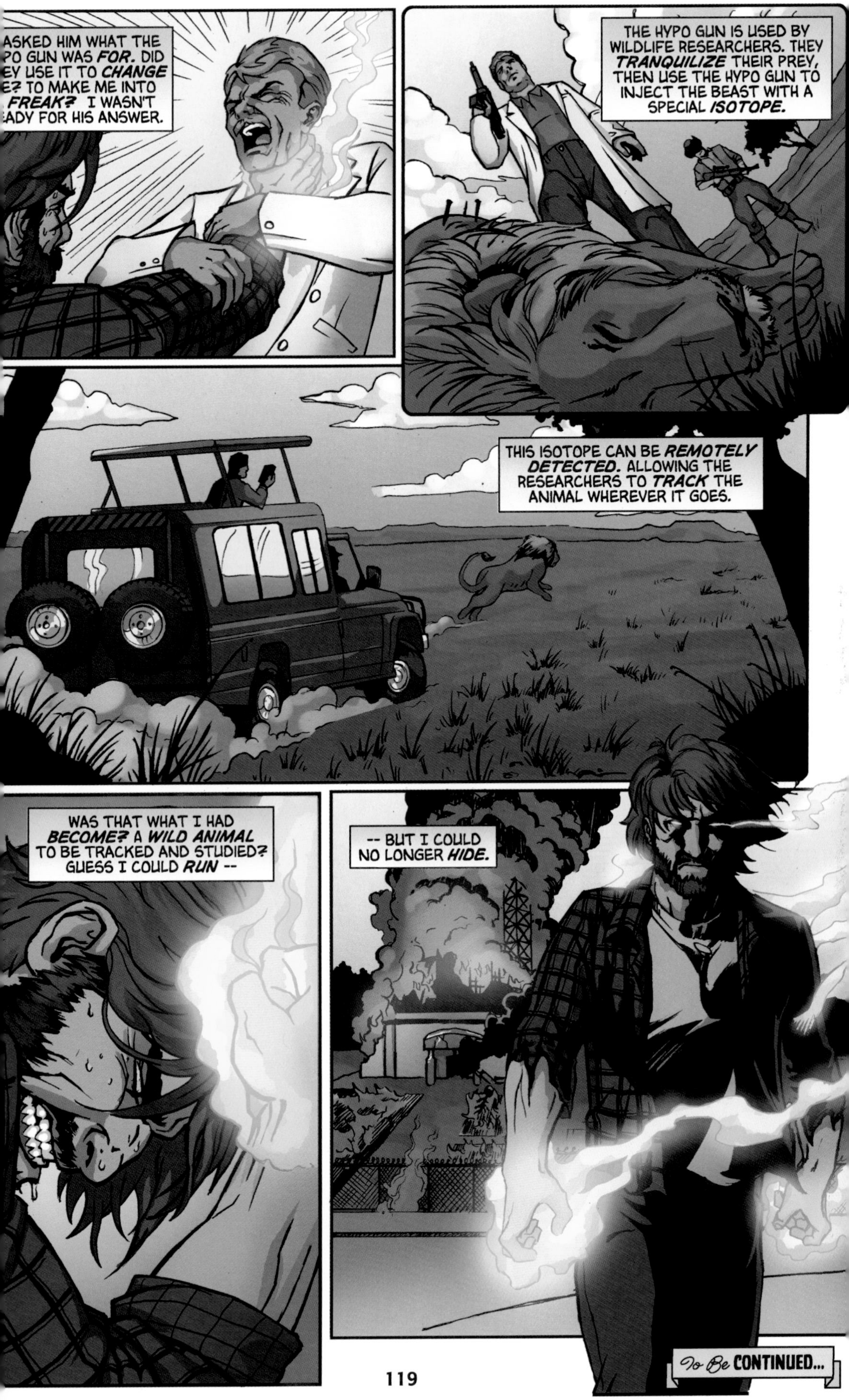
ASKED HIM WHAT THE
PO GUN WAS FOR. DID
EY USE IT TO CHANGE
E? TO MAKE ME INTO
FREAK? I WASN'T
EADY FOR HIS ANSWER.
THE HYPO GUN IS USED BY
WILDLIFE RESEARCHERS. THEY
TRANQUILIZE THEIR PREY,
THEN USE THE HYPO GUN TO
INJECT THE BEAST WITH A
SPECIAL ISOTOPE.
THIS ISOTOPE CAN BE REMOTELY
DETECTED. ALLOWING THE
RESEARCHERS TO TRACK THE
ANIMAL WHEREVER IT GOES.
WAS THAT WHAT I HAD
BECOME? A WILD ANIMAL
TO BE TRACKED AND STUDIED?
GUESS I COULD RUN --
-- BUT I COULD
NO LONGER HIDE.
To Be CONTINUED...

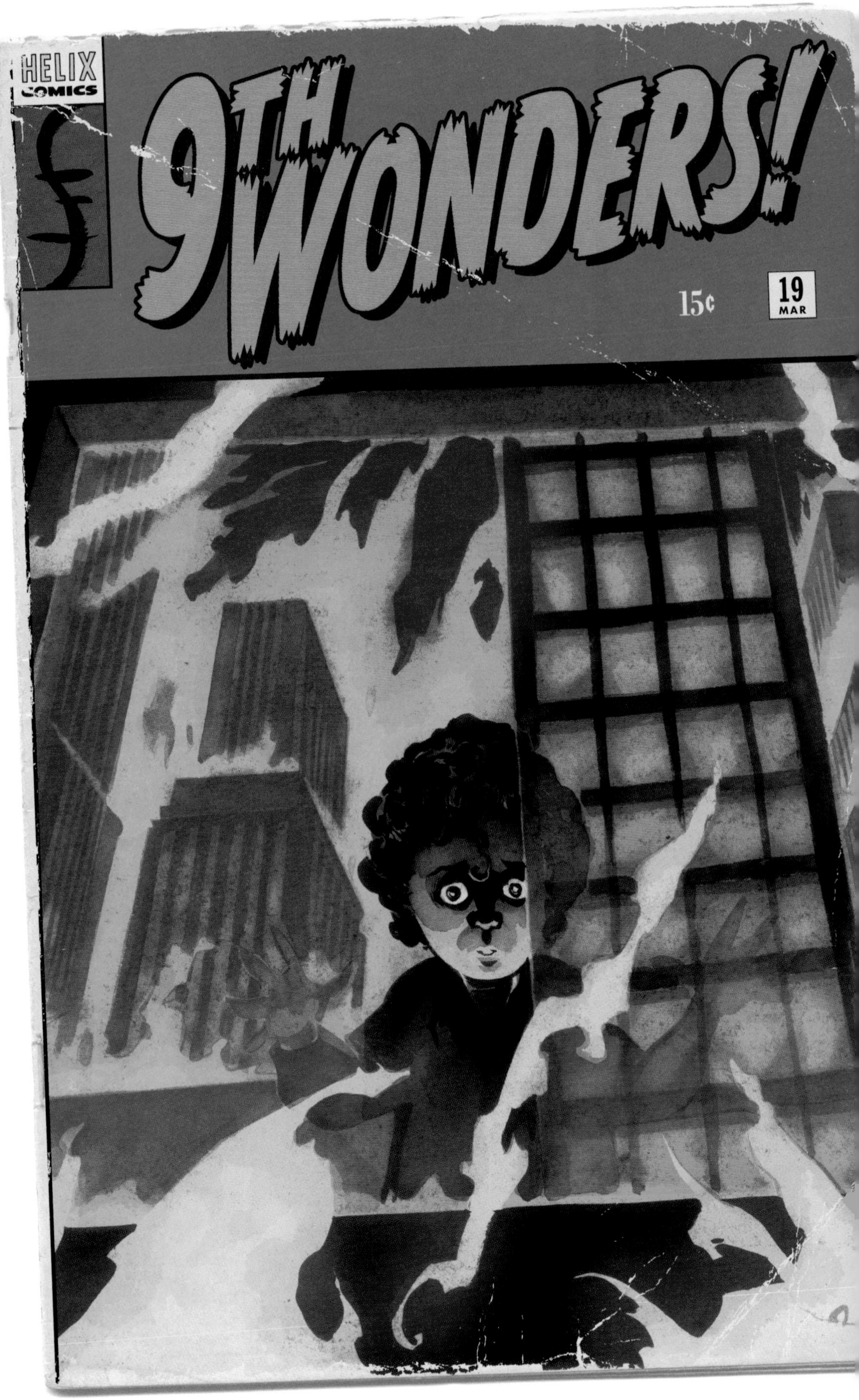
HELIX
COMICS
9TH WONDERS!
15¢
19
MAR

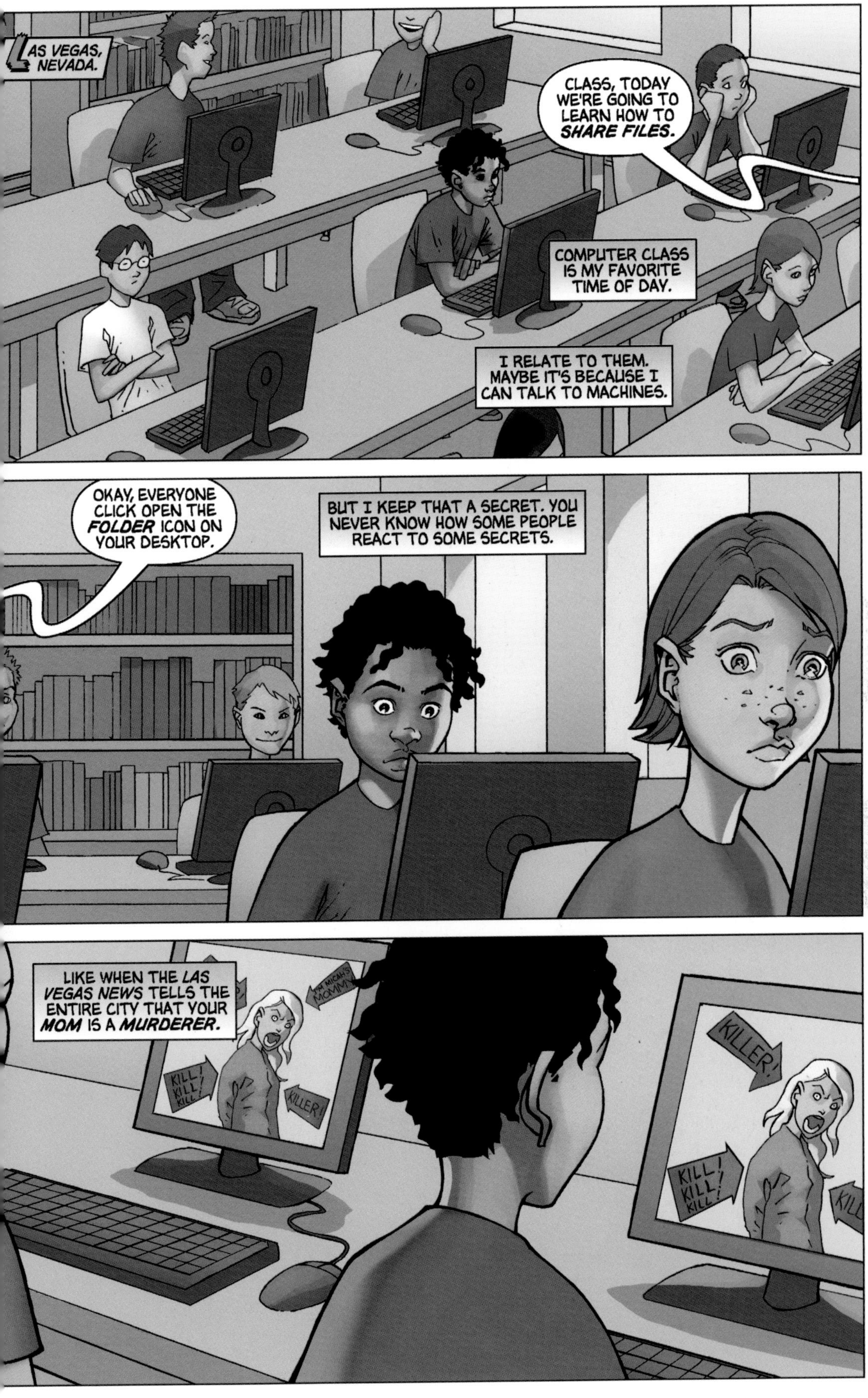
LAS VEGAS, NEVADA.
CLASS, TODAY WE'RE GOING TO LEARN HOW TO *SHARE FILES.*
COMPUTER CLASS IS MY FAVORITE TIME OF DAY.
I RELATE TO THEM. MAYBE IT'S BECAUSE I CAN TALK TO MACHINES.
OKAY, EVERYONE CLICK OPEN THE *FOLDER* ICON ON YOUR DESKTOP.
BUT I KEEP THAT A SECRET. YOU NEVER KNOW HOW SOME PEOPLE REACT TO SOME SECRETS.
LIKE WHEN THE *LAS VEGAS NEWS* TELLS THE ENTIRE CITY THAT YOUR *MOM* IS A *MURDERER*.
I'M MICAH'S MOMMY
KILL! KILL! KILL!
KILLER!
KILLER!
KILL! KILL! KILL!

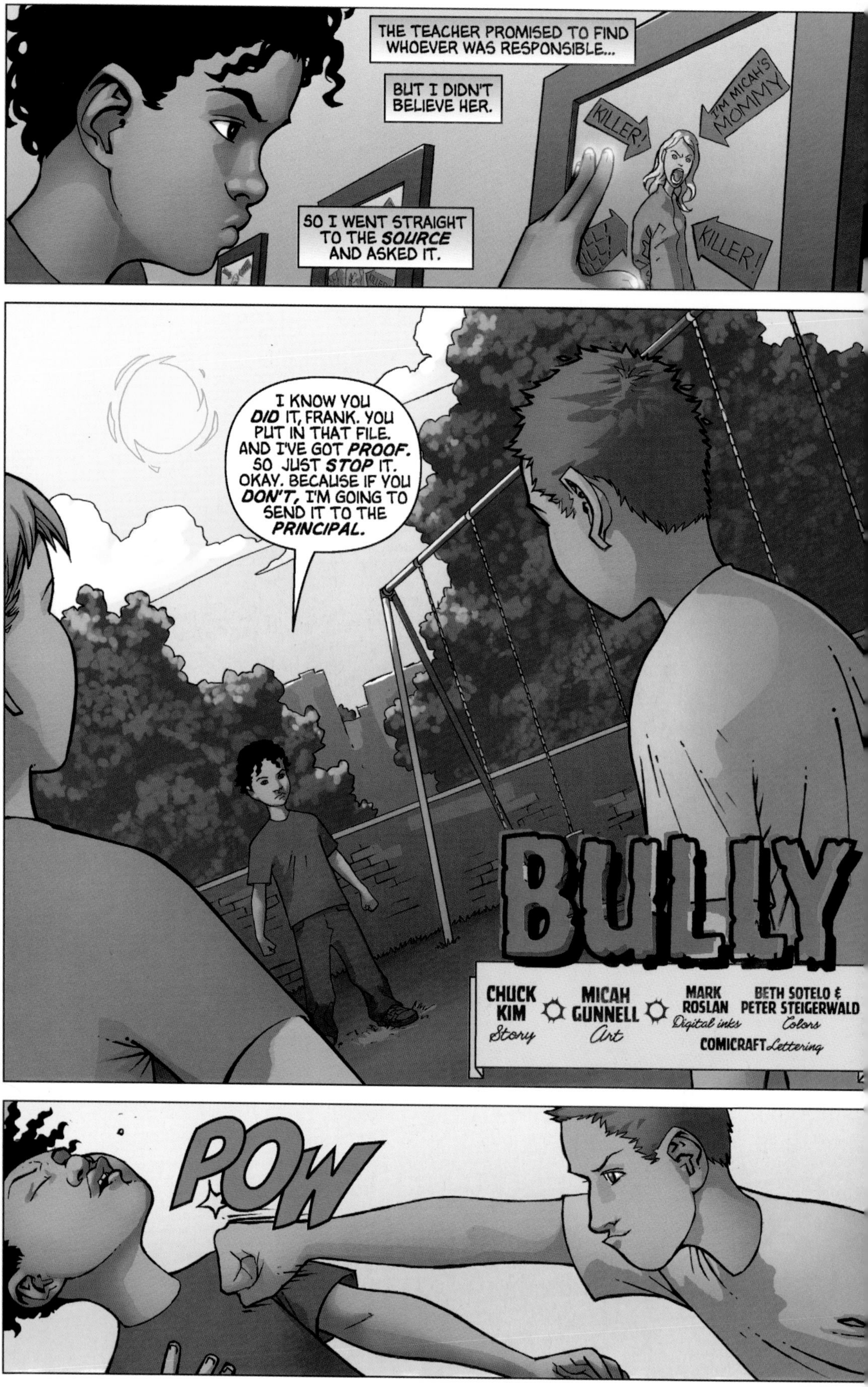
THE TEACHER PROMISED TO FIND WHOEVER WAS RESPONSIBLE...
BUT I DIDN'T BELIEVE HER.
SO I WENT STRAIGHT TO THE SOURCE AND ASKED IT.
KILLER!
I'M MICAH'S MOMMY
KILLER!
I KNOW YOU DID IT, FRANK. YOU PUT IN THAT FILE. AND I'VE GOT PROOF. SO JUST STOP IT. OKAY. BECAUSE IF YOU DON'T, I'M GOING TO SEND IT TO THE PRINCIPAL.
BULLY
CHUCK KIM Story
MICAH GUNNELL Art
MARK ROSLAN Digital inks
BETH SOTELO & PETER STEIGERWALD Colors
COMICRAFT Lettering
POW

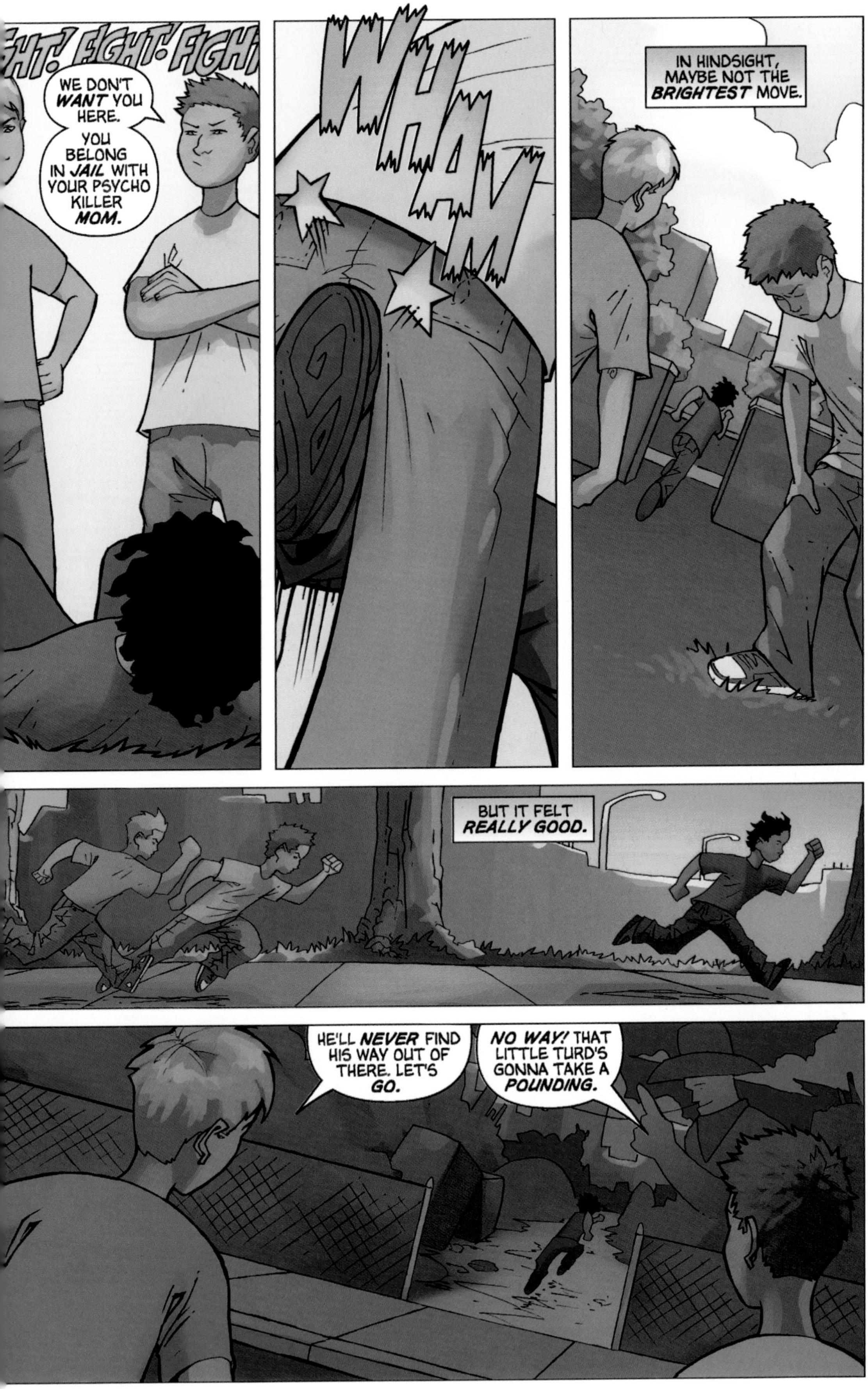
FIGHT! FIGHT! FIGHT
WE DON'T WANT YOU HERE.
YOU BELONG IN JAIL WITH YOUR PSYCHO KILLER MOM.
WHAM
IN HINDSIGHT, MAYBE NOT THE BRIGHTEST MOVE.
BUT IT FELT REALLY GOOD.
HE'LL NEVER FIND HIS WAY OUT OF THERE. LET'S GO.
NO WAY! THAT LITTLE TURD'S GONNA TAKE A POUNDING.

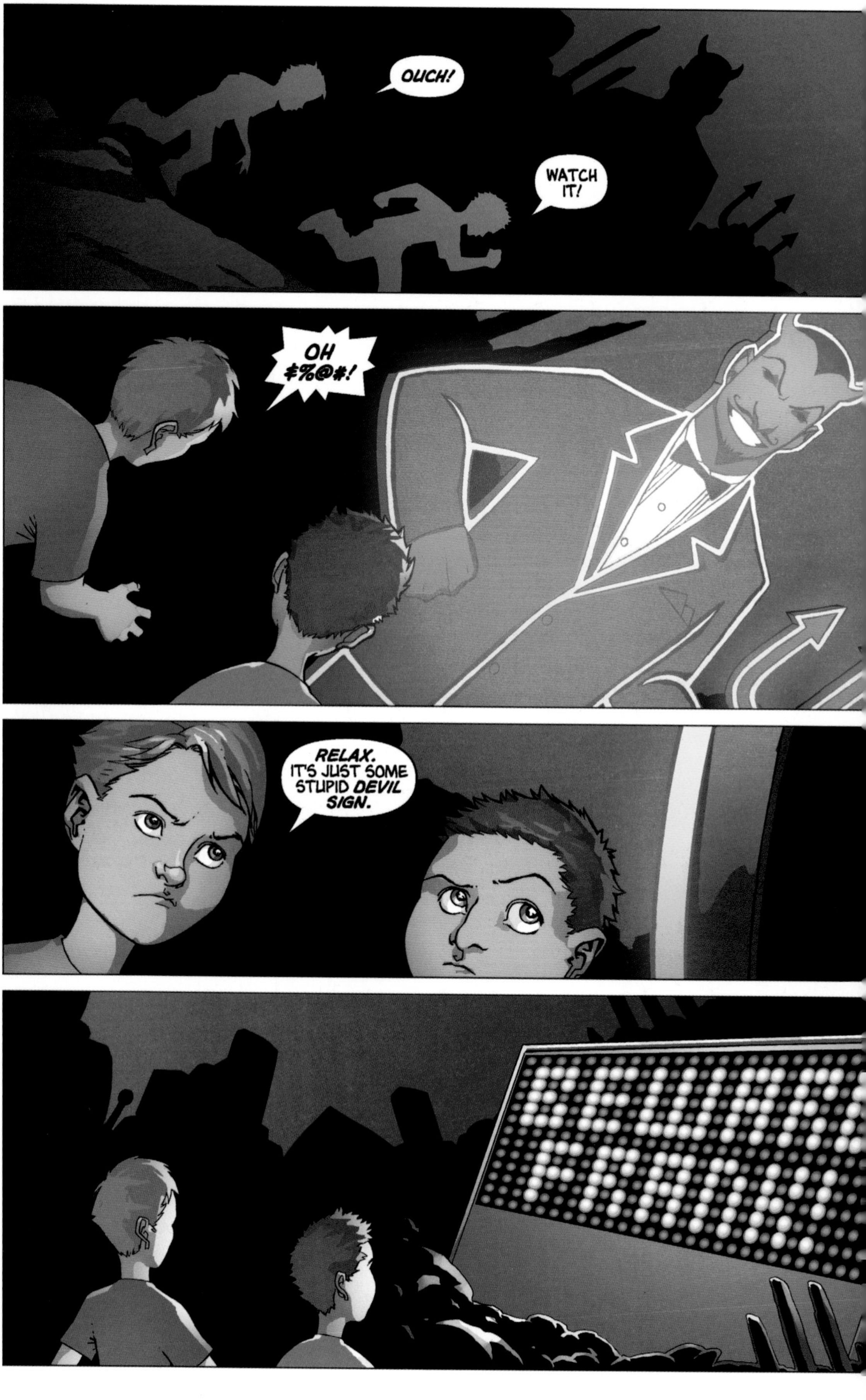
OUCH!
WATCH IT!
OH ¢%@#!
RELAX. IT'S JUST SOME STUPID DEVIL SIGN.

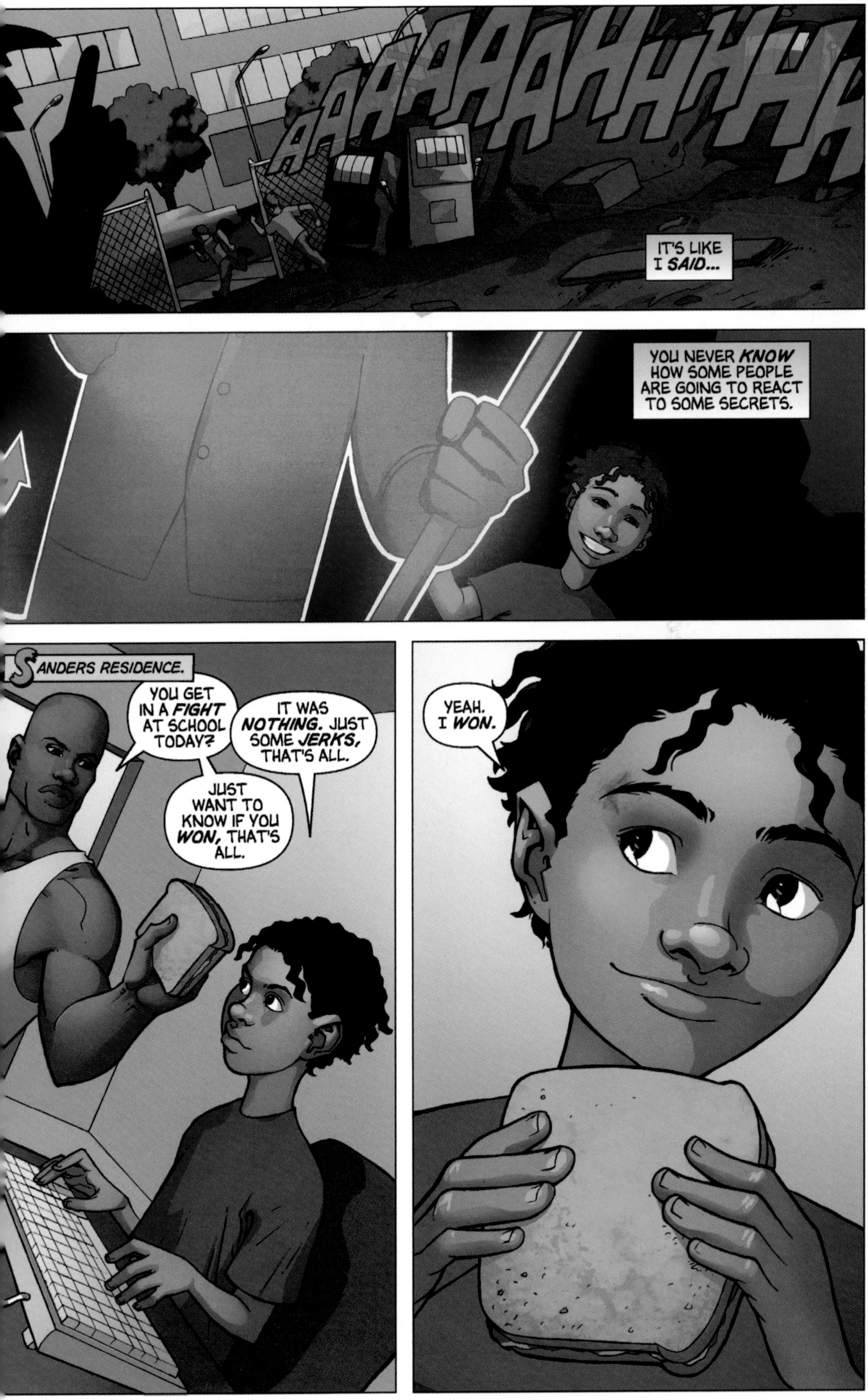
AAAAAAHHHHHHHHH
IT'S LIKE I SAID...
YOU NEVER KNOW HOW SOME PEOPLE ARE GOING TO REACT TO SOME SECRETS.
SANDERS RESIDENCE.
YOU GET IN A FIGHT AT SCHOOL TODAY?
IT WAS NOTHING. JUST SOME JERKS, THAT'S ALL.
JUST WANT TO KNOW IF YOU WON, THAT'S ALL.
YEAH. I WON.

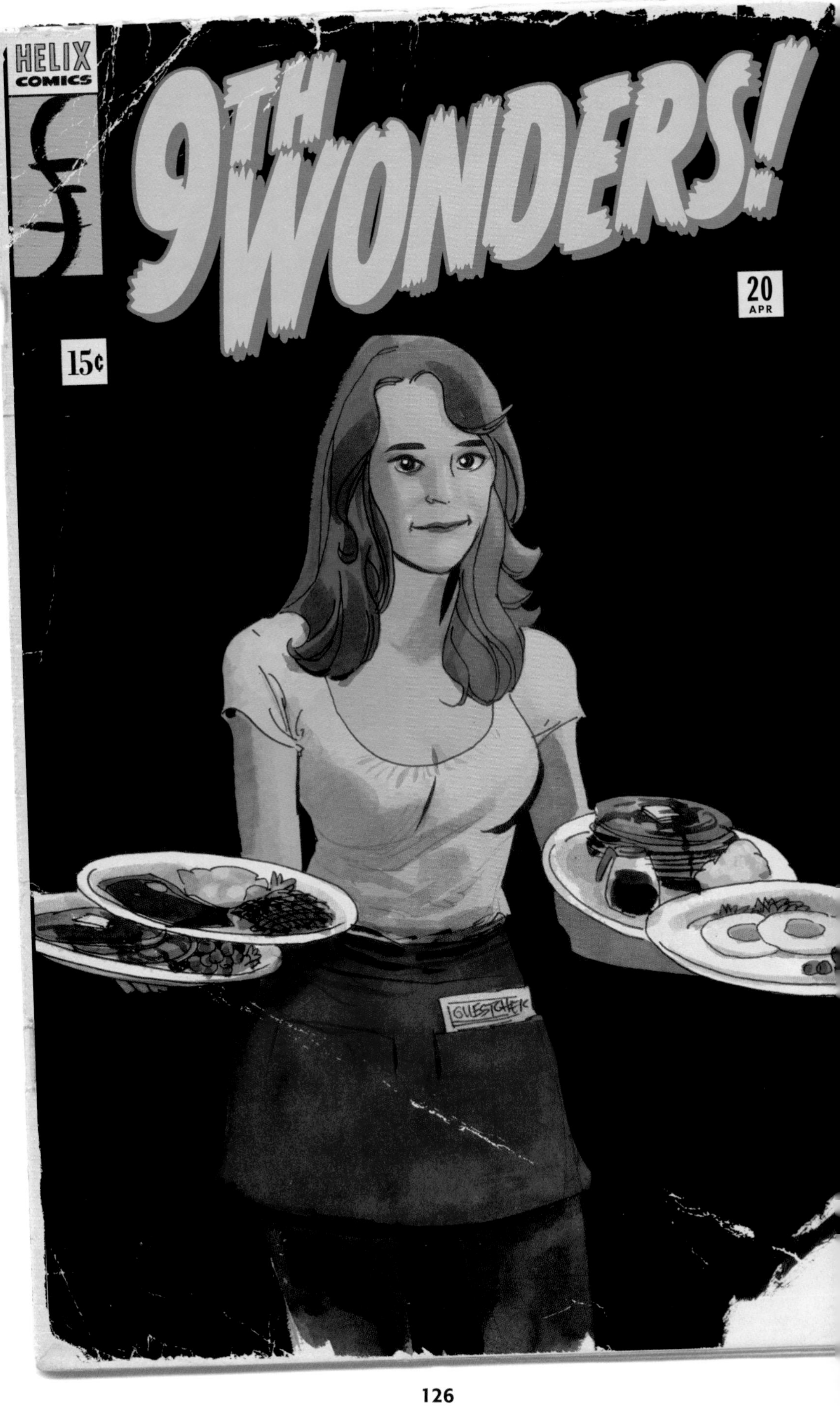
HELIX
COMICS
9TH WONDERS!
20
APR
15¢
GUESTCHECK

TWO DAYS AGO.

ODESSA GAS

ODESSA BUTTON WORKS

OPEN

CAPTURED, TORTURED, THEN INJURED. IN *PODUNK,* TEXAS.

THESE BULLET HOLES WOULDN'T BE A *PROBLEM* IF I HAD JUST GOTTEN THAT *CHEERLEADER.*

HER DADDY WAS A DAMN GOOD *SHOT* FOR A GUY WHO NEEDS *CORRECTIVE LENSES.*

BUT NOT GOOD *ENOUGH.*

I CAN'T IMAGINE HE'S *NOT* COMING AFTER ME. AFTER WHAT I DID TO HIS *DAUGHTER.*

NOT TO MENTION HIS *WIFE.*

President drew fire for welfare comments

O'Grady Farm to be purchased back from C...

NEED TO GET AS *FAR* AWAY FROM HERE AS POSSIBLE.

BEER

WHICH MEANS I NEED A *RIDE.*

BEER

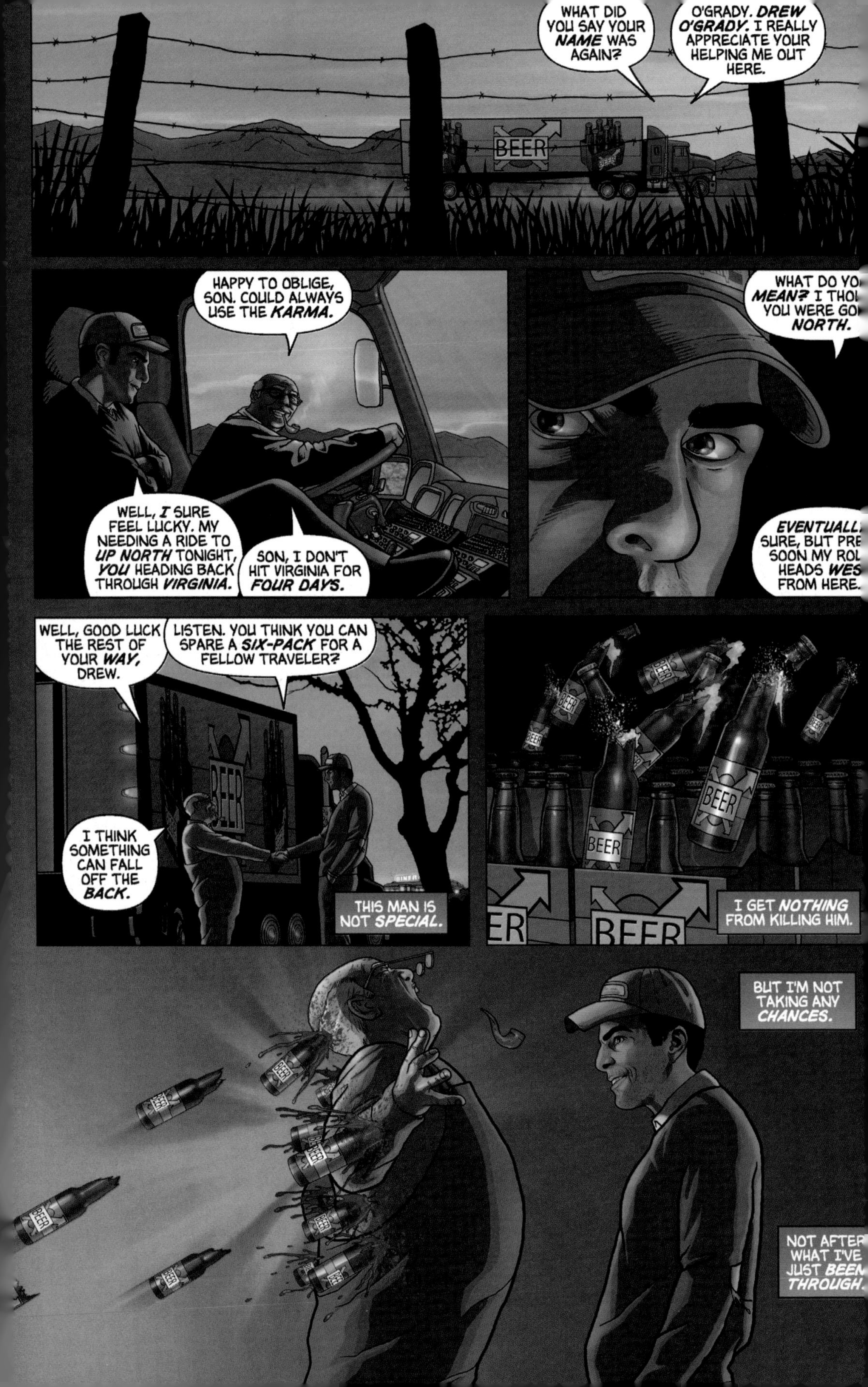
WHAT DID YOU SAY YOUR NAME WAS AGAIN?
O'GRADY. DREW O'GRADY. I REALLY APPRECIATE YOUR HELPING ME OUT HERE.
BEER
HAPPY TO OBLIGE, SON. COULD ALWAYS USE THE KARMA.
WELL, I SURE FEEL LUCKY. MY NEEDING A RIDE TO UP NORTH TONIGHT, YOU HEADING BACK THROUGH VIRGINIA.
SON, I DON'T HIT VIRGINIA FOR FOUR DAYS.
WHAT DO YO MEAN? I THO YOU WERE GO NORTH.
EVENTUALL SURE, BUT PRE SOON MY RO HEADS WES FROM HERE.
WELL, GOOD LUCK THE REST OF YOUR WAY, DREW.
LISTEN. YOU THINK YOU CAN SPARE A SIX-PACK FOR A FELLOW TRAVELER?
I THINK SOMETHING CAN FALL OFF THE BACK.
THIS MAN IS NOT SPECIAL.
I GET NOTHING FROM KILLING HIM.
BUT I'M NOT TAKING ANY CHANCES.
NOT AFTER WHAT I'VE JUST BEEN THROUGH.

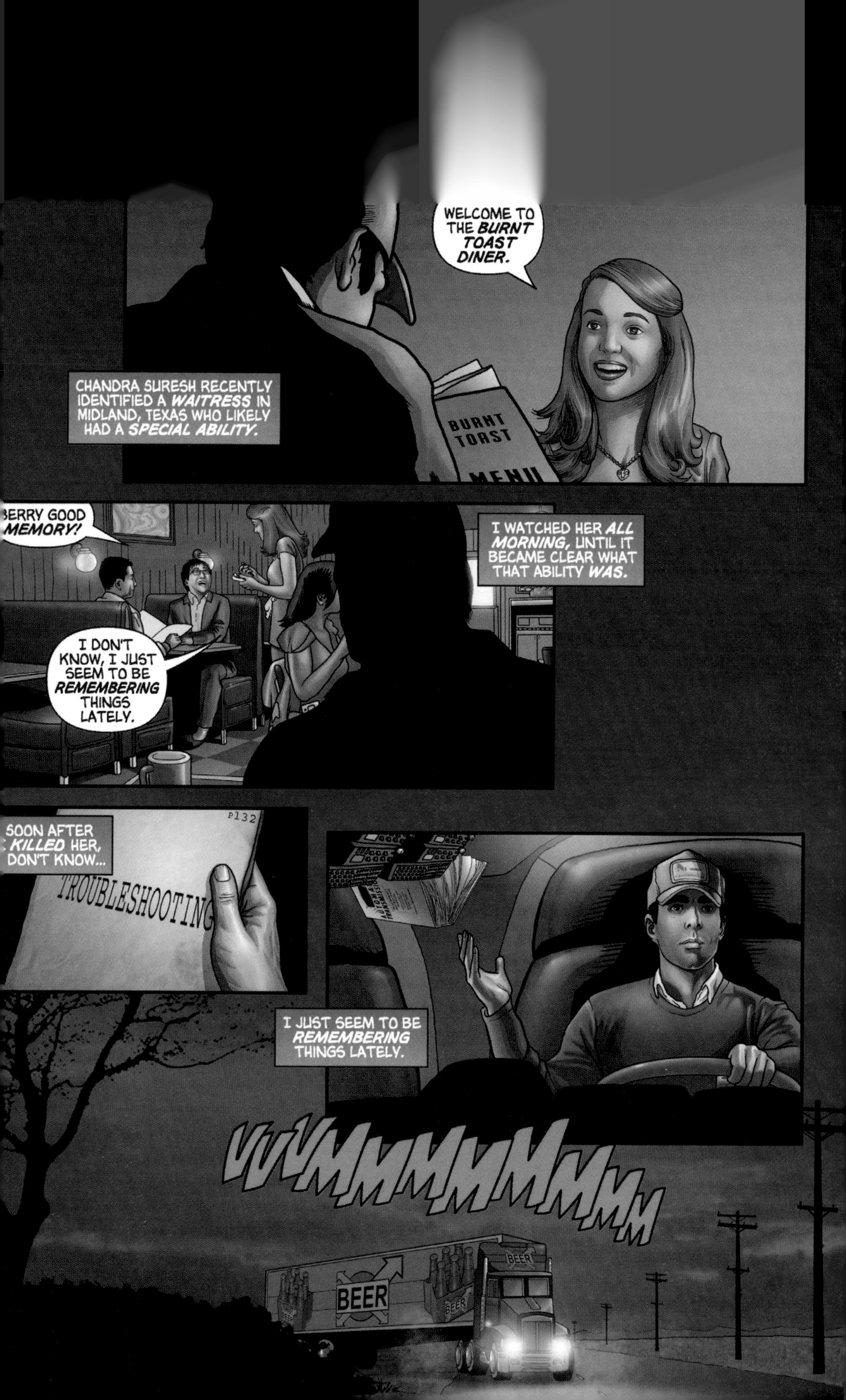
WELCOME TO THE BURNT TOAST DINER.
CHANDRA SURESH RECENTLY IDENTIFIED A WAITRESS IN MIDLAND, TEXAS WHO LIKELY HAD A SPECIAL ABILITY.
BURNT TOAST MENU
BERRY GOOD MEMORY!
I WATCHED HER ALL MORNING, UNTIL IT BECAME CLEAR WHAT THAT ABILITY WAS.
I DON'T KNOW, I JUST SEEM TO BE REMEMBERING THINGS LATELY.
SOON AFTER KILLED HER, DON'T KNOW...
P132
TROUBLESHOOTING
I JUST SEEM TO BE REMEMBERING THINGS LATELY.
VVVMMMMMMMMMMMM
BEER
BEER
BEER

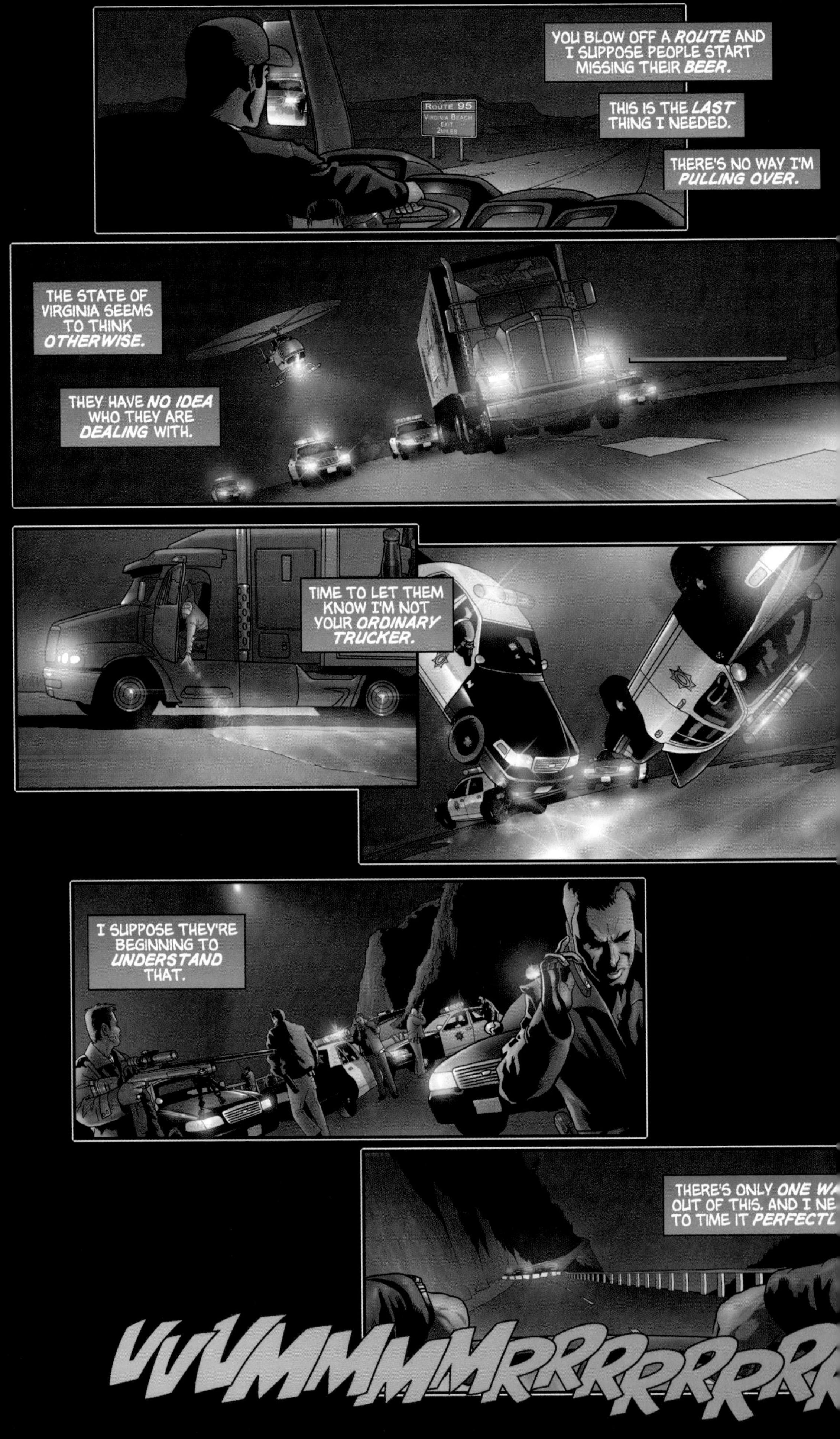
YOU BLOW OFF A ROUTE AND I SUPPOSE PEOPLE START MISSING THEIR BEER.
THIS IS THE LAST THING I NEEDED.
THERE'S NO WAY I'M PULLING OVER.
ROUTE 95
VIRGINIA BEACH EXIT 2MILES
THE STATE OF VIRGINIA SEEMS TO THINK OTHERWISE.
THEY HAVE NO IDEA WHO THEY ARE DEALING WITH.
TIME TO LET THEM KNOW I'M NOT YOUR ORDINARY TRUCKER.
I SUPPOSE THEY'RE BEGINNING TO UNDERSTAND THAT.
THERE'S ONLY ONE WA
OUT OF THIS. AND I NE
TO TIME IT PERFECTL
VVVMMMMRRRRRRRR

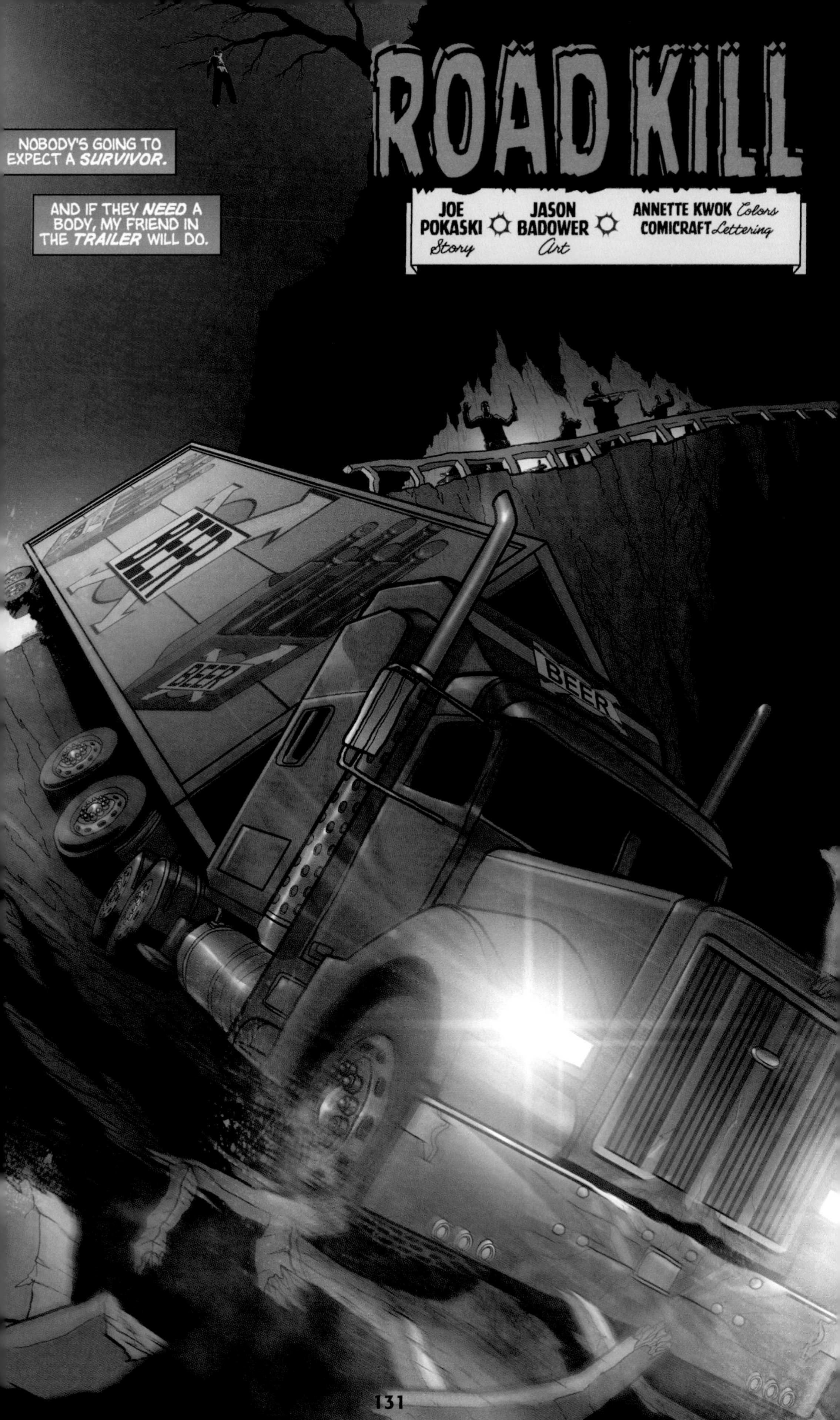
ROAD KILL
NOBODY'S GOING TO EXPECT A SURVIVOR.
AND IF THEY NEED A BODY, MY FRIEND IN THE TRAILER WILL DO.
JOE POKASKI Story
JASON BADOWER Art
ANNETTE KWOK Colors
COMICRAFT Lettering
BEER
BEER
BEER

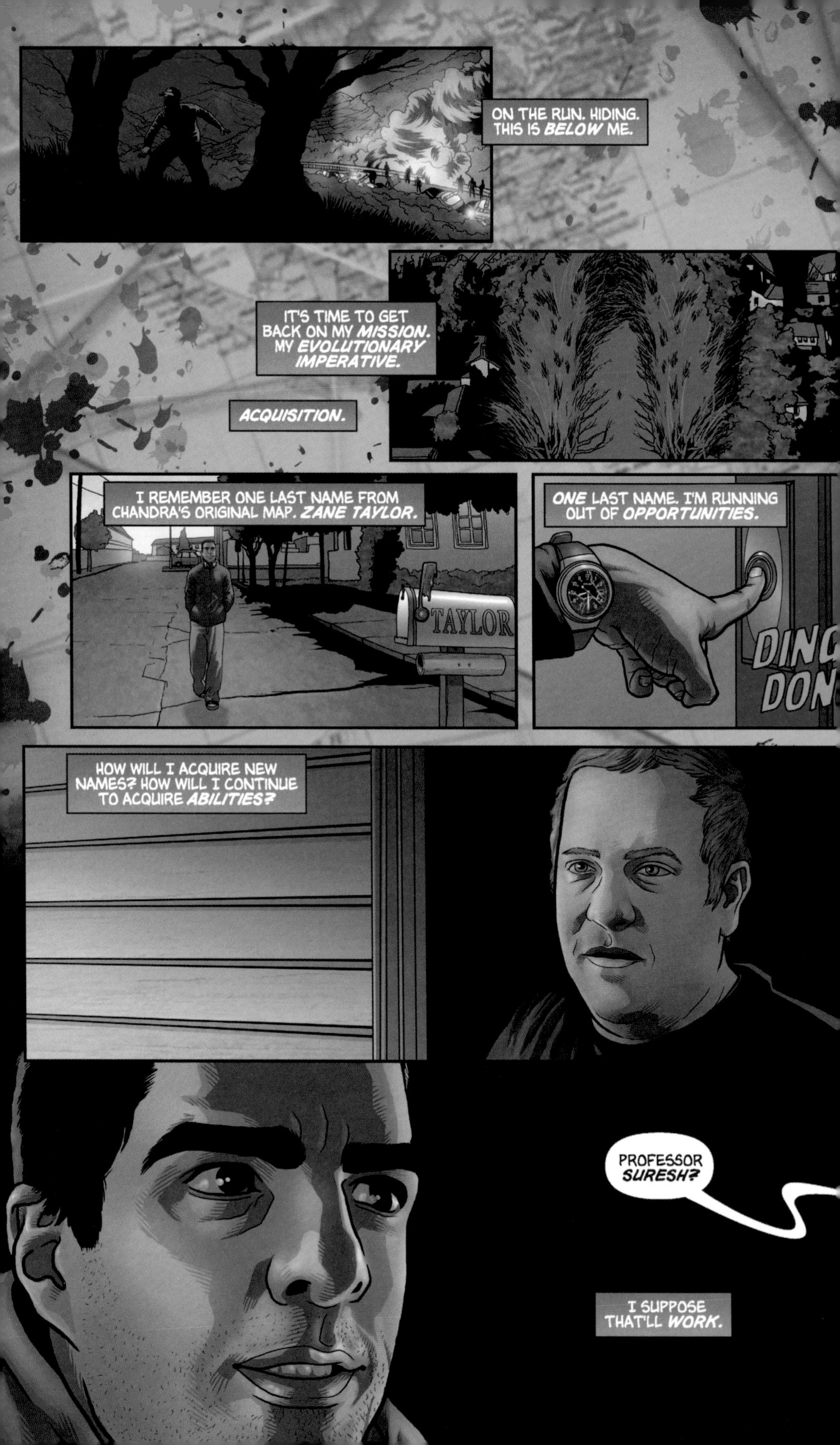

ON THE RUN. HIDING. THIS IS BELOW ME.
IT'S TIME TO GET BACK ON MY MISSION. MY EVOLUTIONARY IMPERATIVE.
ACQUISITION.
I REMEMBER ONE LAST NAME FROM CHANDRA'S ORIGINAL MAP. ZANE TAYLOR.
TAYLOR
ONE LAST NAME. I'M RUNNING OUT OF OPPORTUNITIES.
DING
DON
HOW WILL I ACQUIRE NEW NAMES? HOW WILL I CONTINUE TO ACQUIRE ABILITIES?
PROFESSOR SURESH?
I SUPPOSE THAT'LL WORK.

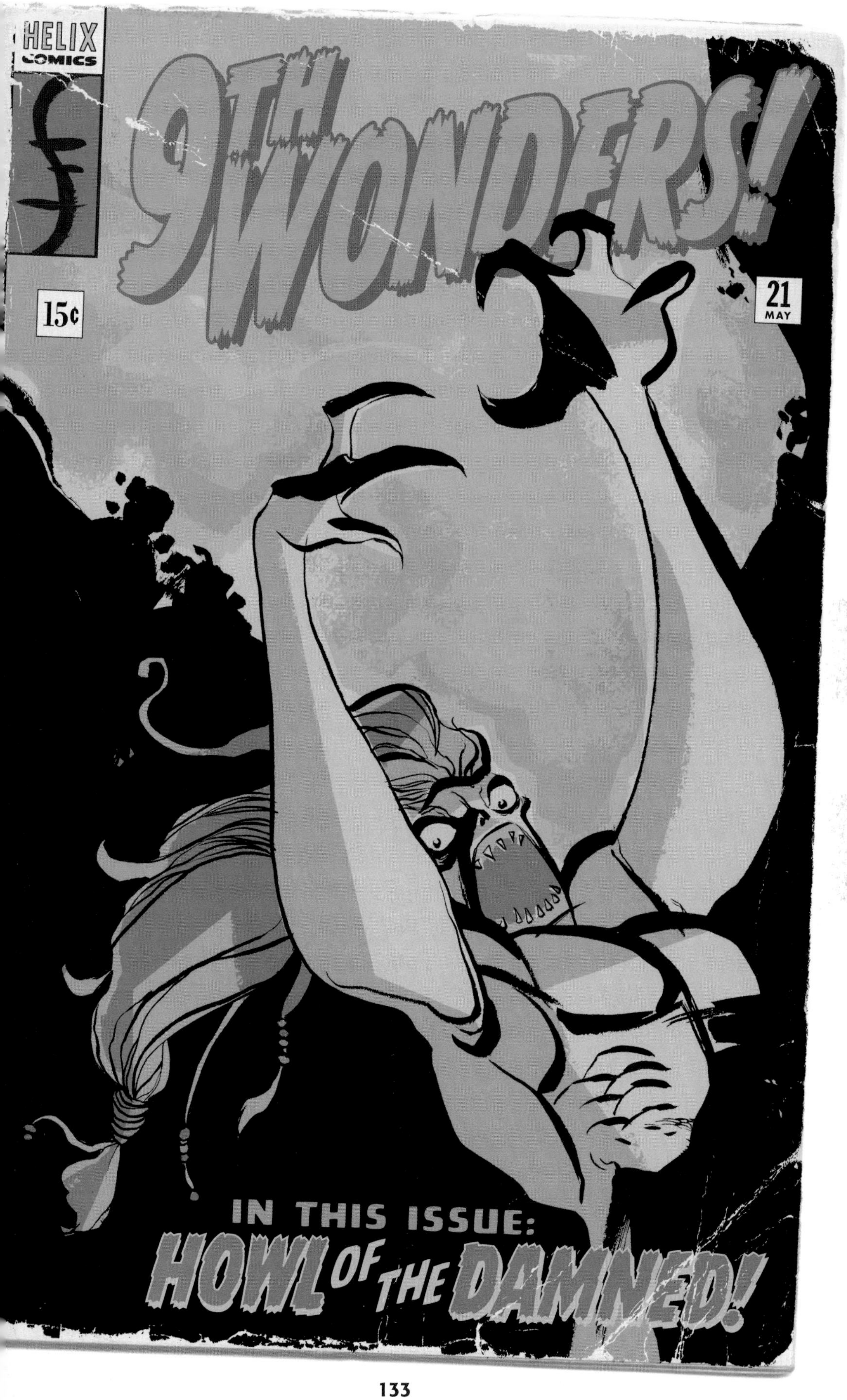
HELIX COMICS
9TH WONDERS!
15¢
21 MAY
IN THIS ISSUE:
HOWL OF THE DAMNED!

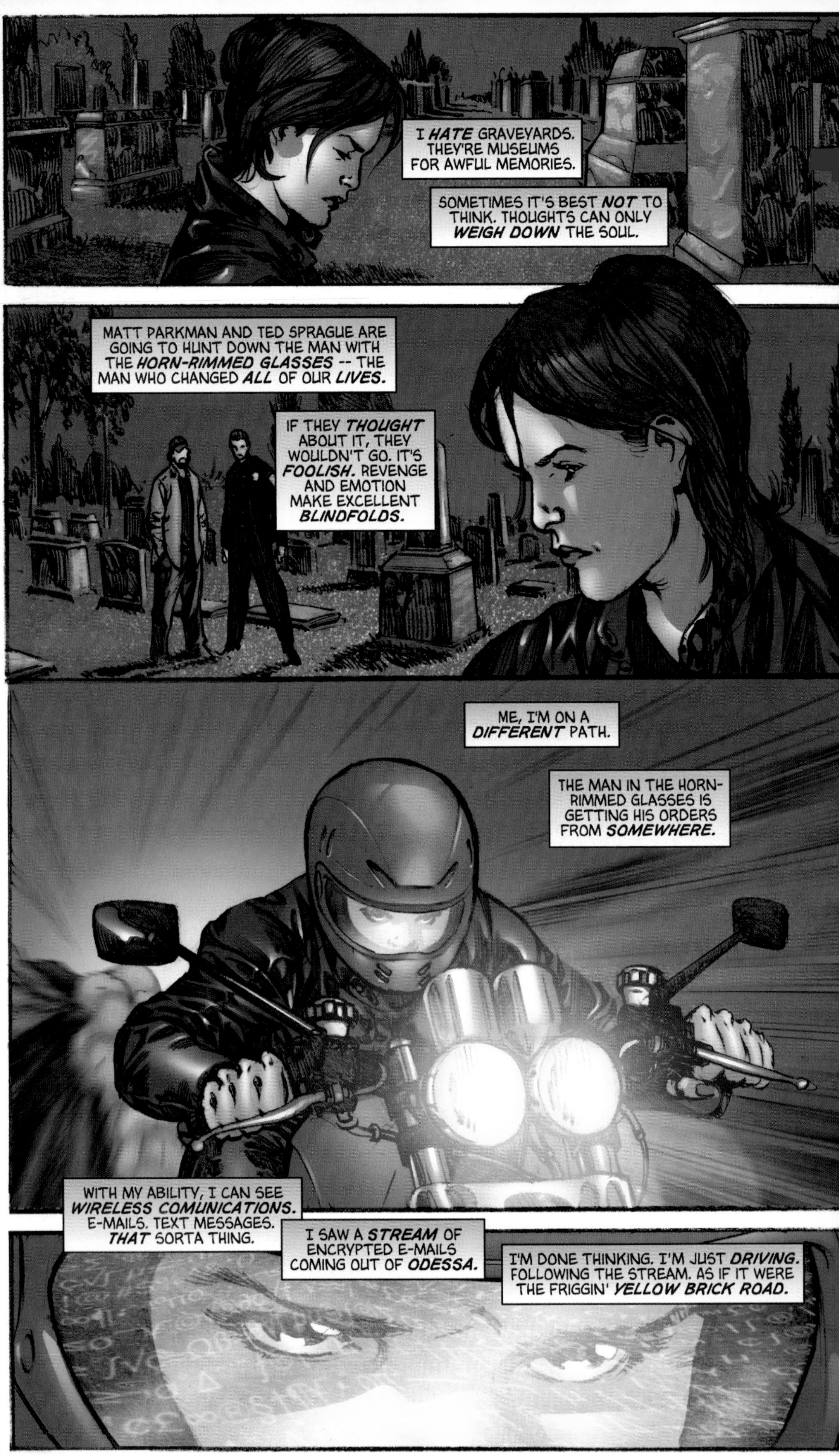
I HATE GRAVEYARDS. THEY'RE MUSEUMS FOR AWFUL MEMORIES.
SOMETIMES IT'S BEST NOT TO THINK. THOUGHTS CAN ONLY WEIGH DOWN THE SOUL.
MATT PARKMAN AND TED SPRAGUE ARE GOING TO HUNT DOWN THE MAN WITH THE HORN-RIMMED GLASSES -- THE MAN WHO CHANGED ALL OF OUR LIVES.
IF THEY THOUGHT ABOUT IT, THEY WOULDN'T GO. IT'S FOOLISH. REVENGE AND EMOTION MAKE EXCELLENT BLINDFOLDS.
ME, I'M ON A DIFFERENT PATH.
THE MAN IN THE HORN-RIMMED GLASSES IS GETTING HIS ORDERS FROM SOMEWHERE.
WITH MY ABILITY, I CAN SEE WIRELESS COMUNICATIONS. E-MAILS. TEXT MESSAGES. THAT SORTA THING.
I SAW A STREAM OF ENCRYPTED E-MAILS COMING OUT OF ODESSA.
I'M DONE THINKING. I'M JUST DRIVING. FOLLOWING THE STREAM. AS IF IT WERE THE FRIGGIN' YELLOW BRICK ROAD.

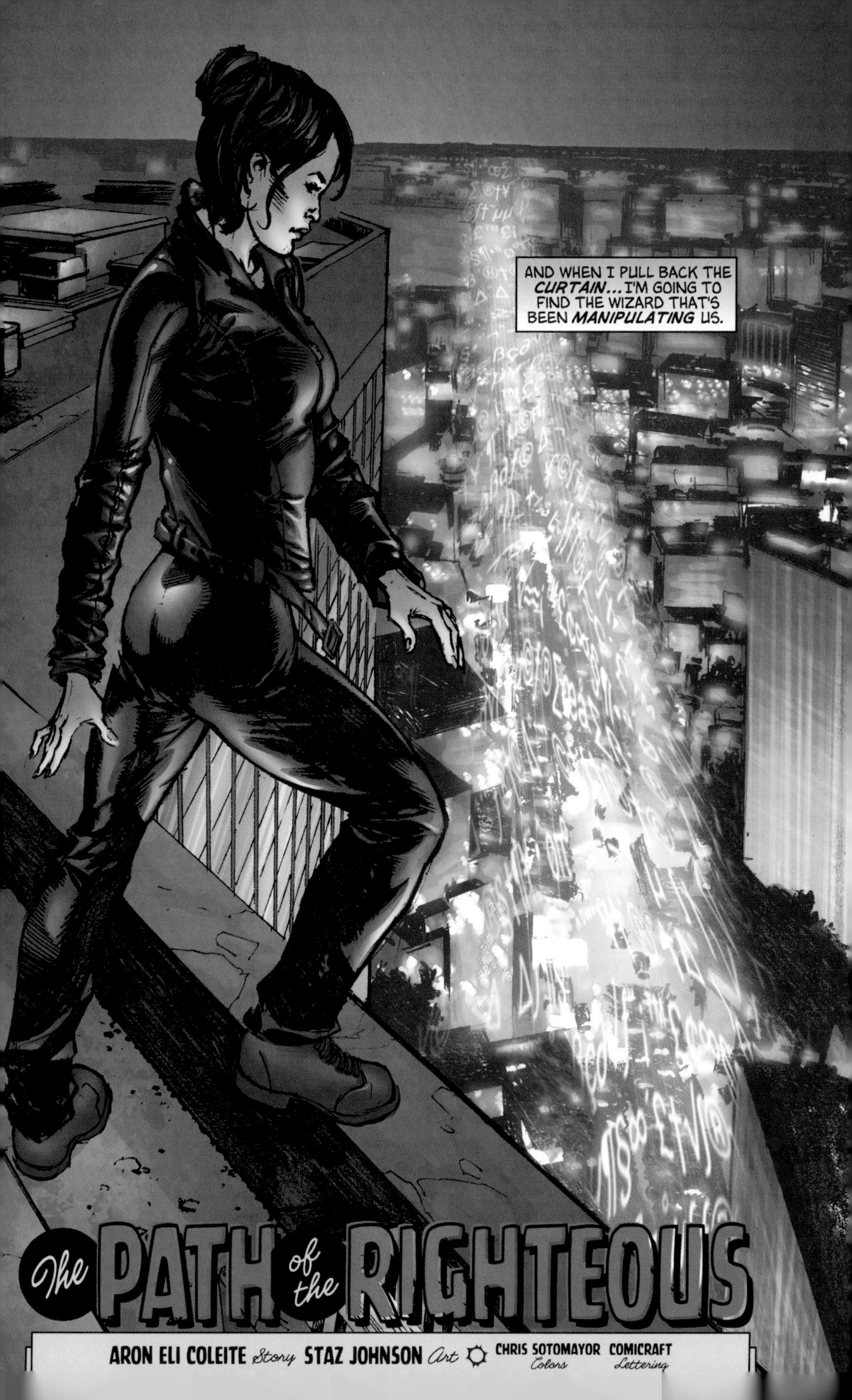
AND WHEN I PULL BACK THE *CURTAIN*... I'M GOING TO FIND THE WIZARD THAT'S BEEN *MANIPULATING* US.
The PATH of the RIGHTEOUS
ARON ELI COLEITE Story STAZ JOHNSON Art CHRIS SOTOMAYOR Colors COMICRAFT Lettering

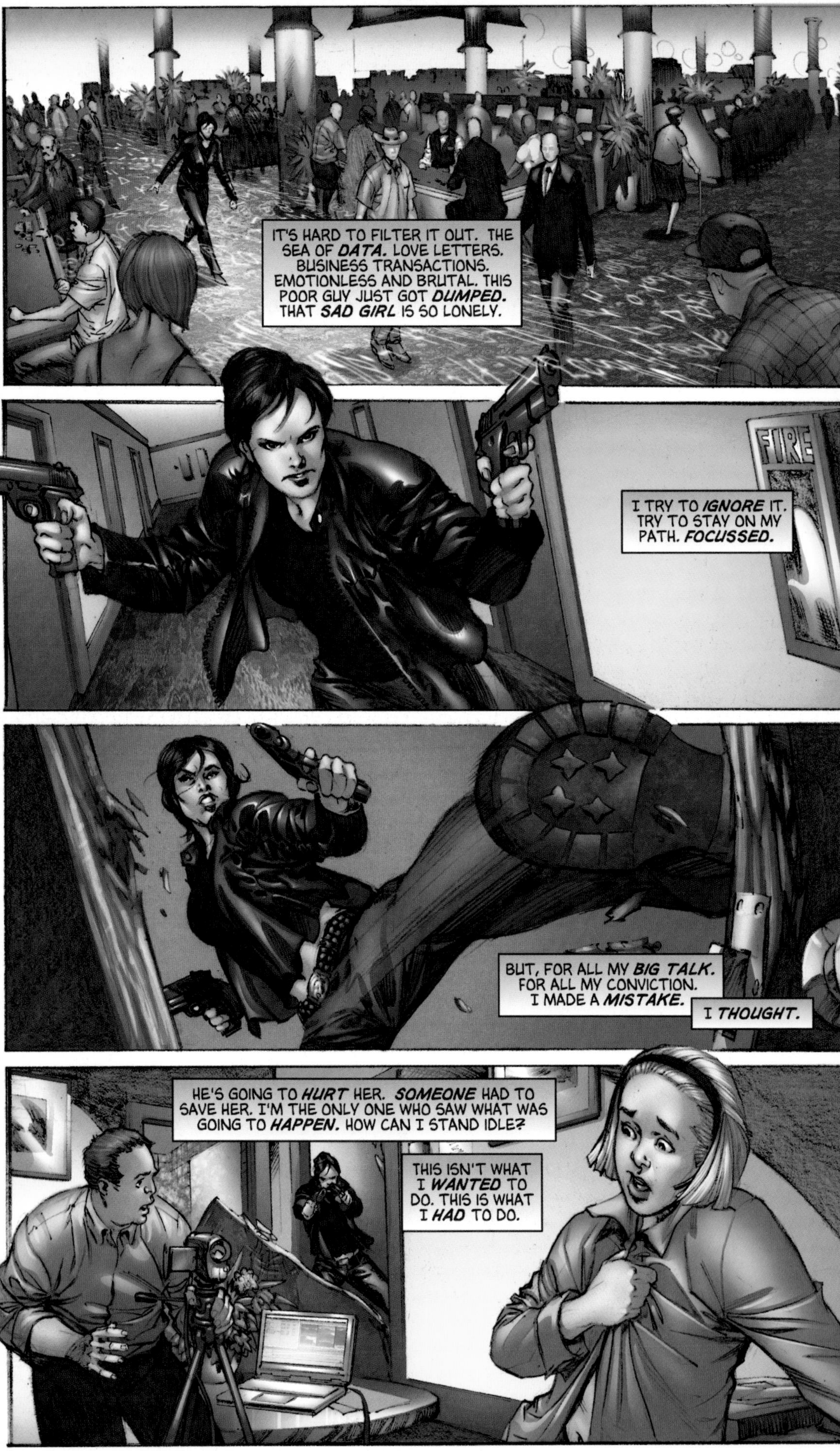
IT'S HARD TO FILTER IT OUT. THE SEA OF DATA. LOVE LETTERS. BUSINESS TRANSACTIONS. EMOTIONLESS AND BRUTAL. THIS POOR GUY JUST GOT DUMPED. THAT SAD GIRL IS SO LONELY.
FIRE
I TRY TO IGNORE IT. TRY TO STAY ON MY PATH. FOCUSSED.
BUT, FOR ALL MY BIG TALK. FOR ALL MY CONVICTION. I MADE A MISTAKE.
I THOUGHT.
HE'S GOING TO HURT HER. SOMEONE HAD TO SAVE HER. I'M THE ONLY ONE WHO SAW WHAT WAS GOING TO HAPPEN. HOW CAN I STAND IDLE?
THIS ISN'T WHAT I WANTED TO DO. THIS IS WHAT I HAD TO DO.

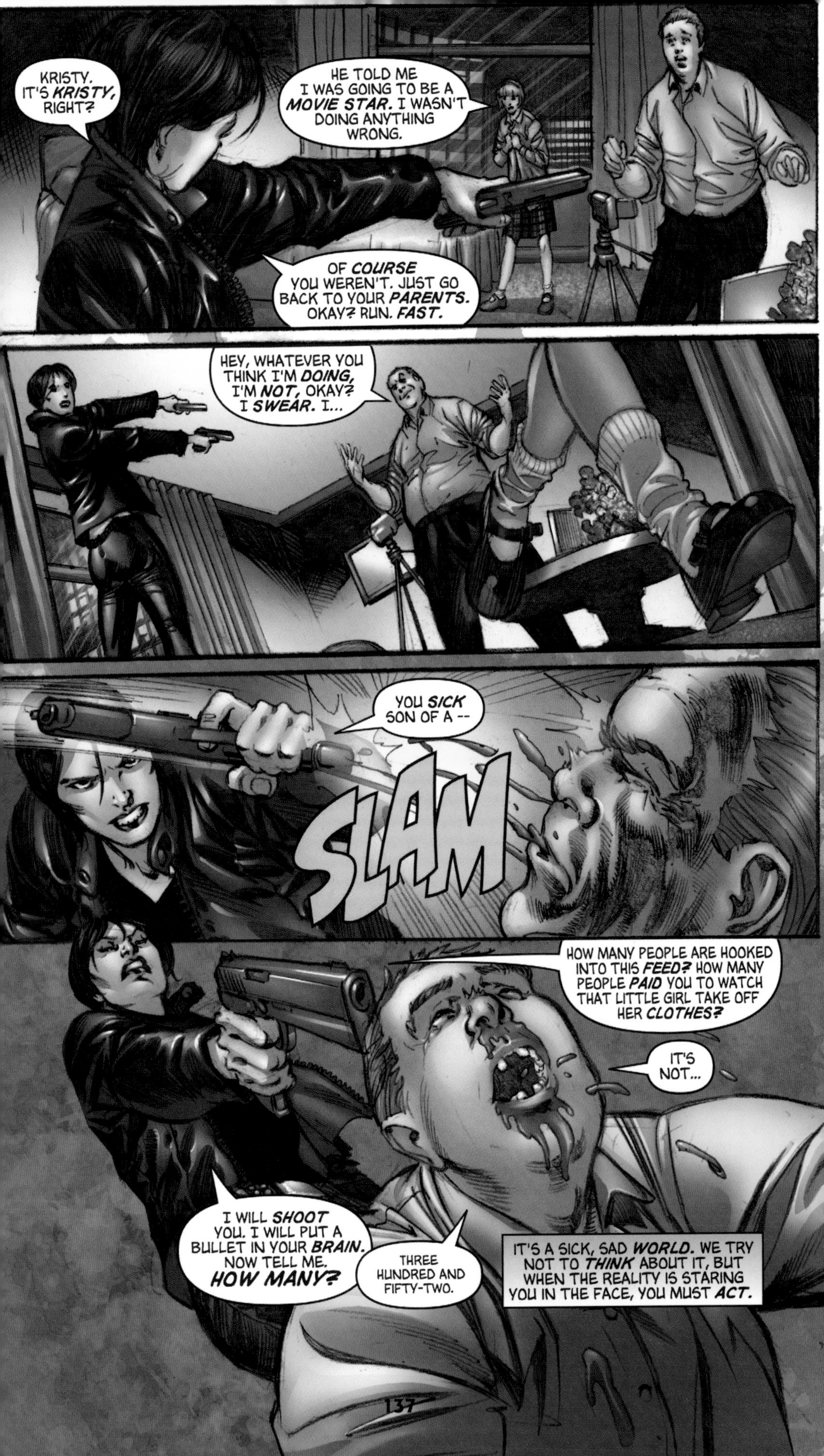
KRISTY. IT'S KRISTY, RIGHT?
HE TOLD ME I WAS GOING TO BE A MOVIE STAR. I WASN'T DOING ANYTHING WRONG.
OF COURSE YOU WEREN'T. JUST GO BACK TO YOUR PARENTS. OKAY? RUN. FAST.
HEY, WHATEVER YOU THINK I'M DOING, I'M NOT, OKAY? I SWEAR. I...
YOU SICK SON OF A --
SLAM
HOW MANY PEOPLE ARE HOOKED INTO THIS FEED? HOW MANY PEOPLE PAID YOU TO WATCH THAT LITTLE GIRL TAKE OFF HER CLOTHES?
IT'S NOT...
I WILL SHOOT YOU. I WILL PUT A BULLET IN YOUR BRAIN. NOW TELL ME. HOW MANY?
THREE HUNDRED AND FIFTY-TWO.
IT'S A SICK, SAD WORLD. WE TRY NOT TO THINK ABOUT IT, BUT WHEN THE REALITY IS STARING YOU IN THE FACE, YOU MUST ACT.

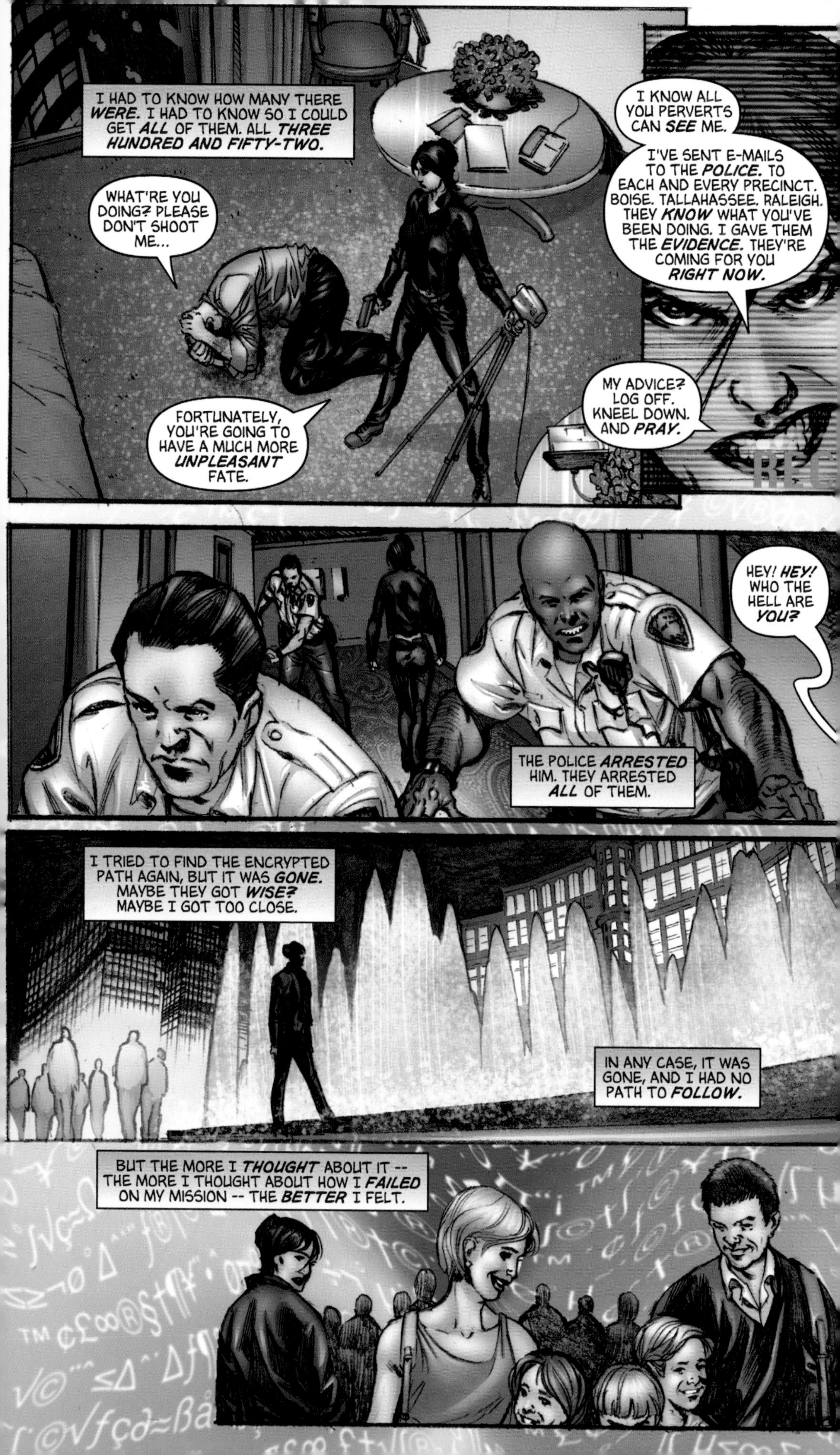

I HAD TO KNOW HOW MANY THERE WERE. I HAD TO KNOW SO I COULD GET ALL OF THEM. ALL THREE HUNDRED AND FIFTY-TWO.
WHAT'RE YOU DOING? PLEASE DON'T SHOOT ME...
FORTUNATELY, YOU'RE GOING TO HAVE A MUCH MORE UNPLEASANT FATE.
I KNOW ALL YOU PERVERTS CAN SEE ME.
I'VE SENT E-MAILS TO THE POLICE. TO EACH AND EVERY PRECINCT. BOISE. TALLAHASSEE. RALEIGH. THEY KNOW WHAT YOU'VE BEEN DOING. I GAVE THEM THE EVIDENCE. THEY'RE COMING FOR YOU RIGHT NOW.
MY ADVICE? LOG OFF. KNEEL DOWN. AND PRAY.
REC
HEY! HEY! WHO THE HELL ARE YOU?
THE POLICE ARRESTED HIM. THEY ARRESTED ALL OF THEM.
I TRIED TO FIND THE ENCRYPTED PATH AGAIN, BUT IT WAS GONE. MAYBE THEY GOT WISE? MAYBE I GOT TOO CLOSE.
IN ANY CASE, IT WAS GONE, AND I HAD NO PATH TO FOLLOW.
BUT THE MORE I THOUGHT ABOUT IT -- THE MORE I THOUGHT ABOUT HOW I FAILED ON MY MISSION -- THE BETTER I FELT.

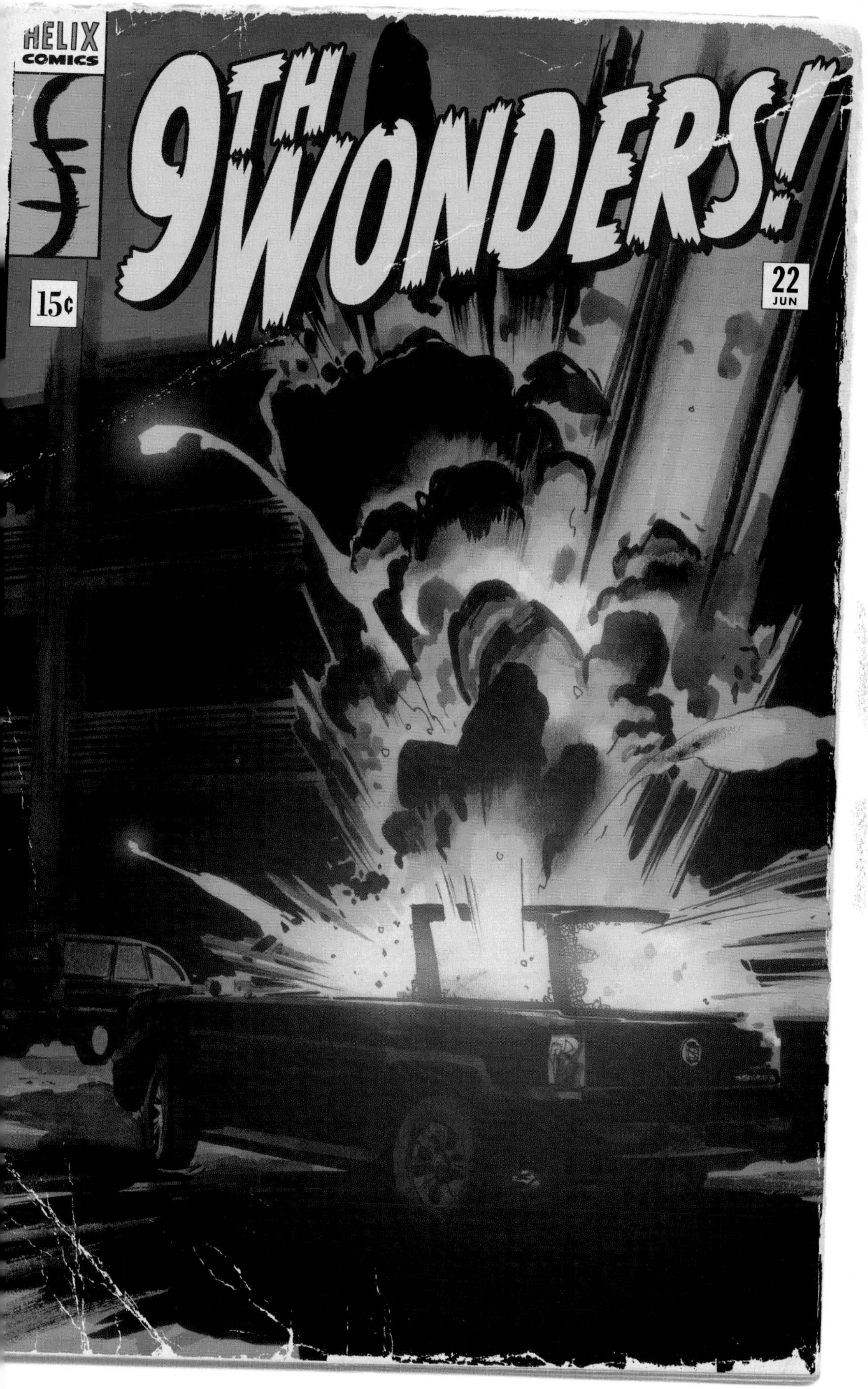
HELIX
COMICS
9TH WONDERS!
15¢
22
JUN

TEXAS. AFTER MIDNIGHT. 1992.

IT WASN'T THE *FIRST* BAG AND TAG THAT I'D RUN WITH CLAUDE.

THIS WOMAN WE'RE AFTER, HAS SHE MANIFESTED AN *ABILITY?*

NOT A *CLUE.* BUT THAT'S THE *FUN,* RIGHT? NEVER KNOWIN' *WHAT* WE'RE GONNA GET.

WE'D BEEN PARTNERS FOR A WHILE. I WAS STILL A ROOKIE. HE WAS THE *PRO.*

ISN'T THIS *DANGEROUS?* NOT KNOWING WHAT WE'RE WALKING *INTO?*

"WE'RE" NOT WALKING INTO ANYTHING *YOU'RE* STAYING OUT HER AND KEEPING *WATCH* LIK A GOOD DOGGY, WHILE *I* D THE HEAVY LIFTIN'.

CLAUDE COULD MAKE HIMSELF *INVISIBLE.* I THINK THAT MADE HIM FEEL *UNTOUCHABLE.*

BUT WHAT IF SHE *SPOTS* YOU?

IT'S FORTY WINKS PAST *2 AM,* ROOKIE. AND I'M BLOODY *TRANSPARENT.* SHE'S NOT GONNA SPOT ME UNLESS I SAY *"BOO."*

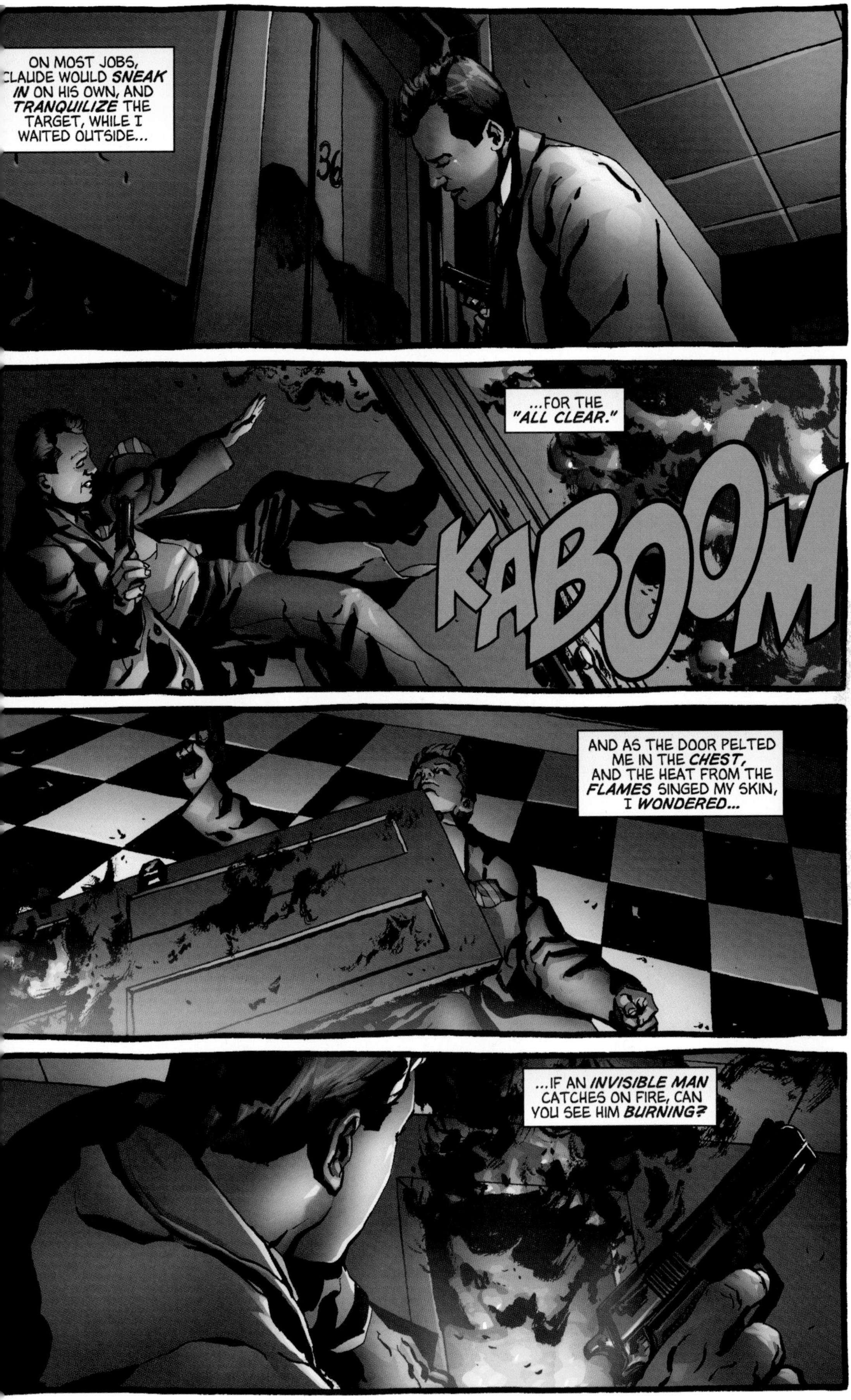
ON MOST JOBS, CLAUDE WOULD SNEAK IN ON HIS OWN, AND TRANQUILIZE THE TARGET, WHILE I WAITED OUTSIDE...
...FOR THE "ALL CLEAR."
KABOOM
AND AS THE DOOR PELTED ME IN THE CHEST, AND THE HEAT FROM THE FLAMES SINGED MY SKIN, I WONDERED...
...IF AN INVISIBLE MAN CATCHES ON FIRE, CAN YOU SEE HIM BURNING?

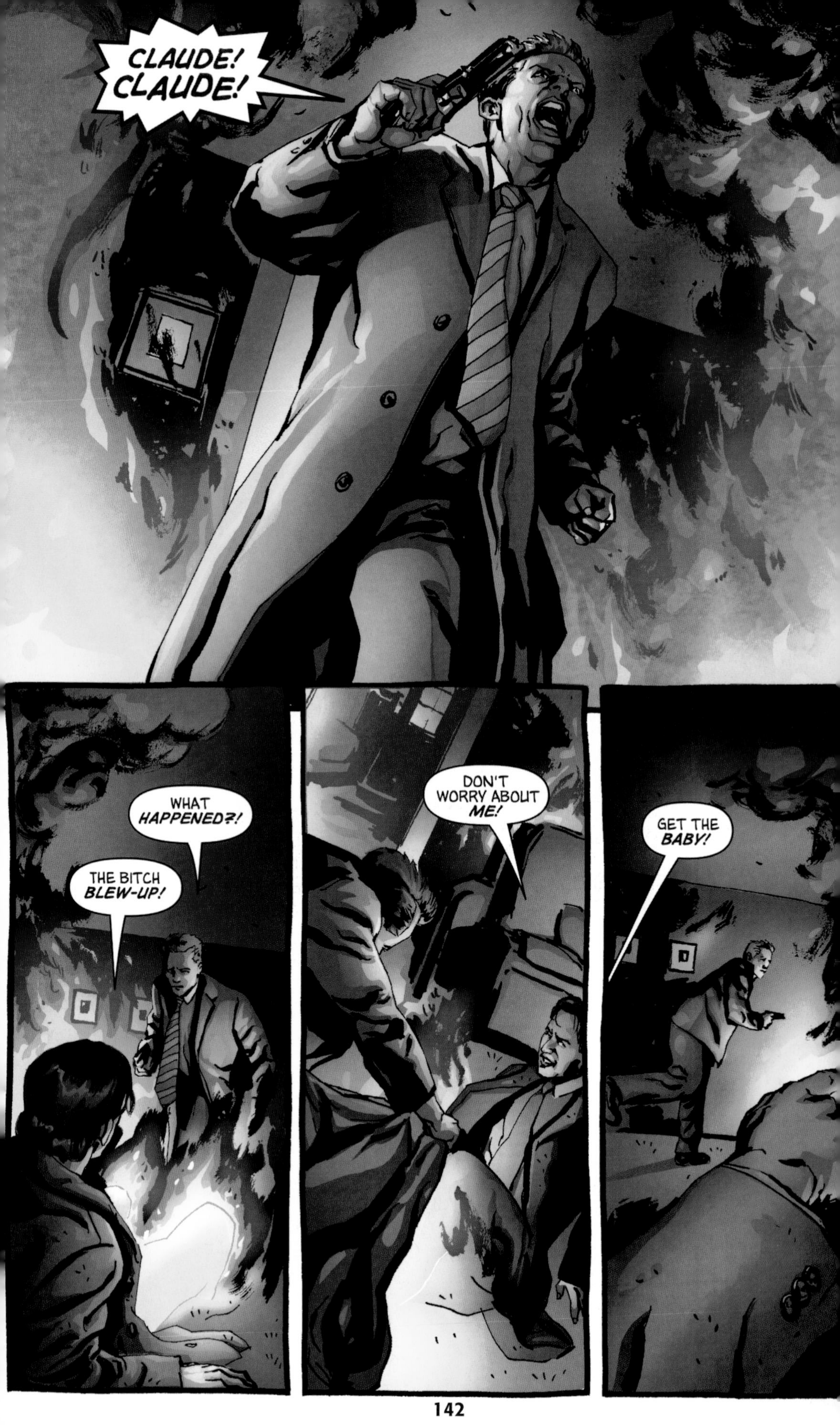
CLAUDE! CLAUDE!
WHAT HAPPENED?!
THE BITCH BLEW-UP!
DON'T WORRY ABOUT ME!
GET THE BABY!

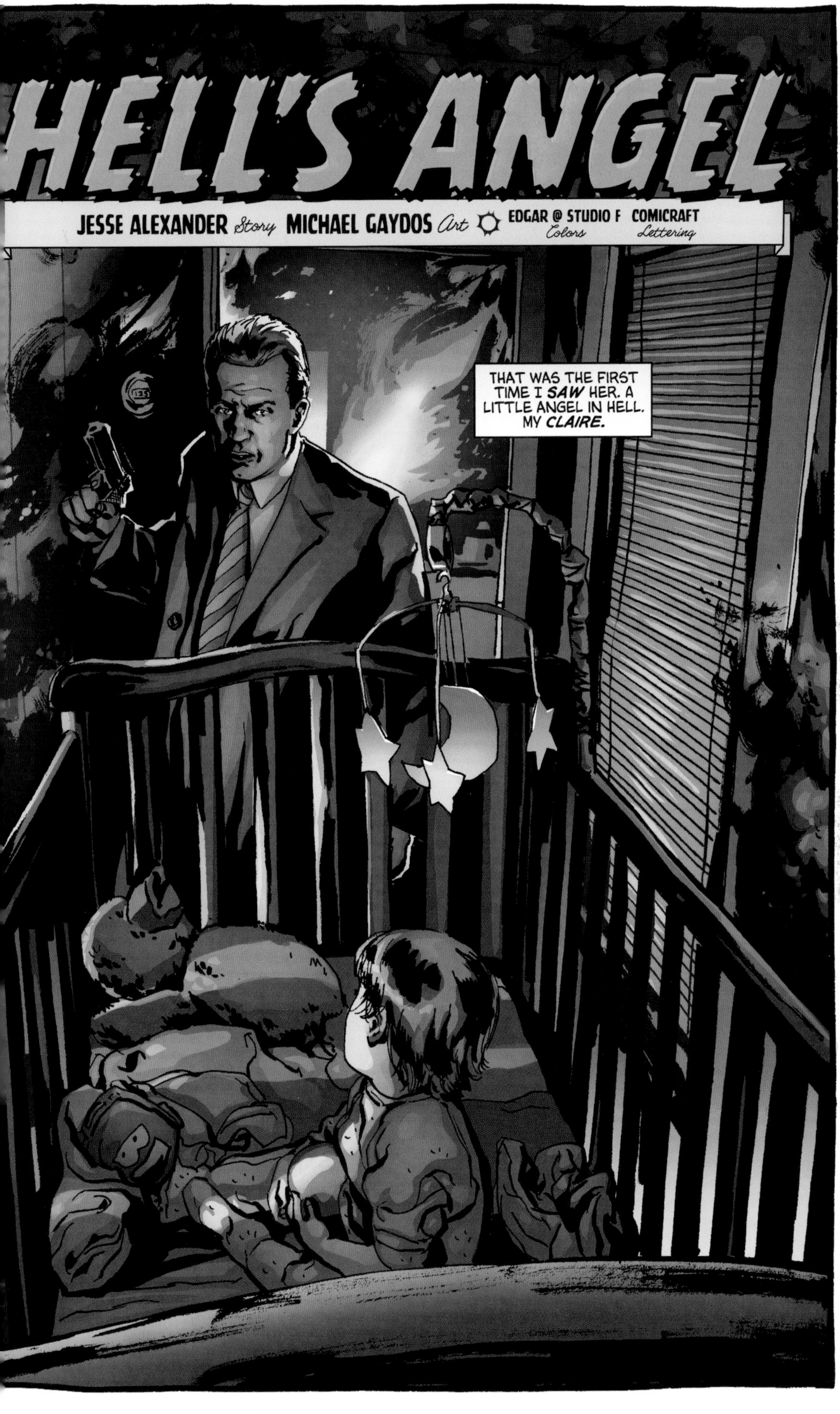
HELL'S ANGEL
JESSE ALEXANDER Story MICHAEL GAYDOS Art EDGAR @ STUDIO F Colors COMICRAFT Lettering
THAT WAS THE FIRST TIME I SAW HER. A LITTLE ANGEL IN HELL. MY CLAIRE.

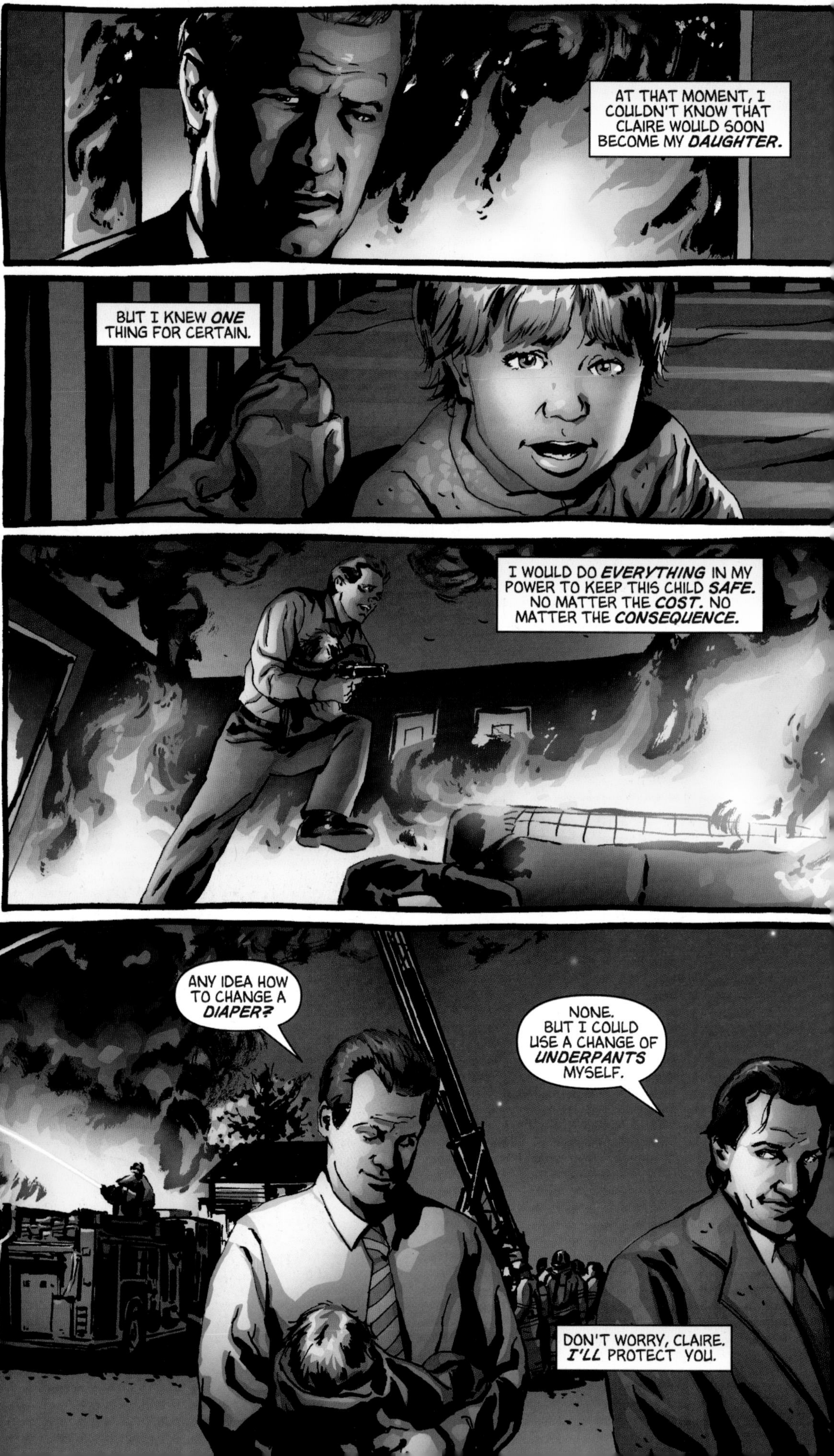

AT THAT MOMENT, I COULDN'T KNOW THAT CLAIRE WOULD SOON BECOME MY DAUGHTER.
BUT I KNEW ONE THING FOR CERTAIN.
I WOULD DO EVERYTHING IN MY POWER TO KEEP THIS CHILD SAFE. NO MATTER THE COST. NO MATTER THE CONSEQUENCE.
ANY IDEA HOW TO CHANGE A DIAPER?
NONE. BUT I COULD USE A CHANGE OF UNDERPANTS MYSELF.
DON'T WORRY, CLAIRE. I'LL PROTECT YOU.

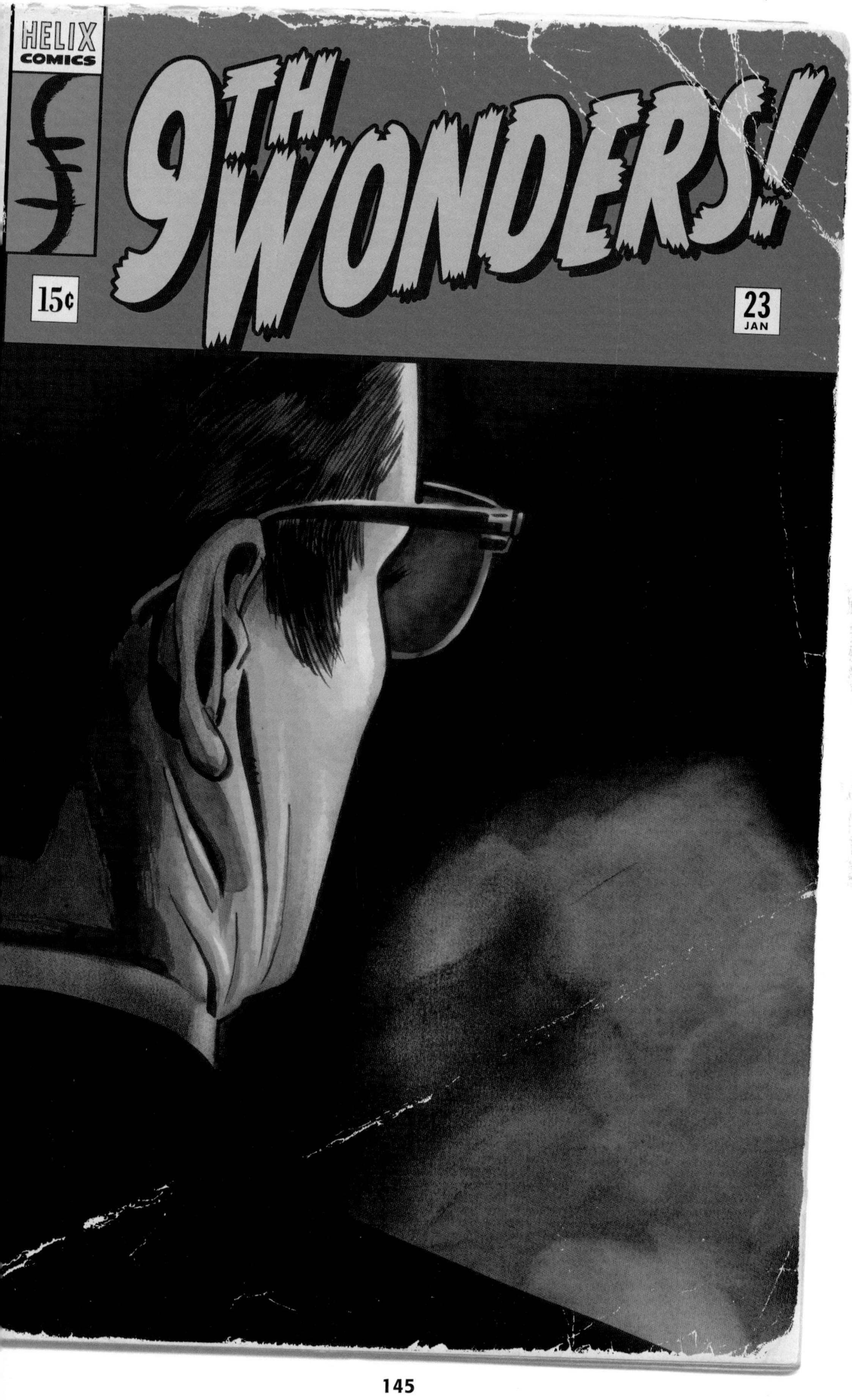
HELIX
COMICS
9TH WONDERS!
15¢
23
JAN

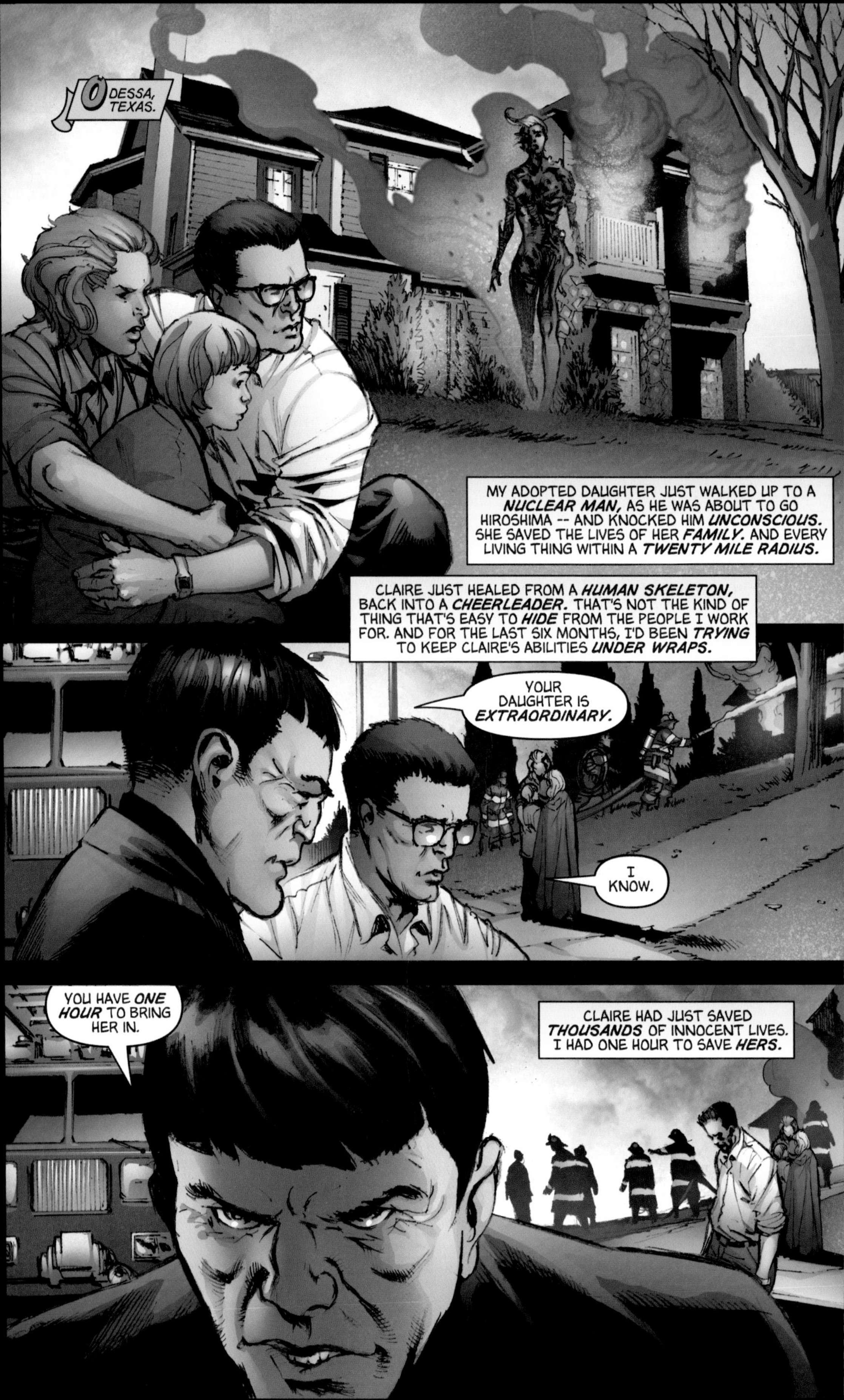
ODESSA, TEXAS.
MY ADOPTED DAUGHTER JUST WALKED UP TO A NUCLEAR MAN, AS HE WAS ABOUT TO GO HIROSHIMA -- AND KNOCKED HIM UNCONSCIOUS. SHE SAVED THE LIVES OF HER FAMILY. AND EVERY LIVING THING WITHIN A TWENTY MILE RADIUS.
CLAIRE JUST HEALED FROM A HUMAN SKELETON, BACK INTO A CHEERLEADER. THAT'S NOT THE KIND OF THING THAT'S EASY TO HIDE FROM THE PEOPLE I WORK FOR. AND FOR THE LAST SIX MONTHS, I'D BEEN TRYING TO KEEP CLAIRE'S ABILITIES UNDER WRAPS.
YOUR DAUGHTER IS EXTRAORDINARY.
I KNOW.
YOU HAVE ONE HOUR TO BRING HER IN.
CLAIRE HAD JUST SAVED THOUSANDS OF INNOCENT LIVES. I HAD ONE HOUR TO SAVE HERS.

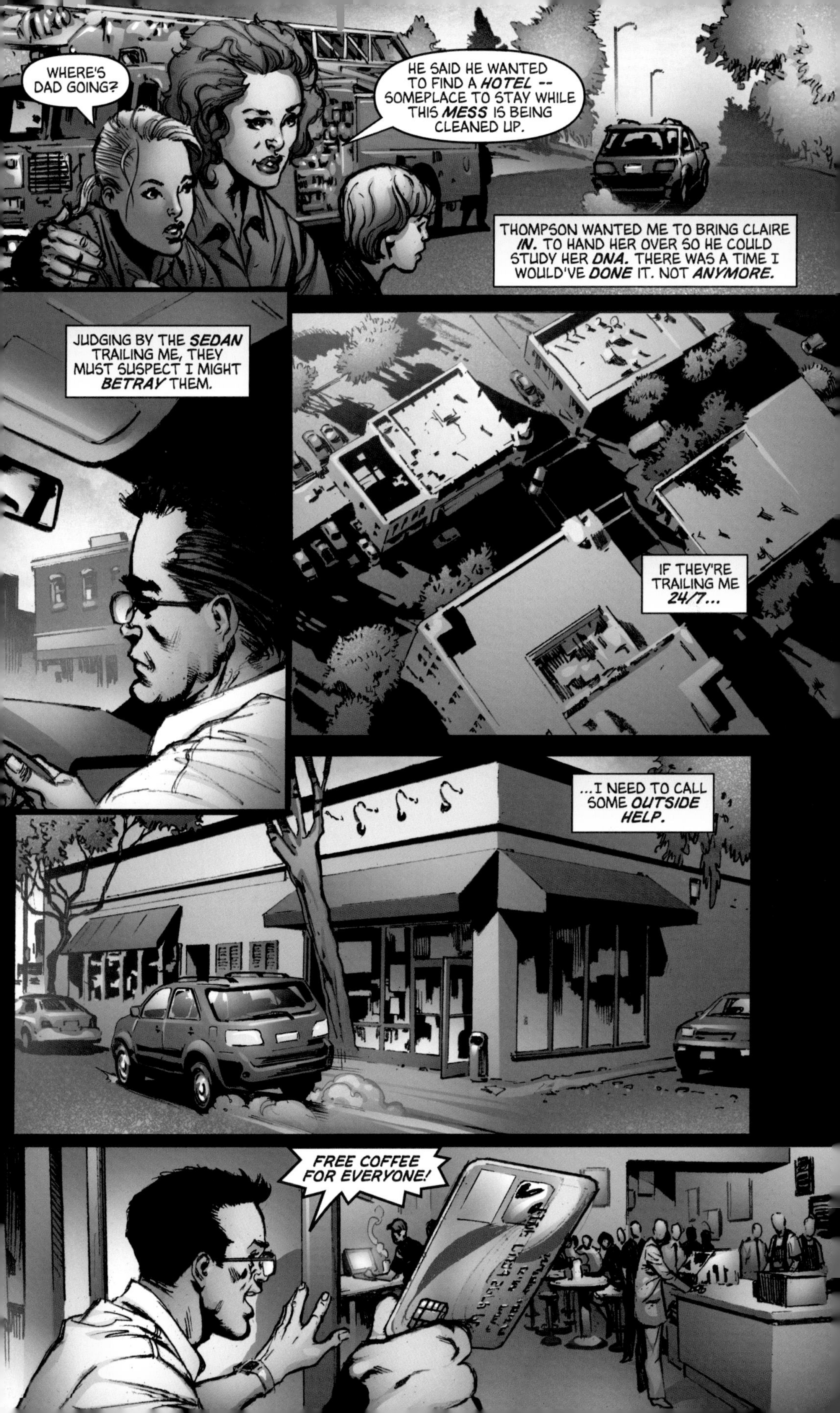
WHERE'S DAD GOING?
HE SAID HE WANTED TO FIND A HOTEL -- SOMEPLACE TO STAY WHILE THIS MESS IS BEING CLEANED UP.
THOMPSON WANTED ME TO BRING CLAIRE IN. TO HAND HER OVER SO HE COULD STUDY HER DNA. THERE WAS A TIME I WOULD'VE DONE IT. NOT ANYMORE.
JUDGING BY THE SEDAN TRAILING ME, THEY MUST SUSPECT I MIGHT BETRAY THEM.
IF THEY'RE TRAILING ME 24/7...
...I NEED TO CALL SOME OUTSIDE HELP.
FREE COFFEE FOR EVERYONE!

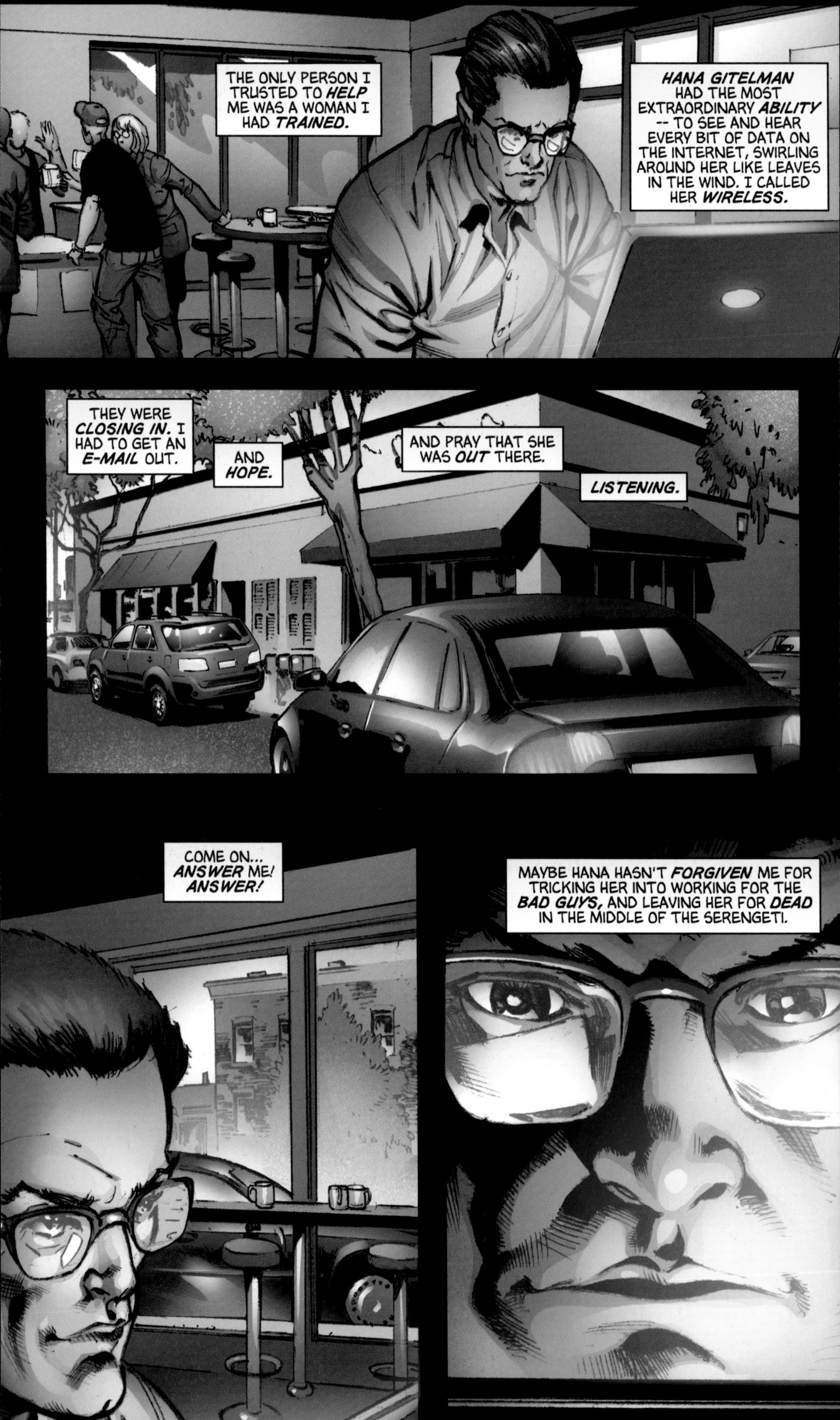

THE ONLY PERSON I TRUSTED TO *HELP* ME WAS A WOMAN I HAD *TRAINED.*
HANA GITELMAN HAD THE MOST EXTRAORDINARY *ABILITY* -- TO SEE AND HEAR EVERY BIT OF DATA ON THE INTERNET, SWIRLING AROUND HER LIKE LEAVES IN THE WIND. I CALLED HER *WIRELESS.*
THEY WERE *CLOSING IN.* I HAD TO GET AN *E-MAIL* OUT.
AND *HOPE.*
AND PRAY THAT SHE WAS *OUT* THERE.
LISTENING.
COME ON... *ANSWER* ME! *ANSWER!*
MAYBE HANA HASN'T *FORGIVEN* ME FOR TRICKING HER INTO WORKING FOR THE *BAD GUYS,* AND LEAVING HER FOR *DEAD* IN THE MIDDLE OF THE SERENGETI.

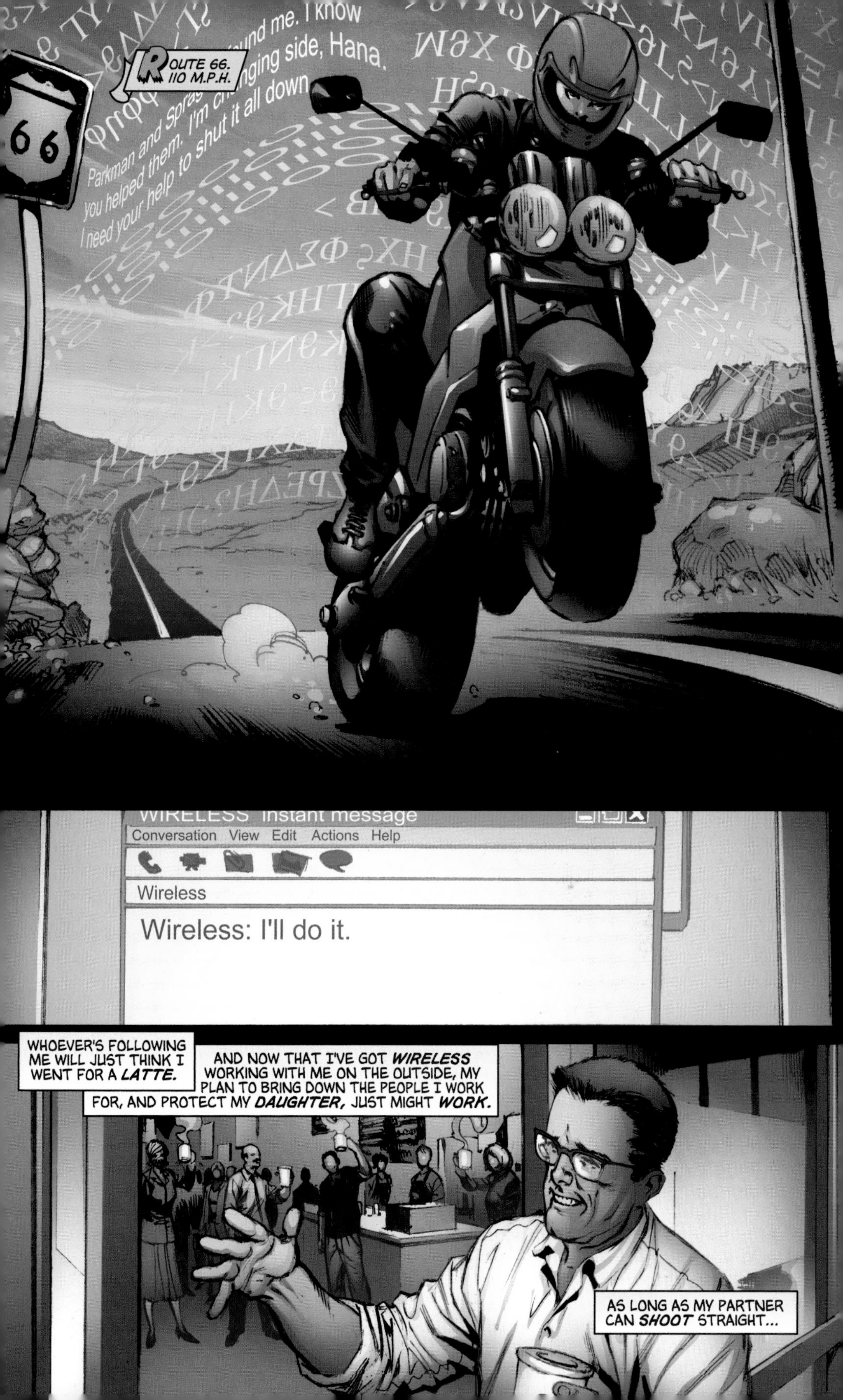

ROUTE 66. 110 M.P.H.
66
und me. I know
nging side, Hana.
Parkman and Spra
you helped them. I'm ch
I need your help to shut it all down
WIRELESS instant message
Conversation View Edit Actions Help
Wireless
Wireless: I'll do it.
WHOEVER'S FOLLOWING ME WILL JUST THINK I WENT FOR A LATTE.
AND NOW THAT I'VE GOT WIRELESS WORKING WITH ME ON THE OUTSIDE, MY PLAN TO BRING DOWN THE PEOPLE I WORK FOR, AND PROTECT MY DAUGHTER, JUST MIGHT WORK.
AS LONG AS MY PARTNER CAN SHOOT STRAIGHT...

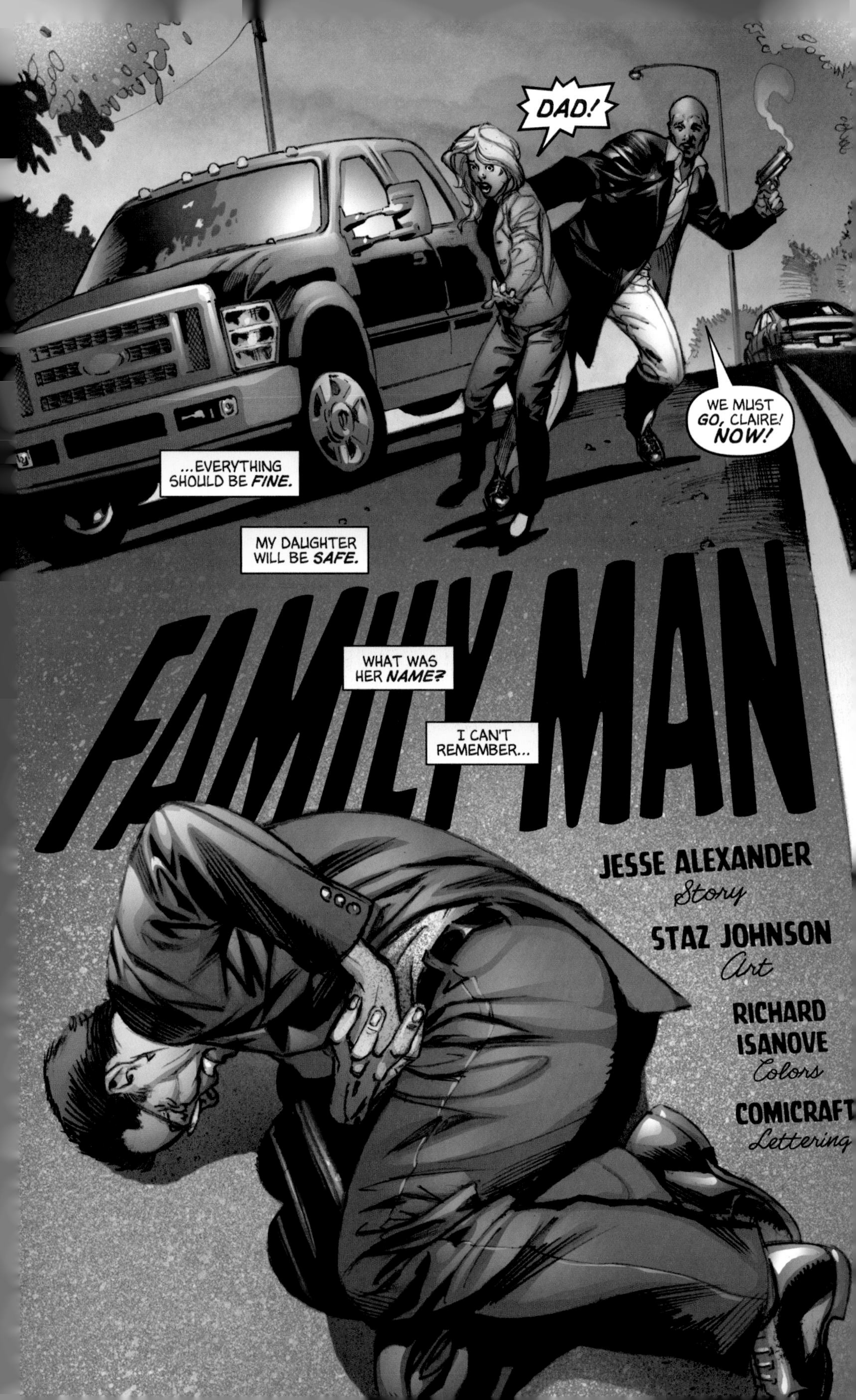
DAD!
WE MUST GO, CLAIRE! NOW!
...EVERYTHING SHOULD BE FINE.
MY DAUGHTER WILL BE SAFE.
FAMILY MAN
WHAT WAS HER NAME?
I CAN'T REMEMBER...
JESSE ALEXANDER Story
STAZ JOHNSON Art
RICHARD ISANOVE Colors
COMICRAFT Lettering

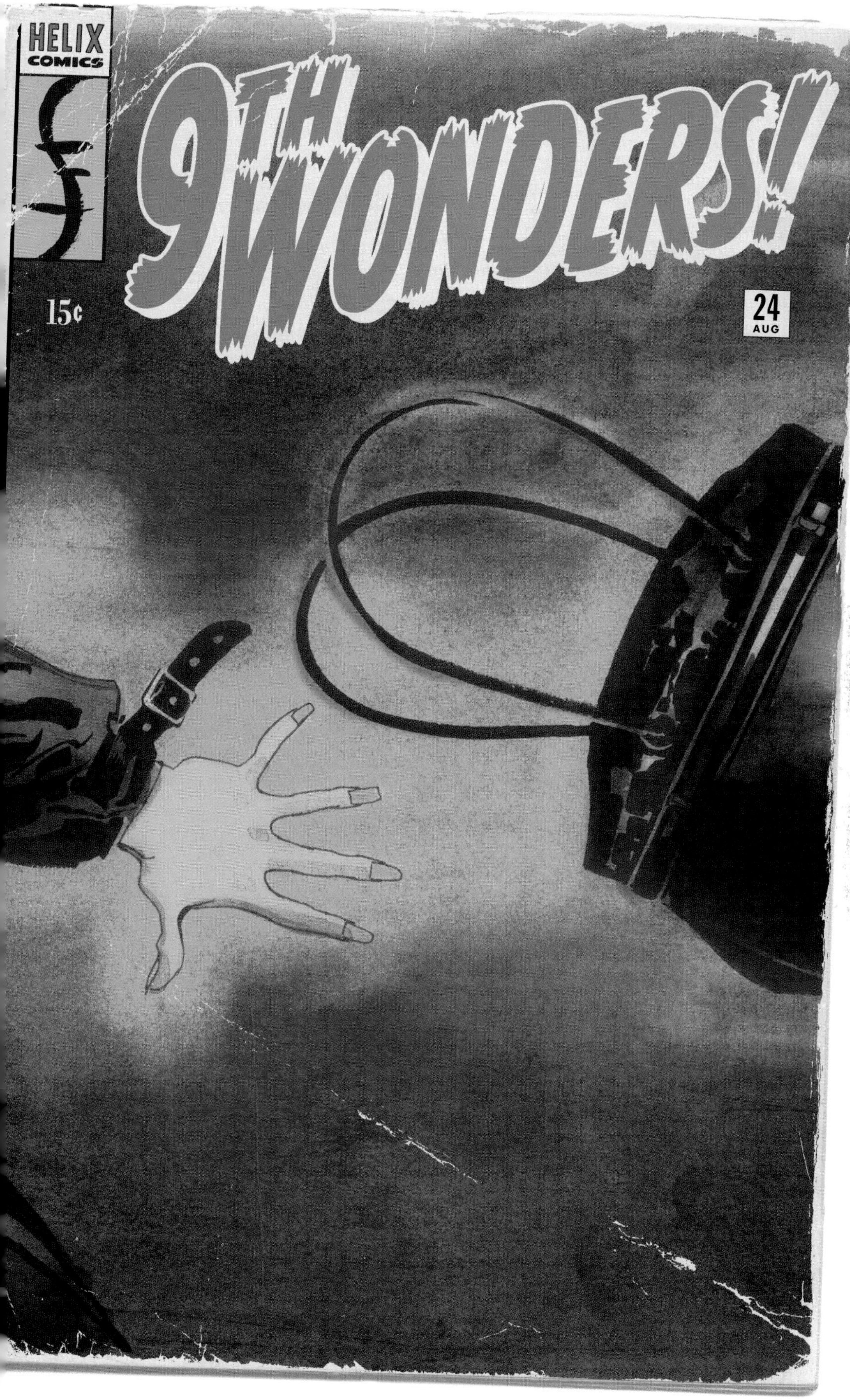
HELIX COMICS
9TH WONDERS!
15¢
24 AUG

MY NAME IS *HANA GITELMAN*. I CAN SEE, HEAR AND MANIPULATE THE VORTEX OF *WIRELESS DIGITAL INFORMATION* SWIRLING AROUND THE EARTH.

YES, I KNOW. I'M A *WALKING BLACKBERRY.*

WAR BUDDIES
THE LONESTAR FILE

Part 1 of Six

DO I *TRUST* HIM?

YESTERDAY, I WANTED *VENGEANCE* ON THE MAN IN THE HORN-RIMMED GLASSES -- *BENNET.*

HE *MANIPULATED* ME. *USED* ME. AND WHEN I NEEDED HIM MOST -- HE THREW ME TO THE *WOLVES.*

TODAY, HE TURNED TO ME FOR *HELP.* SO THE QUESTION IS --

MARK WARSHAW *Story* **STEVEN LEJEUNE** *Art* **EDGAR DELGADO** *Colors* **COMICRAFT** *Lettering*

BENNET SAYS THAT *HE'S* A VICTIM TOO. MANIPULATED BY THE COMPANY.

THAT WE'RE BOTH ON THE SIDE OF THE *ANGELS.* THAT IT'S UP TO *US* TO TAKE DOWN THE COMPANY.

TO HELP ME -- BENNET GAVE ME ONE *FILE NUMBER.* THAT'S IT. *ONE.* ACCORDING TO HIM, ONE FILE WOULD HELP ME TAKE DOWN THE *ENTIRE KINGDOM.*

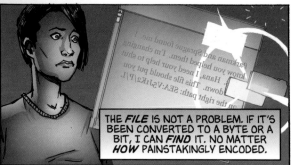

THE *FILE* IS NOT A PROBLEM. IF IT'S BEEN CONVERTED TO A BYTE OR A BIT, I CAN *FIND* IT. NO MATTER *HOW* PAINSTAKINGLY ENCODED.

SEA:V5J1K2/P/L

STORAGE TYPE: PAPER

BUT EVEN *I* HAVE MY LIMITS.

AND I WAS OUT OF *OPTIONS.* SO, REALLY WHAT *CHOICE* DID I HA

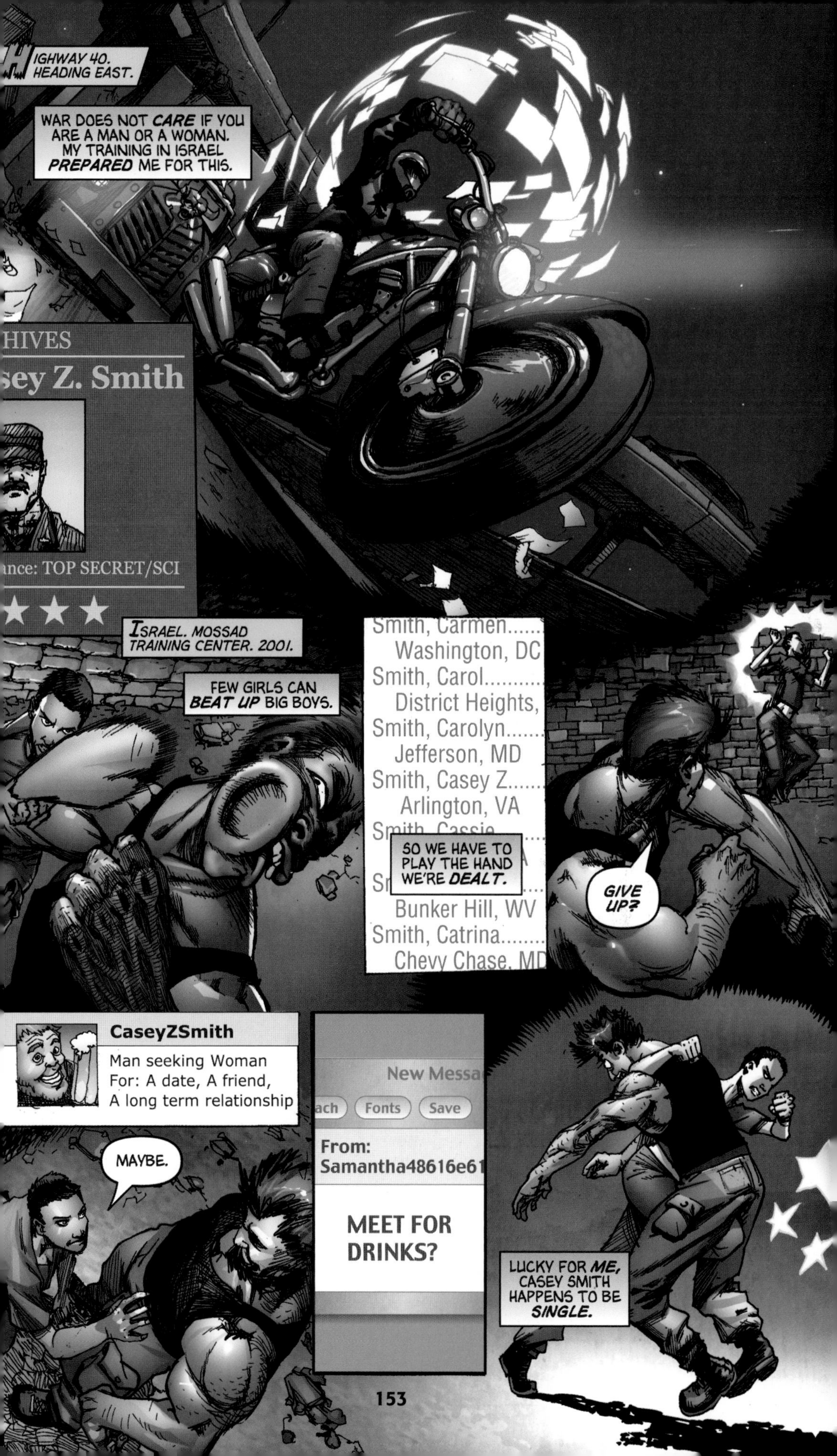

HIGHWAY 40. HEADING EAST.
WAR DOES NOT CARE IF YOU ARE A MAN OR A WOMAN. MY TRAINING IN ISRAEL PREPARED ME FOR THIS.
HIVES
sey Z. Smith
ance: TOP SECRET/SCI
ISRAEL. MOSSAD TRAINING CENTER. 2001.
FEW GIRLS CAN BEAT UP BIG BOYS.
Smith, Carmen......
Washington, DC
Smith, Carol..........
District Heights,
Smith, Carolyn.......
Jefferson, MD
Smith, Casey Z.......
Arlington, VA
SO WE HAVE TO PLAY THE HAND WE'RE DEALT.
Bunker Hill, WV
Smith, Catrina........
Chevy Chase, MD
GIVE UP?
CaseyZSmith
Man seeking Woman
For: A date, A friend,
A long term relationship
MAYBE.
New Messa
ach
Fonts
Save
From:
Samantha48616e61
MEET FOR DRINKS?
LUCKY FOR ME, CASEY SMITH HAPPENS TO BE SINGLE.

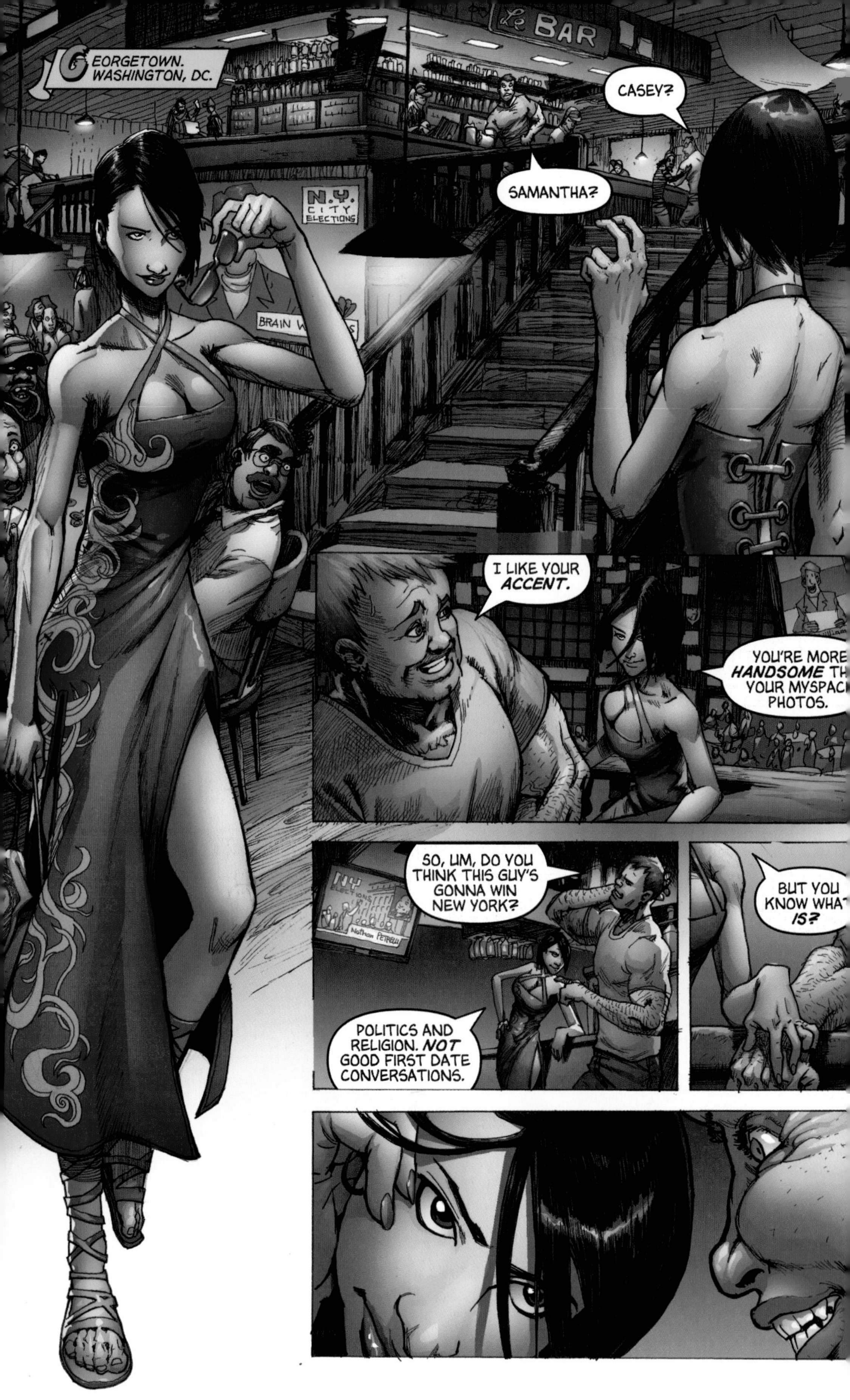
GEORGETOWN. WASHINGTON, DC.
Le BAR
N.Y. CITY ELECTIONS
BRAIN W
CASEY?
SAMANTHA?
I LIKE YOUR ACCENT.
YOU'RE MORE HANDSOME TH YOUR MYSPAC PHOTOS.
SO, UM, DO YOU THINK THIS GUY'S GONNA WIN NEW YORK?
NY ELECTIONS
Nathan Petrelli
POLITICS AND RELIGION. NOT GOOD FIRST DATE CONVERSATIONS.
BUT YOU KNOW WHAT IS?

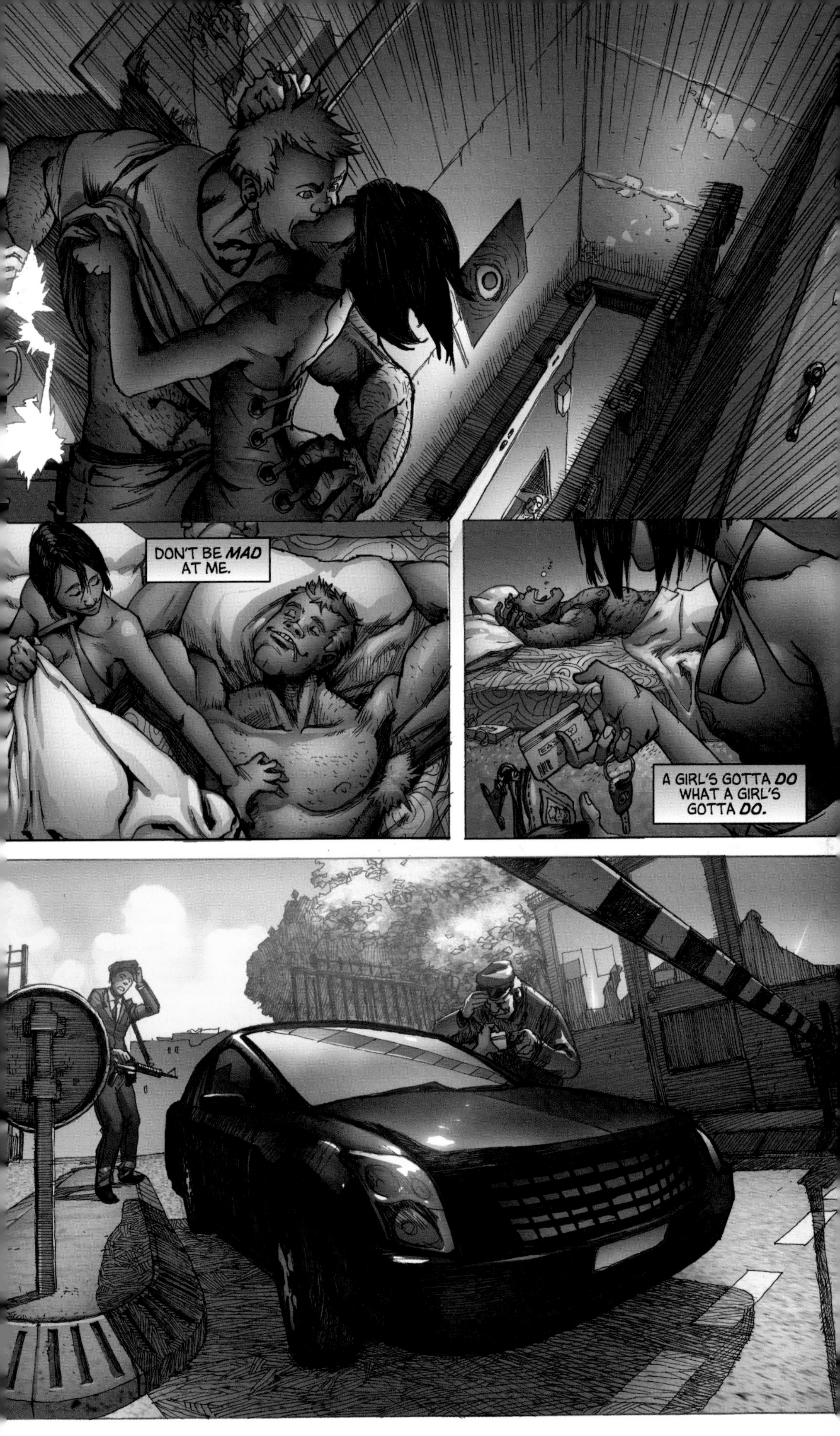
DON'T BE MAD AT ME.
A GIRL'S GOTTA DO WHAT A GIRL'S GOTTA DO.

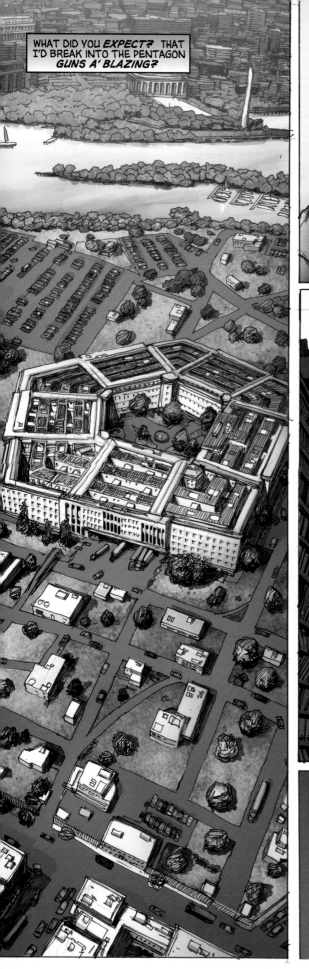

WHAT DID YOU *EXPECT?* THAT I'D BREAK INTO THE PENTAGON *GUNS A' BLAZING?*

I NEED TO ACCOMPLISH THIS *MISSION.*

I NEED *ANSWERS* TO MY QUESTIONS.

LOOKS LIKE I'M OFF TO A *GOOD START.*

To Be Continued...

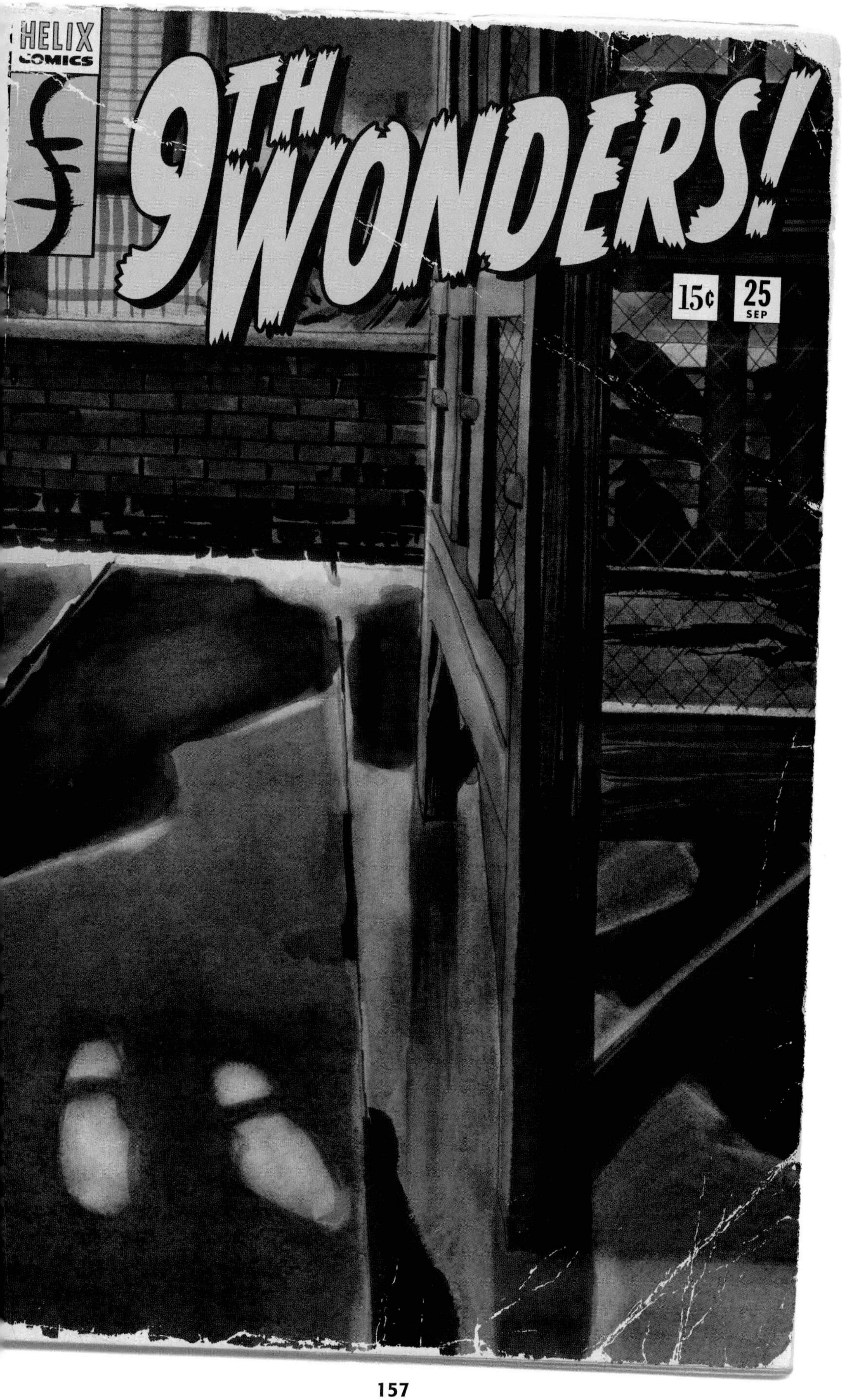
HELIX COMICS
9TH WONDERS!
15¢
25
SEP

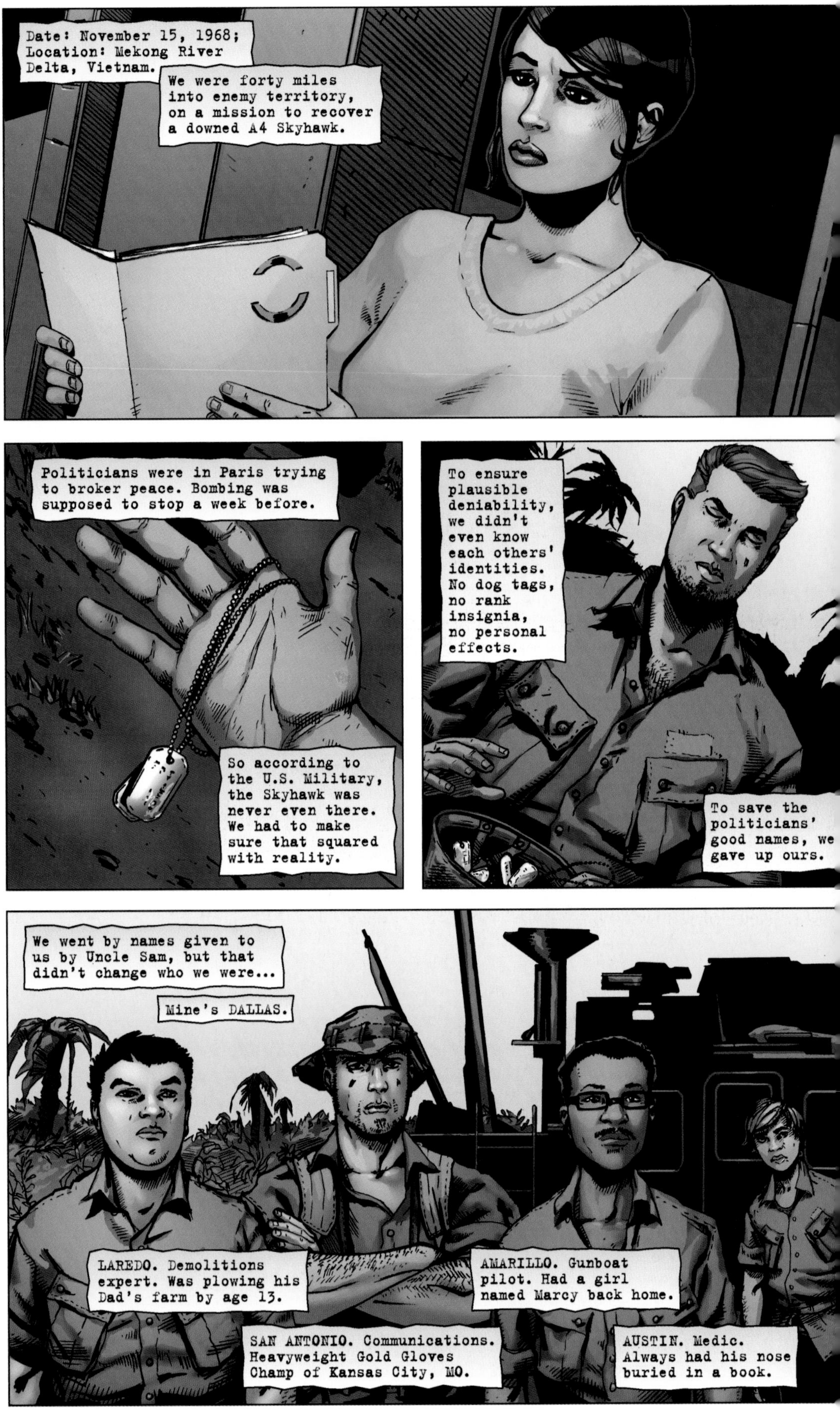
Date: November 15, 1968; Location: Mekong River Delta, Vietnam.
We were forty miles into enemy territory, on a mission to recover a downed A4 Skyhawk.
Politicians were in Paris trying to broker peace. Bombing was supposed to stop a week before.
So according to the U.S. Military, the Skyhawk was never even there. We had to make sure that squared with reality.
To ensure plausible deniability, we didn't even know each others' identities. No dog tags, no rank insignia, no personal effects.
To save the politicians' good names, we gave up ours.
We went by names given to us by Uncle Sam, but that didn't change who we were...
Mine's DALLAS.
LAREDO. Demolitions expert. Was plowing his Dad's farm by age 13.
AMARILLO. Gunboat pilot. Had a girl named Marcy back home.
SAN ANTONIO. Communications. Heavyweight Gold Gloves Champ of Kansas City, MO.
AUSTIN. Medic. Always had his nose buried in a book.

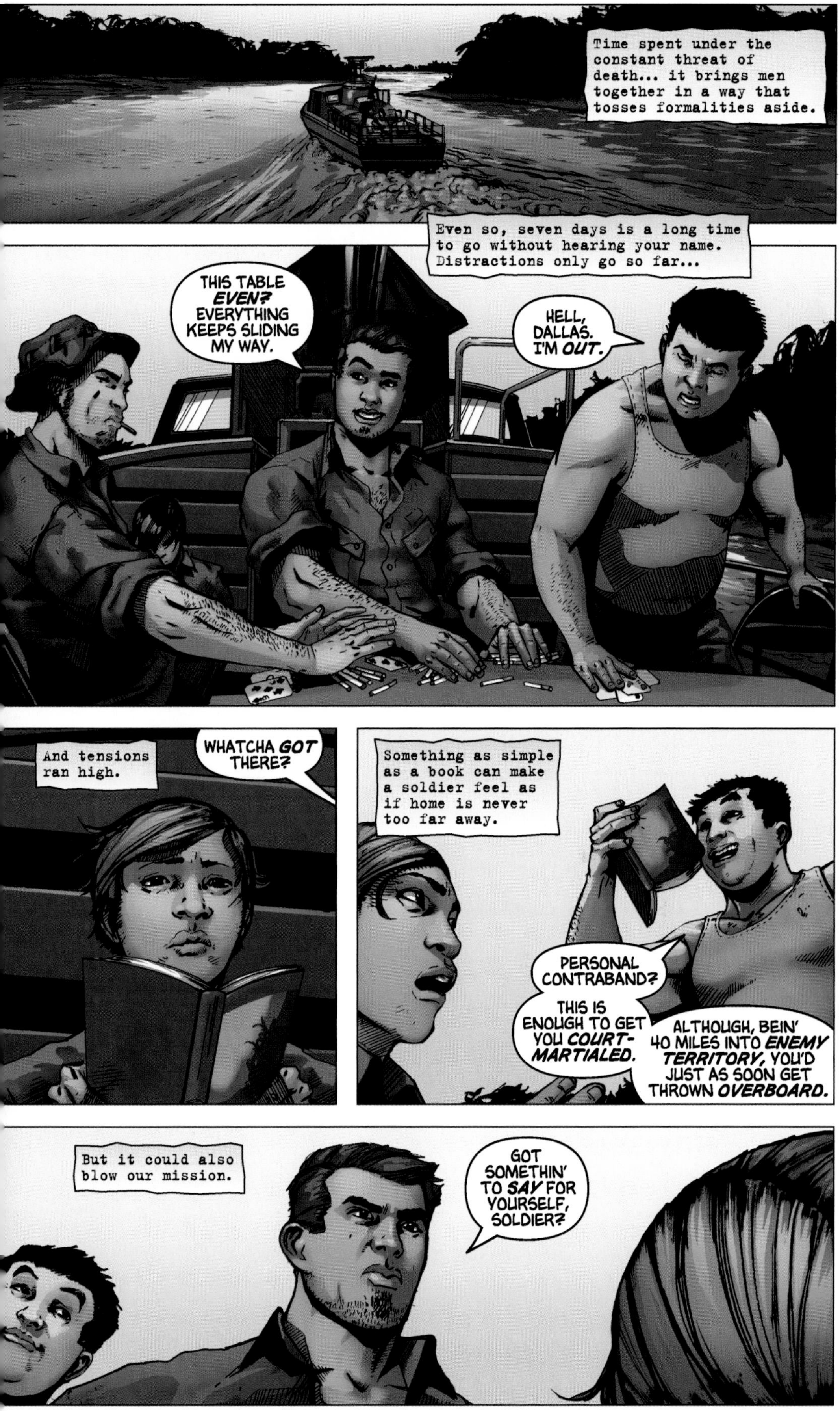
Time spent under the constant threat of death... it brings men together in a way that tosses formalities aside.
Even so, seven days is a long time to go without hearing your name. Distractions only go so far...
THIS TABLE EVEN? EVERYTHING KEEPS SLIDING MY WAY.
HELL, DALLAS. I'M OUT.
And tensions ran high.
WHATCHA GOT THERE?
Something as simple as a book can make a soldier feel as if home is never too far away.
PERSONAL CONTRABAND?
THIS IS ENOUGH TO GET YOU COURT-MARTIALED.
ALTHOUGH, BEIN' 40 MILES INTO ENEMY TERRITORY, YOU'D JUST AS SOON GET THROWN OVERBOARD.
But it could also blow our mission.
GOT SOMETHIN' TO SAY FOR YOURSELF, SOLDIER?

Truth is, I was just as guilty of possessing personal contraband as he was.

WE ALL NEED TO HOLD ON TO A PIECE OF *OURSELVES* OUT HERE.

I shared a letter from my family with Austin, hoping he would open up...

ould have een here to ee our son. e took his irst steps esterday. e's going o make us roud one day.

...but he had nothing.

YOU GOT *FAMILY*, AUSTIN?

NO, SIR. BEEN ON MY OWN FOR A *WHILE* NOW.

PFFFFT

ish you uld have en here to e our son. e took his rst steps

roud one day.

As I showed Austin the letter, our position was compromised to Viet Cong scouts. I took enemy fire to the chest.

Out in the jungle you can lose yourself without even realizing it.

...

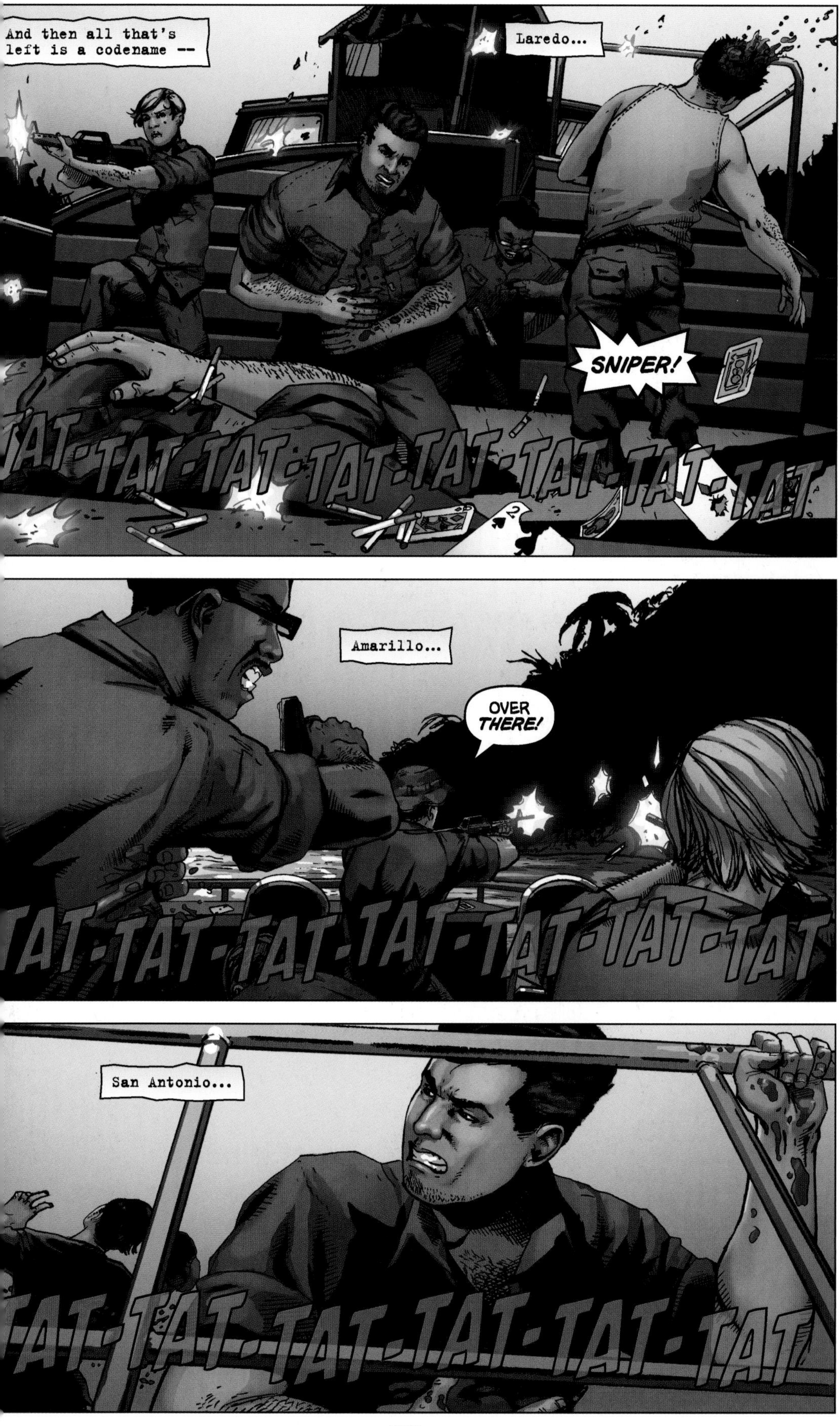
And then all that's left is a codename --
Laredo...
SNIPER!
TAT-TAT-TAT-TAT-TAT-TAT-TAT-TAT
Amarillo...
OVER THERE!
TAT-TAT-TAT-TAT-TAT-TAT-TAT
San Antonio...
TAT-TAT-TAT-TAT-TAT-TAT-TAT

During the firefight, the gunboat crew sustained heavy casualties, leaving Austin and myself, ████████ ███████, as the only survivors.

CLEAR!

...AUSTIN...

Sometimes the soldiers you expect the least from, give you the most.

I'd like to go on record, that while there is no evidence to support my statement...

HOLD ON. THE BULLET WENT *CLEAN THROUGH.*

JUST RELAX.

████████████████████ ████████████████████

I'VE DONE THIS *BEFORE.*

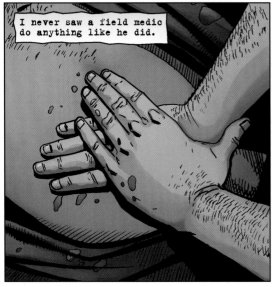

I never saw a field medic do anything like he did.

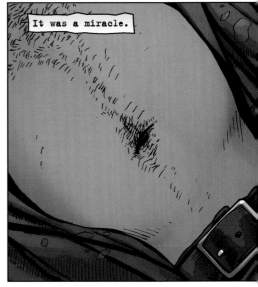

It was a miracle.

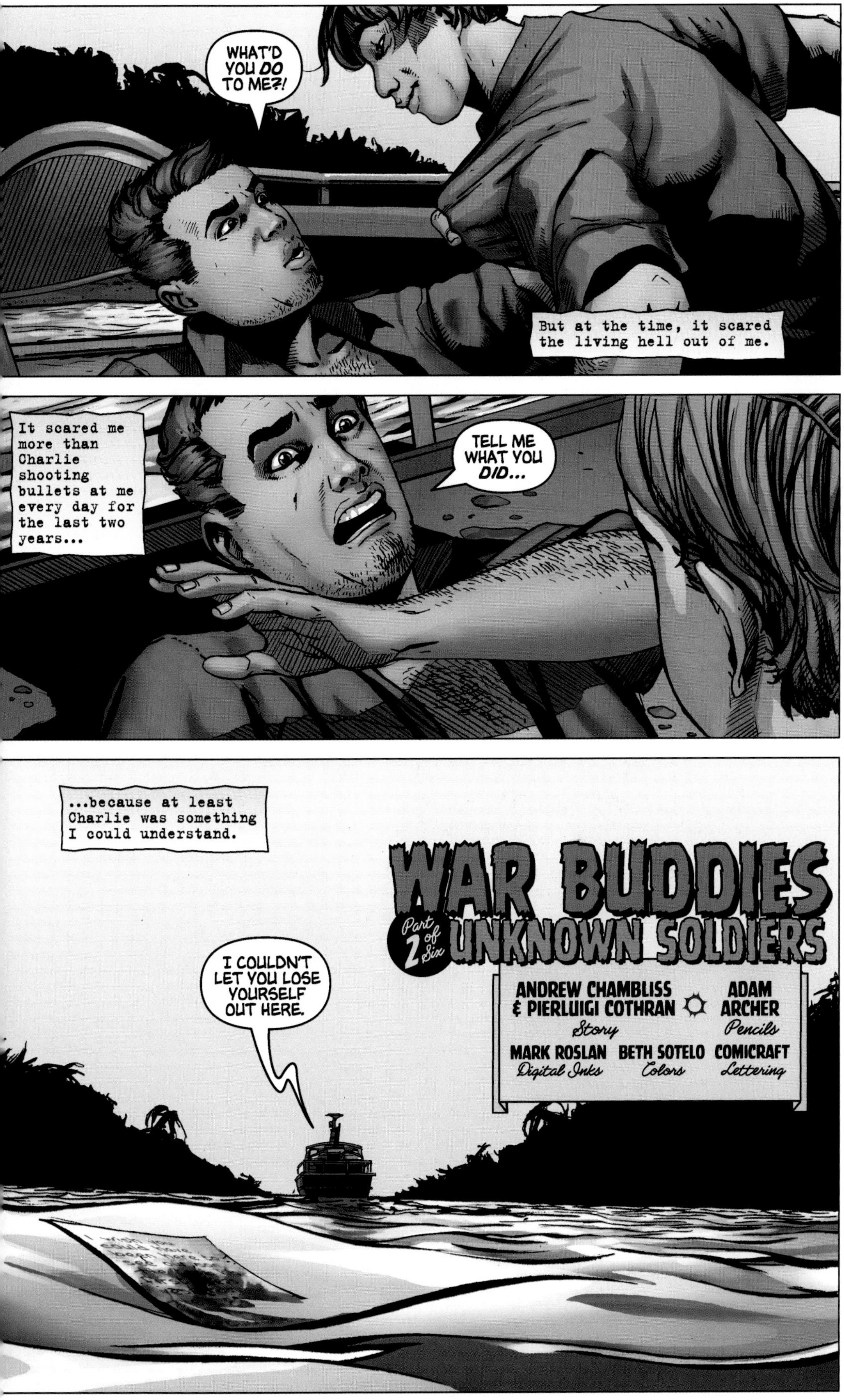
WHAT'D YOU DO TO ME?!
But at the time, it scared the living hell out of me.
It scared me more than Charlie shooting bullets at me every day for the last two years...
TELL ME WHAT YOU DID...
...because at least Charlie was something I could understand.
WAR BUDDIES
Part 2 of Six
UNKNOWN SOLDIERS
ANDREW CHAMBLISS & PIERLUIGI COTHRAN Story
ADAM ARCHER Pencils
MARK ROSLAN Digital Inks
BETH SOTELO Colors
COMICRAFT Lettering
I COULDN'T LET YOU LOSE YOURSELF OUT HERE.

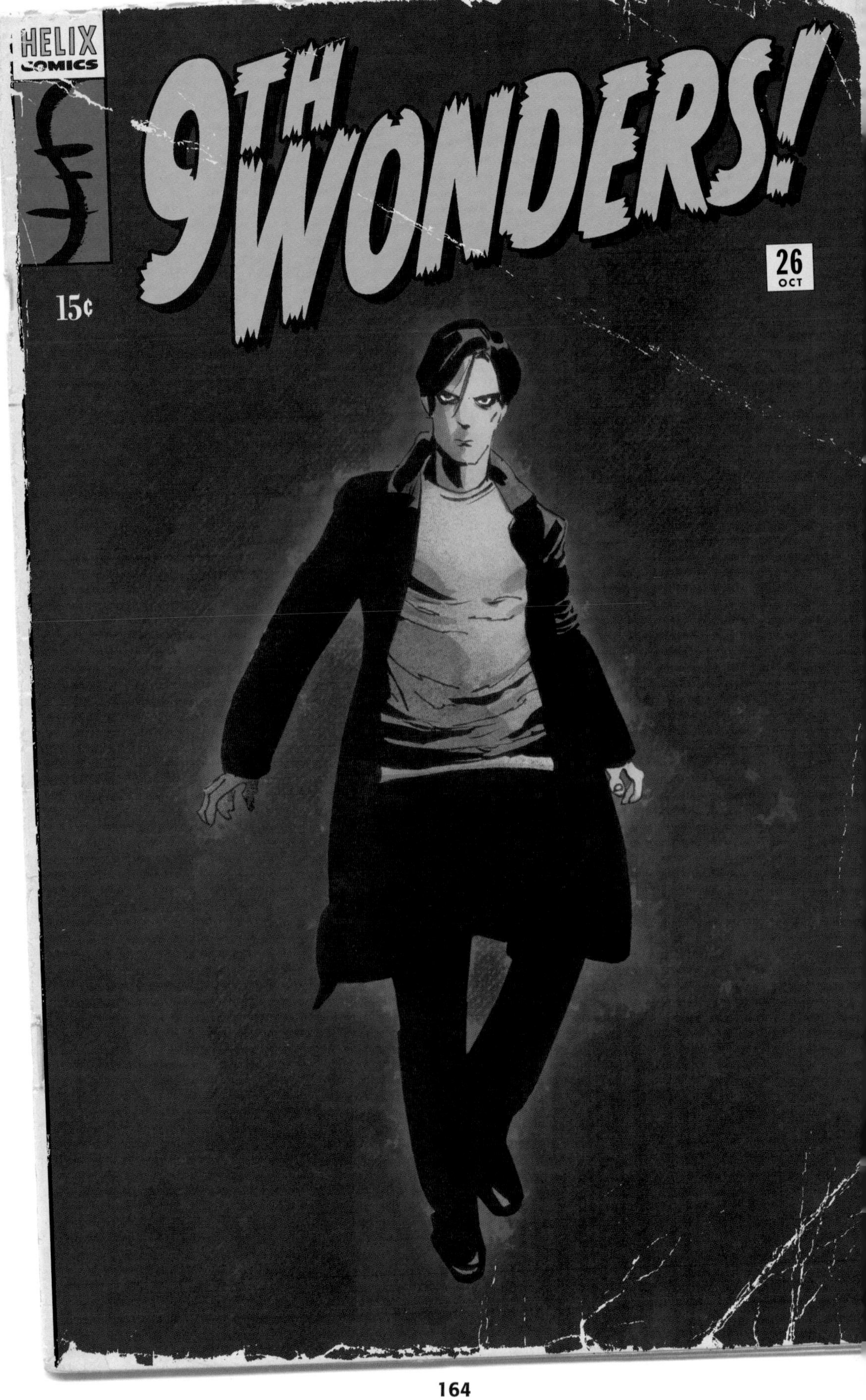
HELIX
COMICS
9TH WONDERS!
26
OCT
15¢

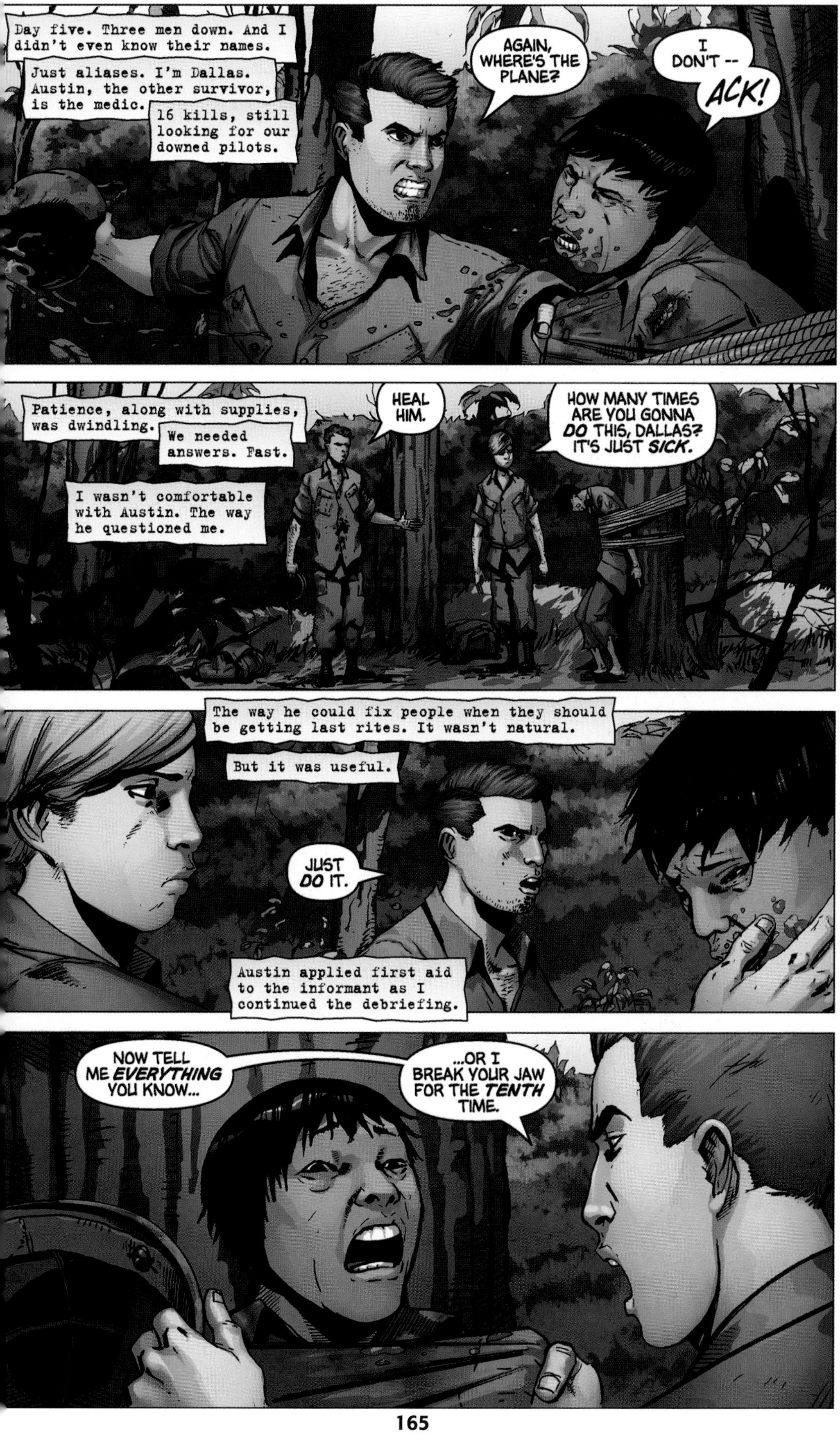
Day five. Three men down. And I didn't even know their names.
Just aliases. I'm Dallas. Austin, the other survivor, is the medic.
16 kills, still looking for our downed pilots.
AGAIN, WHERE'S THE PLANE?
I DON'T -- ACK!
Patience, along with supplies, was dwindling.
We needed answers. Fast.
I wasn't comfortable with Austin. The way he questioned me.
HEAL HIM.
HOW MANY TIMES ARE YOU GONNA DO THIS, DALLAS? IT'S JUST SICK.
The way he could fix people when they should be getting last rites. It wasn't natural.
But it was useful.
JUST DO IT.
Austin applied first aid to the informant as I continued the debriefing.
NOW TELL ME EVERYTHING YOU KNOW...
...OR I BREAK YOUR JAW FOR THE TENTH TIME.

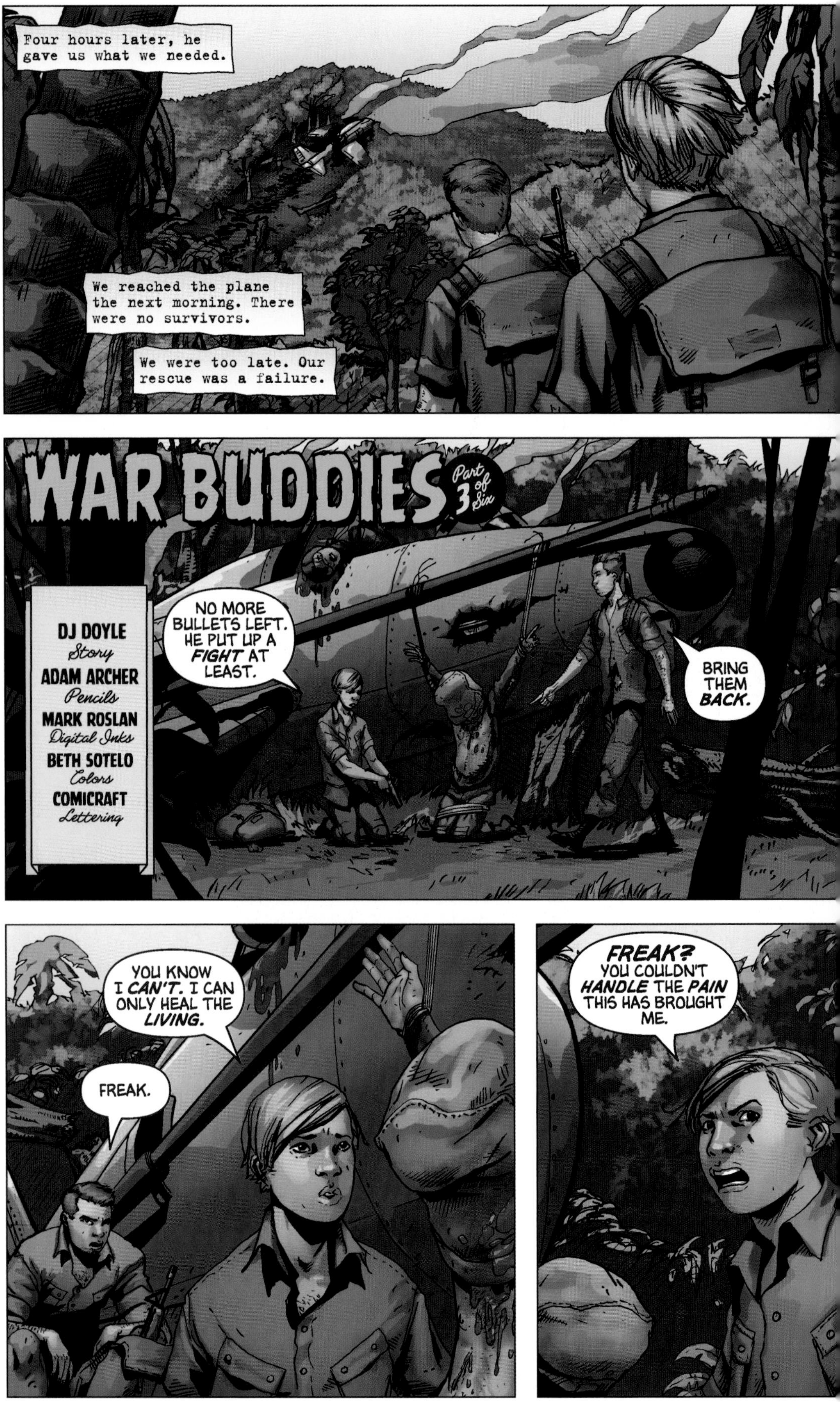
Four hours later, he gave us what we needed.
We reached the plane the next morning. There were no survivors.
We were too late. Our rescue was a failure.
WAR BUDDIES Part 3 of Six
DJ DOYLE Story
ADAM ARCHER Pencils
MARK ROSLAN Digital Inks
BETH SOTELO Colors
COMICRAFT Lettering
NO MORE BULLETS LEFT. HE PUT UP A FIGHT AT LEAST.
BRING THEM BACK.
YOU KNOW I CAN'T. I CAN ONLY HEAL THE LIVING.
FREAK.
FREAK? YOU COULDN'T HANDLE THE PAIN THIS HAS BROUGHT ME.

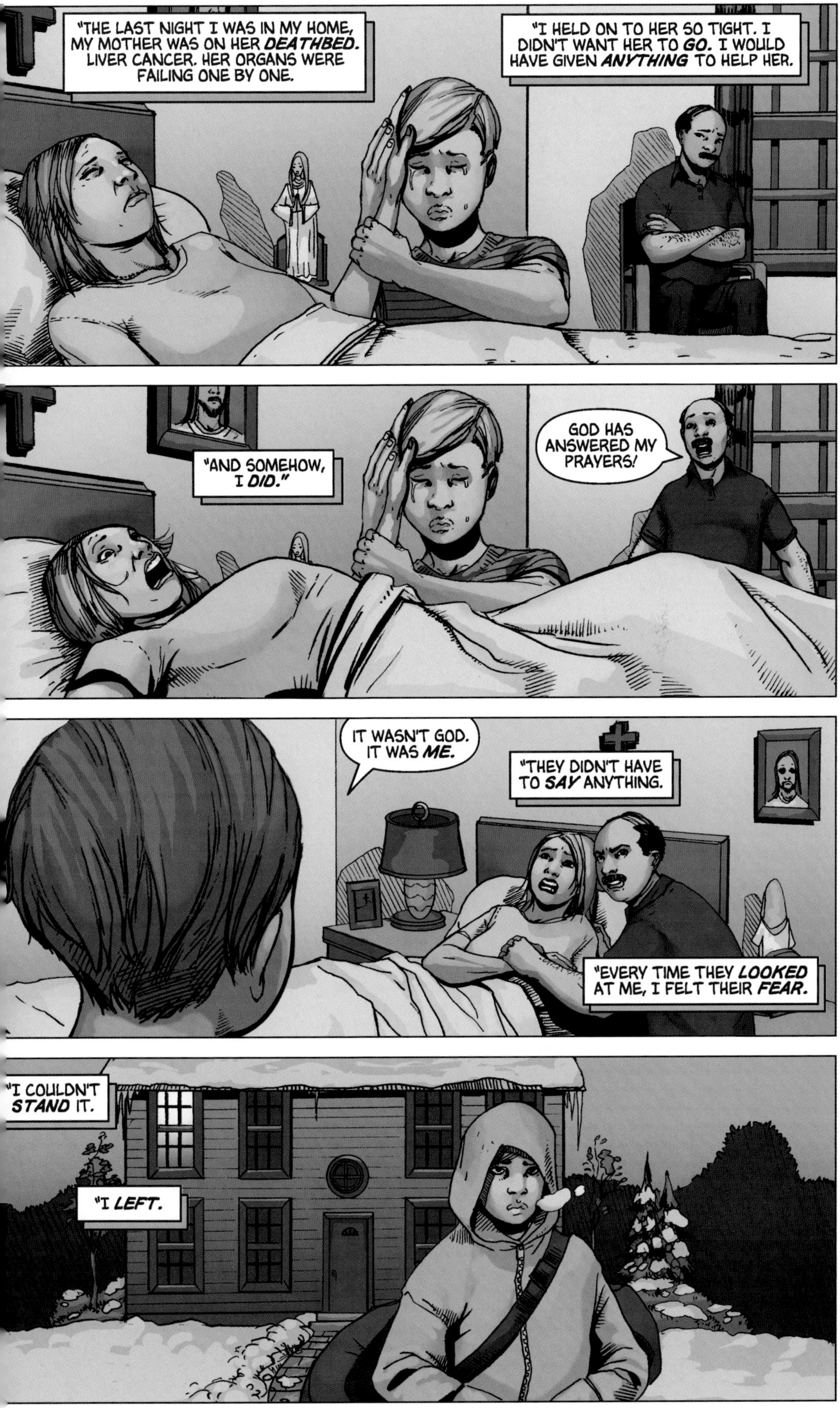
"THE LAST NIGHT I WAS IN MY HOME, MY MOTHER WAS ON HER DEATHBED. LIVER CANCER. HER ORGANS WERE FAILING ONE BY ONE.
"I HELD ON TO HER SO TIGHT. I DIDN'T WANT HER TO GO. I WOULD HAVE GIVEN ANYTHING TO HELP HER.
"AND SOMEHOW, I DID."
GOD HAS ANSWERED MY PRAYERS!
IT WASN'T GOD. IT WAS ME.
"THEY DIDN'T HAVE TO SAY ANYTHING.
"EVERY TIME THEY LOOKED AT ME, I FELT THEIR FEAR.
"I COULDN'T STAND IT.
"I LEFT.

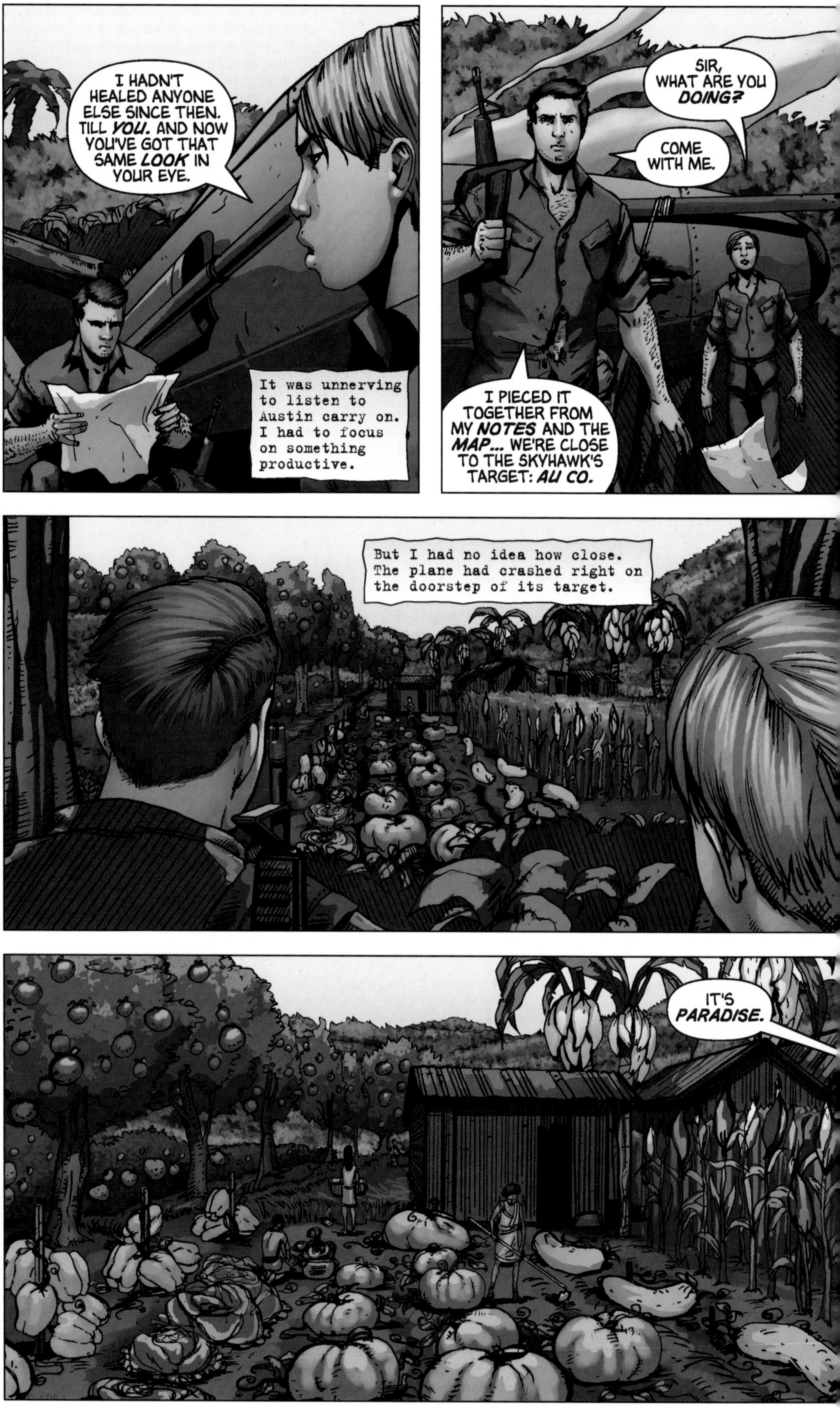
I HADN'T HEALED ANYONE ELSE SINCE THEN. TILL *YOU.* AND NOW YOU'VE GOT THAT SAME *LOOK* IN YOUR EYE.
It was unnerving to listen to Austin carry on. I had to focus on something productive.
SIR, WHAT ARE YOU *DOING?*
COME WITH ME.
I PIECED IT TOGETHER FROM MY *NOTES* AND THE *MAP...* WE'RE CLOSE TO THE SKYHAWK'S TARGET: *AU CO.*
But I had no idea how close. The plane had crashed right on the doorstep of its target.
IT'S *PARADISE.*

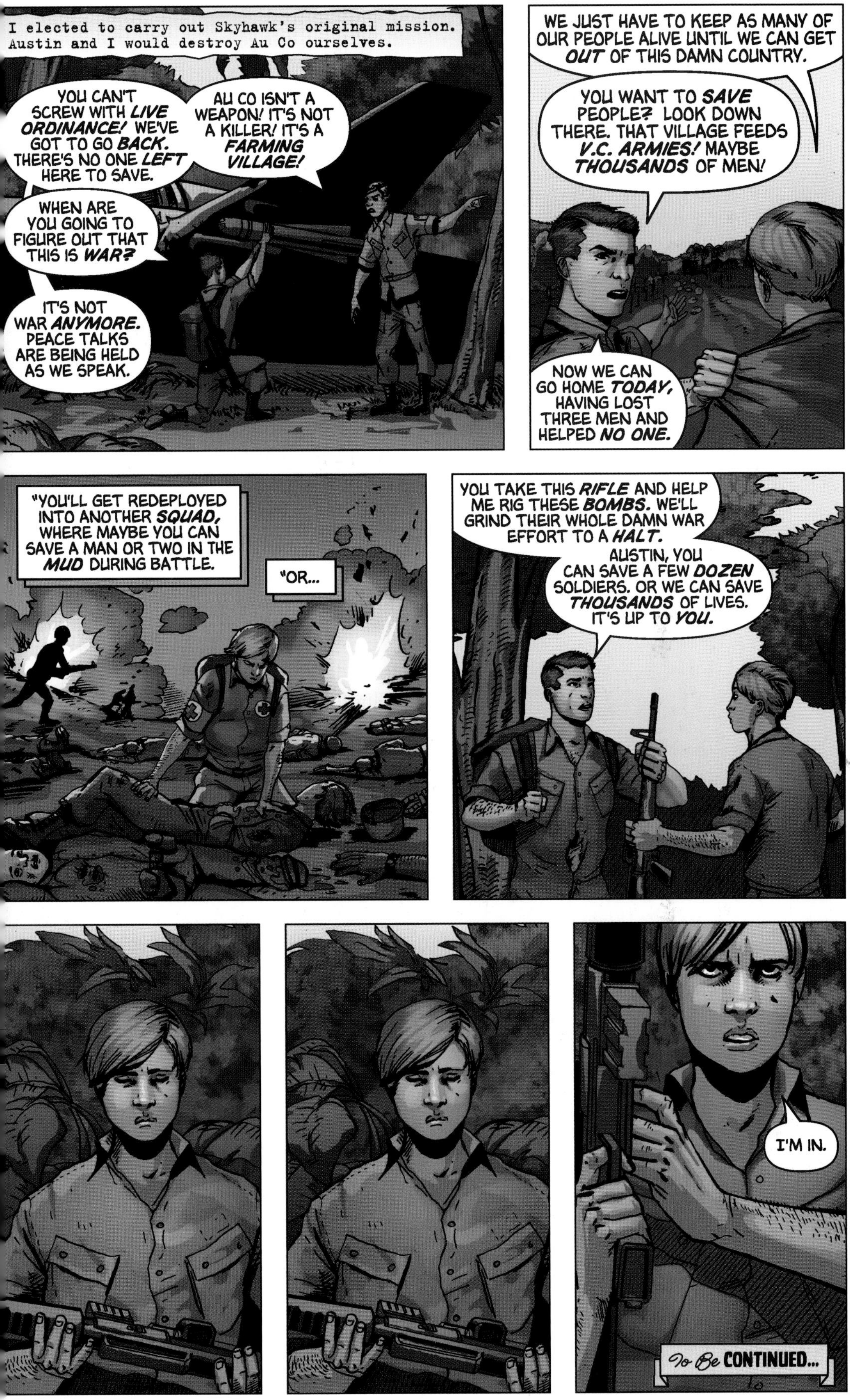
I elected to carry out Skyhawk's original mission. Austin and I would destroy Au Co ourselves.
YOU CAN'T SCREW WITH *LIVE ORDINANCE!* WE'VE GOT TO GO *BACK.* THERE'S NO ONE *LEFT* HERE TO SAVE.
AU CO ISN'T A WEAPON! IT'S NOT A KILLER! IT'S A *FARMING VILLAGE!*
WHEN ARE YOU GOING TO FIGURE OUT THAT THIS IS *WAR?*
IT'S NOT WAR *ANYMORE.* PEACE TALKS ARE BEING HELD AS WE SPEAK.
WE JUST HAVE TO KEEP AS MANY OF OUR PEOPLE ALIVE UNTIL WE CAN GET *OUT* OF THIS DAMN COUNTRY.
YOU WANT TO *SAVE* PEOPLE? LOOK DOWN THERE. THAT VILLAGE FEEDS *V.C. ARMIES!* MAYBE *THOUSANDS* OF MEN!
NOW WE CAN GO HOME *TODAY,* HAVING LOST THREE MEN AND HELPED *NO ONE.*
"YOU'LL GET REDEPLOYED INTO ANOTHER *SQUAD,* WHERE MAYBE YOU CAN SAVE A MAN OR TWO IN THE *MUD* DURING BATTLE.
"OR...
YOU TAKE THIS *RIFLE* AND HELP ME RIG THESE *BOMBS.* WE'LL GRIND THEIR WHOLE DAMN WAR EFFORT TO A *HALT.*
AUSTIN, YOU CAN SAVE A FEW *DOZEN* SOLDIERS. OR WE CAN SAVE *THOUSANDS* OF LIVES. IT'S UP TO *YOU.*
I'M IN.
To Be CONTINUED...

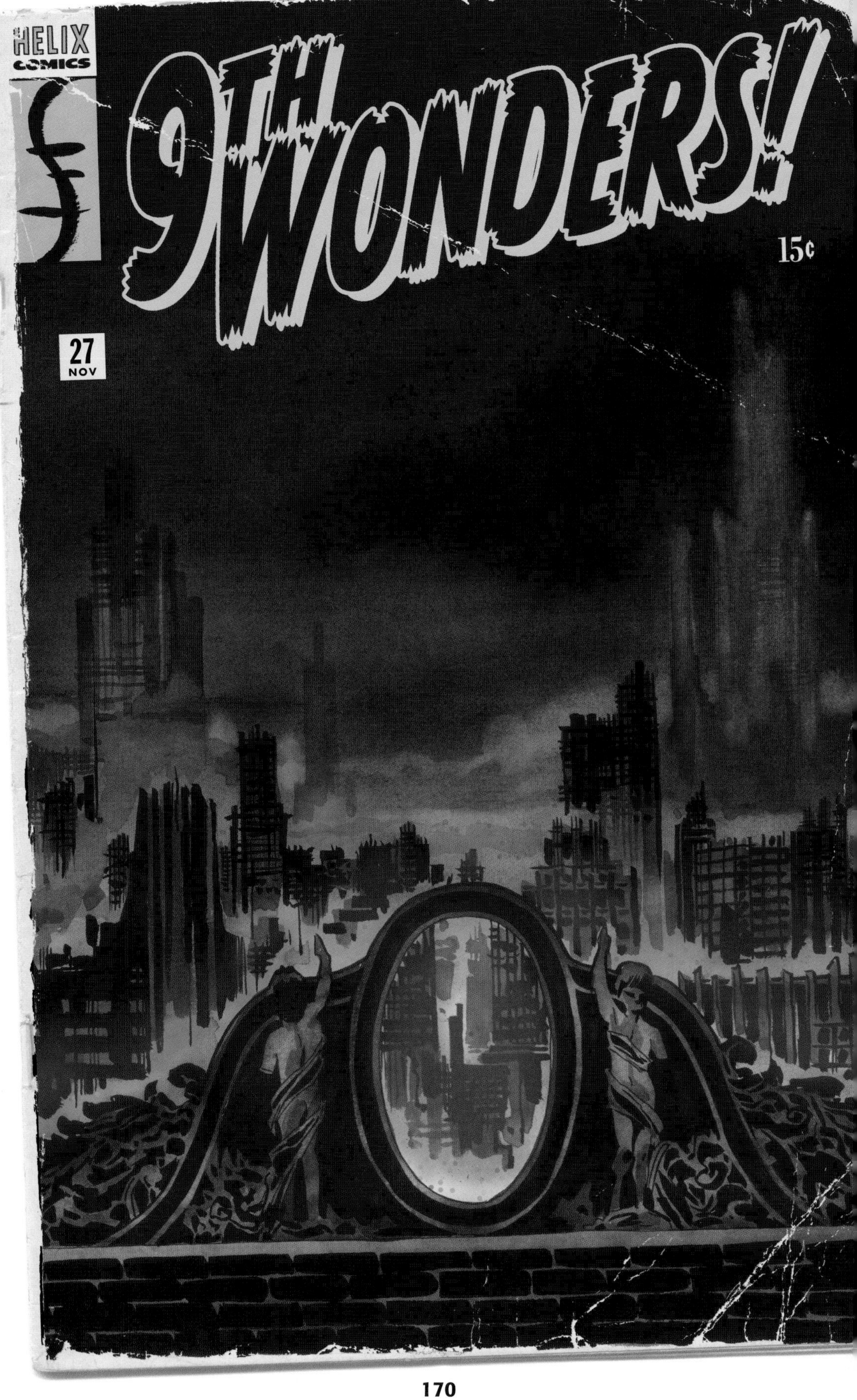
HELIX
COMICS
9TH WONDERS!
15¢
27
NOV

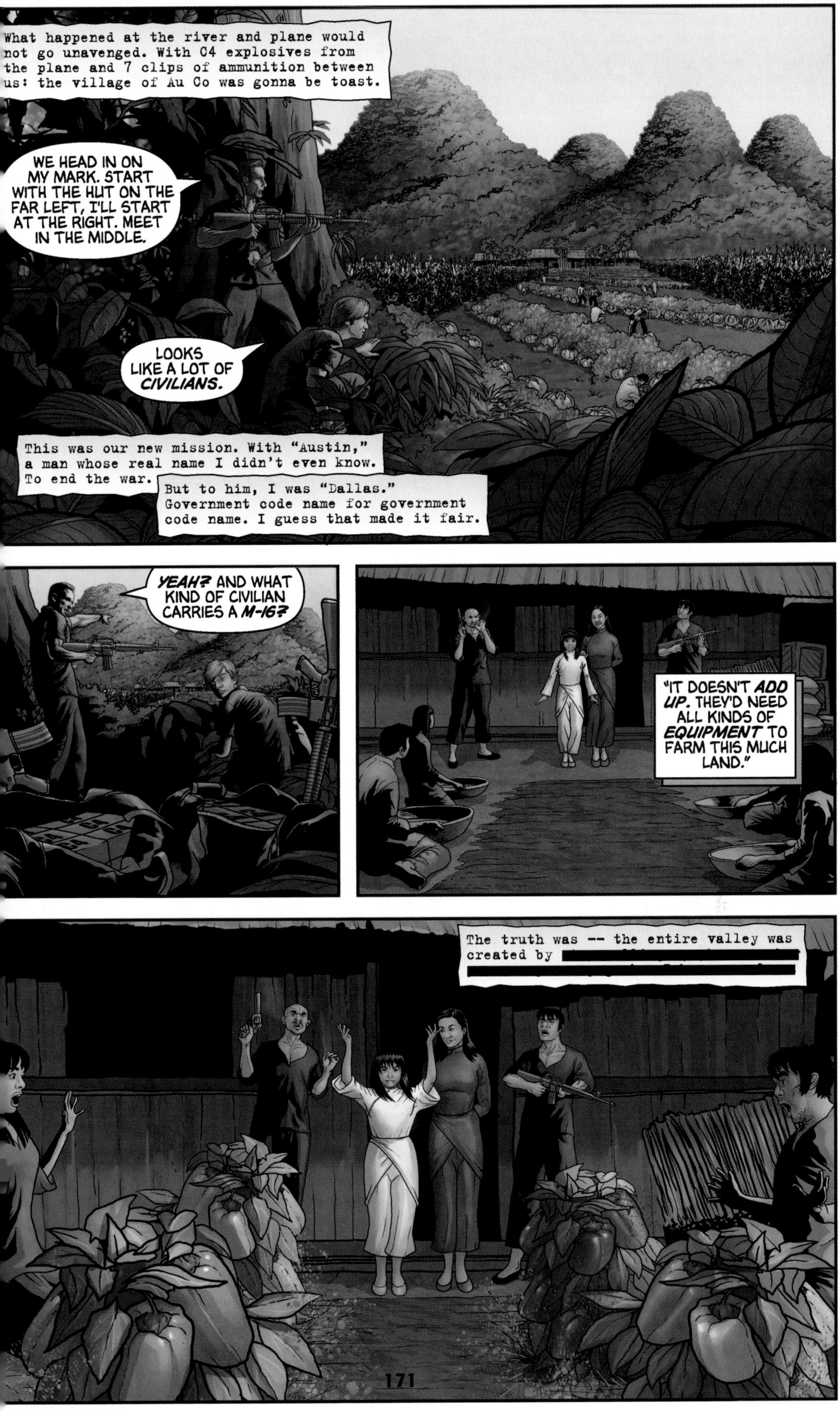
What happened at the river and plane would not go unavenged. With C4 explosives from the plane and 7 clips of ammunition between us: the village of Au Co was gonna be toast.
WE HEAD IN ON MY MARK. START WITH THE HUT ON THE FAR LEFT, I'LL START AT THE RIGHT. MEET IN THE MIDDLE.
LOOKS LIKE A LOT OF *CIVILIANS.*
This was our new mission. With "Austin," a man whose real name I didn't even know. To end the war.
But to him, I was "Dallas." Government code name for government code name. I guess that made it fair.
YEAH? AND WHAT KIND OF CIVILIAN CARRIES A *M-16?*
"IT DOESN'T *ADD UP.* THEY'D NEED ALL KINDS OF *EQUIPMENT* TO FARM THIS MUCH LAND."
The truth was -- the entire valley was created by [redacted]

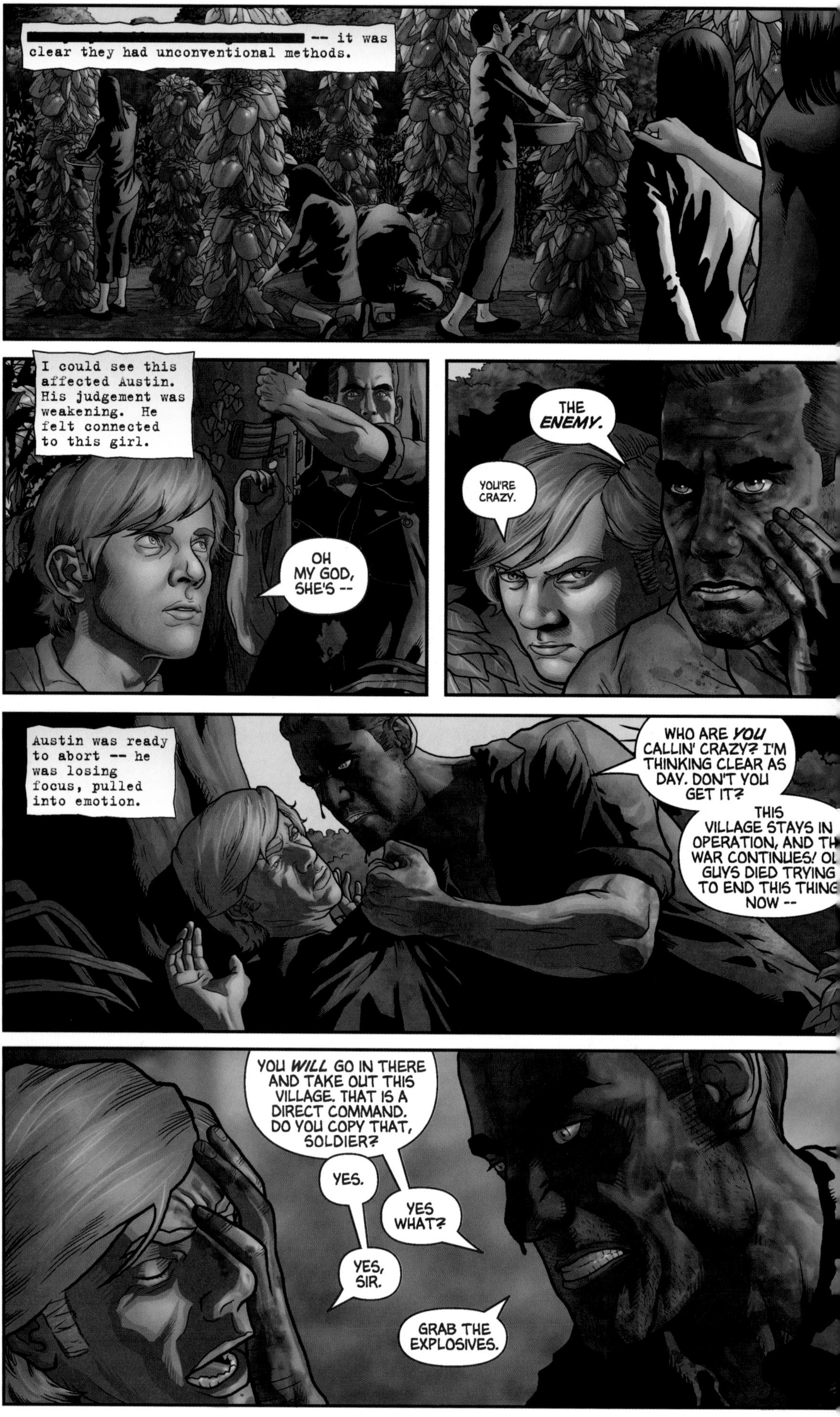
[redacted] -- it was clear they had unconventional methods.
I could see this affected Austin. His judgement was weakening. He felt connected to this girl.
OH MY GOD, SHE'S --
THE *ENEMY.*
YOU'RE CRAZY.
Austin was ready to abort -- he was losing focus, pulled into emotion.
WHO ARE *YOU* CALLIN' CRAZY? I'M THINKING CLEAR AS DAY. DON'T YOU GET IT?
THIS VILLAGE STAYS IN OPERATION, AND TH WAR CONTINUES! OU GUYS DIED TRYING TO END THIS THING NOW --
YOU *WILL* GO IN THERE AND TAKE OUT THIS VILLAGE. THAT IS A DIRECT COMMAND. DO YOU COPY THAT, SOLDIER?
YES.
YES WHAT?
YES, SIR.
GRAB THE EXPLOSIVES.

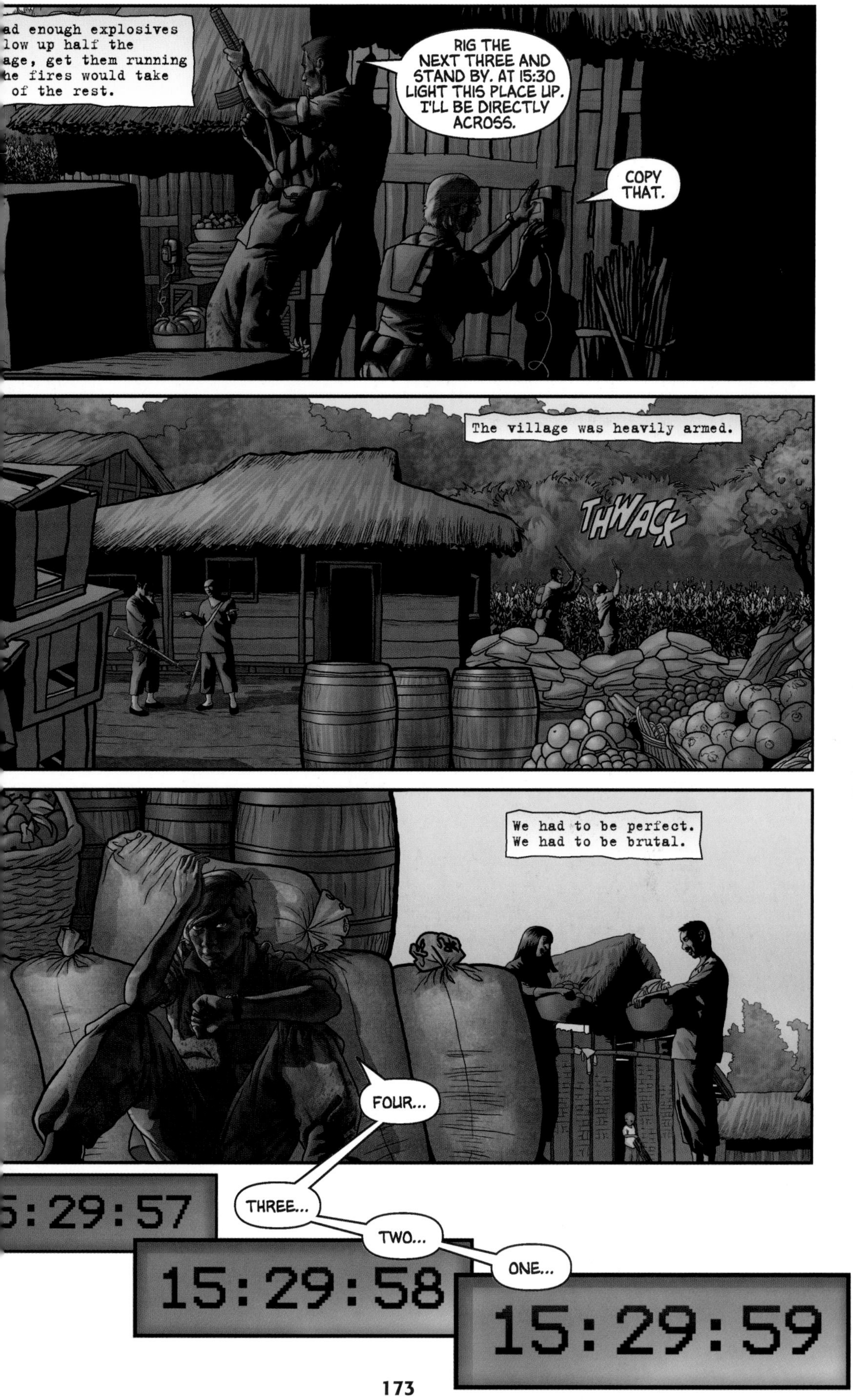
ad enough explosives
low up half the
age, get them running
he fires would take
of the rest.
RIG THE NEXT THREE AND STAND BY. AT 15:30 LIGHT THIS PLACE UP. I'LL BE DIRECTLY ACROSS.
COPY THAT.
The village was heavily armed.
THWACK
We had to be perfect.
We had to be brutal.
FOUR...
5:29:57
THREE...
TWO...
15:29:58
ONE...
15:29:59

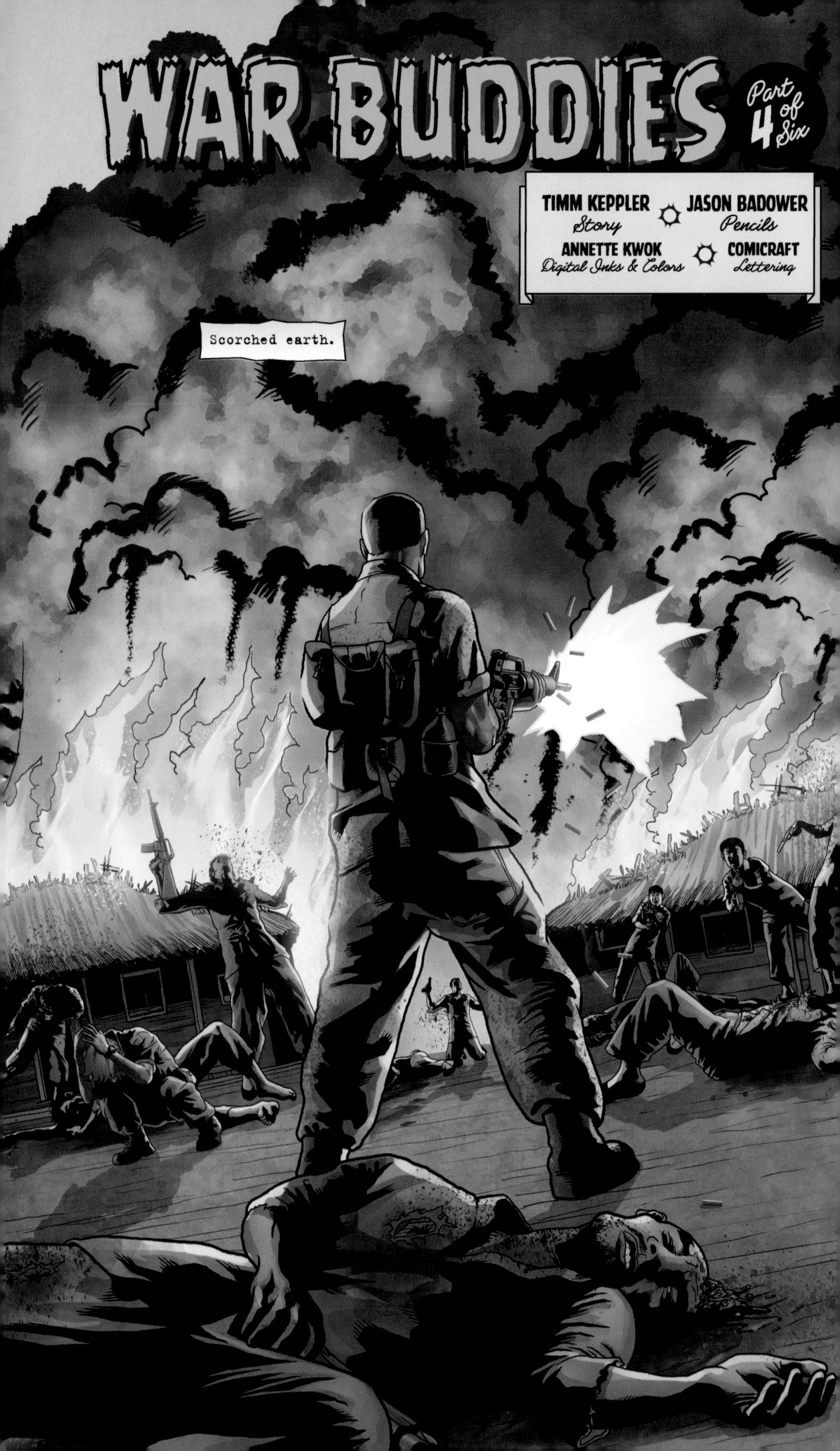

WAR BUDDIES
Part 4 of Six
TIMM KEPPLER Story
JASON BADOWER Pencils
ANNETTE KWOK Digital Inks & Colors
COMICRAFT Lettering
Scorched earth.

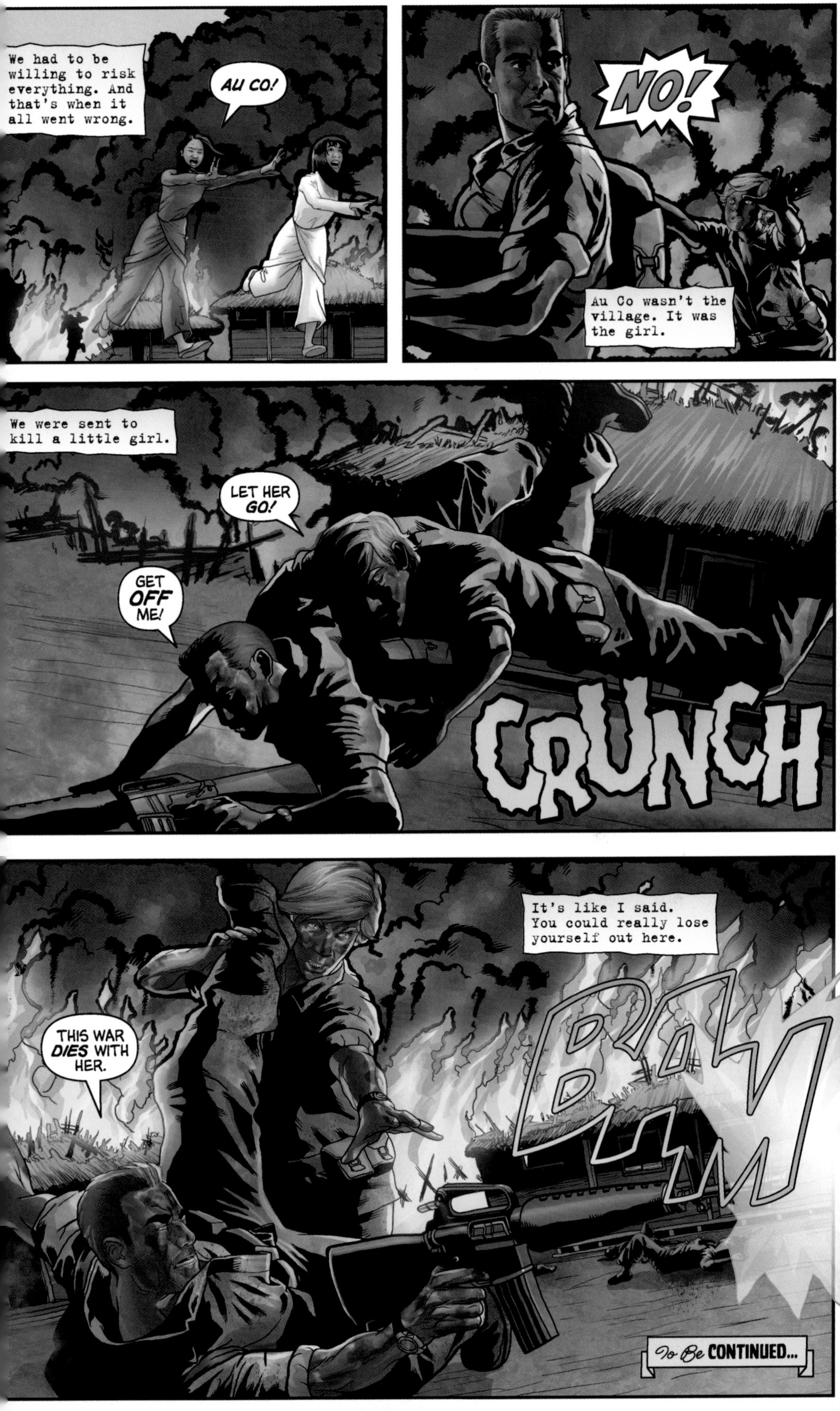
We had to be willing to risk everything. And that's when it all went wrong.
AU CO!
NO!
Au Co wasn't the village. It was the girl.
We were sent to kill a little girl.
LET HER GO!
GET OFF ME!
CRUNCH
It's like I said. You could really lose yourself out here.
THIS WAR DIES WITH HER.
BLAM
To Be CONTINUED...

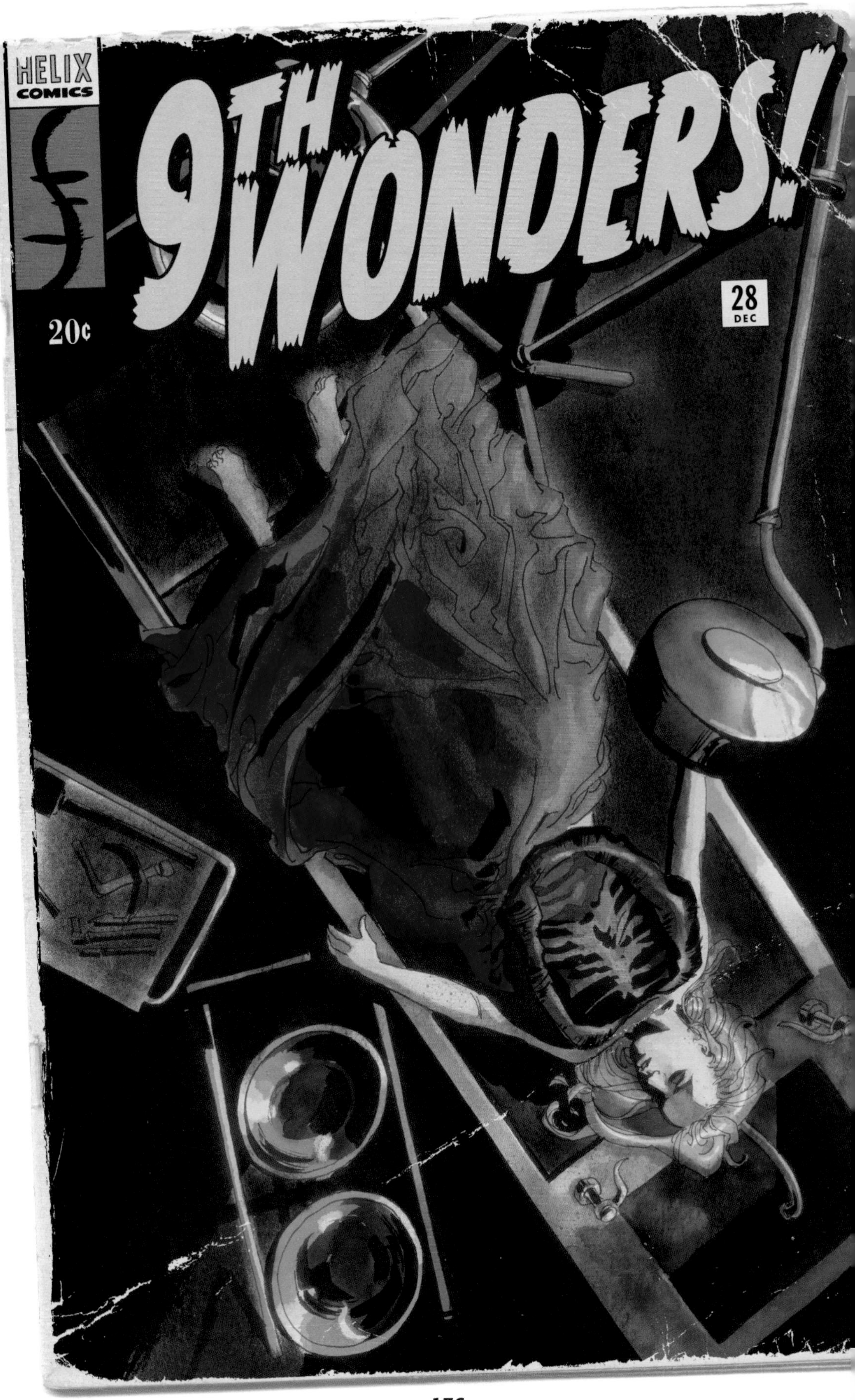
HELIX
COMICS
9TH WONDERS!
28
DEC
20¢

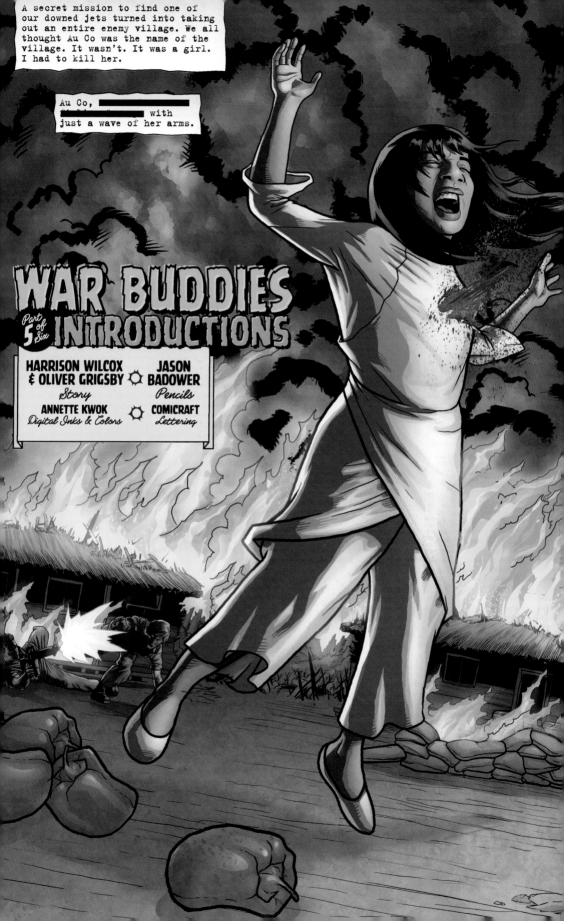

A secret mission to find one of our downed jets turned into taking out an entire enemy village. We all thought Au Co was the name of the village. It wasn't. It was a girl. I had to kill her.

Au Co, ▮▮▮▮▮▮▮▮ with just a wave of her arms.

WAR BUDDIES
INTRODUCTIONS
Part 5 of Six

HARRISON WILCOX & OLIVER GRIGSBY
Story

JASON BADOWER
Pencils

ANNETTE KWOK
Digital Inks & Colors

COMICRAFT
Lettering

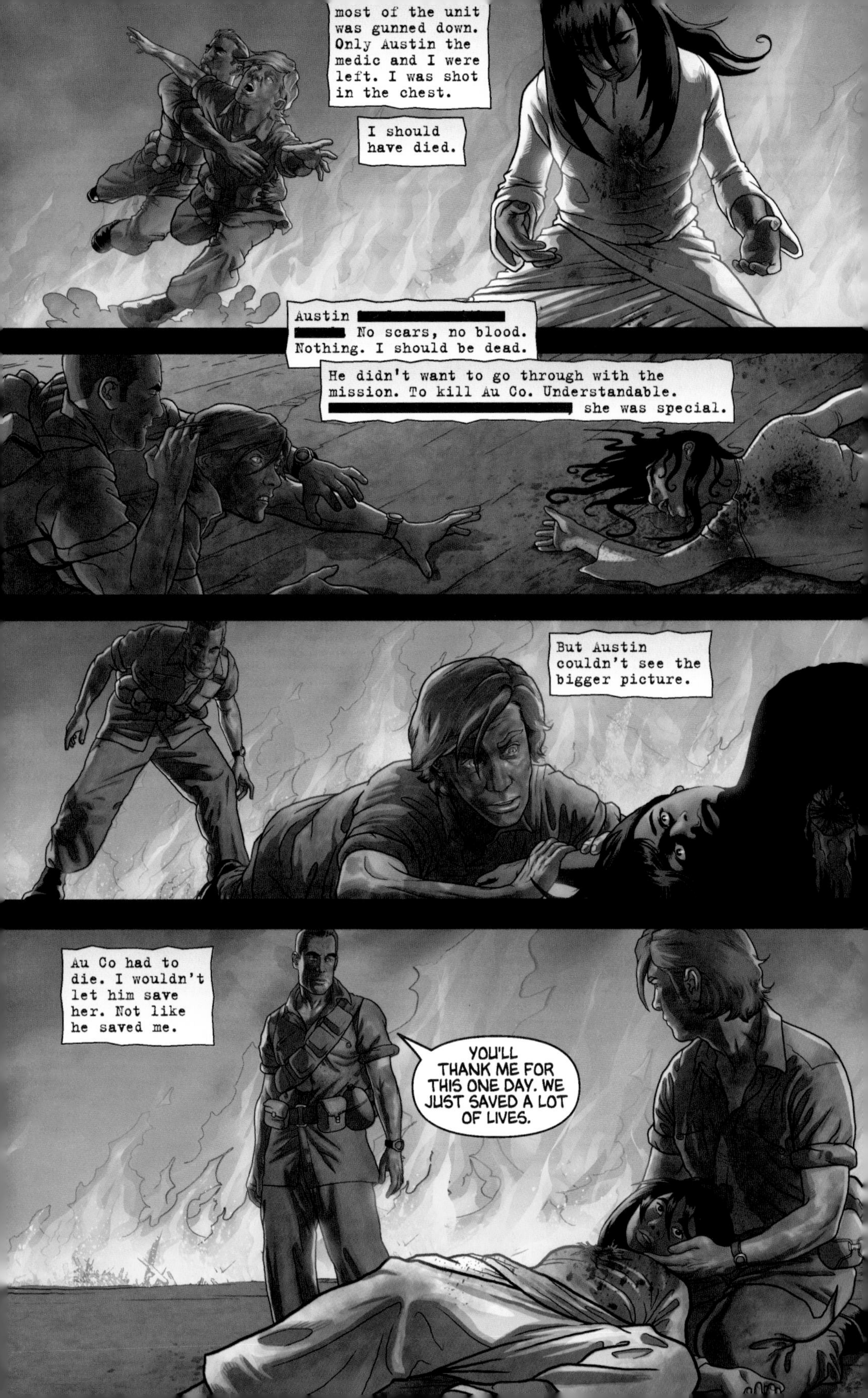
most of the unit was gunned down. Only Austin the medic and I were left. I was shot in the chest.
I should have died.
Austin [redacted] No scars, no blood. Nothing. I should be dead.
He didn't want to go through with the mission. To kill Au Co. Understandable. [redacted] she was special.
But Austin couldn't see the bigger picture.
Au Co had to die. I wouldn't let him save her. Not like he saved me.
YOU'LL THANK ME FOR THIS ONE DAY. WE JUST SAVED A LOT OF LIVES.

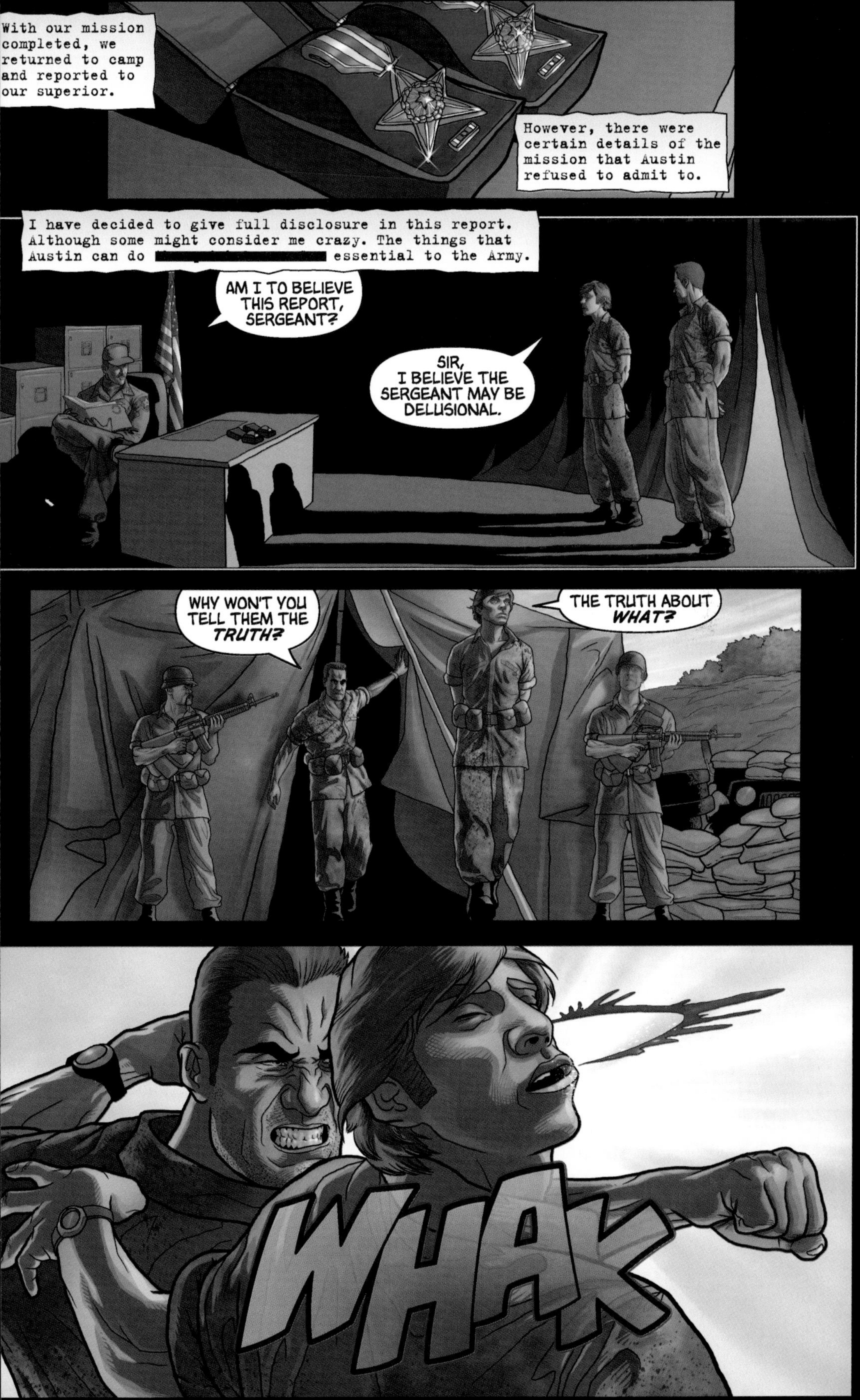
With our mission completed, we returned to camp and reported to our superior.
However, there were certain details of the mission that Austin refused to admit to.
I have decided to give full disclosure in this report. Although some might consider me crazy. The things that Austin can do [redacted] essential to the Army.
AM I TO BELIEVE THIS REPORT, SERGEANT?
SIR, I BELIEVE THE SERGEANT MAY BE DELUSIONAL.
WHY WON'T YOU TELL THEM THE *TRUTH?*
THE TRUTH ABOUT *WHAT?*
WHAK

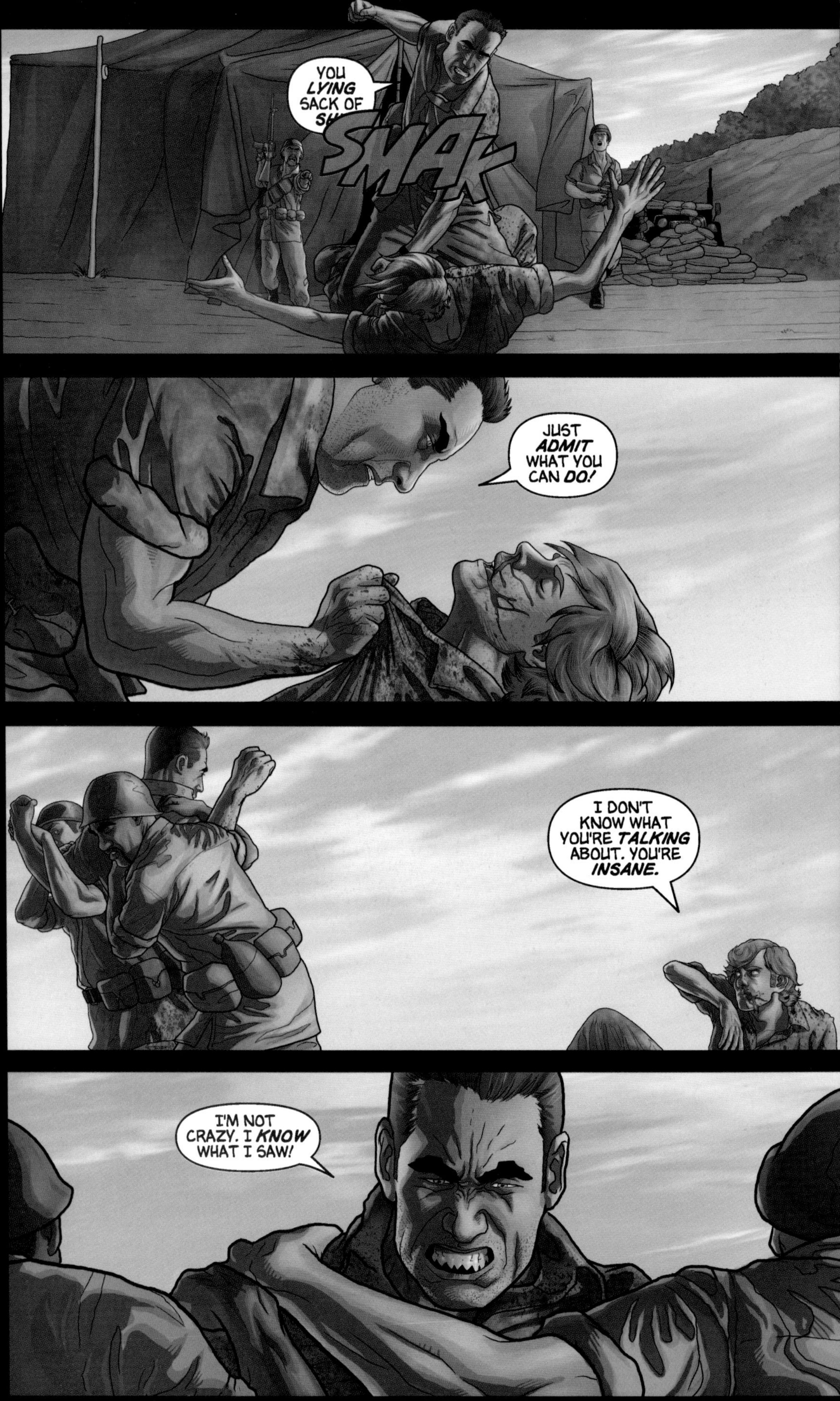
YOU LYING SACK OF SH--
SMAK
JUST ADMIT WHAT YOU CAN DO!
I DON'T KNOW WHAT YOU'RE TALKING ABOUT. YOU'RE INSANE.
I'M NOT CRAZY. I KNOW WHAT I SAW!

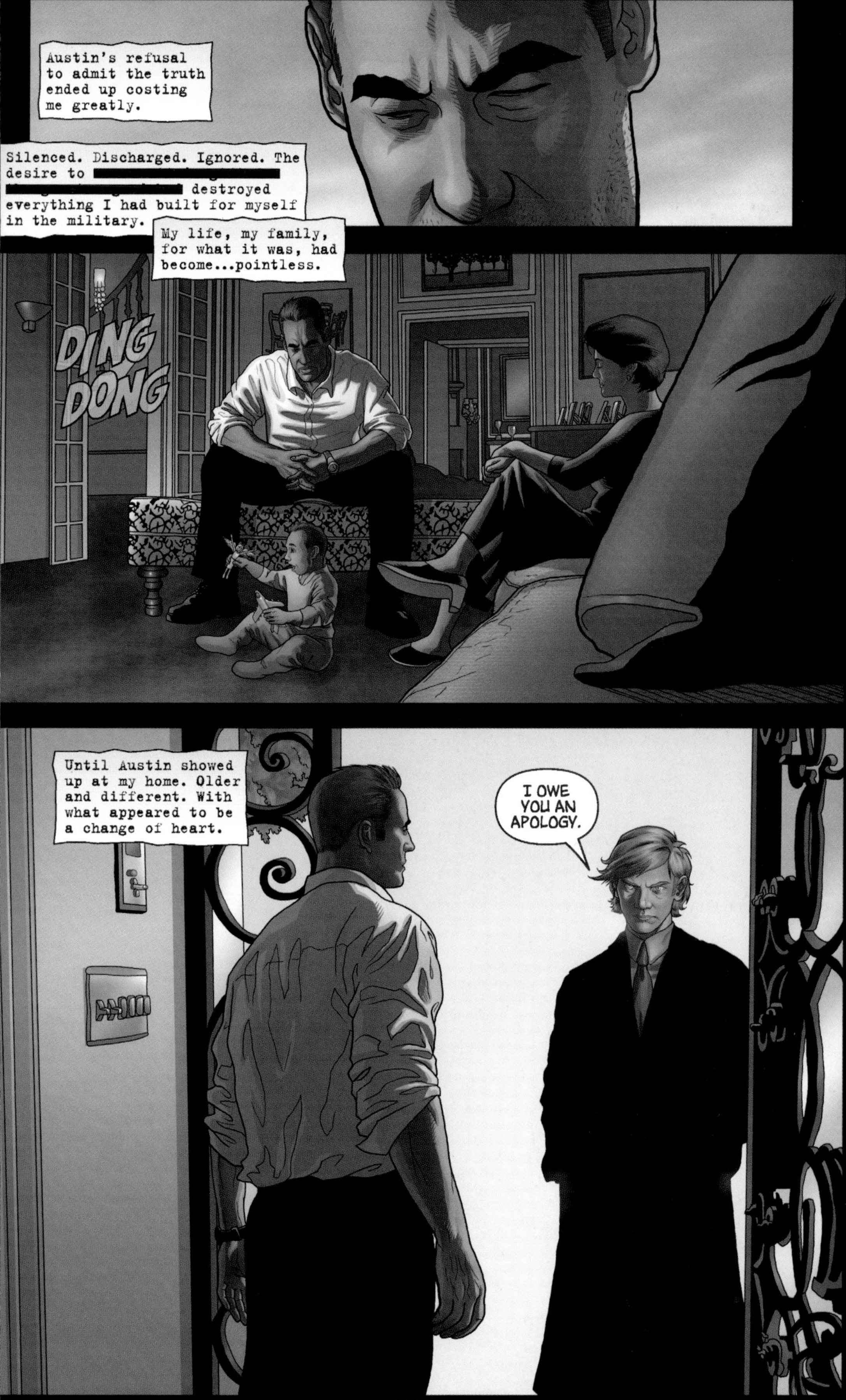
Austin's refusal to admit the truth ended up costing me greatly.
Silenced. Discharged. Ignored. The desire to [redacted] destroyed everything I had built for myself in the military.
My life, my family, for what it was, had become...pointless.
DING DONG
Until Austin showed up at my home. Older and different. With what appeared to be a change of heart.
I OWE YOU AN APOLOGY.

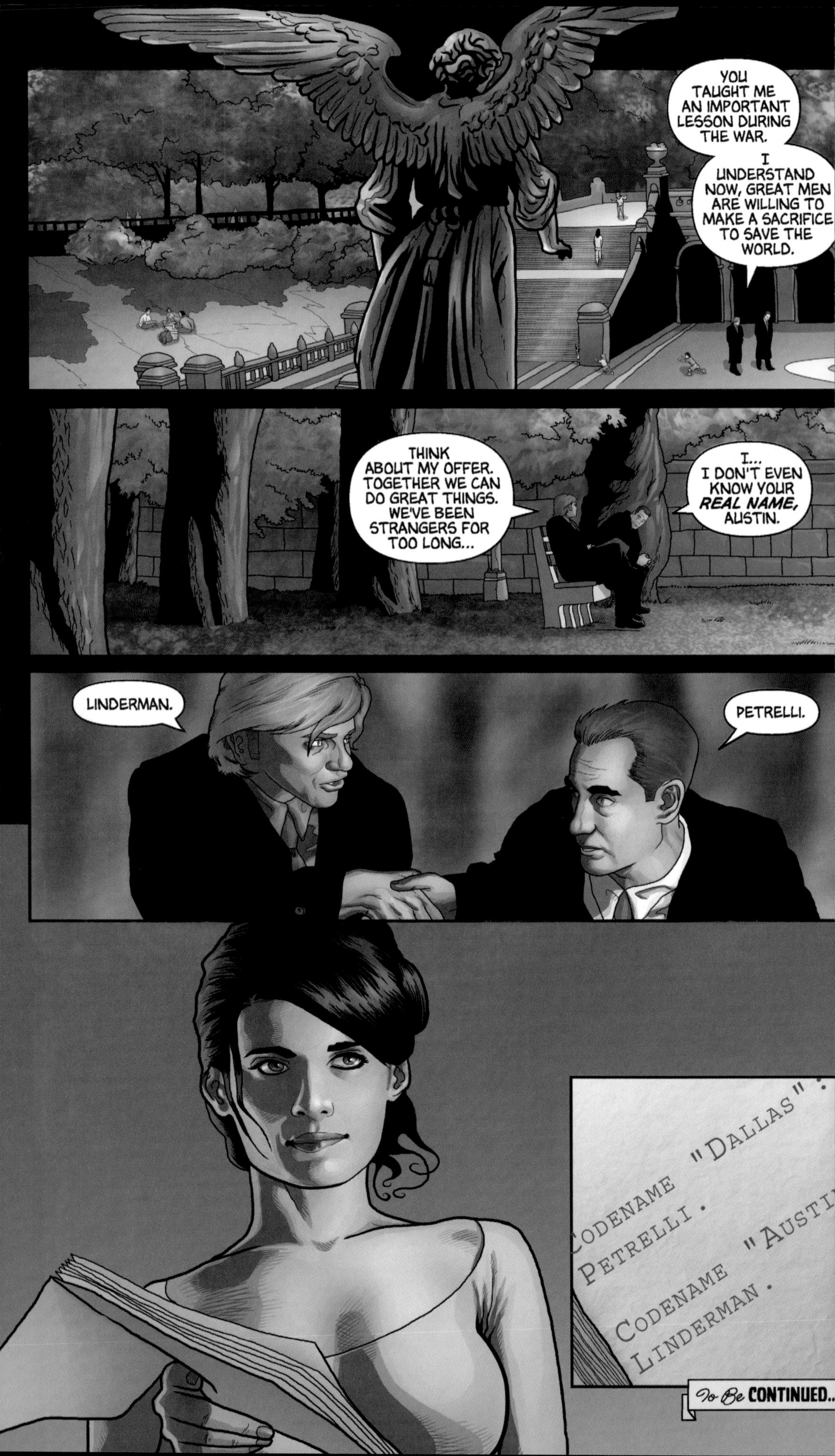
YOU TAUGHT ME AN IMPORTANT LESSON DURING THE WAR.
I UNDERSTAND NOW, GREAT MEN ARE WILLING TO MAKE A SACRIFICE TO SAVE THE WORLD.
THINK ABOUT MY OFFER. TOGETHER WE CAN DO GREAT THINGS. WE'VE BEEN STRANGERS FOR TOO LONG...
I... I DON'T EVEN KNOW YOUR REAL NAME, AUSTIN.
LINDERMAN.
PETRELLI.
CODENAME "DALLAS": PETRELLI.
CODENAME "AUSTI
LINDERMAN.
To Be CONTINUED...

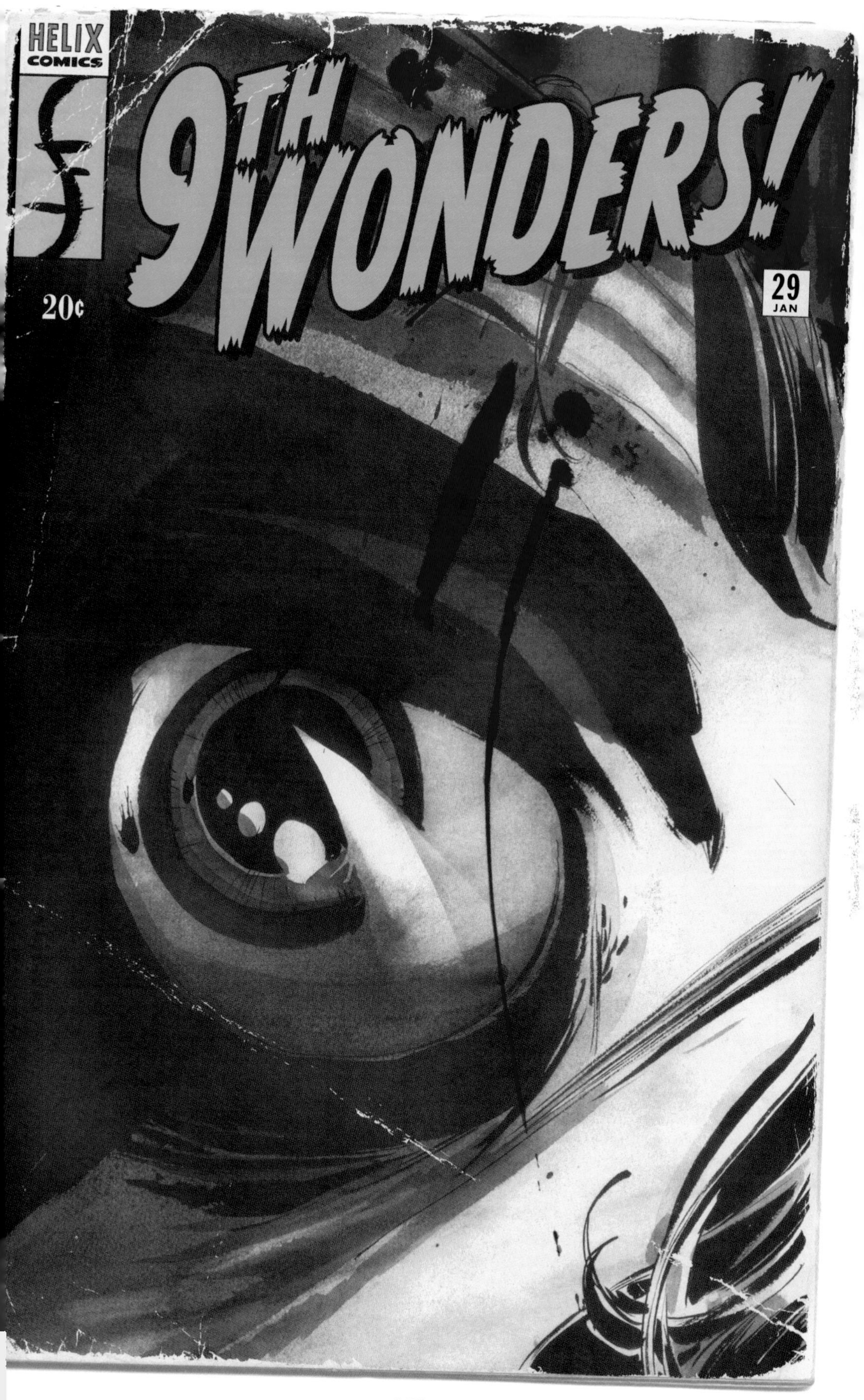
HELIX COMICS
9TH WONDERS!
20¢
29
JAN

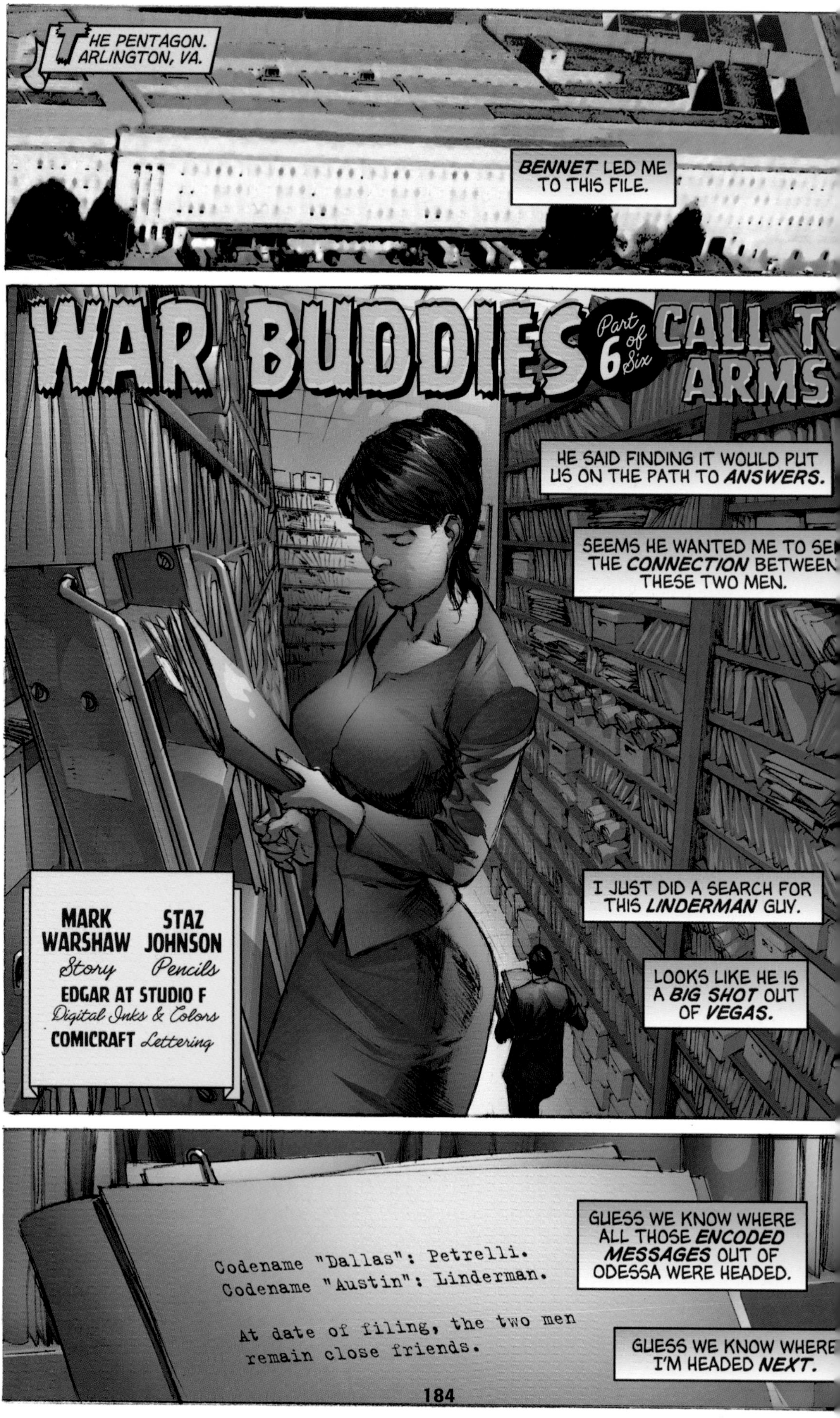
THE PENTAGON. ARLINGTON, VA.
BENNET LED ME TO THIS FILE.
WAR BUDDIES Part 6 of Six CALL TO ARMS
HE SAID FINDING IT WOULD PUT US ON THE PATH TO ANSWERS.
SEEMS HE WANTED ME TO SEE THE CONNECTION BETWEEN THESE TWO MEN.
I JUST DID A SEARCH FOR THIS LINDERMAN GUY.
LOOKS LIKE HE IS A BIG SHOT OUT OF VEGAS.
MARK WARSHAW Story
STAZ JOHNSON Pencils
EDGAR AT STUDIO F Digital Inks & Colors
COMICRAFT Lettering
Codename "Dallas": Petrelli.
Codename "Austin": Linderman.
At date of filing, the two men remain close friends.
GUESS WE KNOW WHERE ALL THOSE ENCODED MESSAGES OUT OF ODESSA WERE HEADED.
GUESS WE KNOW WHERE I'M HEADED NEXT.

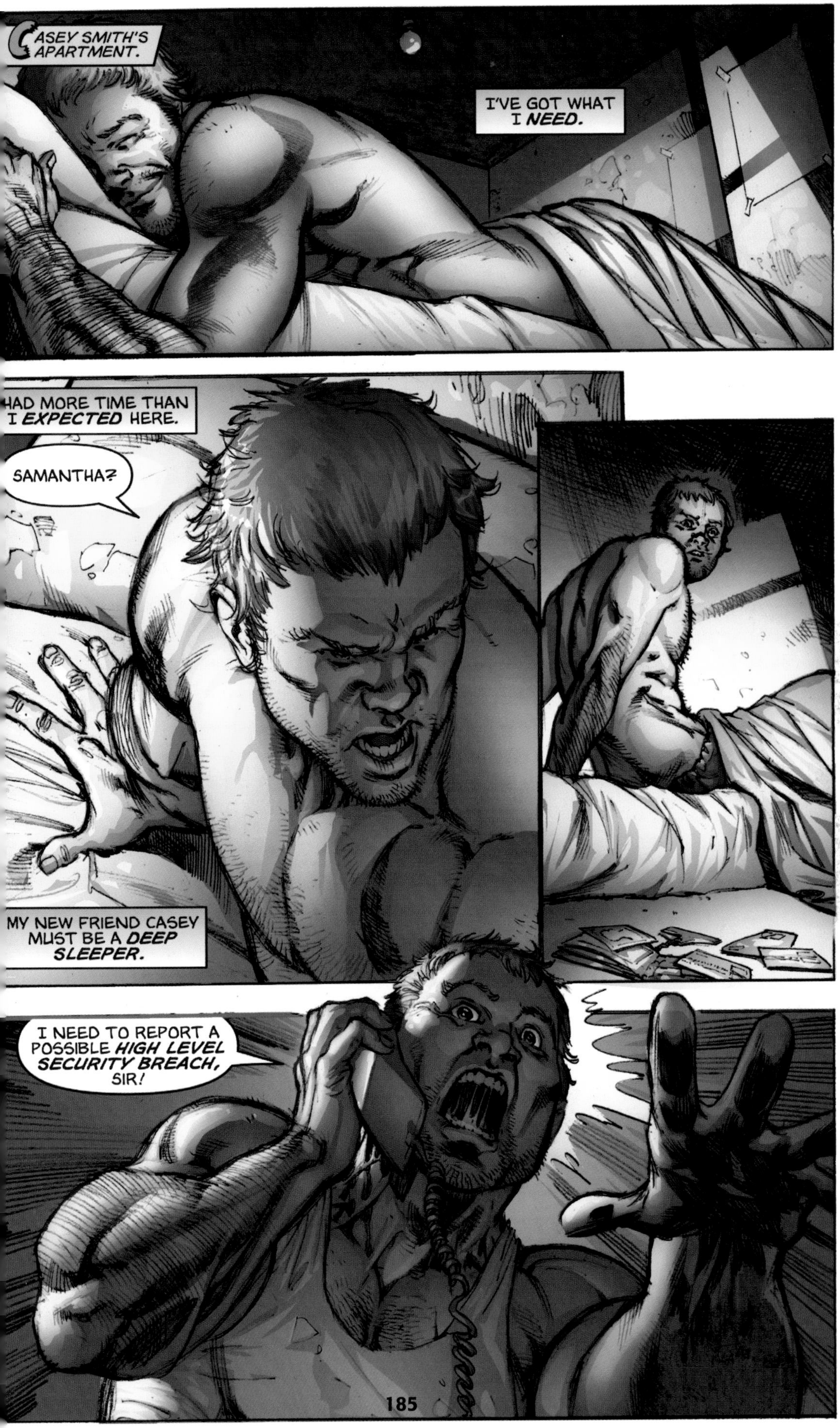
CASEY SMITH'S APARTMENT.
I'VE GOT WHAT I NEED.
HAD MORE TIME THAN I EXPECTED HERE.
SAMANTHA?
MY NEW FRIEND CASEY MUST BE A DEEP SLEEPER.
I NEED TO REPORT A POSSIBLE HIGH LEVEL SECURITY BREACH, SIR!

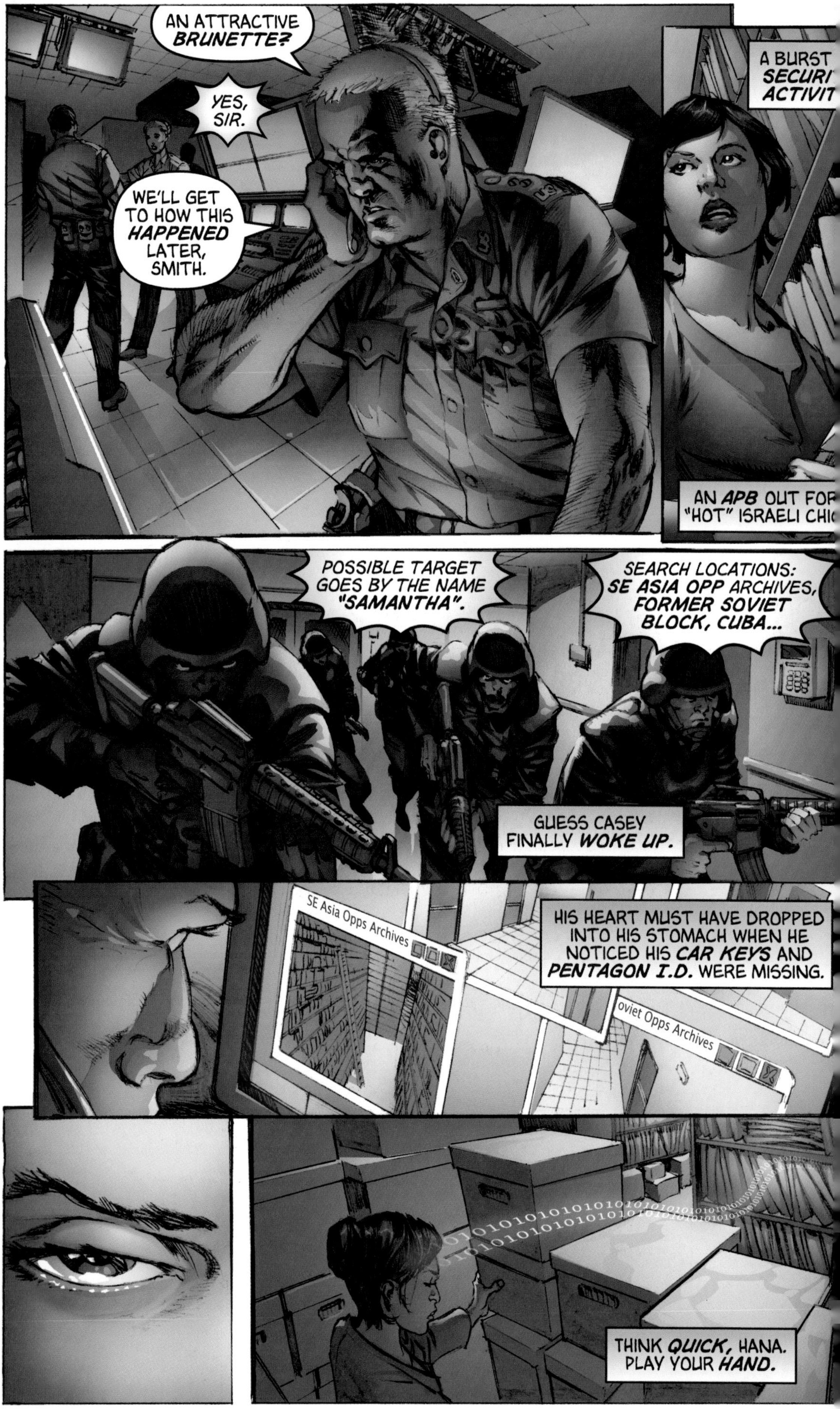
AN ATTRACTIVE BRUNETTE?
YES, SIR.
WE'LL GET TO HOW THIS HAPPENED LATER, SMITH.
A BURST SECURI ACTIVIT
AN APB OUT FOR "HOT" ISRAELI CHI
POSSIBLE TARGET GOES BY THE NAME "SAMANTHA".
SEARCH LOCATIONS: SE ASIA OPP ARCHIVES, FORMER SOVIET BLOCK, CUBA...
GUESS CASEY FINALLY WOKE UP.
SE Asia Opps Archives
HIS HEART MUST HAVE DROPPED INTO HIS STOMACH WHEN HE NOTICED HIS CAR KEYS AND PENTAGON I.D. WERE MISSING.
oviet Opps Archives
THINK QUICK, HANA. PLAY YOUR HAND.

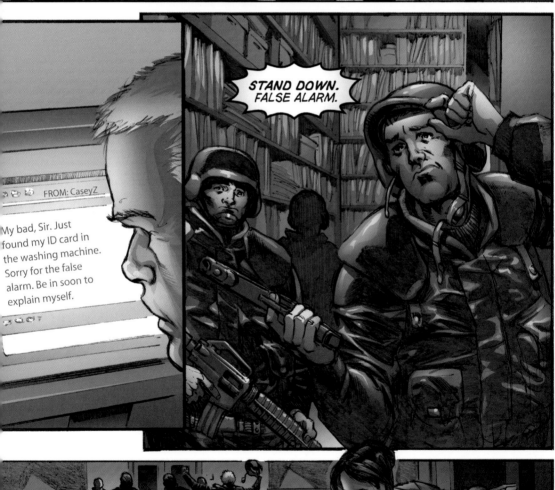

STAND DOWN. FALSE ALARM.

FROM: CaseyZ

My bad, Sir. Just found my ID card in the washing machine. Sorry for the false alarm. Be in soon to explain myself.

MORE EXCITEMENT THAN WE'VE HAD IN *WEEKS*.

TIME TO GET THE HELL *OUT* OF HERE.

ARCHIVES

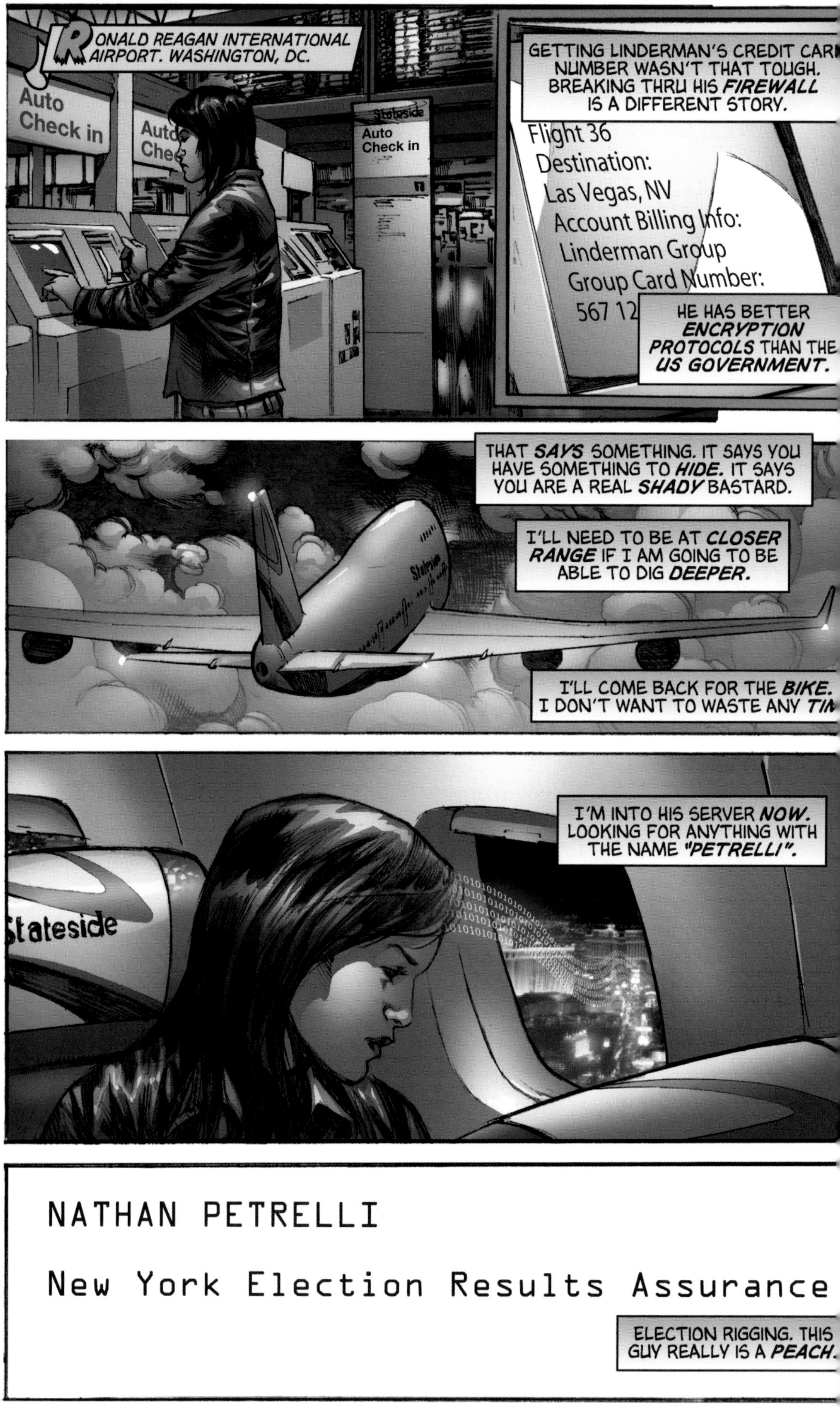

RONALD REAGAN INTERNATIONAL AIRPORT. WASHINGTON, DC.
Auto Check in
Stateside
Auto Check in
GETTING LINDERMAN'S CREDIT CAR NUMBER WASN'T THAT TOUGH. BREAKING THRU HIS FIREWALL IS A DIFFERENT STORY.
Flight 36
Destination:
Las Vegas, NV
Account Billing Info:
Linderman Group
Group Card Number:
567 12
HE HAS BETTER ENCRYPTION PROTOCOLS THAN THE US GOVERNMENT.
THAT SAYS SOMETHING. IT SAYS YOU HAVE SOMETHING TO HIDE. IT SAYS YOU ARE A REAL SHADY BASTARD.
I'LL NEED TO BE AT CLOSER RANGE IF I AM GOING TO BE ABLE TO DIG DEEPER.
I'LL COME BACK FOR THE BIKE. I DON'T WANT TO WASTE ANY TIM
I'M INTO HIS SERVER NOW. LOOKING FOR ANYTHING WITH THE NAME "PETRELLI".
Stateside
NATHAN PETRELLI
New York Election Results Assurance
ELECTION RIGGING. THIS GUY REALLY IS A PEACH.

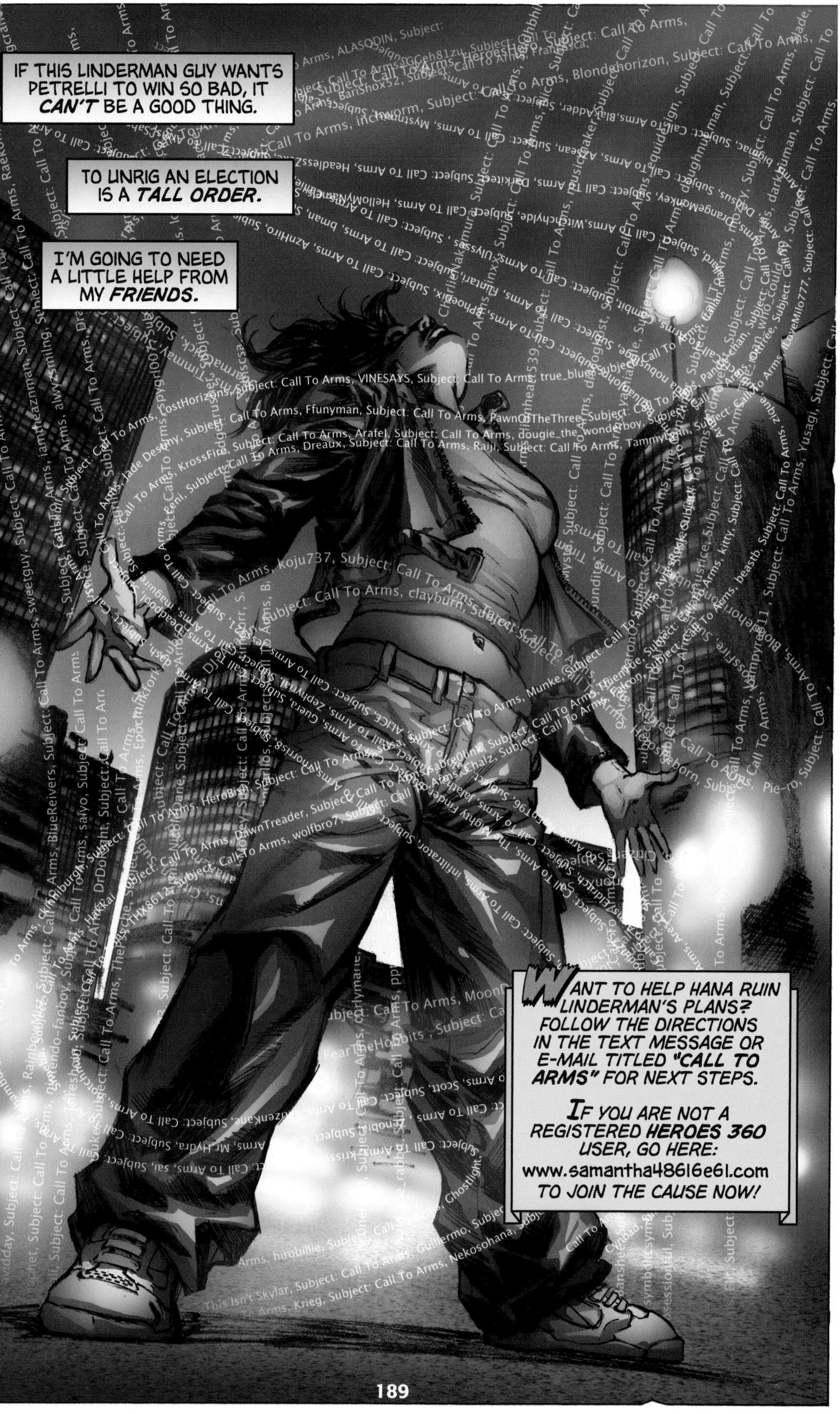
IF THIS LINDERMAN GUY WANTS PETRELLI TO WIN SO BAD, IT CAN'T BE A GOOD THING.
TO UNRIG AN ELECTION IS A TALL ORDER.
I'M GOING TO NEED A LITTLE HELP FROM MY FRIENDS.
WANT TO HELP HANA RUIN LINDERMAN'S PLANS? FOLLOW THE DIRECTIONS IN THE TEXT MESSAGE OR E-MAIL TITLED "CALL TO ARMS" FOR NEXT STEPS.
IF YOU ARE NOT A REGISTERED HEROES 360 USER, GO HERE: www.samantha48616e61.com TO JOIN THE CAUSE NOW!

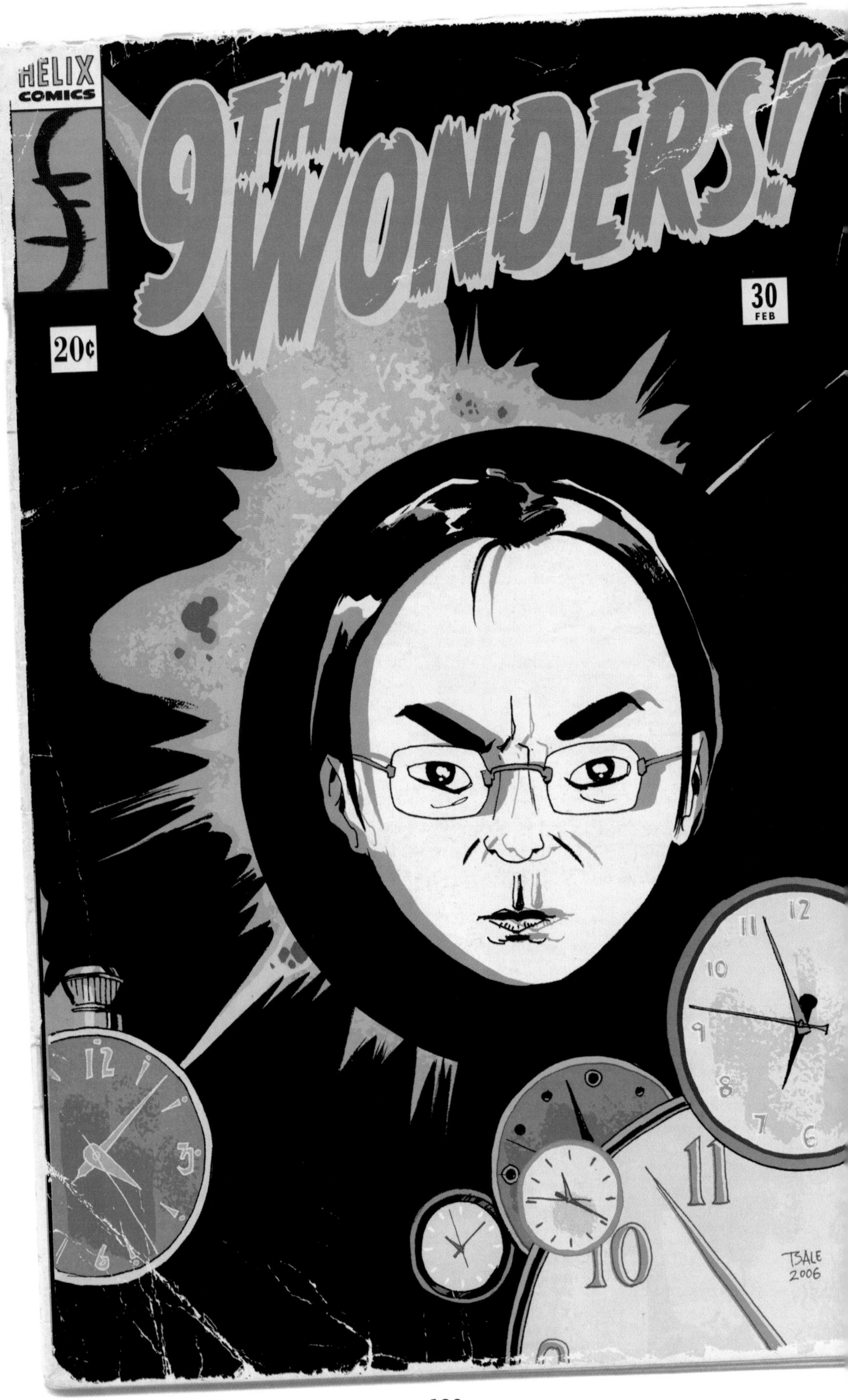
HELIX
COMICS
9TH WONDERS!
30
FEB
20¢
12
11
10
9
8
7
6
12
3
6
11
10
TSALE
2006

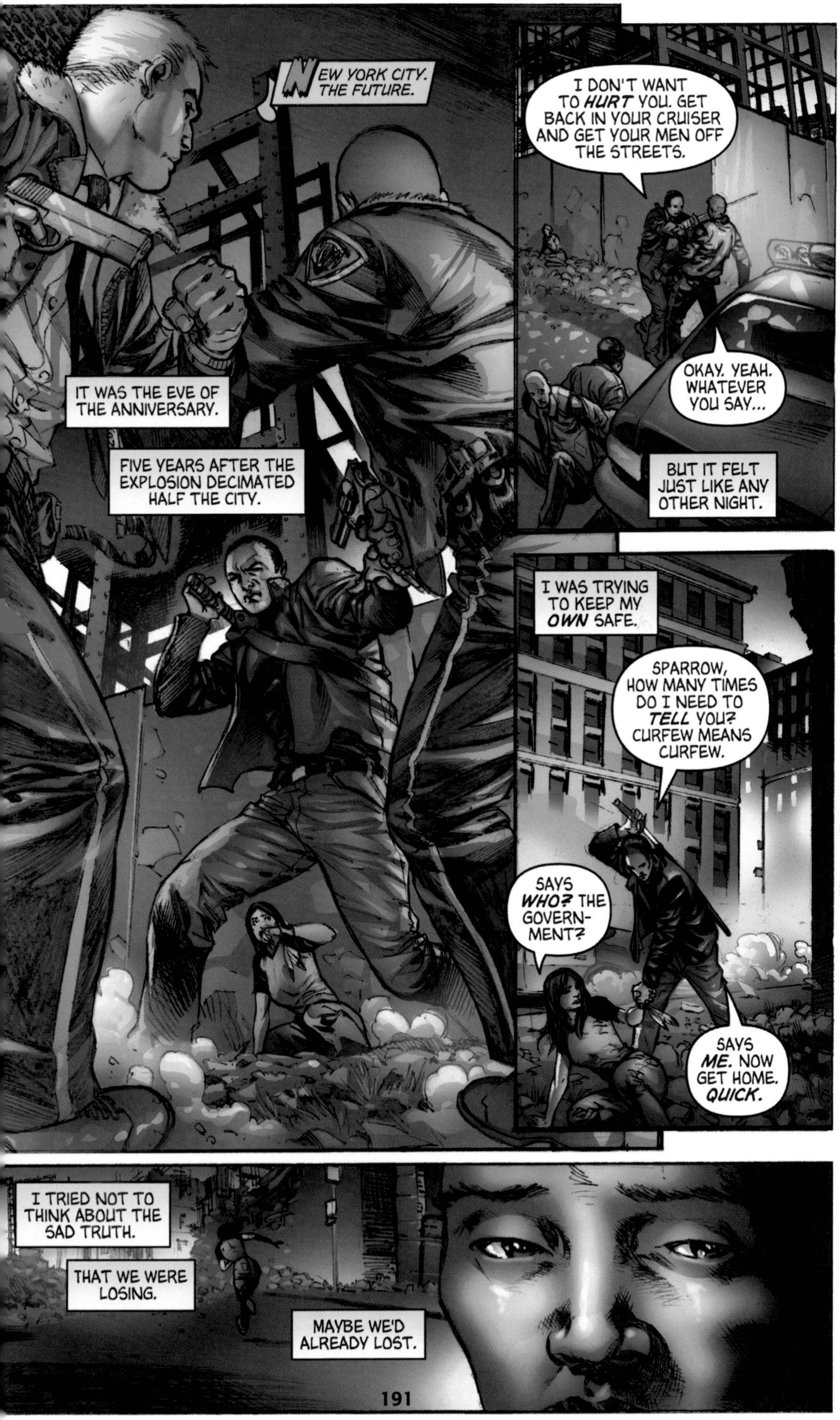
NEW YORK CITY. THE FUTURE.
IT WAS THE EVE OF THE ANNIVERSARY.
FIVE YEARS AFTER THE EXPLOSION DECIMATED HALF THE CITY.
I DON'T WANT TO HURT YOU. GET BACK IN YOUR CRUISER AND GET YOUR MEN OFF THE STREETS.
OKAY. YEAH. WHATEVER YOU SAY...
BUT IT FELT JUST LIKE ANY OTHER NIGHT.
I WAS TRYING TO KEEP MY OWN SAFE.
SPARROW, HOW MANY TIMES DO I NEED TO TELL YOU? CURFEW MEANS CURFEW.
SAYS WHO? THE GOVERNMENT?
SAYS ME. NOW GET HOME. QUICK.
I TRIED NOT TO THINK ABOUT THE SAD TRUTH.
THAT WE WERE LOSING.
MAYBE WE'D ALREADY LOST.

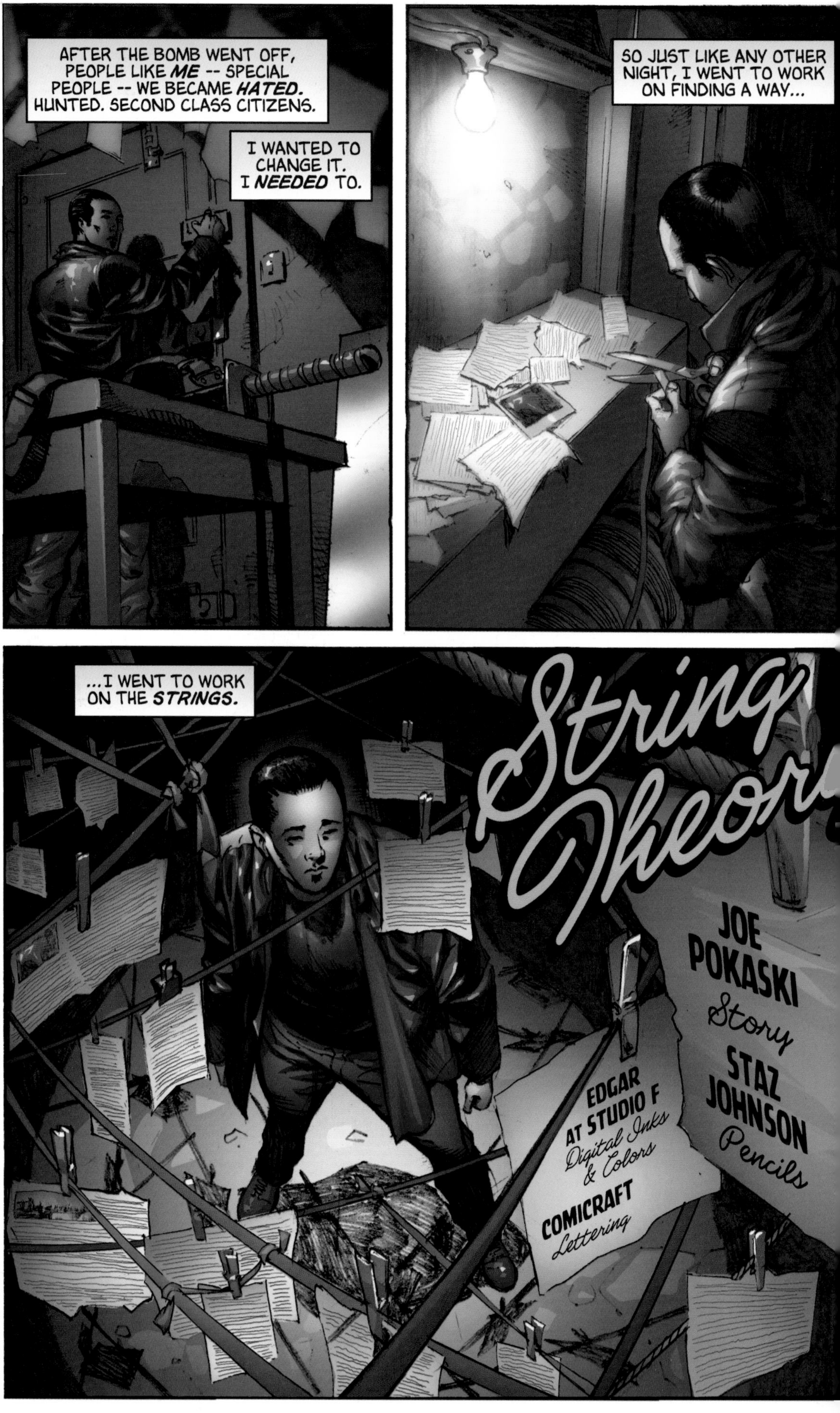
AFTER THE BOMB WENT OFF, PEOPLE LIKE ME -- SPECIAL PEOPLE -- WE BECAME HATED. HUNTED. SECOND CLASS CITIZENS.
I WANTED TO CHANGE IT. I NEEDED TO.
SO JUST LIKE ANY OTHER NIGHT, I WENT TO WORK ON FINDING A WAY...
...I WENT TO WORK ON THE STRINGS.
String Theor
JOE POKASKI Story
STAZ JOHNSON Pencils
EDGAR AT STUDIO F Digital Inks & Colors
COMICRAFT Lettering

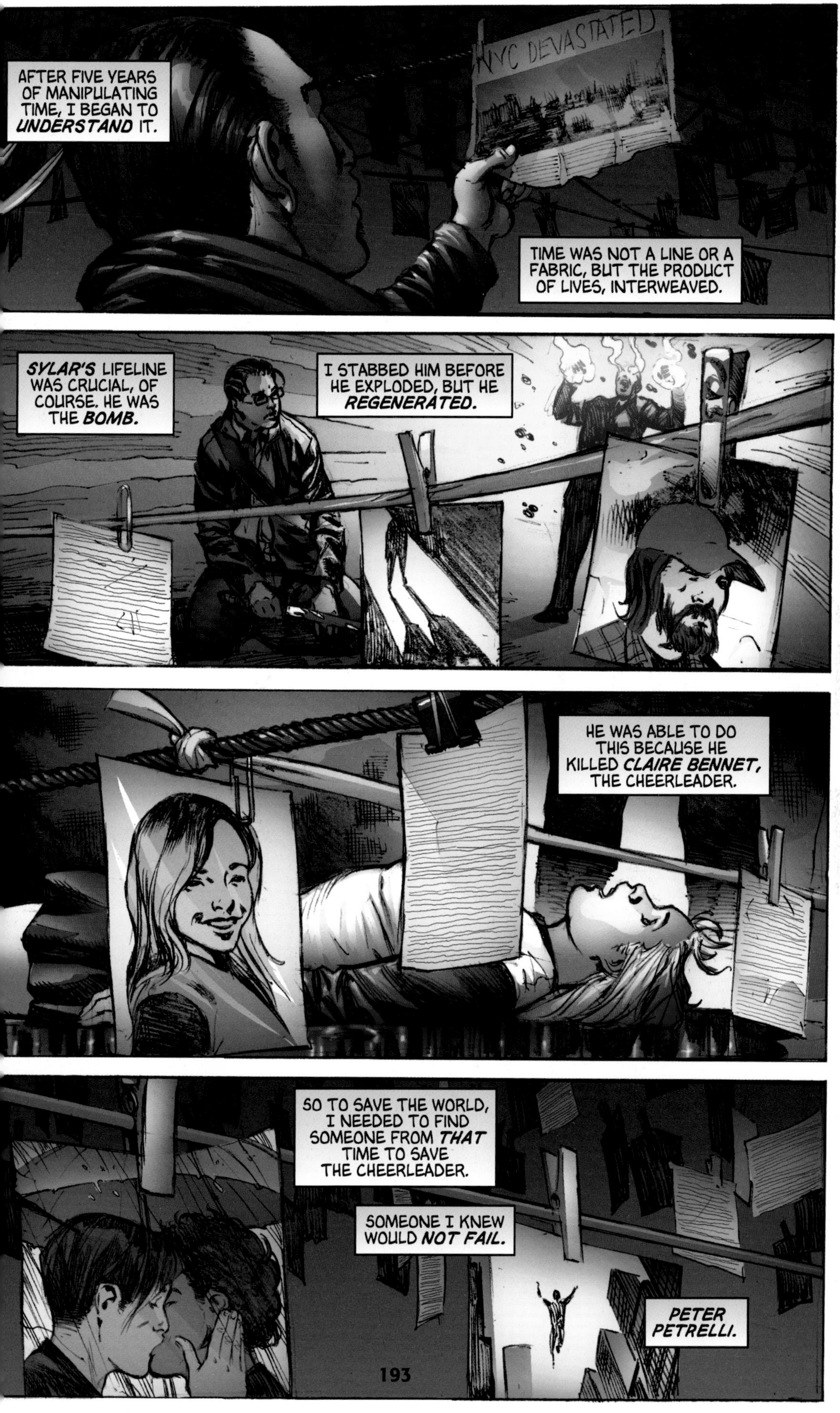
AFTER FIVE YEARS OF MANIPULATING TIME, I BEGAN TO UNDERSTAND IT.
NYC DEVASTATED
TIME WAS NOT A LINE OR A FABRIC, BUT THE PRODUCT OF LIVES, INTERWEAVED.
SYLAR'S LIFELINE WAS CRUCIAL, OF COURSE. HE WAS THE BOMB.
I STABBED HIM BEFORE HE EXPLODED, BUT HE REGENERATED.
HE WAS ABLE TO DO THIS BECAUSE HE KILLED CLAIRE BENNET, THE CHEERLEADER.
SO TO SAVE THE WORLD, I NEEDED TO FIND SOMEONE FROM THAT TIME TO SAVE THE CHEERLEADER.
SOMEONE I KNEW WOULD NOT FAIL.
PETER PETRELLI.

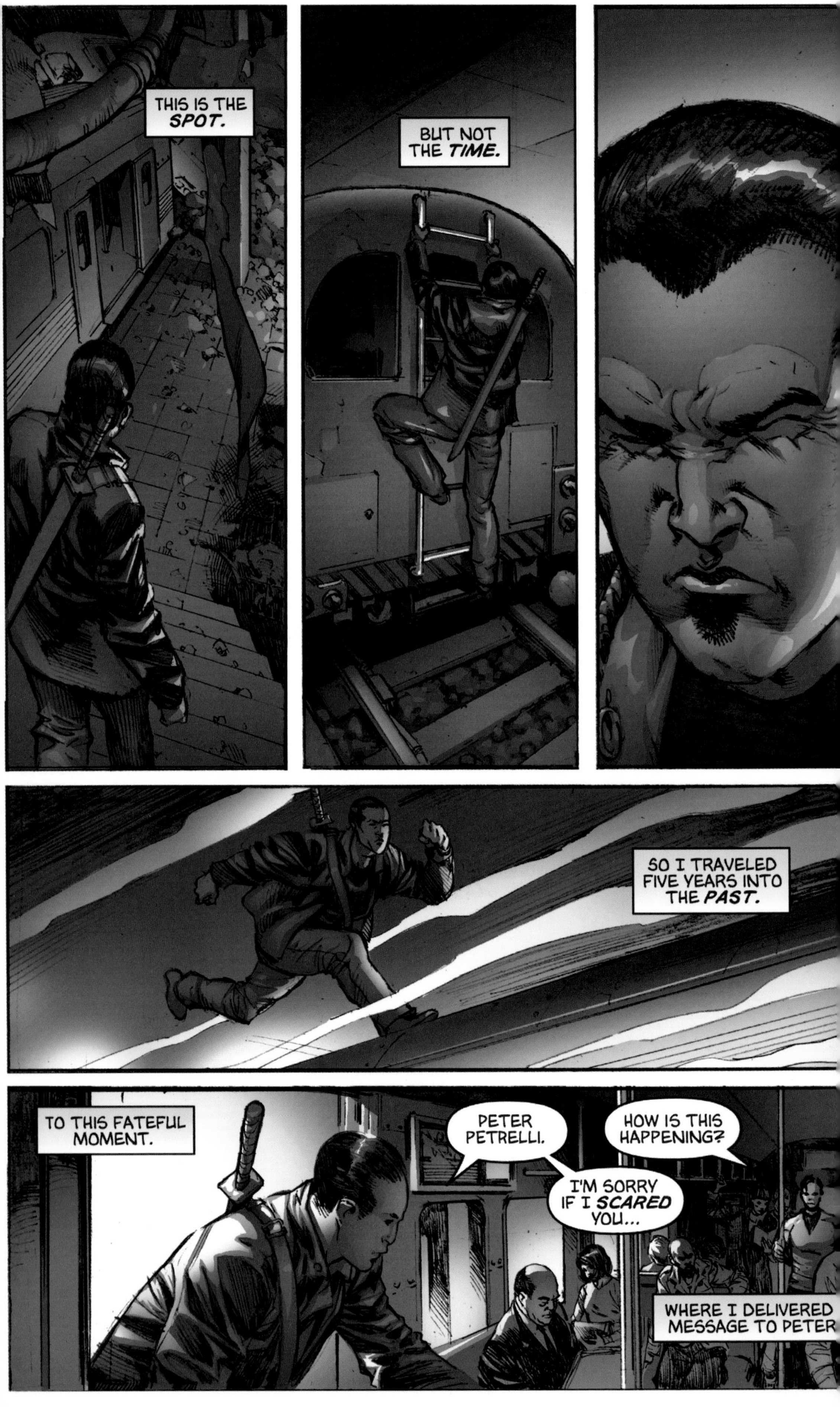

THIS IS THE SPOT.
BUT NOT THE TIME.
SO I TRAVELED FIVE YEARS INTO THE PAST.
TO THIS FATEFUL MOMENT.
PETER PETRELLI.
I'M SORRY IF I SCARED YOU...
HOW IS THIS HAPPENING?
WHERE I DELIVERED MESSAGE TO PETER

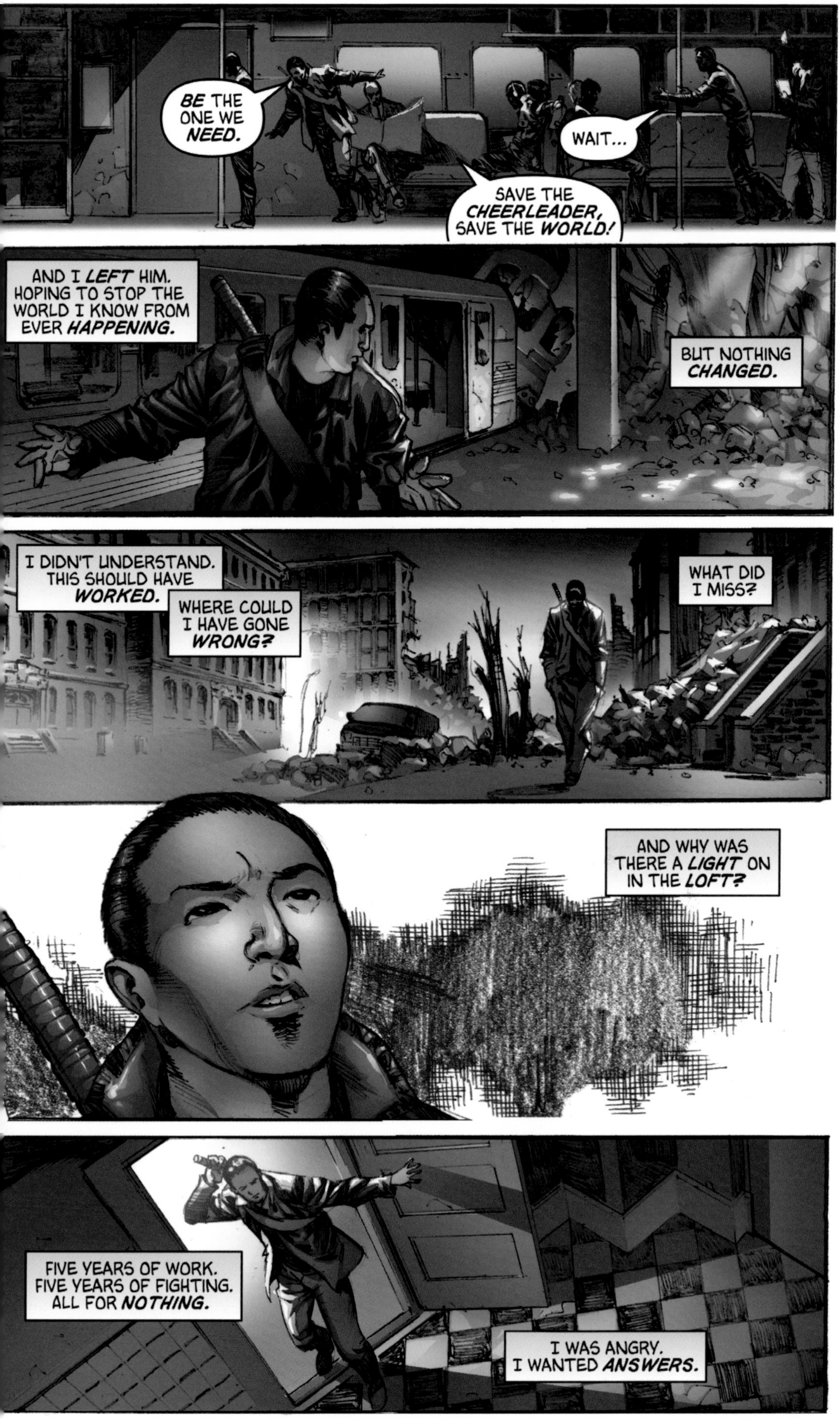
BE THE ONE WE NEED.
WAIT...
SAVE THE CHEERLEADER, SAVE THE WORLD!
AND I LEFT HIM. HOPING TO STOP THE WORLD I KNOW FROM EVER HAPPENING.
BUT NOTHING CHANGED.
I DIDN'T UNDERSTAND. THIS SHOULD HAVE WORKED.
WHERE COULD I HAVE GONE WRONG?
WHAT DID I MISS?
AND WHY WAS THERE A LIGHT ON IN THE LOFT?
FIVE YEARS OF WORK. FIVE YEARS OF FIGHTING. ALL FOR NOTHING.
I WAS ANGRY. I WANTED ANSWERS.

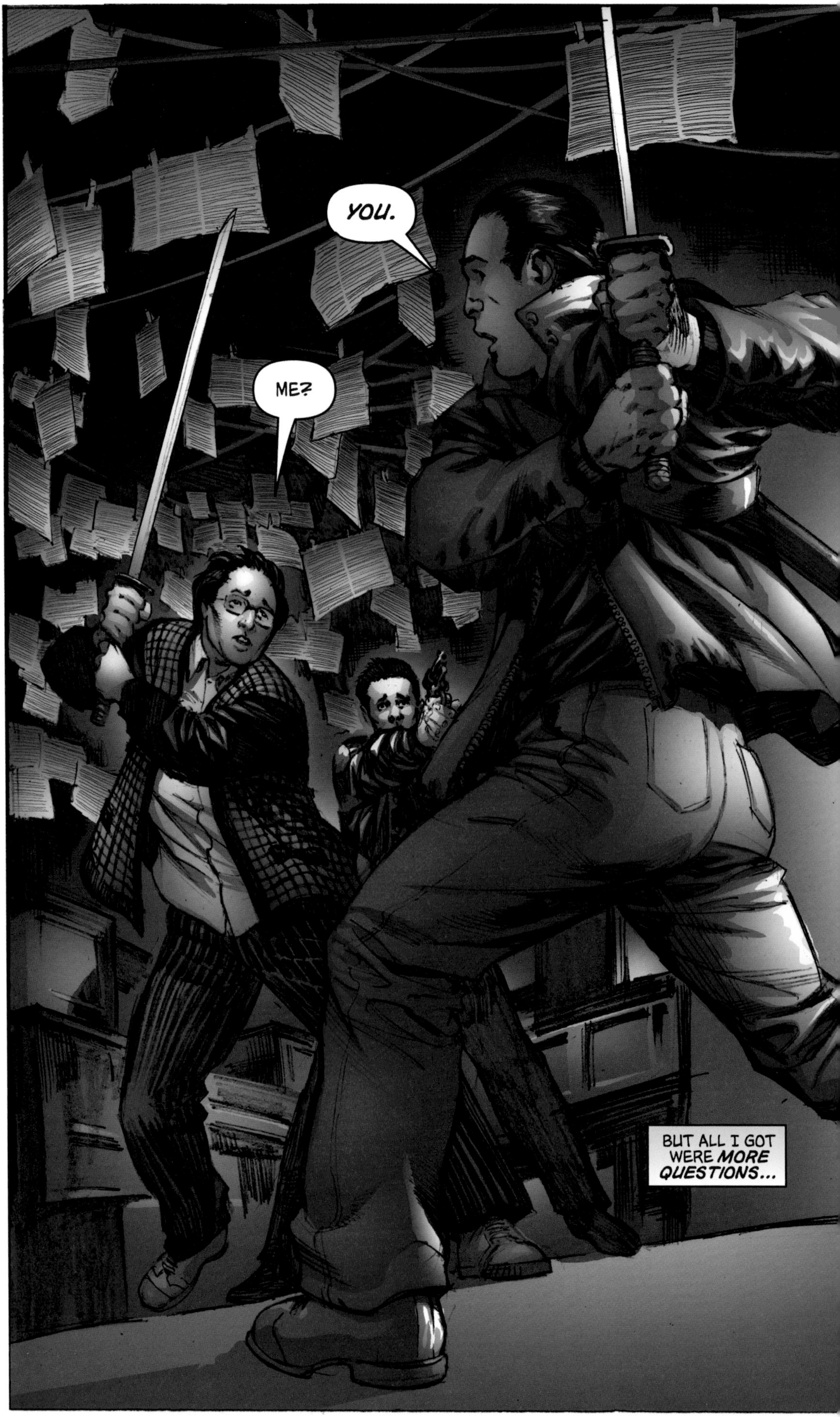
YOU.
ME?
BUT ALL I GOT WERE *MORE QUESTIONS...*

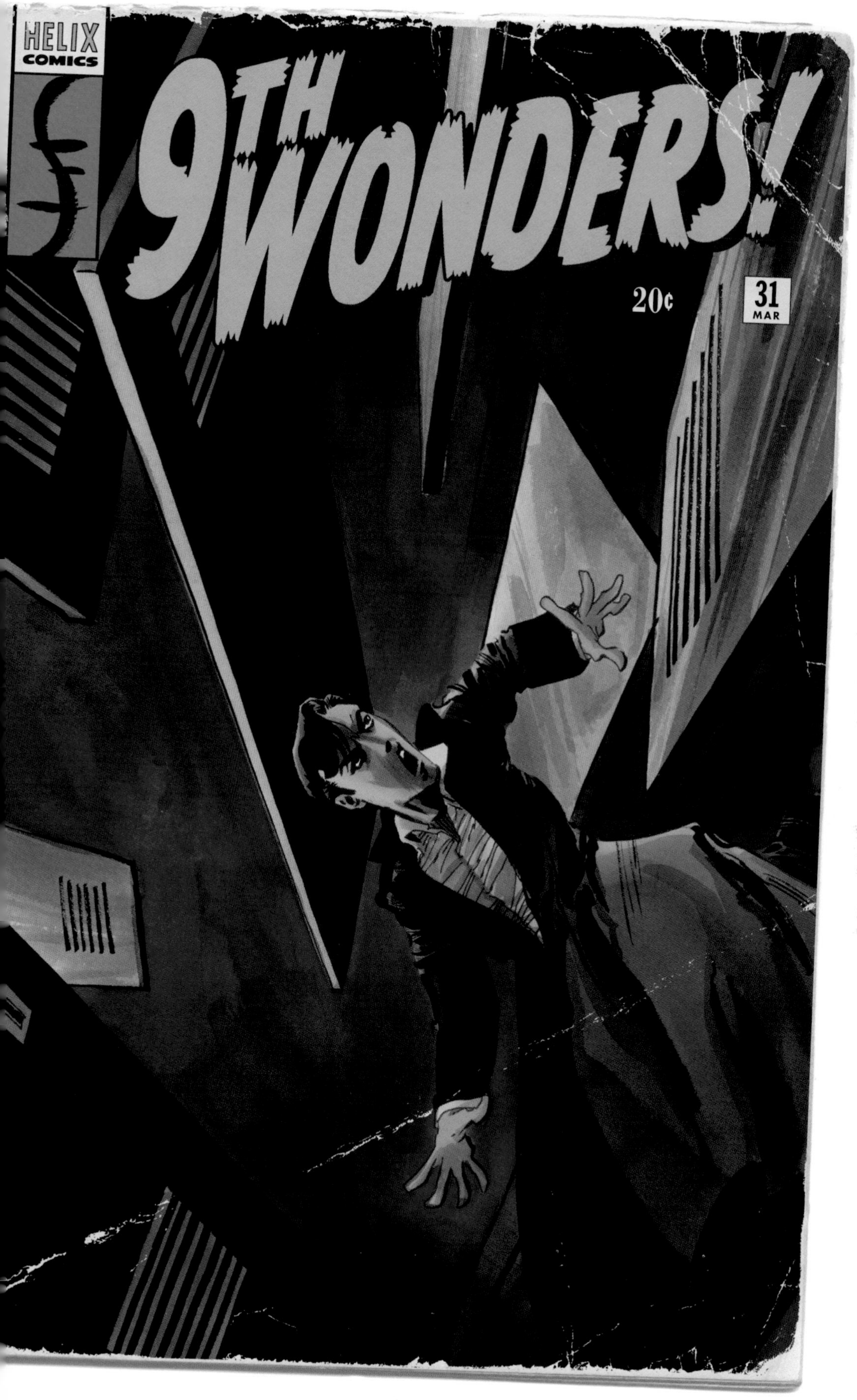
HELIX
COMICS
9TH WONDERS!
20¢
31
MAR

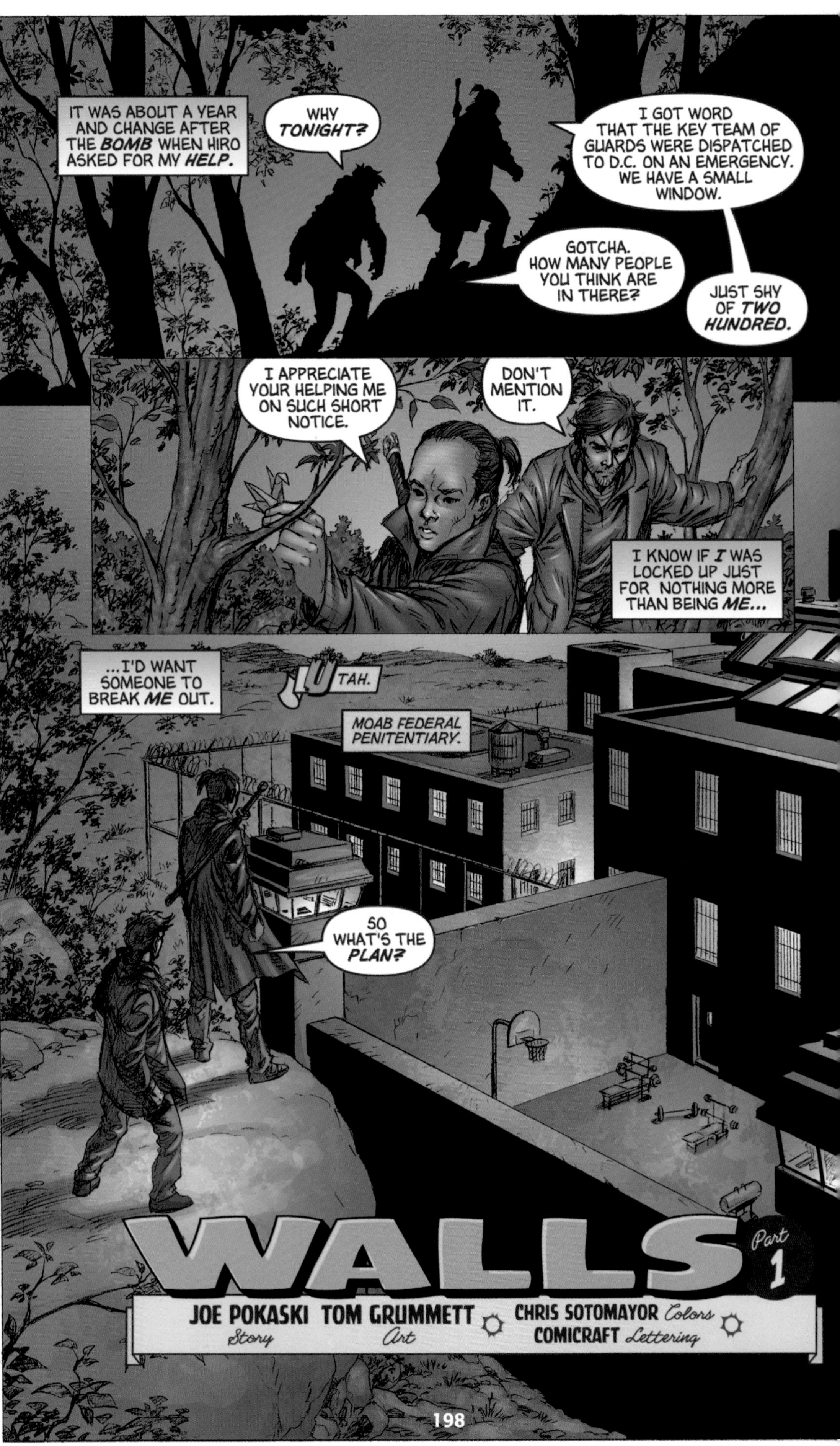
IT WAS ABOUT A YEAR AND CHANGE AFTER THE BOMB WHEN HIRO ASKED FOR MY HELP.
WHY TONIGHT?
I GOT WORD THAT THE KEY TEAM OF GUARDS WERE DISPATCHED TO D.C. ON AN EMERGENCY. WE HAVE A SMALL WINDOW.
GOTCHA. HOW MANY PEOPLE YOU THINK ARE IN THERE?
JUST SHY OF TWO HUNDRED.
I APPRECIATE YOUR HELPING ME ON SUCH SHORT NOTICE.
DON'T MENTION IT.
I KNOW IF I WAS LOCKED UP JUST FOR NOTHING MORE THAN BEING ME...
...I'D WANT SOMEONE TO BREAK ME OUT.
UTAH.
MOAB FEDERAL PENITENTIARY.
SO WHAT'S THE PLAN?
WALLS Part 1
JOE POKASKI Story
TOM GRUMMETT Art
CHRIS SOTOMAYOR Colors
COMICRAFT Lettering

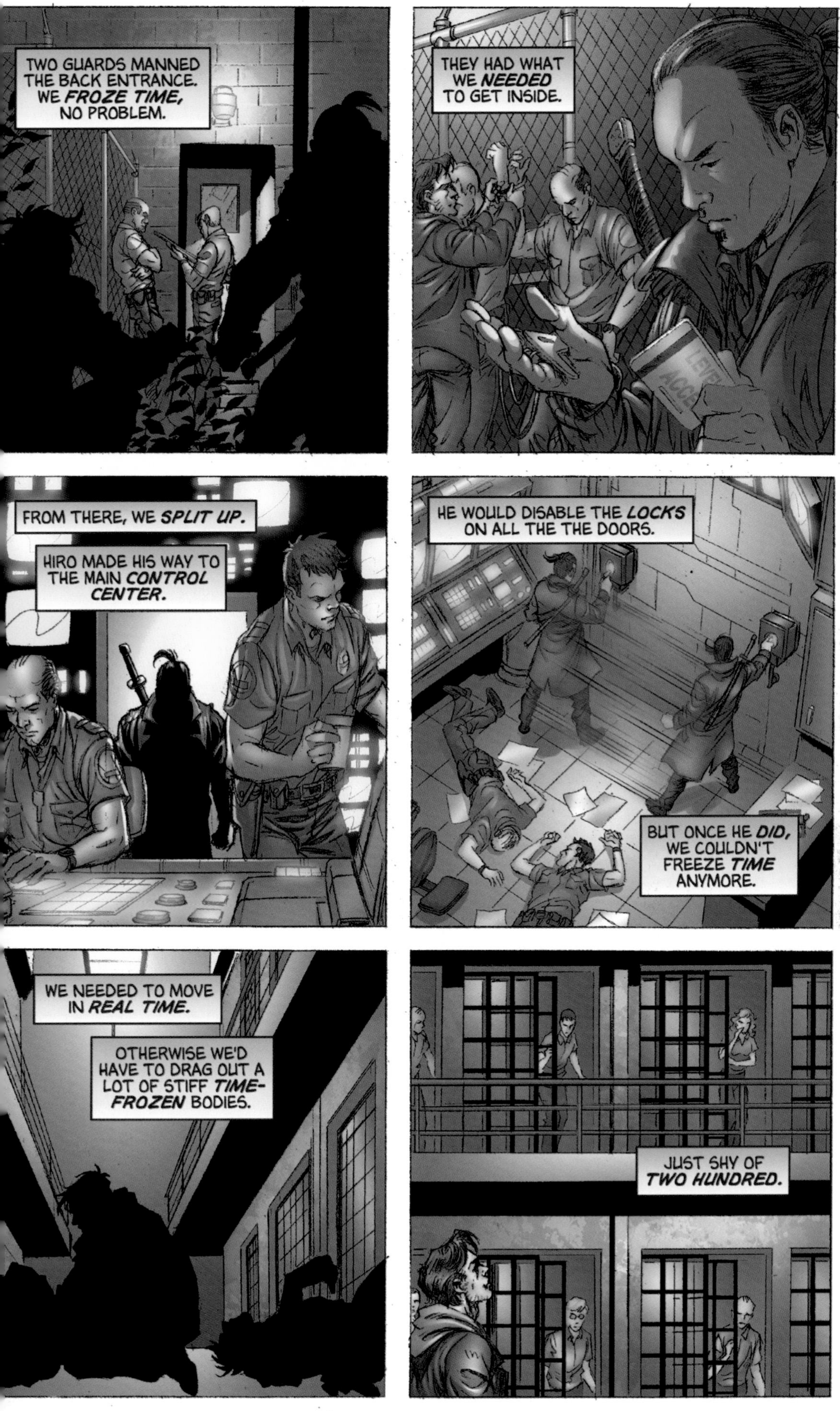
TWO GUARDS MANNED THE BACK ENTRANCE. WE *FROZE TIME,* NO PROBLEM.
THEY HAD WHAT WE *NEEDED* TO GET INSIDE.
FROM THERE, WE *SPLIT UP.*
HIRO MADE HIS WAY TO THE MAIN *CONTROL CENTER.*
HE WOULD DISABLE THE *LOCKS* ON ALL THE THE DOORS.
BUT ONCE HE *DID,* WE COULDN'T FREEZE *TIME* ANYMORE.
WE NEEDED TO MOVE IN *REAL TIME.*
OTHERWISE WE'D HAVE TO DRAG OUT A LOT OF STIFF *TIME-FROZEN* BODIES.
JUST SHY OF *TWO HUNDRED.*

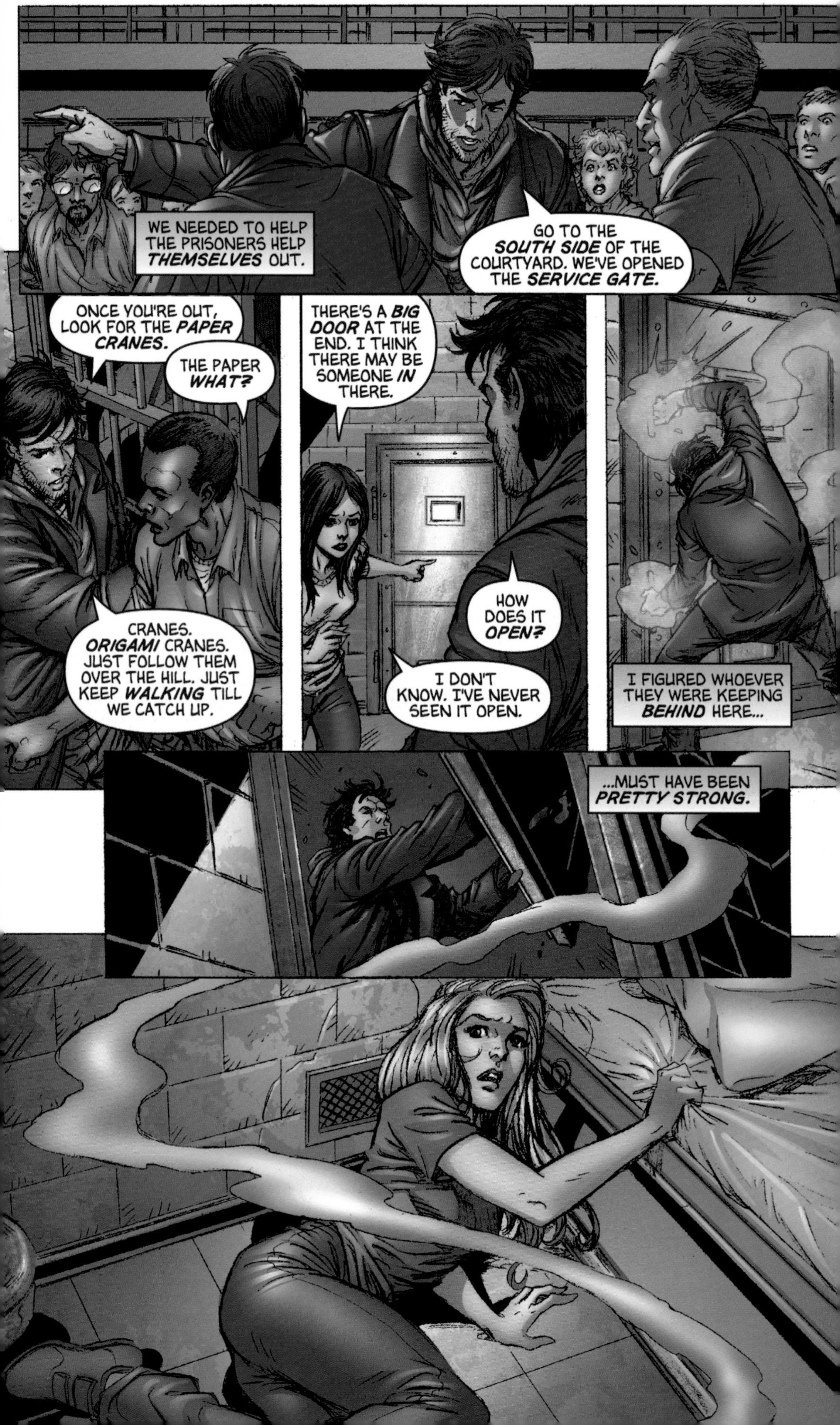
WE NEEDED TO HELP THE PRISONERS HELP THEMSELVES OUT.
GO TO THE SOUTH SIDE OF THE COURTYARD. WE'VE OPENED THE SERVICE GATE.
ONCE YOU'RE OUT, LOOK FOR THE PAPER CRANES.
THE PAPER WHAT?
CRANES. ORIGAMI CRANES. JUST FOLLOW THEM OVER THE HILL. JUST KEEP WALKING TILL WE CATCH UP.
THERE'S A BIG DOOR AT THE END. I THINK THERE MAY BE SOMEONE IN THERE.
HOW DOES IT OPEN?
I DON'T KNOW. I'VE NEVER SEEN IT OPEN.
I FIGURED WHOEVER THEY WERE KEEPING BEHIND HERE...
...MUST HAVE BEEN PRETTY STRONG.

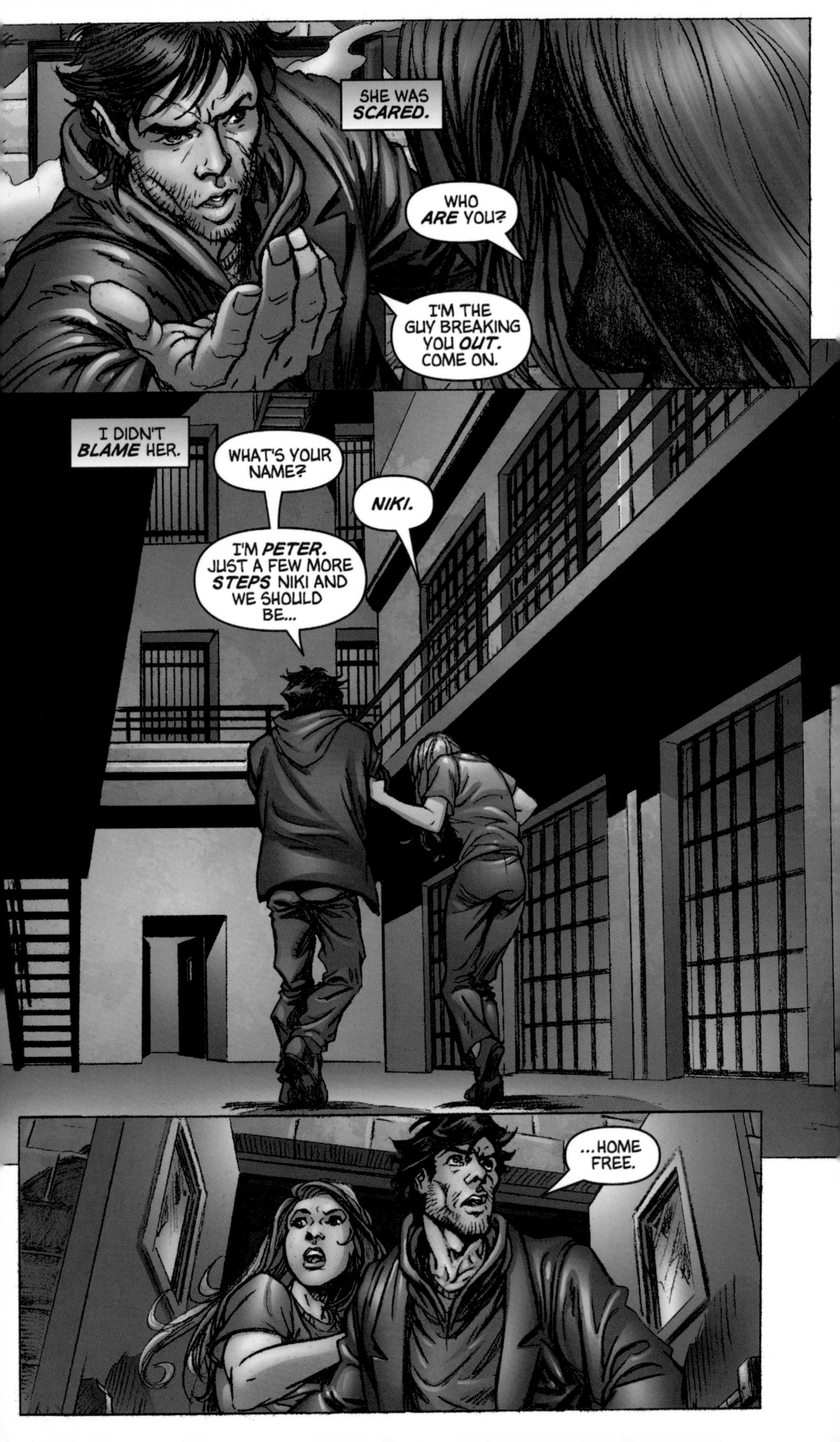
SHE WAS SCARED.
WHO ARE YOU?
I'M THE GUY BREAKING YOU OUT. COME ON.
I DIDN'T BLAME HER.
WHAT'S YOUR NAME?
NIKI.
I'M PETER. JUST A FEW MORE STEPS NIKI AND WE SHOULD BE...
...HOME FREE.

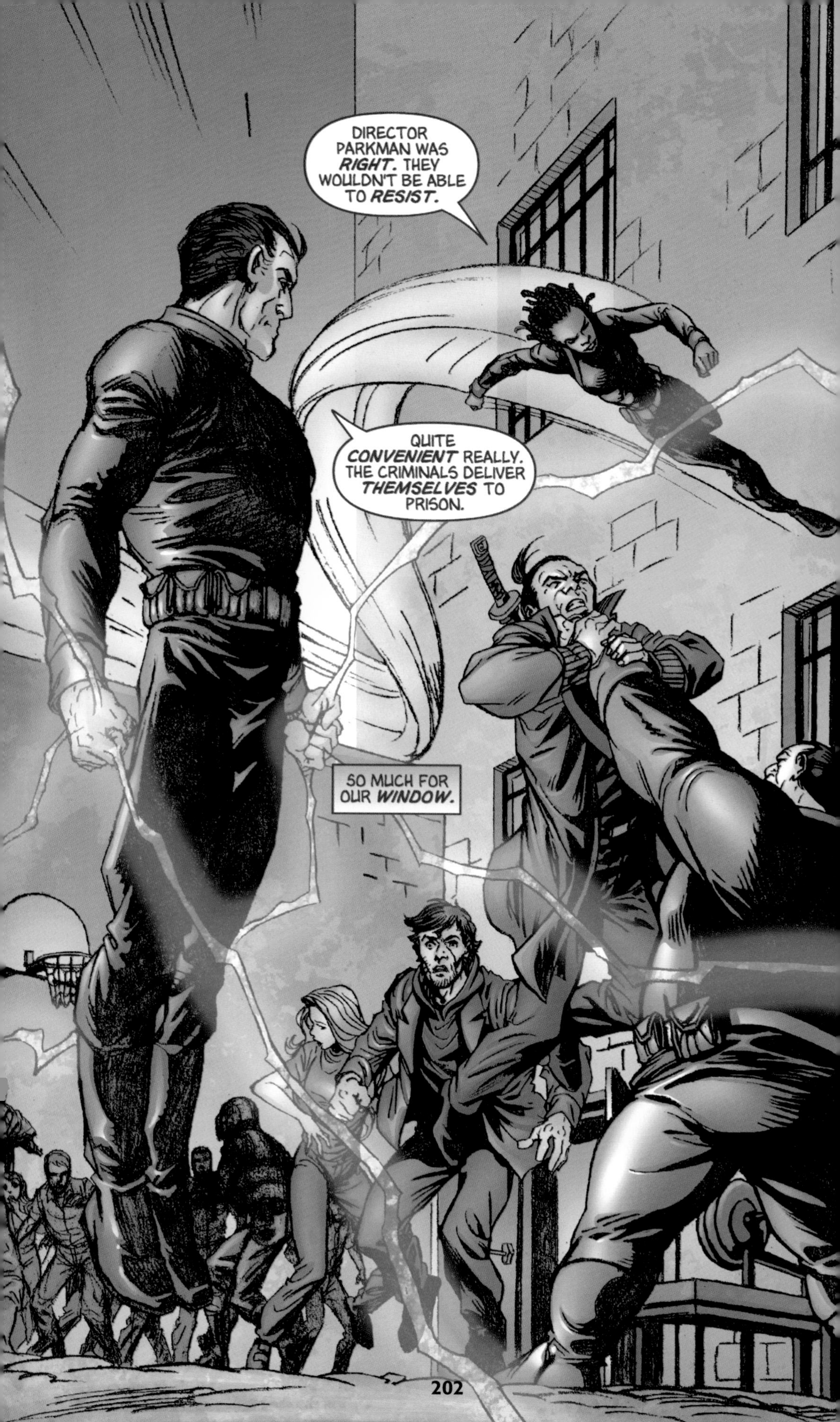
DIRECTOR PARKMAN WAS RIGHT. THEY WOULDN'T BE ABLE TO RESIST.
QUITE CONVENIENT REALLY. THE CRIMINALS DELIVER THEMSELVES TO PRISON.
SO MUCH FOR OUR WINDOW.

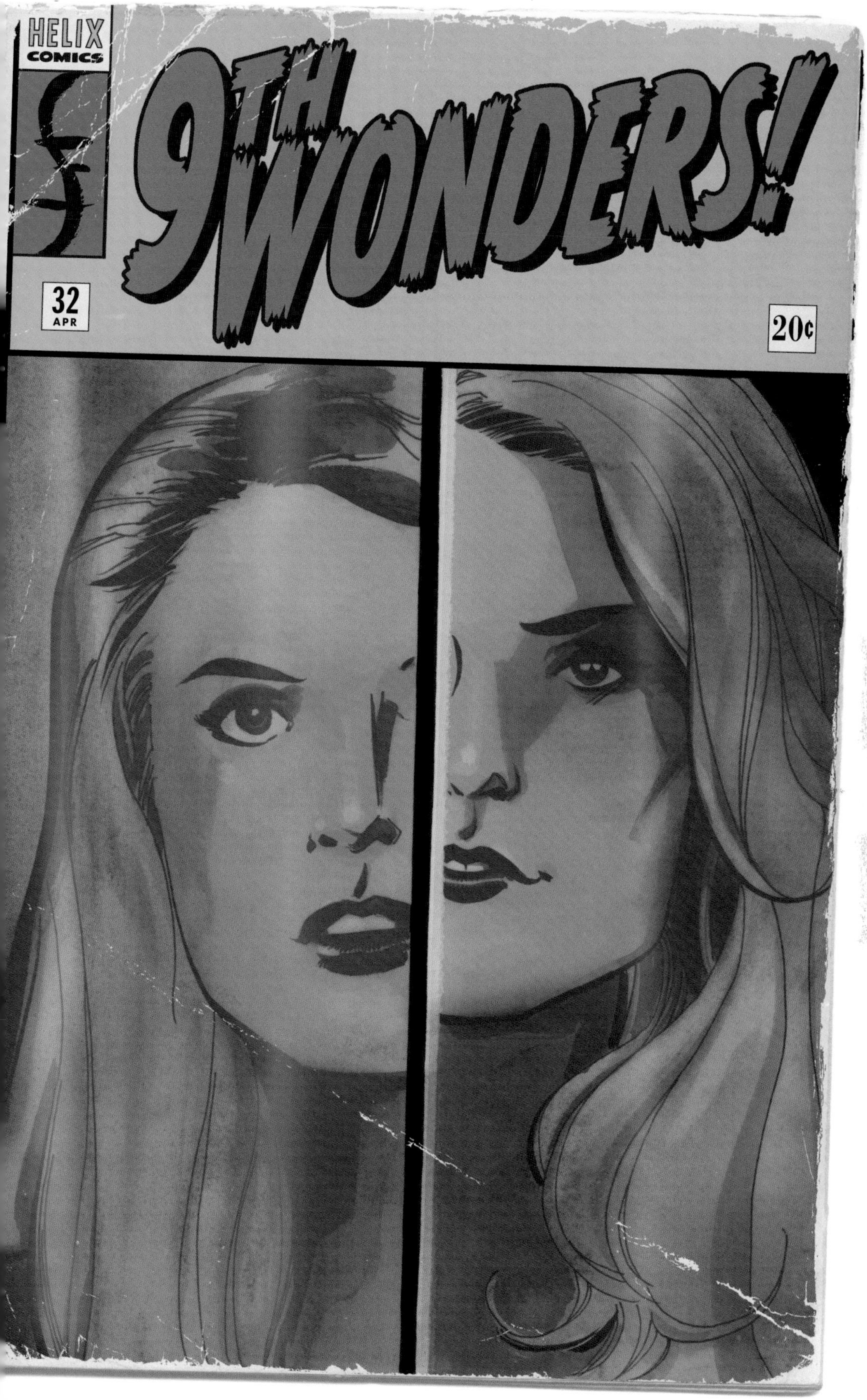
HELIX
COMICS
9TH WONDERS!
32
APR
20¢

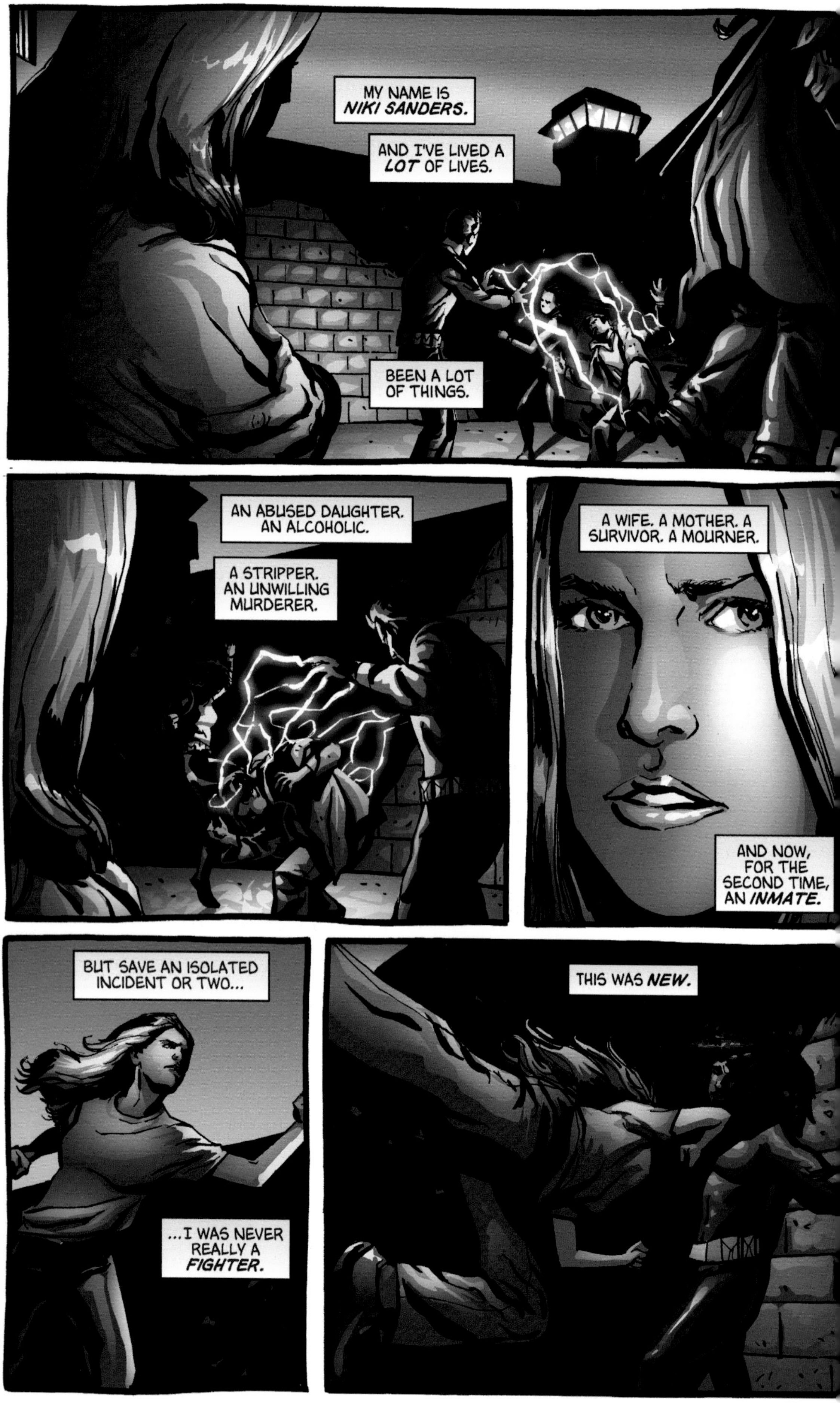

MY NAME IS NIKI SANDERS.
AND I'VE LIVED A LOT OF LIVES.
BEEN A LOT OF THINGS.
AN ABUSED DAUGHTER. AN ALCOHOLIC.
A STRIPPER. AN UNWILLING MURDERER.
A WIFE. A MOTHER. A SURVIVOR. A MOURNER.
AND NOW, FOR THE SECOND TIME, AN INMATE.
BUT SAVE AN ISOLATED INCIDENT OR TWO...
...I WAS NEVER REALLY A FIGHTER.
THIS WAS NEW.

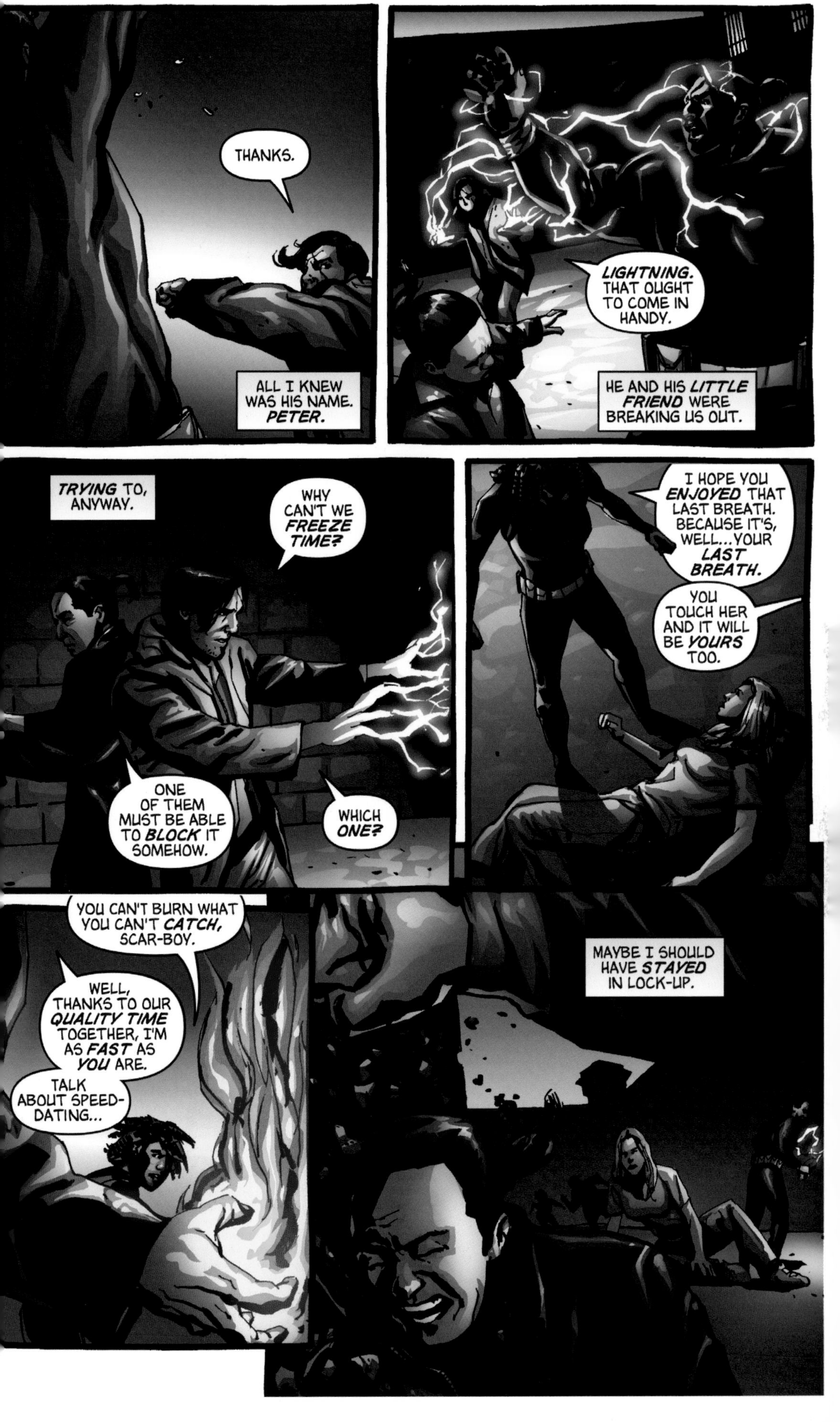
THANKS.
ALL I KNEW WAS HIS NAME. PETER.
LIGHTNING. THAT OUGHT TO COME IN HANDY.
HE AND HIS LITTLE FRIEND WERE BREAKING US OUT.
TRYING TO, ANYWAY.
WHY CAN'T WE FREEZE TIME?
ONE OF THEM MUST BE ABLE TO BLOCK IT SOMEHOW.
WHICH ONE?
I HOPE YOU ENJOYED THAT LAST BREATH. BECAUSE IT'S, WELL...YOUR LAST BREATH.
YOU TOUCH HER AND IT WILL BE YOURS TOO.
YOU CAN'T BURN WHAT YOU CAN'T CATCH, SCAR-BOY.
WELL, THANKS TO OUR QUALITY TIME TOGETHER, I'M AS FAST AS YOU ARE.
TALK ABOUT SPEED-DATING...
MAYBE I SHOULD HAVE STAYED IN LOCK-UP.

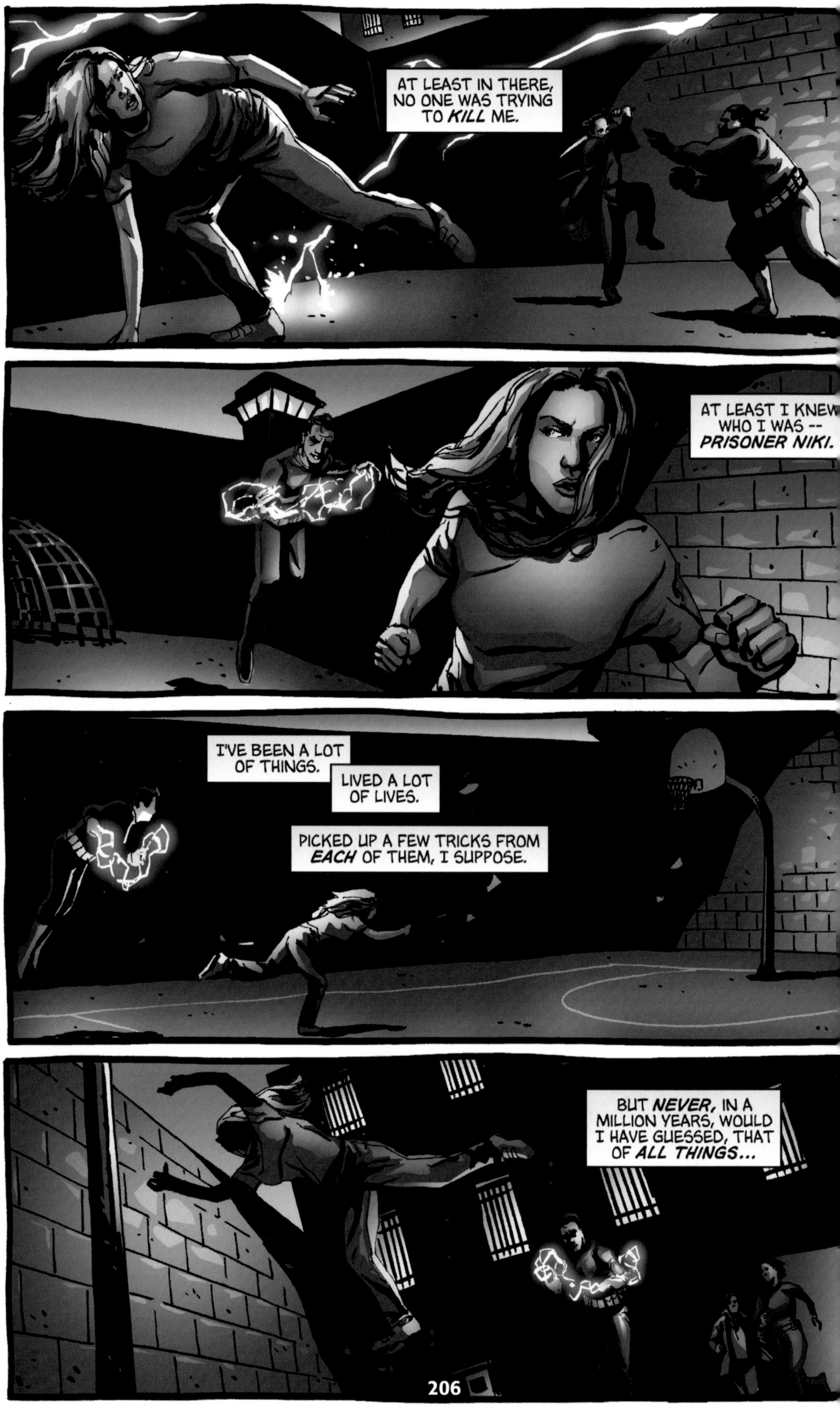
AT LEAST IN THERE, NO ONE WAS TRYING TO KILL ME.
AT LEAST I KNEW WHO I WAS -- PRISONER NIKI.
I'VE BEEN A LOT OF THINGS.
LIVED A LOT OF LIVES.
PICKED UP A FEW TRICKS FROM EACH OF THEM, I SUPPOSE.
BUT NEVER, IN A MILLION YEARS, WOULD I HAVE GUESSED, THAT OF ALL THINGS...

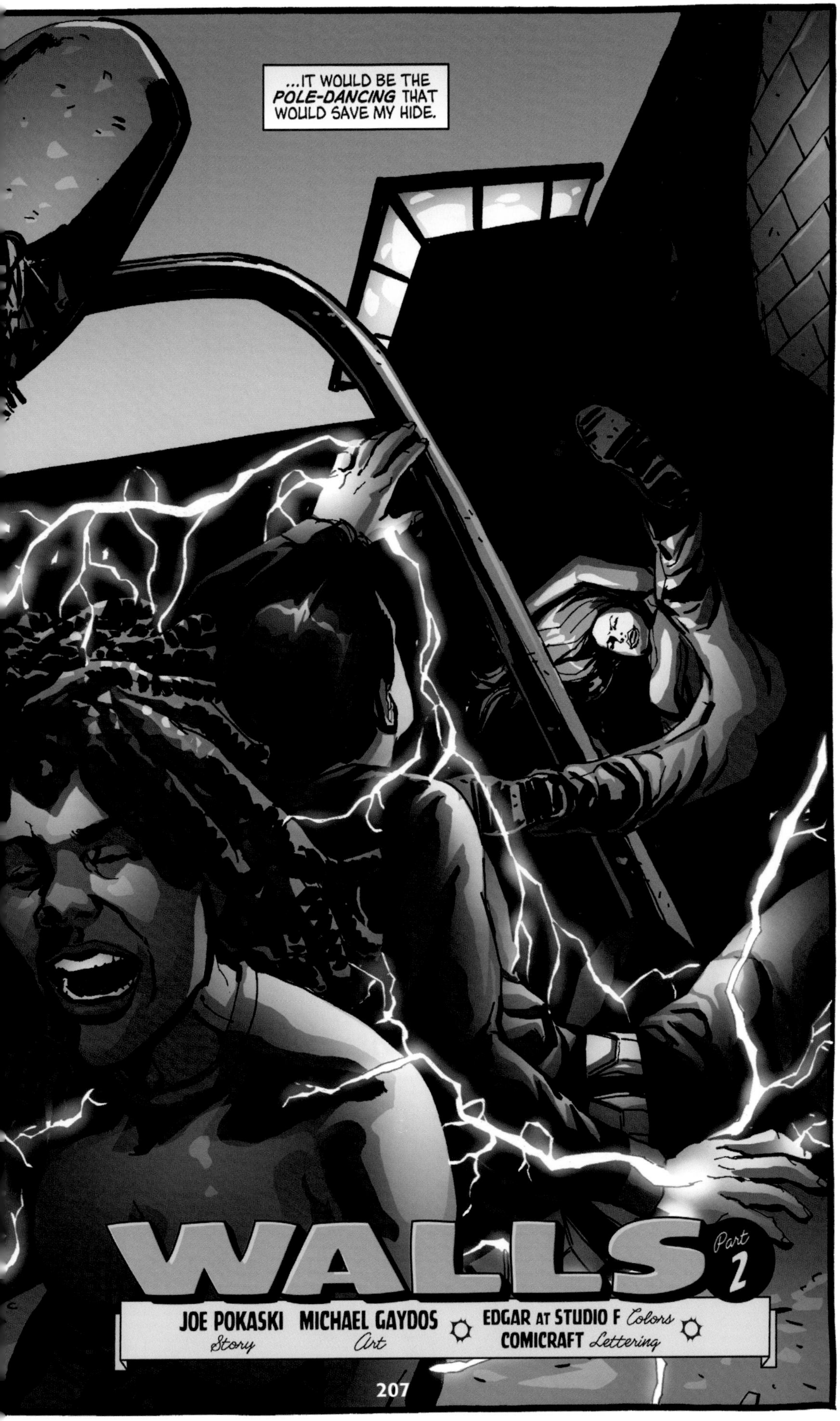
...IT WOULD BE THE *POLE-DANCING* THAT WOULD SAVE MY HIDE.
WALLS Part 2
JOE POKASKI Story
MICHAEL GAYDOS Art
EDGAR AT STUDIO F Colors
COMICRAFT Lettering

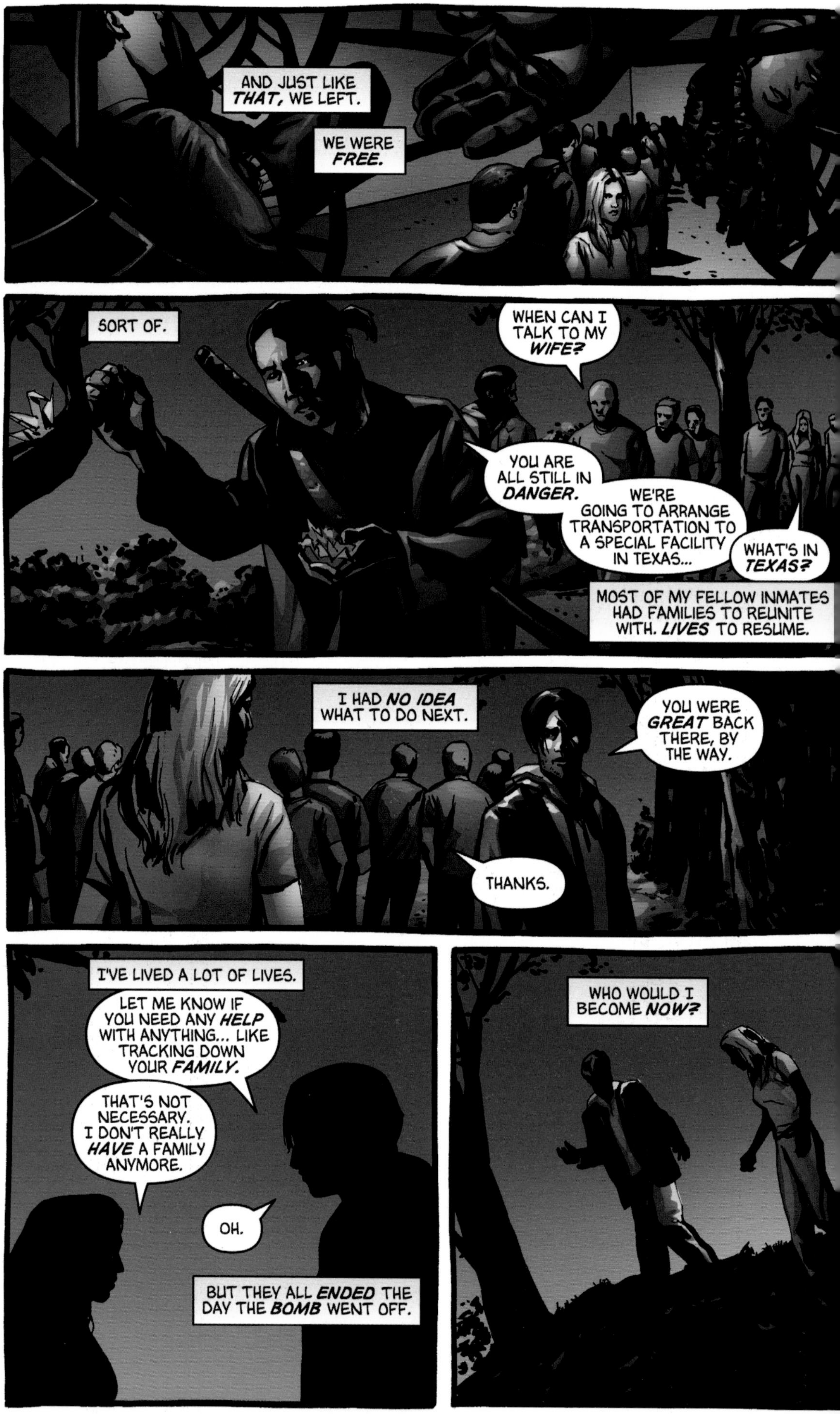
AND JUST LIKE THAT, WE LEFT.
WE WERE FREE.
SORT OF.
WHEN CAN I TALK TO MY WIFE?
YOU ARE ALL STILL IN DANGER.
WE'RE GOING TO ARRANGE TRANSPORTATION TO A SPECIAL FACILITY IN TEXAS...
WHAT'S IN TEXAS?
MOST OF MY FELLOW INMATES HAD FAMILIES TO REUNITE WITH. LIVES TO RESUME.
I HAD NO IDEA WHAT TO DO NEXT.
YOU WERE GREAT BACK THERE, BY THE WAY.
THANKS.
I'VE LIVED A LOT OF LIVES.
LET ME KNOW IF YOU NEED ANY HELP WITH ANYTHING... LIKE TRACKING DOWN YOUR FAMILY.
THAT'S NOT NECESSARY. I DON'T REALLY HAVE A FAMILY ANYMORE.
OH.
BUT THEY ALL ENDED THE DAY THE BOMB WENT OFF.
WHO WOULD I BECOME NOW?

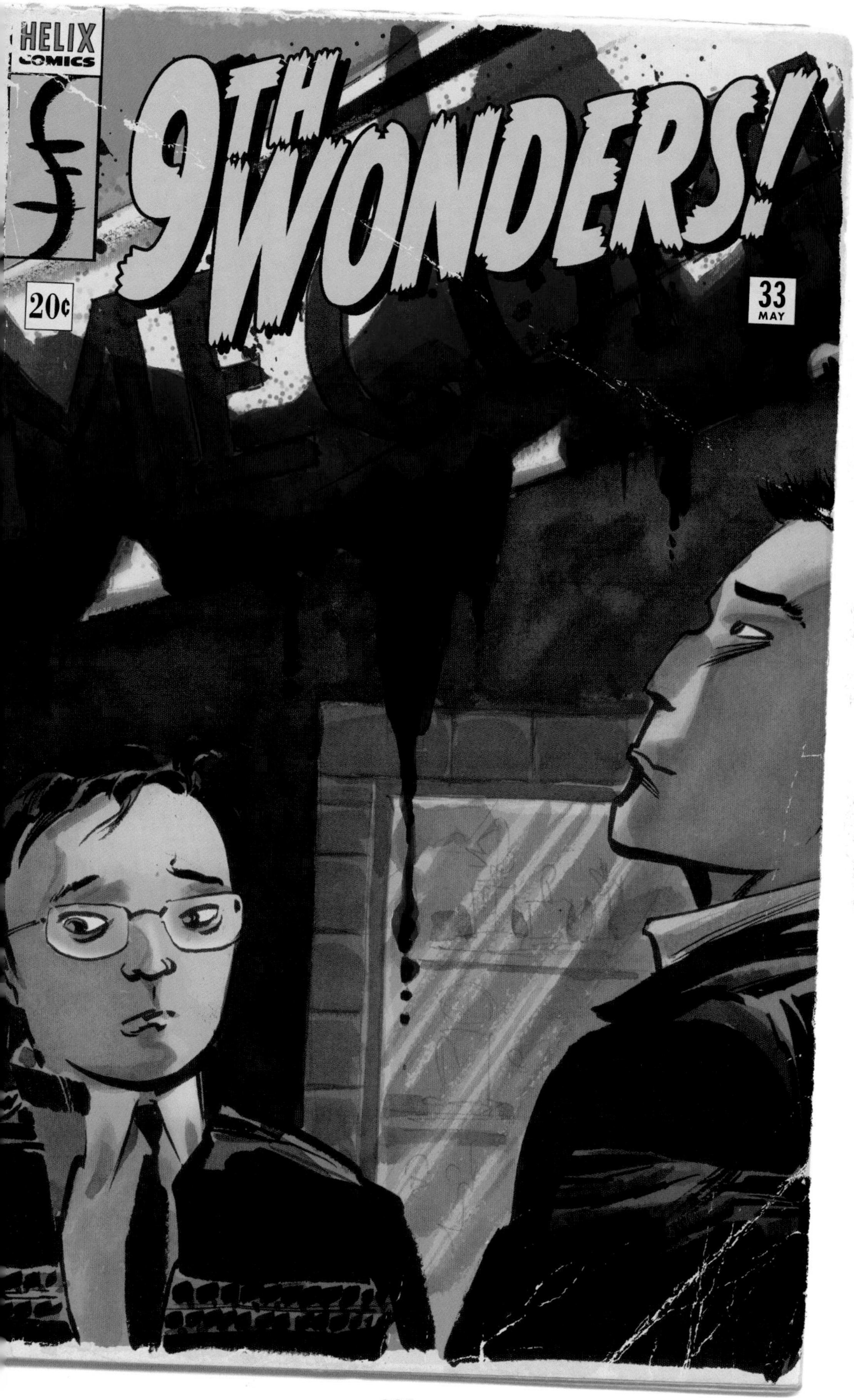
HELIX
COMICS
9TH WONDERS!
20¢
33
MAY

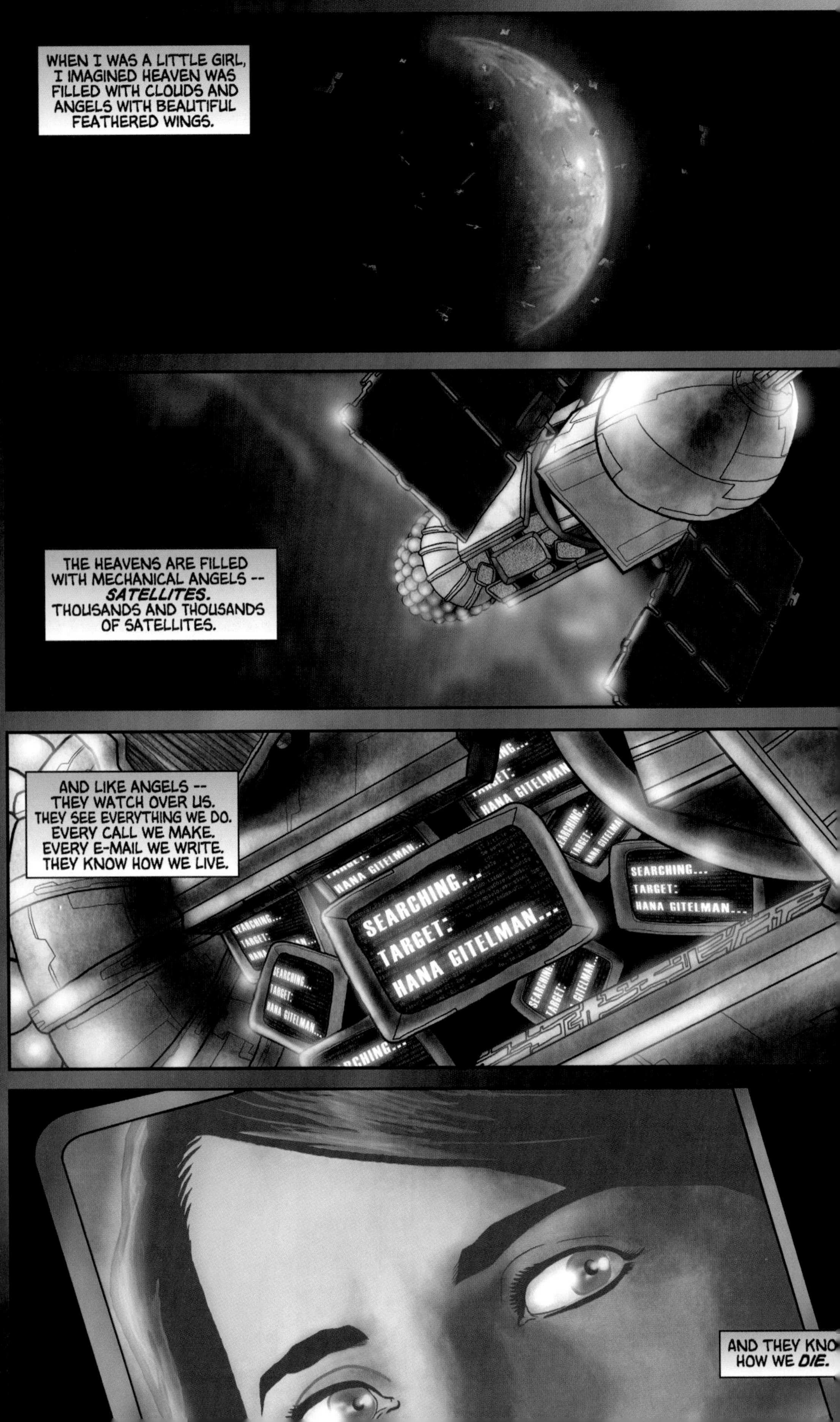
WHEN I WAS A LITTLE GIRL, I IMAGINED HEAVEN WAS FILLED WITH CLOUDS AND ANGELS WITH BEAUTIFUL FEATHERED WINGS.
THE HEAVENS ARE FILLED WITH MECHANICAL ANGELS -- SATELLITES. THOUSANDS AND THOUSANDS OF SATELLITES.
AND LIKE ANGELS -- THEY WATCH OVER US. THEY SEE EVERYTHING WE DO. EVERY CALL WE MAKE. EVERY E-MAIL WE WRITE. THEY KNOW HOW WE LIVE.
SEARCHING... TARGET: HANA GITELMAN...
SEARCHING... TARGET: HANA GITELMAN...
AND THEY KNO HOW WE DIE.

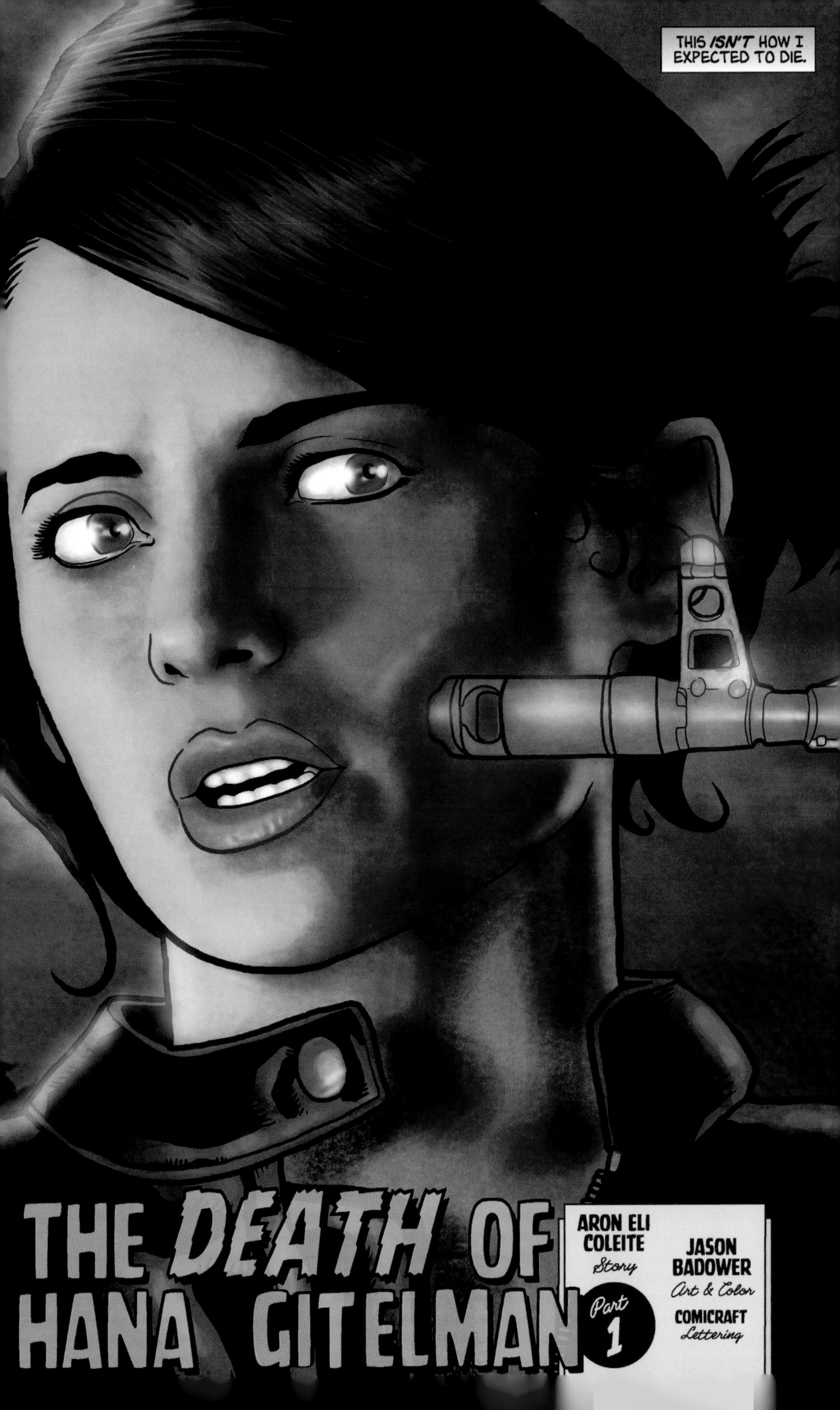

THIS ISN'T HOW I EXPECTED TO DIE.
THE DEATH OF HANA GITELMAN
Part 1
ARON ELI COLEITE Story
JASON BADOWER Art & Color
COMICRAFT Lettering

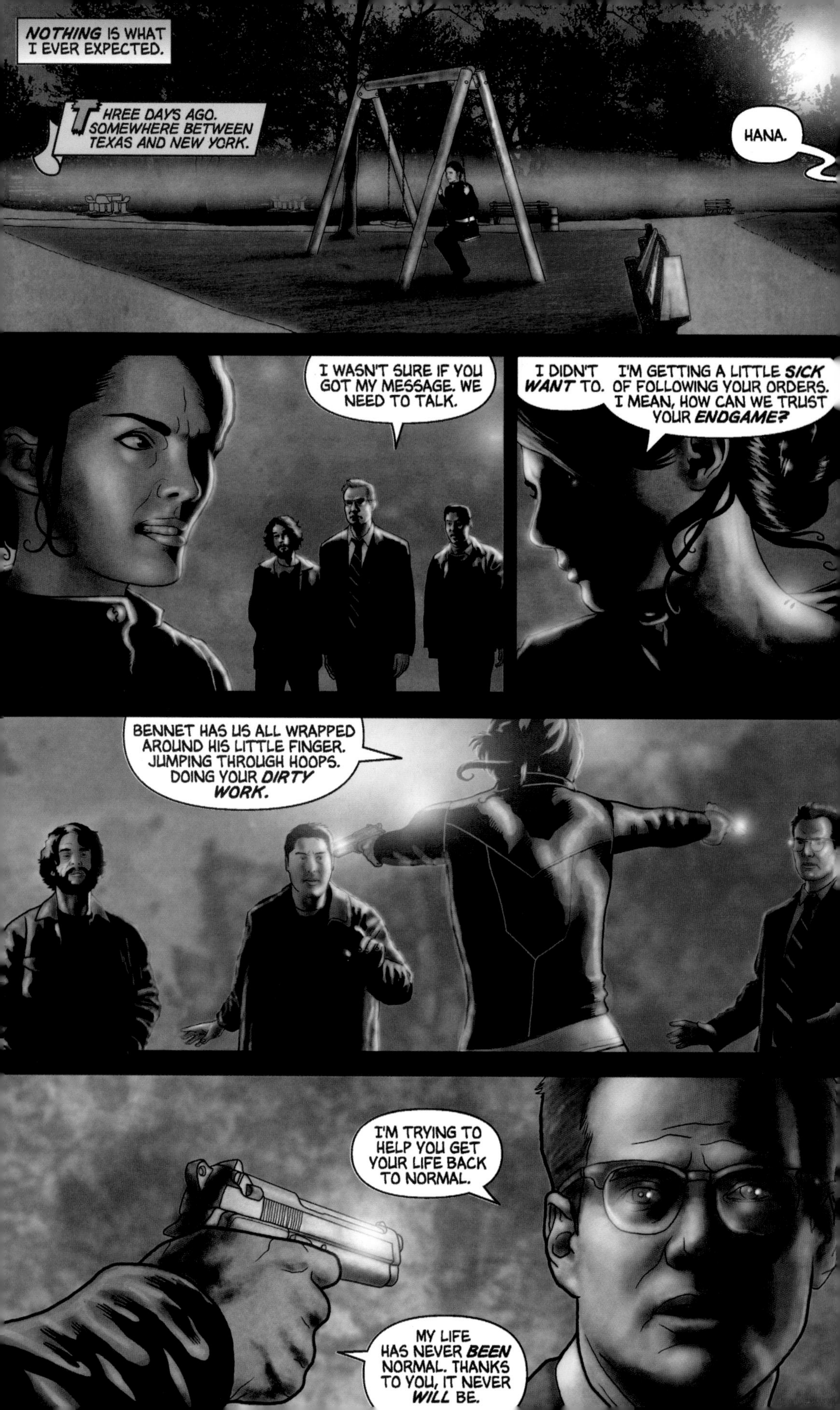
NOTHING IS WHAT I EVER EXPECTED.
THREE DAYS AGO. SOMEWHERE BETWEEN TEXAS AND NEW YORK.
HANA.
I WASN'T SURE IF YOU GOT MY MESSAGE. WE NEED TO TALK.
I DIDN'T WANT TO.
I'M GETTING A LITTLE SICK OF FOLLOWING YOUR ORDERS. I MEAN, HOW CAN WE TRUST YOUR ENDGAME?
BENNET HAS US ALL WRAPPED AROUND HIS LITTLE FINGER. JUMPING THROUGH HOOPS. DOING YOUR DIRTY WORK.
I'M TRYING TO HELP YOU GET YOUR LIFE BACK TO NORMAL.
MY LIFE HAS NEVER BEEN NORMAL. THANKS TO YOU, IT NEVER WILL BE.

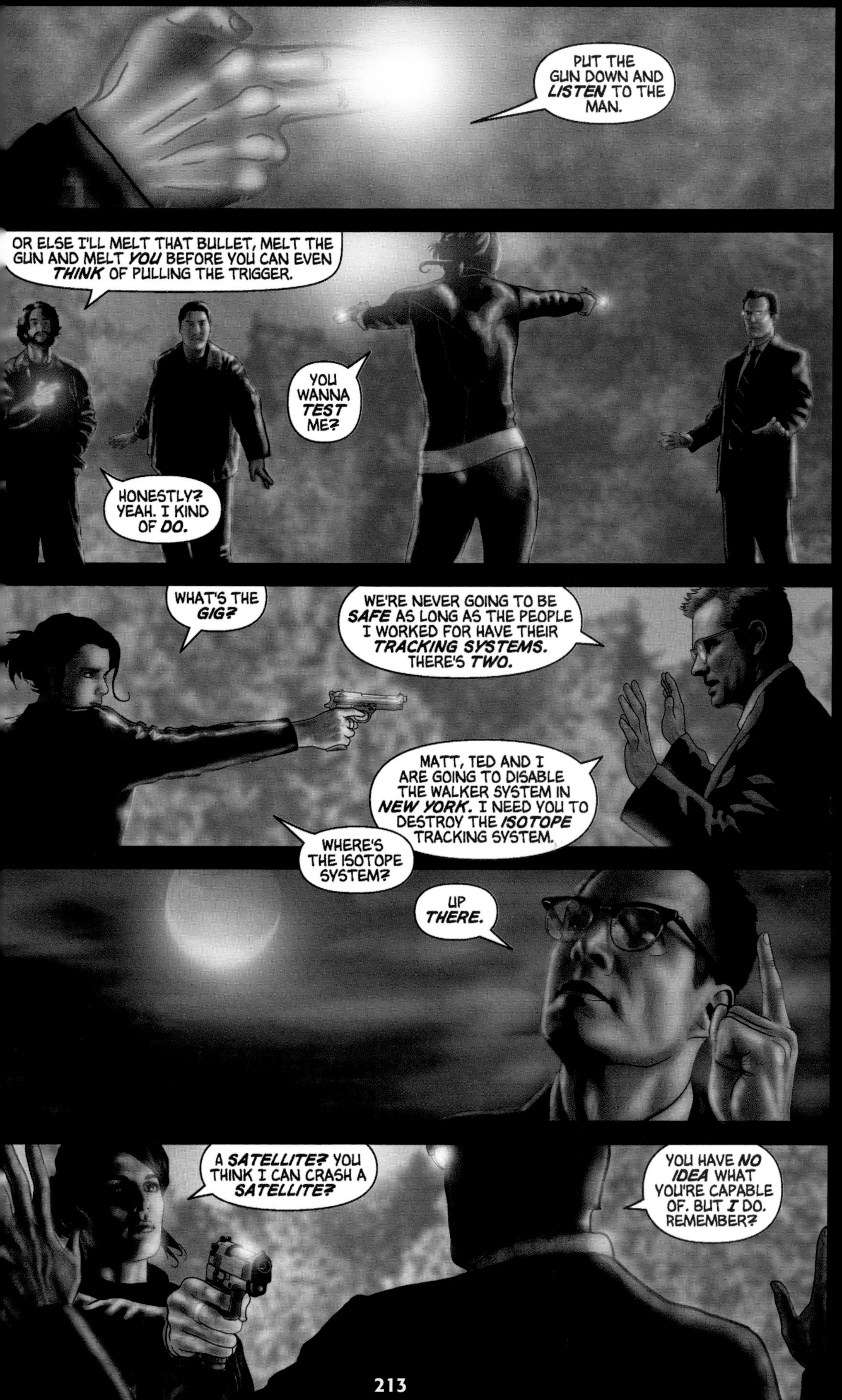
PUT THE GUN DOWN AND LISTEN TO THE MAN.
OR ELSE I'LL MELT THAT BULLET, MELT THE GUN AND MELT YOU BEFORE YOU CAN EVEN THINK OF PULLING THE TRIGGER.
YOU WANNA TEST ME?
HONESTLY? YEAH. I KIND OF DO.
WHAT'S THE GIG?
WE'RE NEVER GOING TO BE SAFE AS LONG AS THE PEOPLE I WORKED FOR HAVE THEIR TRACKING SYSTEMS. THERE'S TWO.
MATT, TED AND I ARE GOING TO DISABLE THE WALKER SYSTEM IN NEW YORK. I NEED YOU TO DESTROY THE ISOTOPE TRACKING SYSTEM.
WHERE'S THE ISOTOPE SYSTEM?
UP THERE.
A SATELLITE? YOU THINK I CAN CRASH A SATELLITE?
YOU HAVE NO IDEA WHAT YOU'RE CAPABLE OF. BUT I DO. REMEMBER?

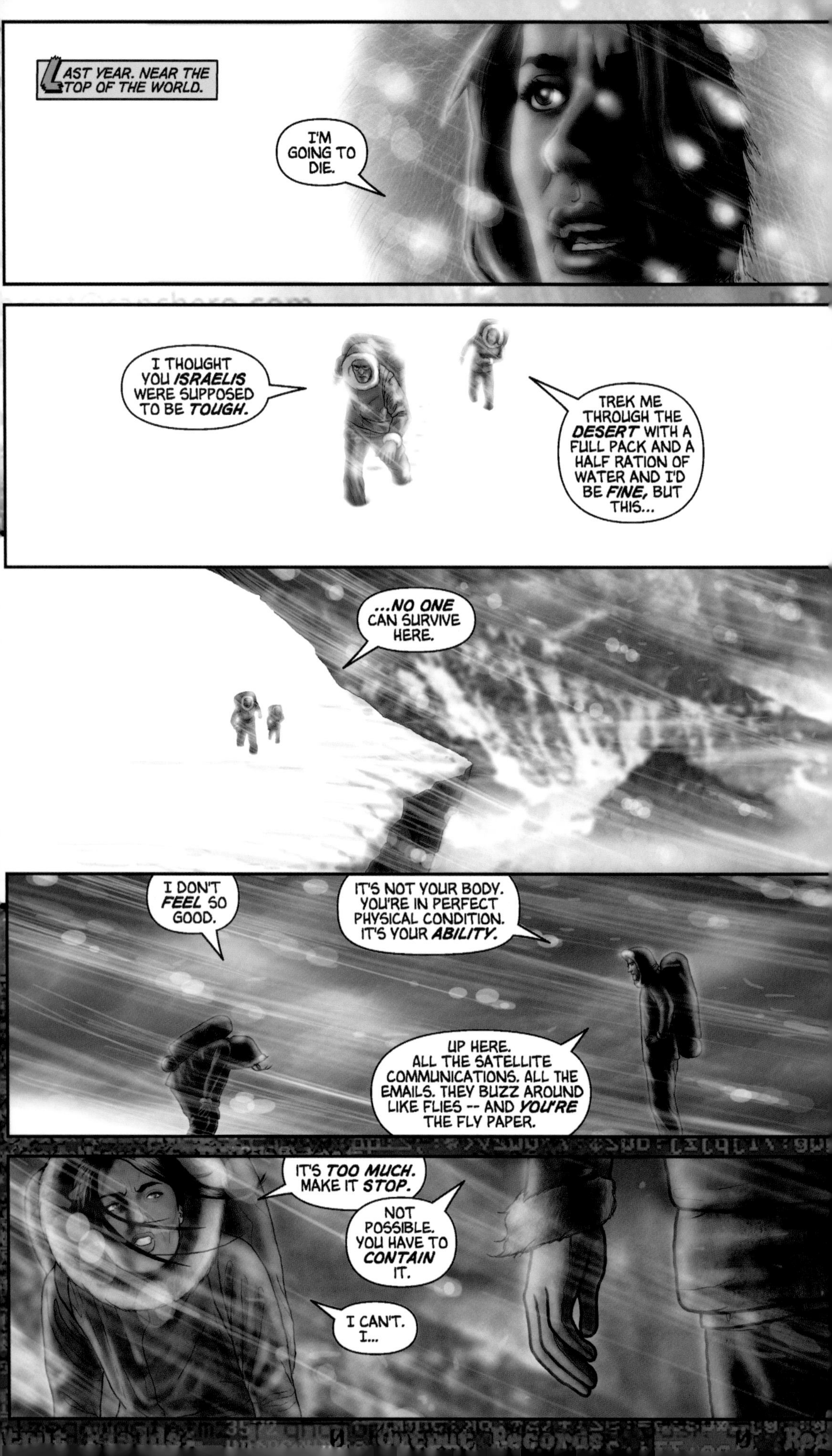
LAST YEAR. NEAR THE TOP OF THE WORLD.
I'M GOING TO DIE.
I THOUGHT YOU ISRAELIS WERE SUPPOSED TO BE TOUGH.
TREK ME THROUGH THE DESERT WITH A FULL PACK AND A HALF RATION OF WATER AND I'D BE FINE, BUT THIS...
...NO ONE CAN SURVIVE HERE.
I DON'T FEEL SO GOOD.
IT'S NOT YOUR BODY. YOU'RE IN PERFECT PHYSICAL CONDITION. IT'S YOUR ABILITY.
UP HERE. ALL THE SATELLITE COMMUNICATIONS. ALL THE EMAILS. THEY BUZZ AROUND LIKE FLIES -- AND YOU'RE THE FLY PAPER.
IT'S TOO MUCH. MAKE IT STOP.
NOT POSSIBLE. YOU HAVE TO CONTAIN IT.
I CAN'T. I...

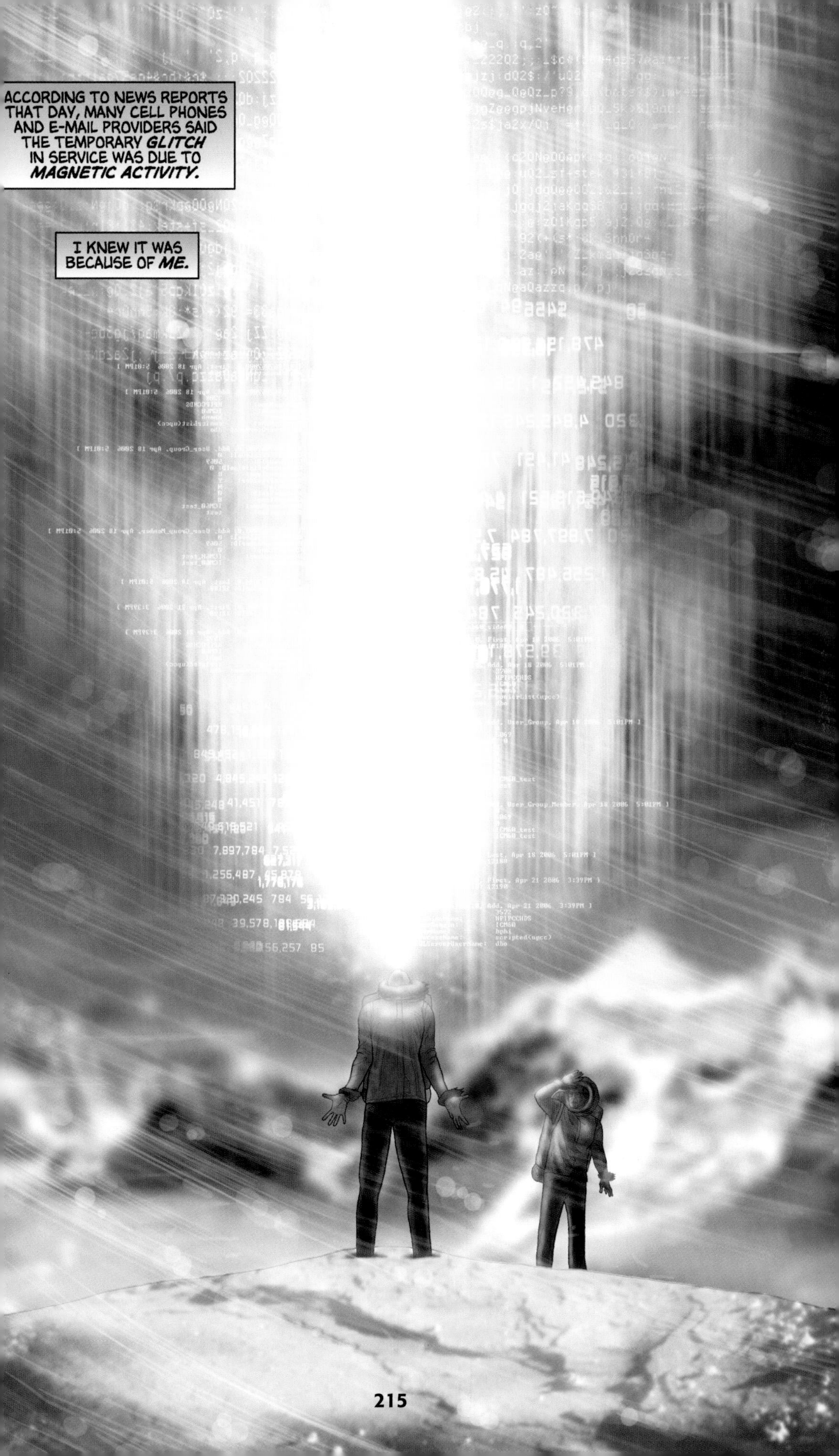
ACCORDING TO NEWS REPORTS THAT DAY, MANY CELL PHONES AND E-MAIL PROVIDERS SAID THE TEMPORARY *GLITCH* IN SERVICE WAS DUE TO ***MAGNETIC ACTIVITY.***
I KNEW IT WAS BECAUSE OF ***ME.***

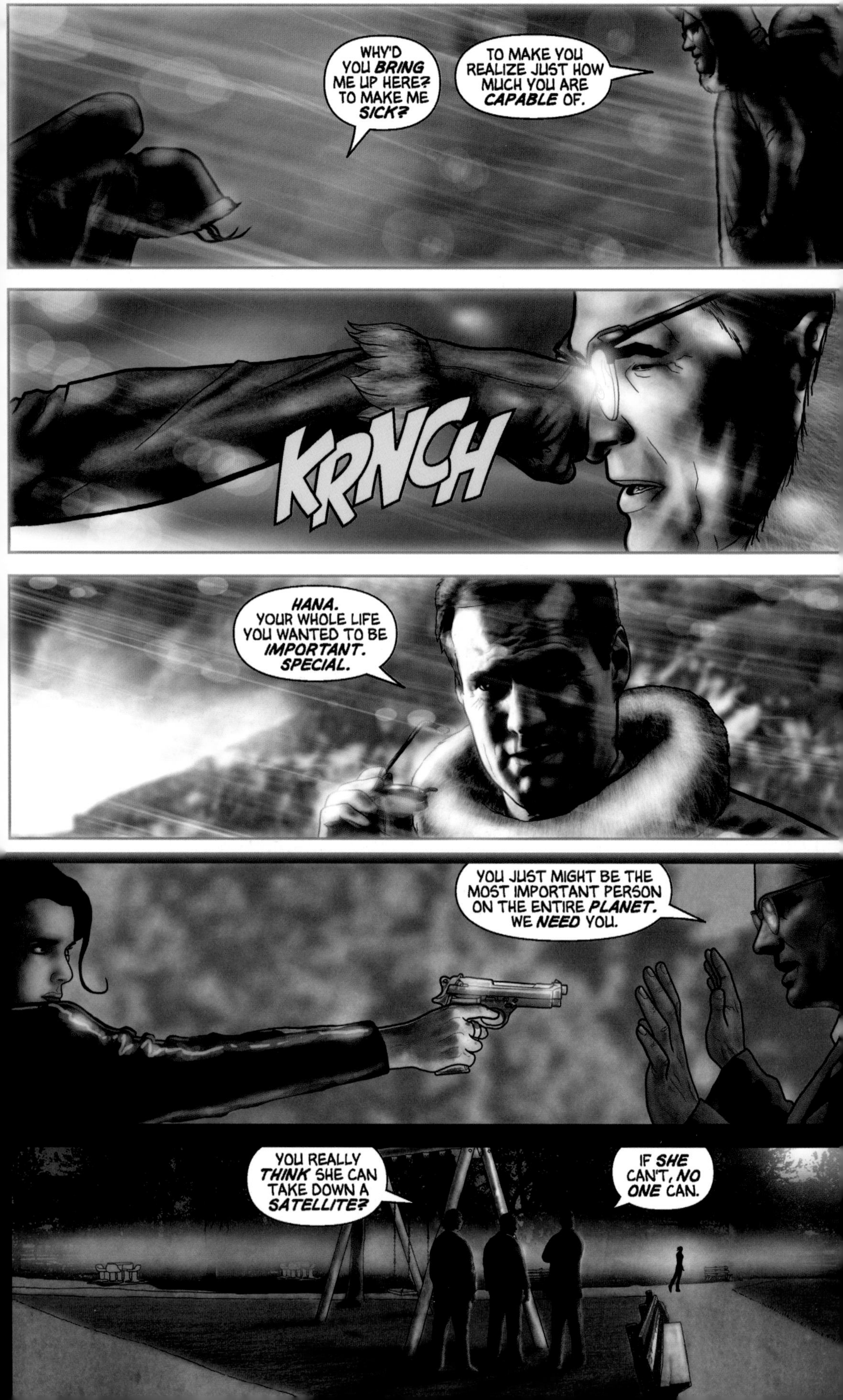
WHY'D YOU BRING ME UP HERE? TO MAKE ME SICK?
TO MAKE YOU REALIZE JUST HOW MUCH YOU ARE CAPABLE OF.
KRNCH
HANA. YOUR WHOLE LIFE YOU WANTED TO BE IMPORTANT. SPECIAL.
YOU JUST MIGHT BE THE MOST IMPORTANT PERSON ON THE ENTIRE PLANET. WE NEED YOU.
YOU REALLY THINK SHE CAN TAKE DOWN A SATELLITE?
IF SHE CAN'T, NO ONE CAN.

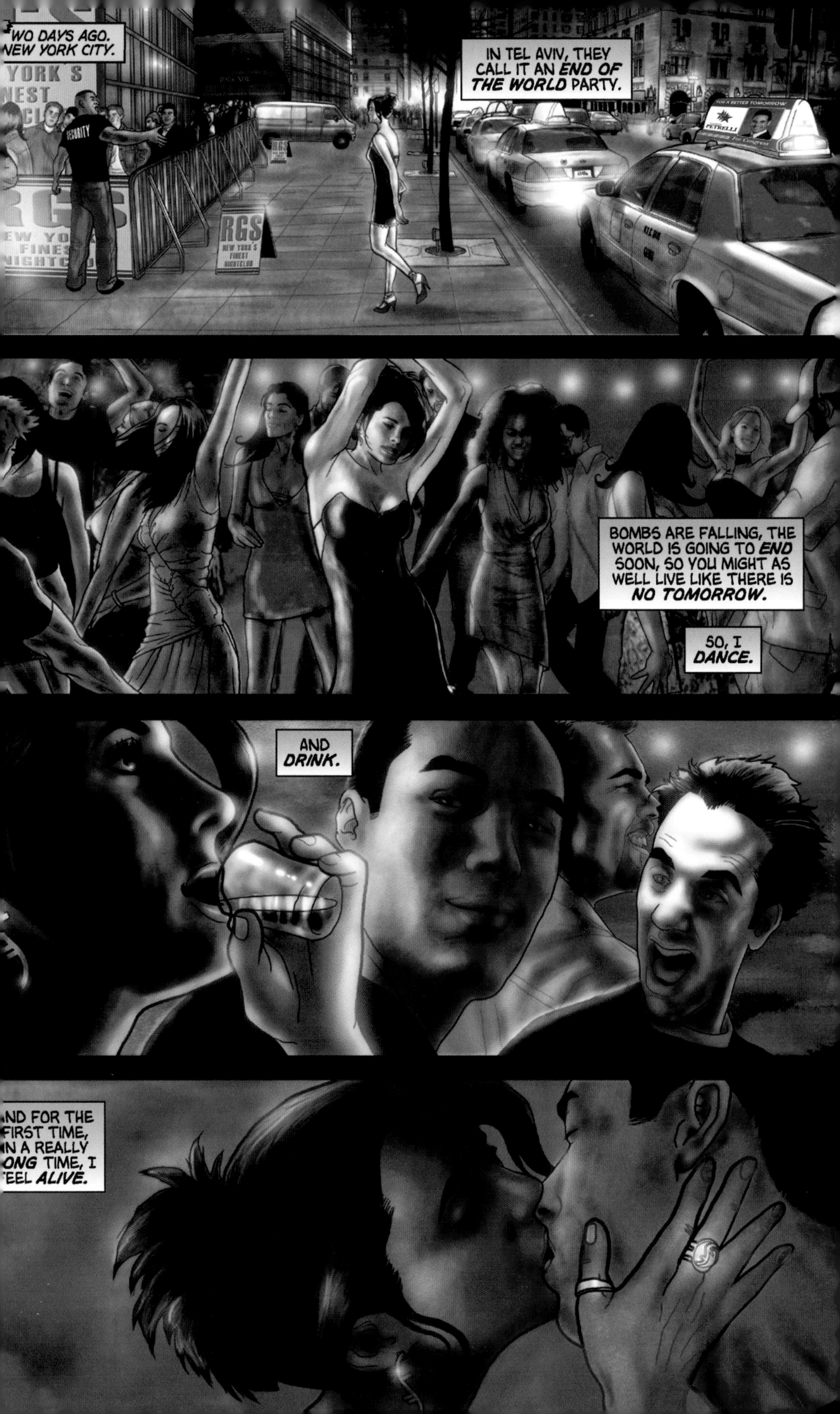
WO DAYS AGO. NEW YORK CITY.
SECURITY
RGS NEW YORK'S FINEST NIGHTCLUB
IN TEL AVIV, THEY CALL IT AN *END OF THE WORLD* PARTY.
FOR A BETTER TOMORROW
PETRELLI
BOMBS ARE FALLING, THE WORLD IS GOING TO *END* SOON, SO YOU MIGHT AS WELL LIVE LIKE THERE IS ***NO TOMORROW.***
SO, I *DANCE.*
AND *DRINK.*
ND FOR THE FIRST TIME, N A REALLY *ONG* TIME, I EEL *ALIVE.*

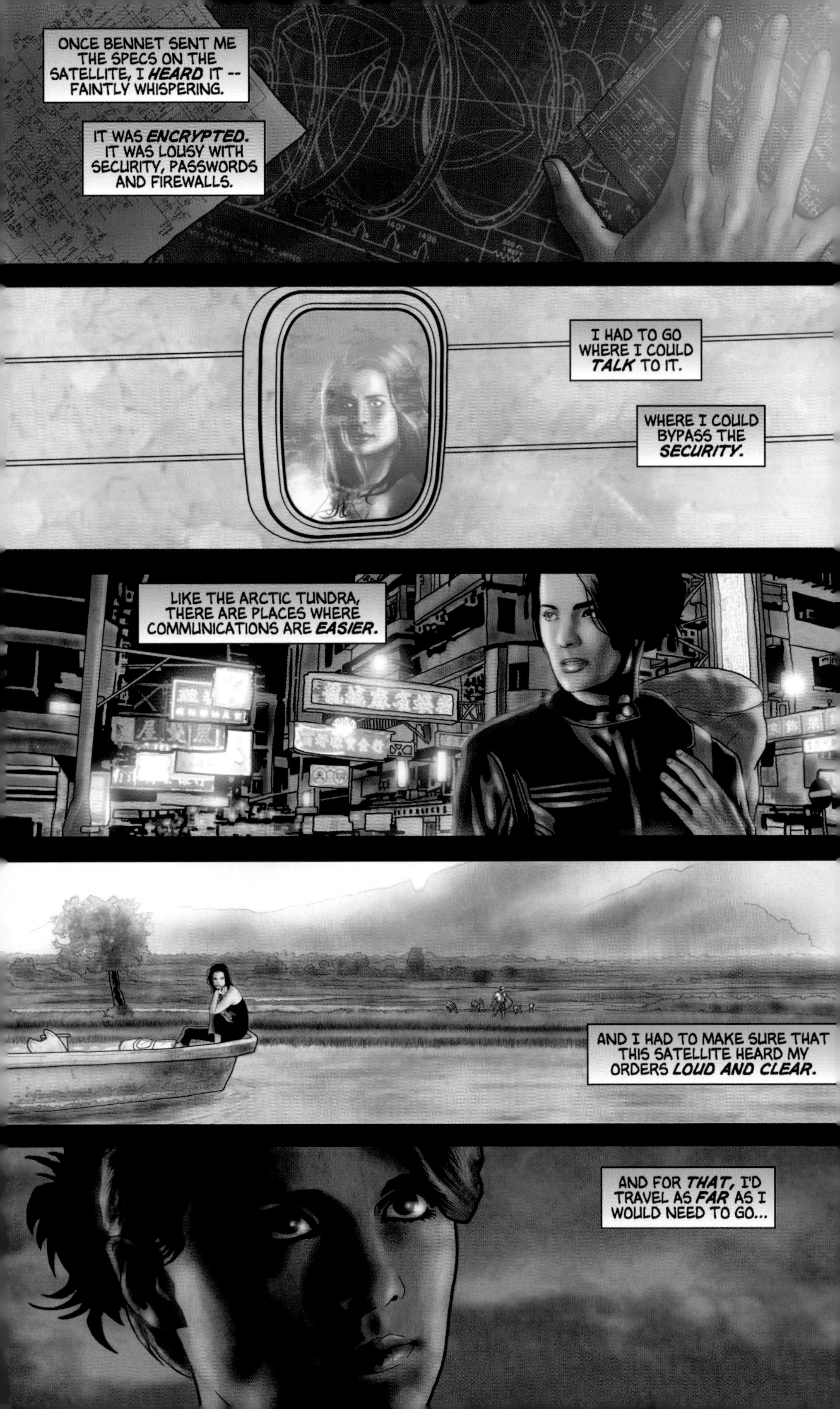

ONCE BENNET SENT ME THE SPECS ON THE SATELLITE, I HEARD IT -- FAINTLY WHISPERING.
IT WAS ENCRYPTED. IT WAS LOUSY WITH SECURITY, PASSWORDS AND FIREWALLS.
I HAD TO GO WHERE I COULD TALK TO IT.
WHERE I COULD BYPASS THE SECURITY.
LIKE THE ARCTIC TUNDRA, THERE ARE PLACES WHERE COMMUNICATIONS ARE EASIER.
AND I HAD TO MAKE SURE THAT THIS SATELLITE HEARD MY ORDERS LOUD AND CLEAR.
AND FOR THAT, I'D TRAVEL AS FAR AS I WOULD NEED TO GO...

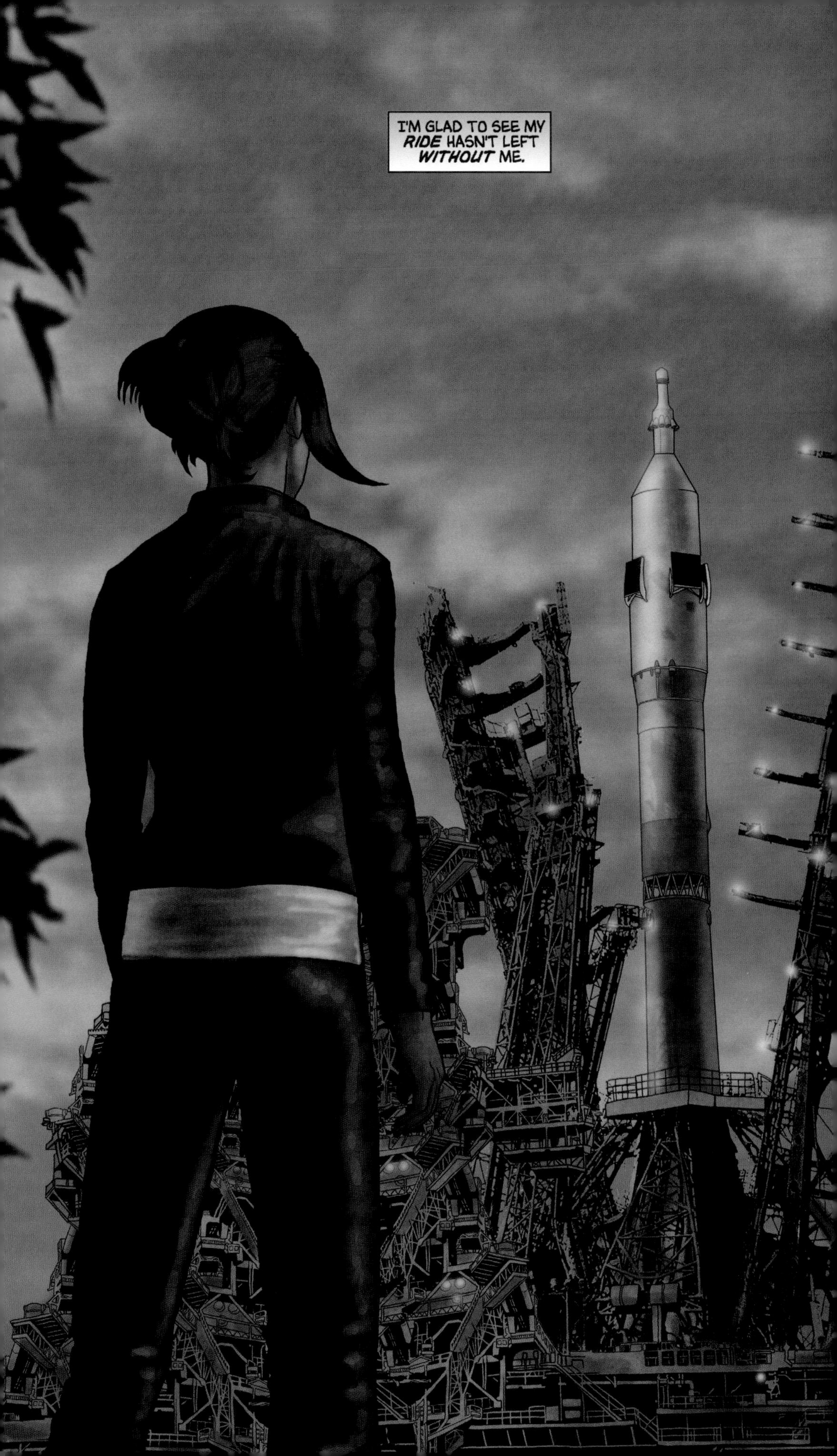
I'M GLAD TO SEE MY RIDE HASN'T LEFT WITHOUT ME.

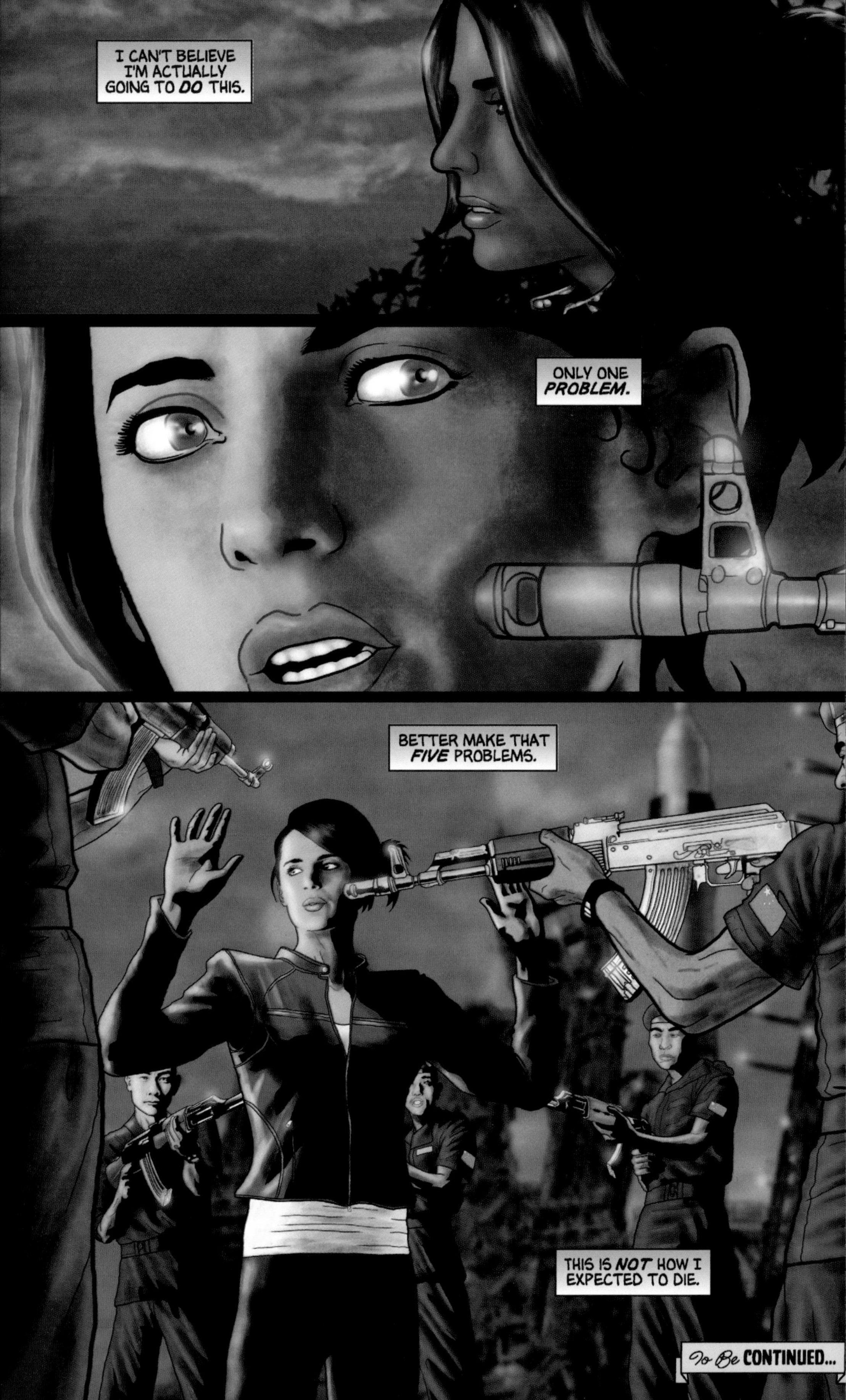
I CAN'T BELIEVE I'M ACTUALLY GOING TO *DO* THIS.
ONLY ONE *PROBLEM.*
BETTER MAKE THAT *FIVE* PROBLEMS.
THIS IS *NOT* HOW I EXPECTED TO DIE.
To Be CONTINUED...

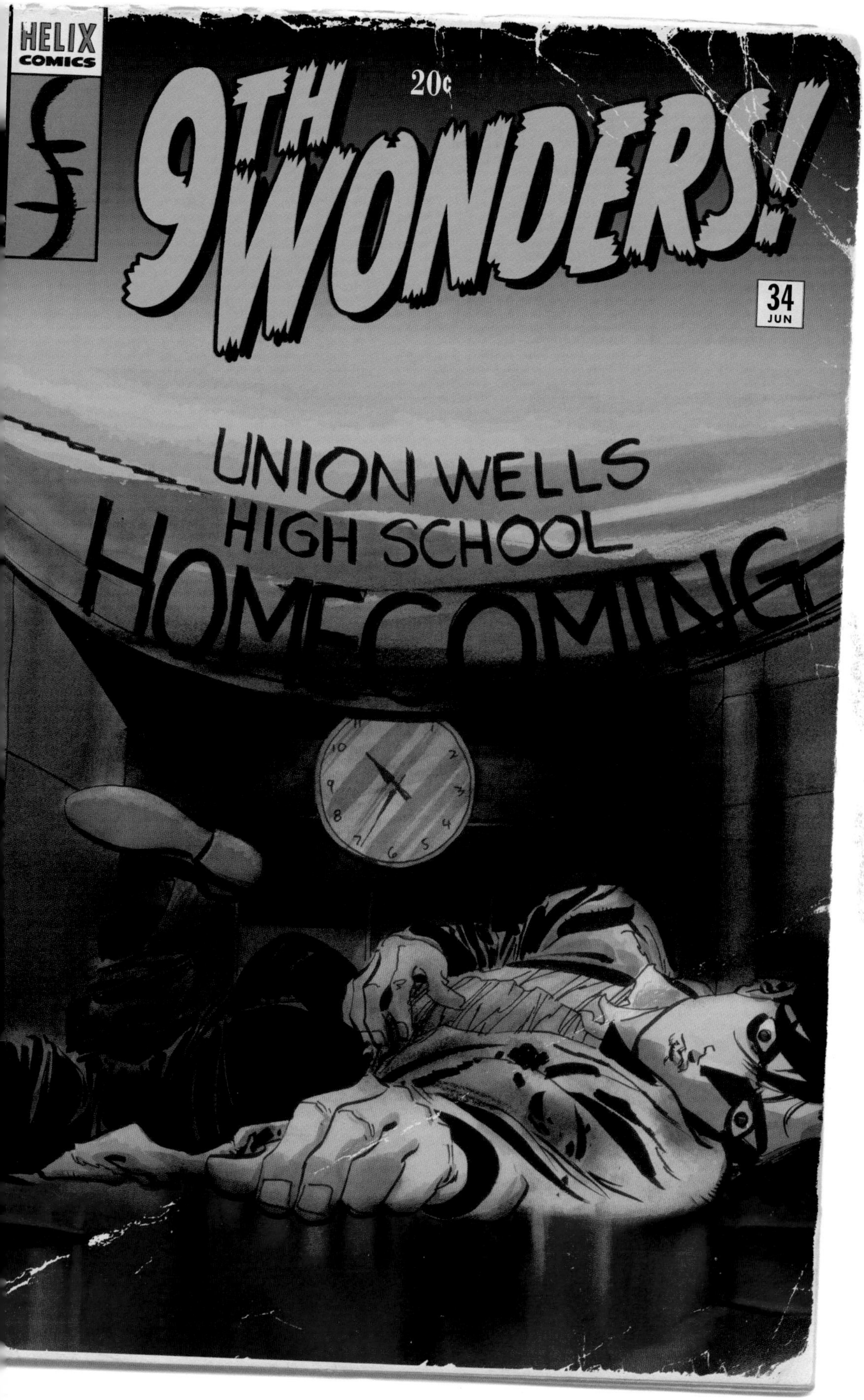
HELIX COMICS
20¢
9TH WONDERS!
34
JUN
UNION WELLS
HIGH SCHOOL
HOMECOMING

THIRTEEN YEARS AGO.

IT'S TRUE WHAT THEY SAY. MOMENTS BEFORE YOU DIE, YOUR LIFE FLASHES BEFORE YOUR EYES. BUT I DIDN'T EXPECT TO REMEMBER *THIS...*

TEL AVIV, ISRAEL.

IT WAS TWO WEEKS AFTER MY MOM AND GRANDMOTHER DIED.

MY *PSYCHOLOGIST* SAID THAT I WAS REACHING OUT FOR ATTENTION. BUT HONESTLY I THOUGHT IT WOULD *WORK.* THAT THE *UMBRELLA* WOULD SLOW ME DOWN.

THAT I COULD *FLY.* LIKE THE *ANGELS.*

I WAS *WRONG.*

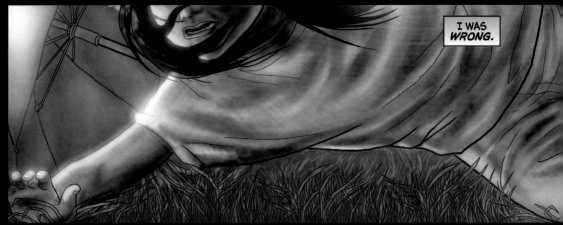

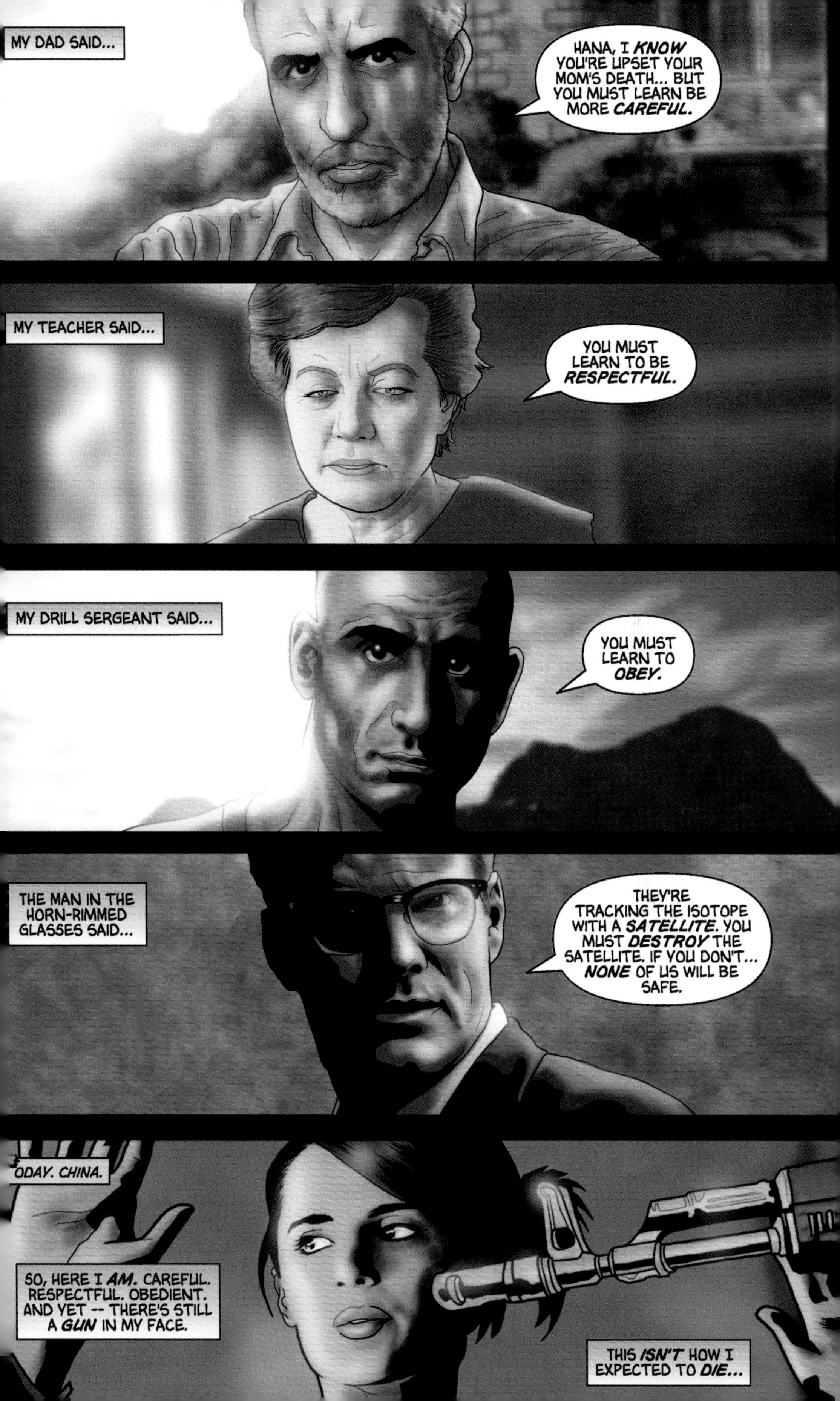
MY DAD SAID...
HANA, I KNOW YOU'RE UPSET YOUR MOM'S DEATH... BUT YOU MUST LEARN BE MORE CAREFUL.
MY TEACHER SAID...
YOU MUST LEARN TO BE RESPECTFUL.
MY DRILL SERGEANT SAID...
YOU MUST LEARN TO OBEY.
THE MAN IN THE HORN-RIMMED GLASSES SAID...
THEY'RE TRACKING THE ISOTOPE WITH A SATELLITE. YOU MUST DESTROY THE SATELLITE. IF YOU DON'T... NONE OF US WILL BE SAFE.
ODAY. CHINA.
SO, HERE I AM. CAREFUL. RESPECTFUL. OBEDIENT. AND YET -- THERE'S STILL A GUN IN MY FACE.
THIS ISN'T HOW I EXPECTED TO DIE...

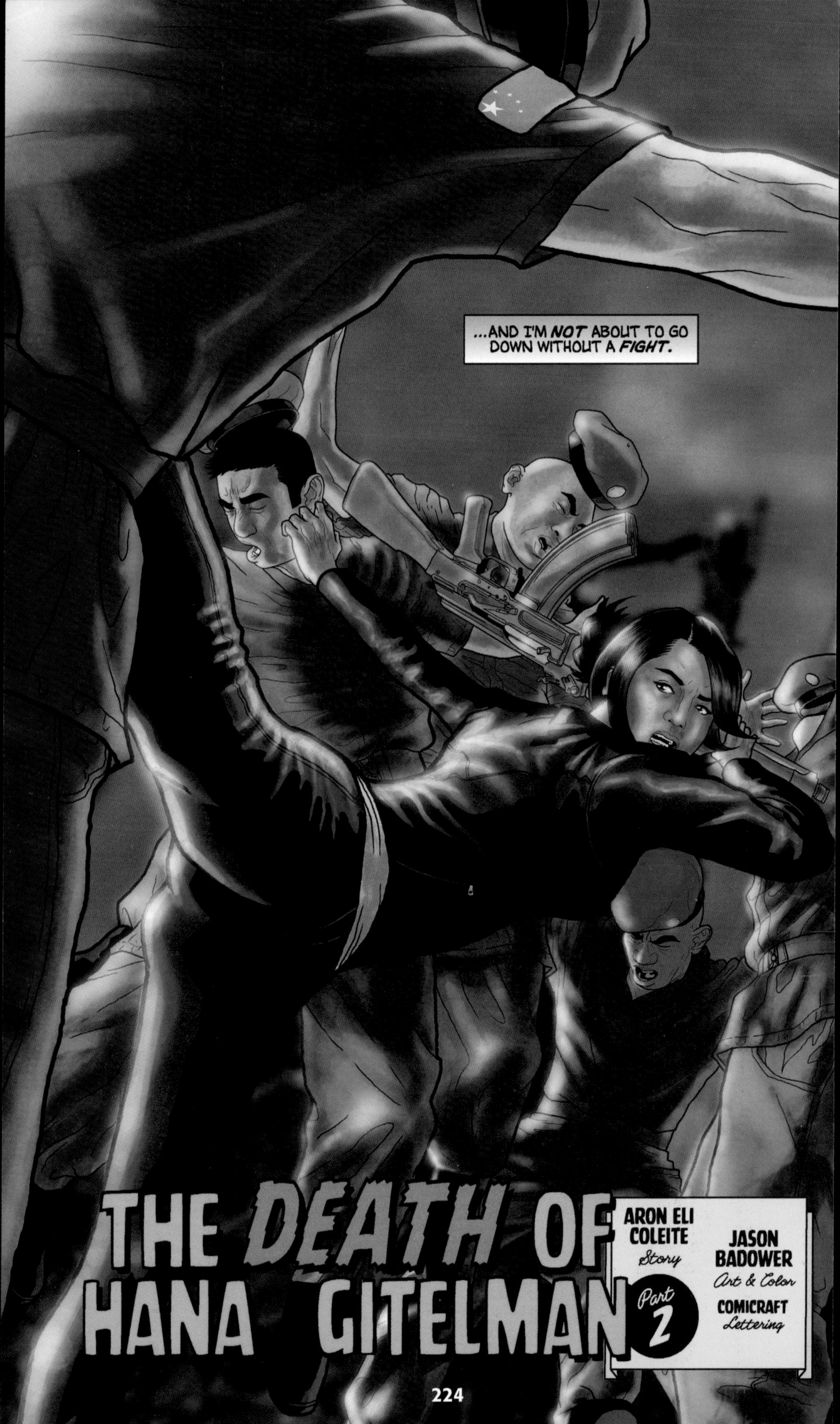
...AND I'M *NOT* ABOUT TO GO DOWN WITHOUT A *FIGHT*.
THE *DEATH* OF HANA GITELMAN
Part 2
ARON ELI COLEITE Story
JASON BADOWER Art & Color
COMICRAFT Lettering

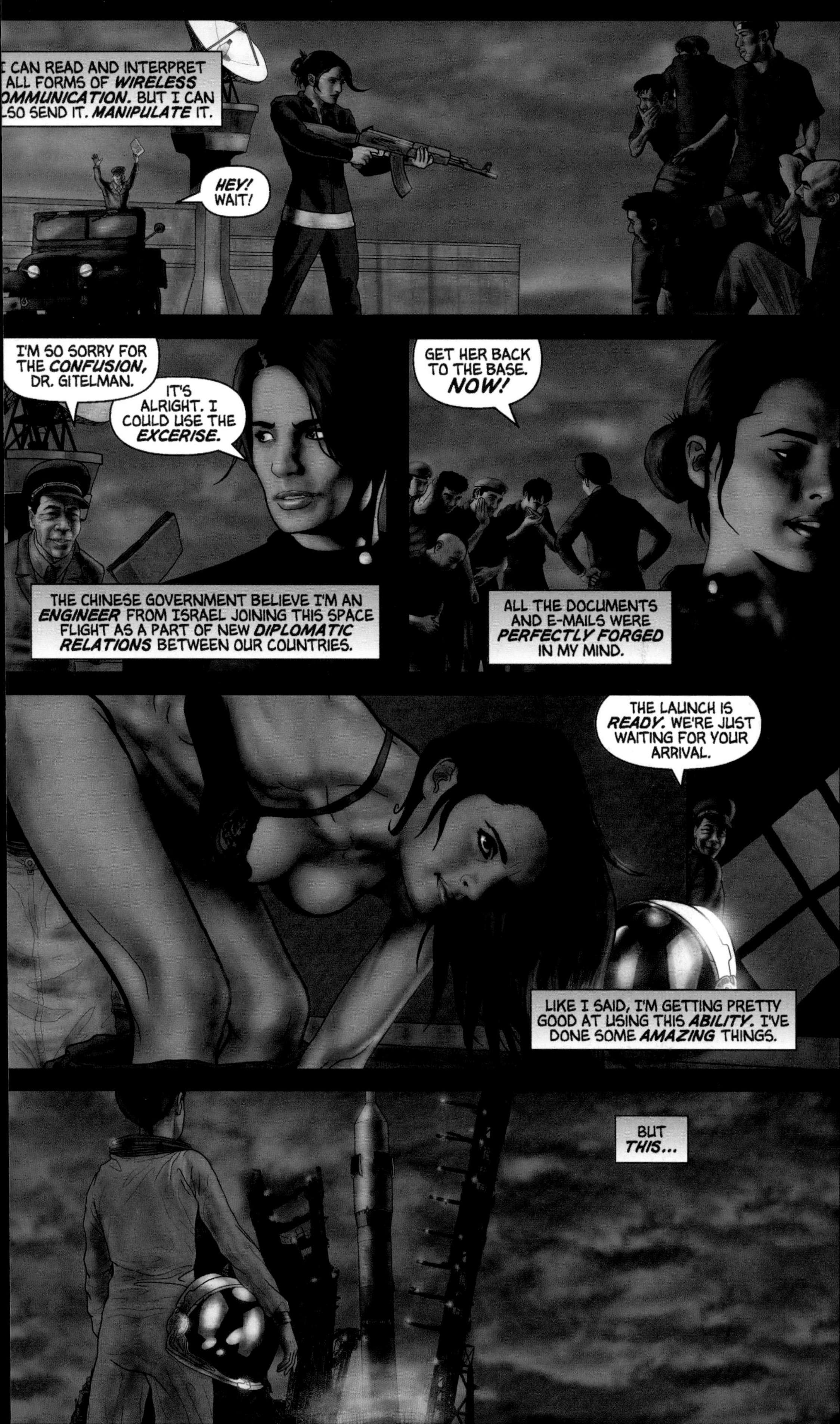

I CAN READ AND INTERPRET ALL FORMS OF WIRELESS COMMUNICATION. BUT I CAN ALSO SEND IT. MANIPULATE IT.
HEY! WAIT!
I'M SO SORRY FOR THE CONFUSION, DR. GITELMAN.
IT'S ALRIGHT. I COULD USE THE EXCERISE.
THE CHINESE GOVERNMENT BELIEVE I'M AN ENGINEER FROM ISRAEL JOINING THIS SPACE FLIGHT AS A PART OF NEW DIPLOMATIC RELATIONS BETWEEN OUR COUNTRIES.
GET HER BACK TO THE BASE. NOW!
ALL THE DOCUMENTS AND E-MAILS WERE PERFECTLY FORGED IN MY MIND.
THE LAUNCH IS READY. WE'RE JUST WAITING FOR YOUR ARRIVAL.
LIKE I SAID, I'M GETTING PRETTY GOOD AT USING THIS ABILITY. I'VE DONE SOME AMAZING THINGS.
BUT THIS...

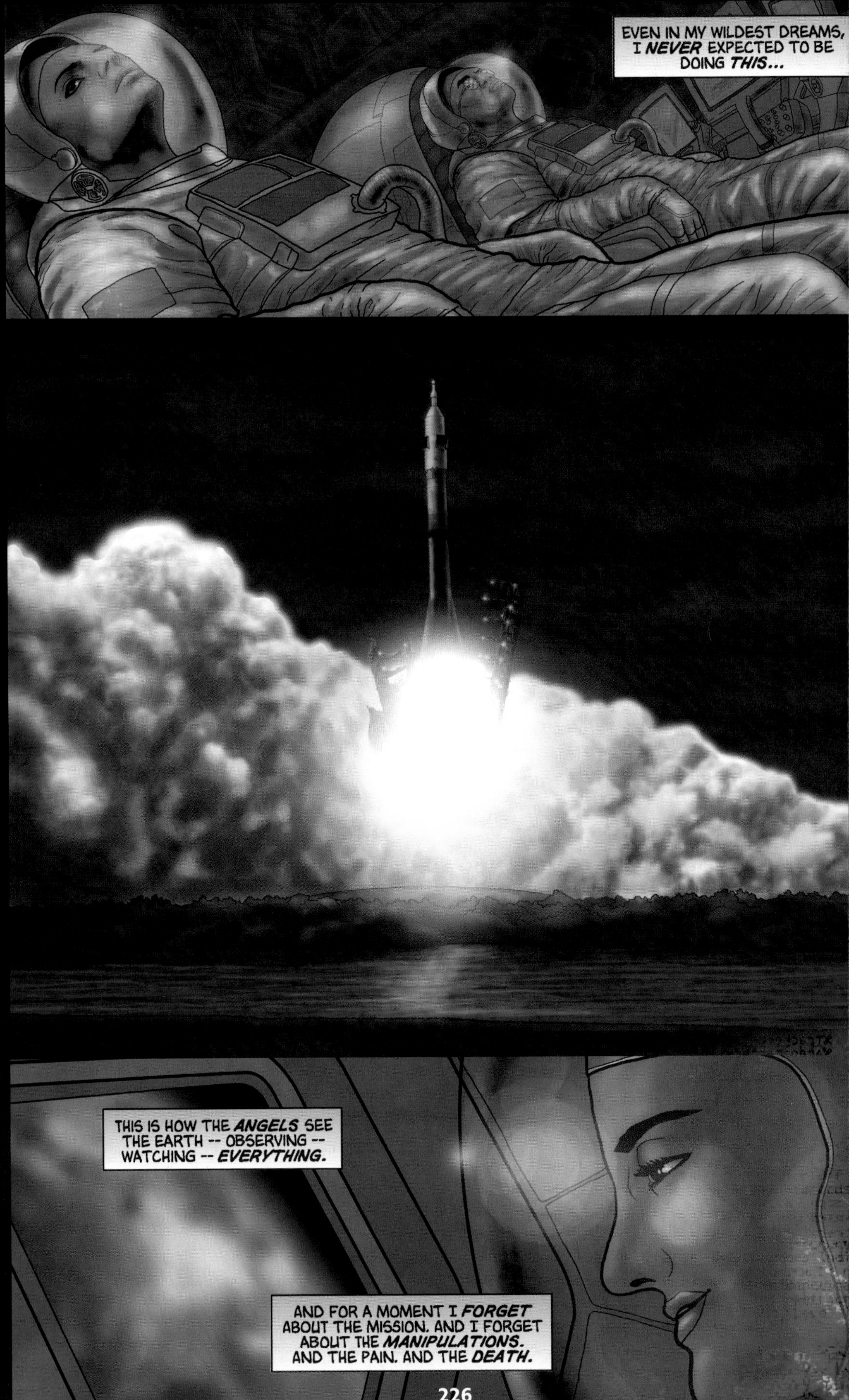
EVEN IN MY WILDEST DREAMS, I NEVER EXPECTED TO BE DOING THIS...
THIS IS HOW THE ANGELS SEE THE EARTH -- OBSERVING -- WATCHING -- EVERYTHING.
AND FOR A MOMENT I FORGET ABOUT THE MISSION. AND I FORGET ABOUT THE MANIPULATIONS. AND THE PAIN. AND THE DEATH.

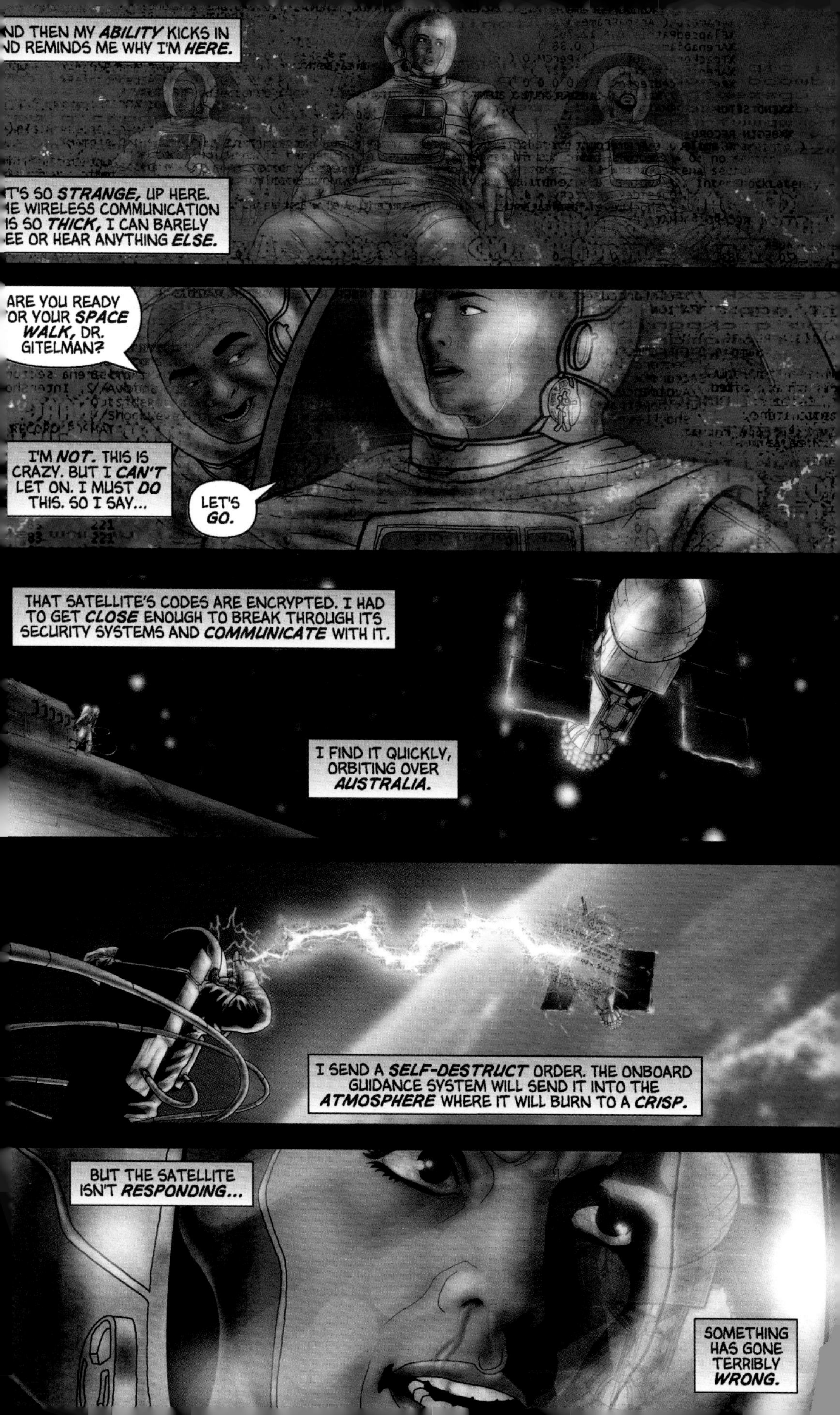
ND THEN MY ABILITY KICKS IN ND REMINDS ME WHY I'M HERE.
T'S SO STRANGE, UP HERE. IE WIRELESS COMMUNICATION IS SO THICK, I CAN BARELY EE OR HEAR ANYTHING ELSE.
ARE YOU READY OR YOUR SPACE WALK, DR. GITELMAN?
I'M NOT. THIS IS CRAZY. BUT I CAN'T LET ON. I MUST DO THIS. SO I SAY...
LET'S GO.
THAT SATELLITE'S CODES ARE ENCRYPTED. I HAD TO GET CLOSE ENOUGH TO BREAK THROUGH ITS SECURITY SYSTEMS AND COMMUNICATE WITH IT.
I FIND IT QUICKLY, ORBITING OVER AUSTRALIA.
I SEND A SELF-DESTRUCT ORDER. THE ONBOARD GUIDANCE SYSTEM WILL SEND IT INTO THE ATMOSPHERE WHERE IT WILL BURN TO A CRISP.
BUT THE SATELLITE ISN'T RESPONDING...
SOMETHING HAS GONE TERRIBLY WRONG.

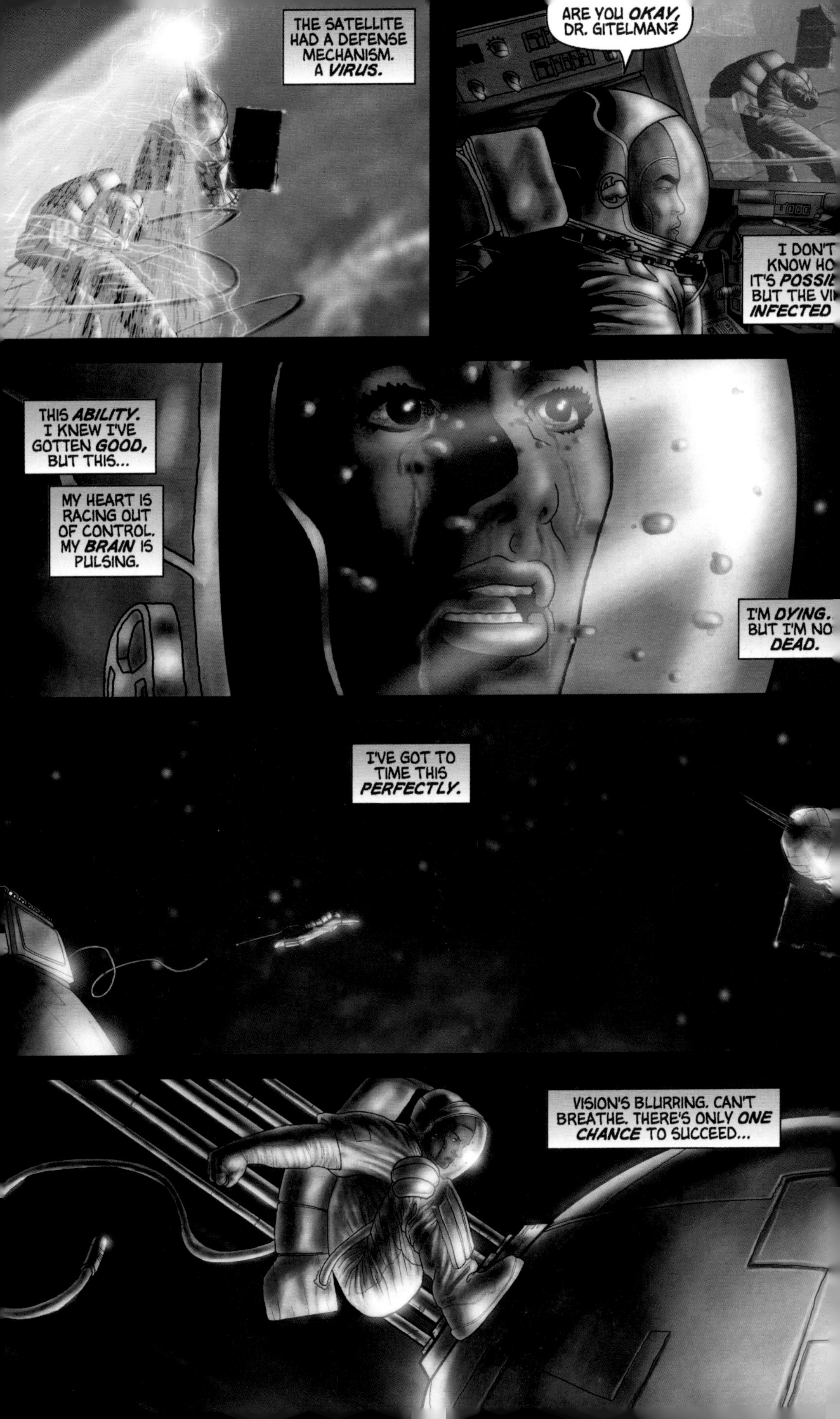
THE SATELLITE HAD A DEFENSE MECHANISM. A VIRUS.
ARE YOU OKAY, DR. GITELMAN?
I DON'T KNOW HO IT'S POSSIL BUT THE VI INFECTED
THIS ABILITY. I KNEW I'VE GOTTEN GOOD, BUT THIS...
MY HEART IS RACING OUT OF CONTROL. MY BRAIN IS PULSING.
I'M DYING. BUT I'M NO DEAD.
I'VE GOT TO TIME THIS PERFECTLY.
VISION'S BLURRING. CAN'T BREATHE. THERE'S ONLY ONE CHANCE TO SUCCEED...

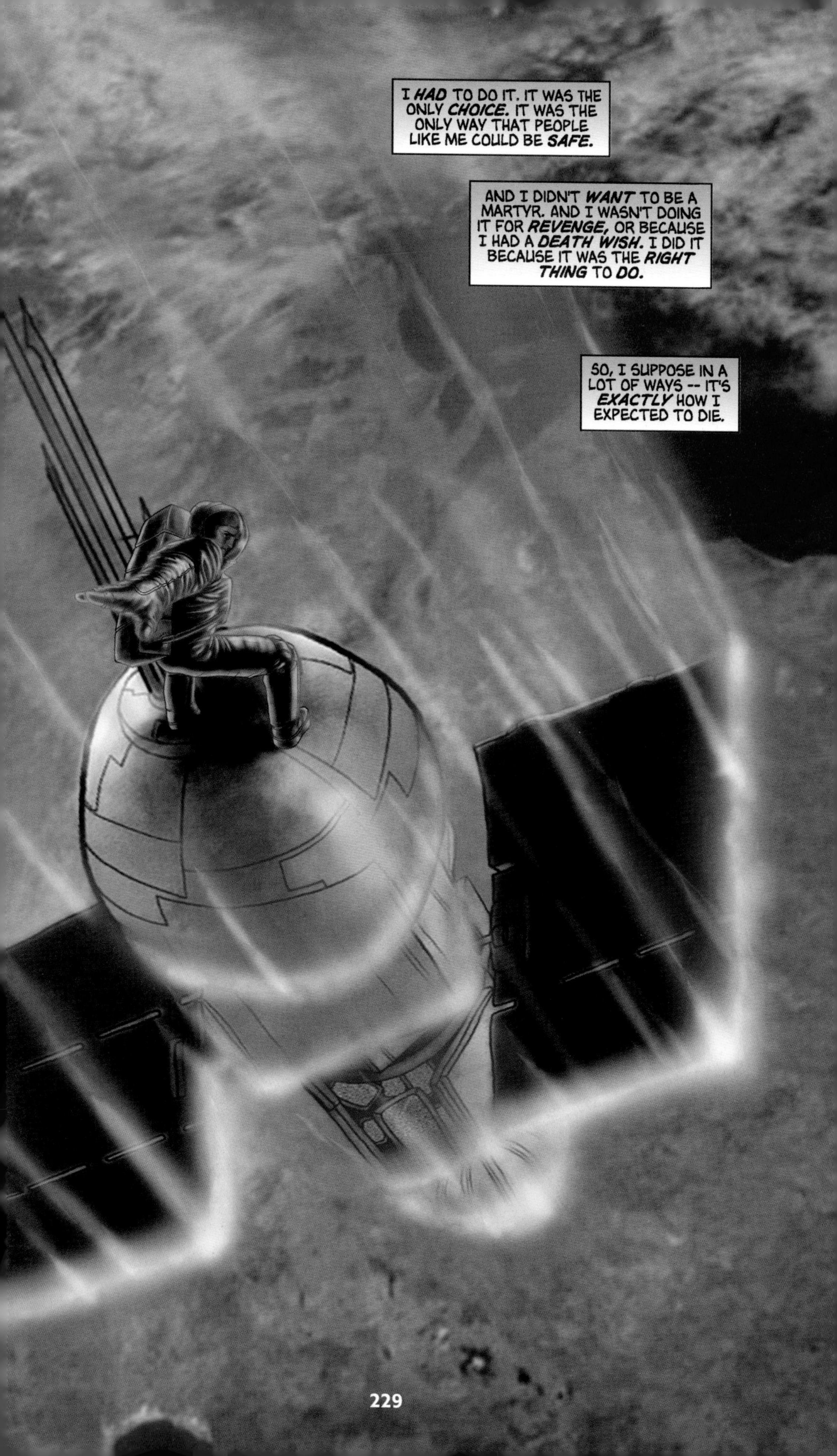
I HAD TO DO IT. IT WAS THE ONLY CHOICE. IT WAS THE ONLY WAY THAT PEOPLE LIKE ME COULD BE SAFE.
AND I DIDN'T WANT TO BE A MARTYR. AND I WASN'T DOING IT FOR REVENGE, OR BECAUSE I HAD A DEATH WISH. I DID IT BECAUSE IT WAS THE RIGHT THING TO DO.
SO, I SUPPOSE IN A LOT OF WAYS -- IT'S EXACTLY HOW I EXPECTED TO DIE.

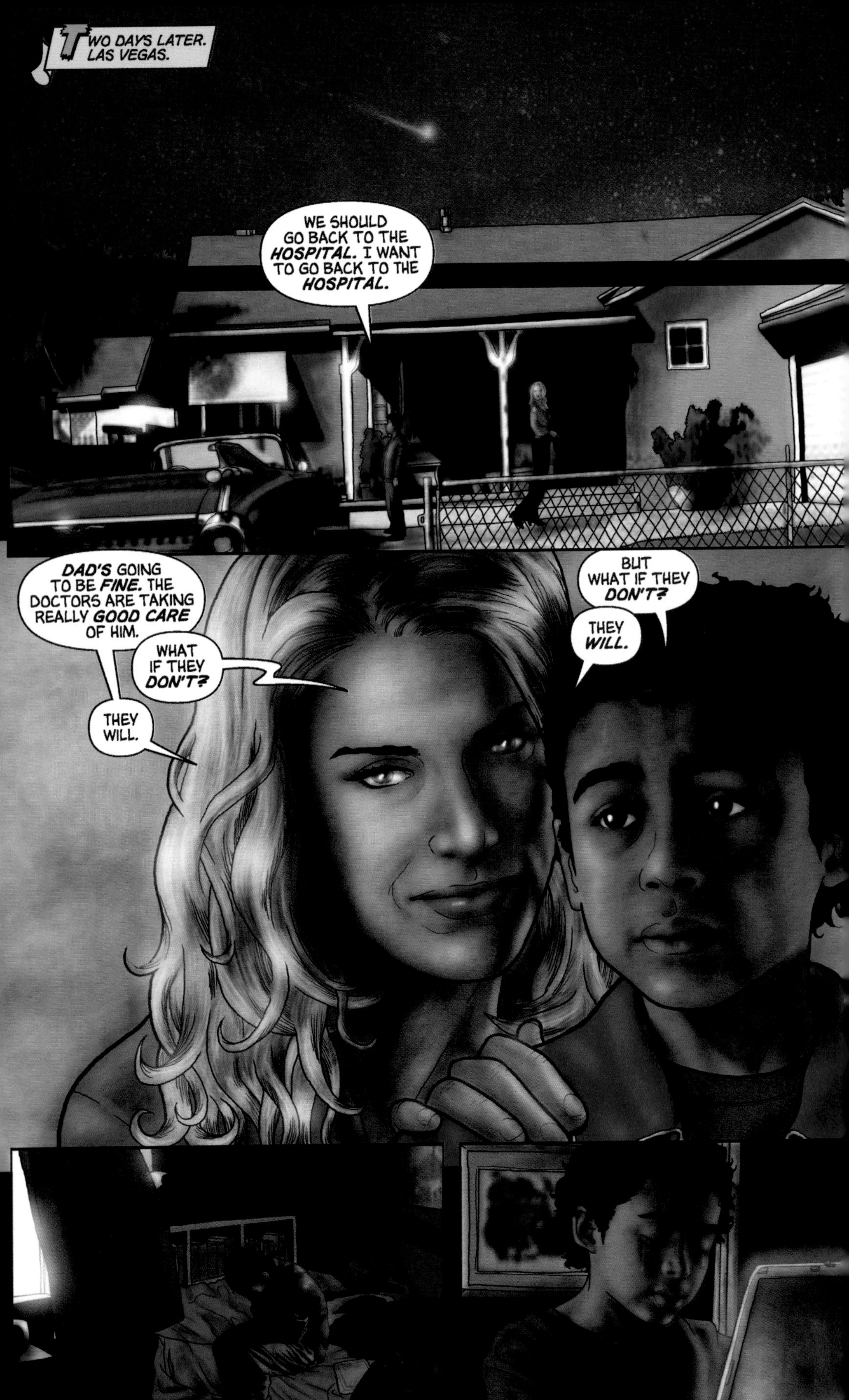
TWO DAYS LATER. LAS VEGAS.
WE SHOULD GO BACK TO THE HOSPITAL. I WANT TO GO BACK TO THE HOSPITAL.
DAD'S GOING TO BE FINE. THE DOCTORS ARE TAKING REALLY GOOD CARE OF HIM.
WHAT IF THEY DON'T?
THEY WILL.
BUT WHAT IF THEY DON'T?
THEY WILL.

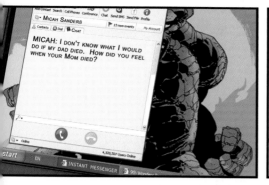

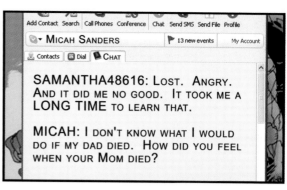

Micah Sanders
MICAH: I don't know what I would do if my dad died. How did you feel when your Mom died?
start
INSTANT MESSENGER
Add Contact Search Call Phones Conference Chat Send SMS Send File Profile
Micah Sanders
13 new events
My Account
Contacts Dial Chat
SAMANTHA48616: Lost. Angry. And it did me no good. It took me a LONG TIME to learn that.
MICAH: I don't know what I would do if my dad died. How did you feel when your Mom died?
Contacts Dial Chat
MICAH: Thank you for chatting with me. What's your name?
Contacts Dial Chat
SAMANTHA48616: My name is Hana Gitelman.
Contacts Dial Chat
SAMANTHA48616: But, you can call me Wireless.
Contacts Dial Chat
SAMANTHA48616: And the truth is, death is never quite what you expect it to be. It might seem like an ending, but really...

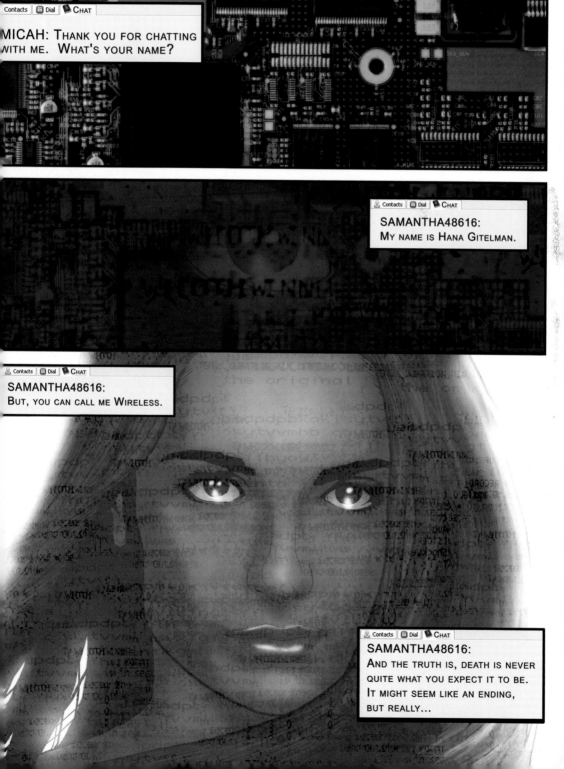

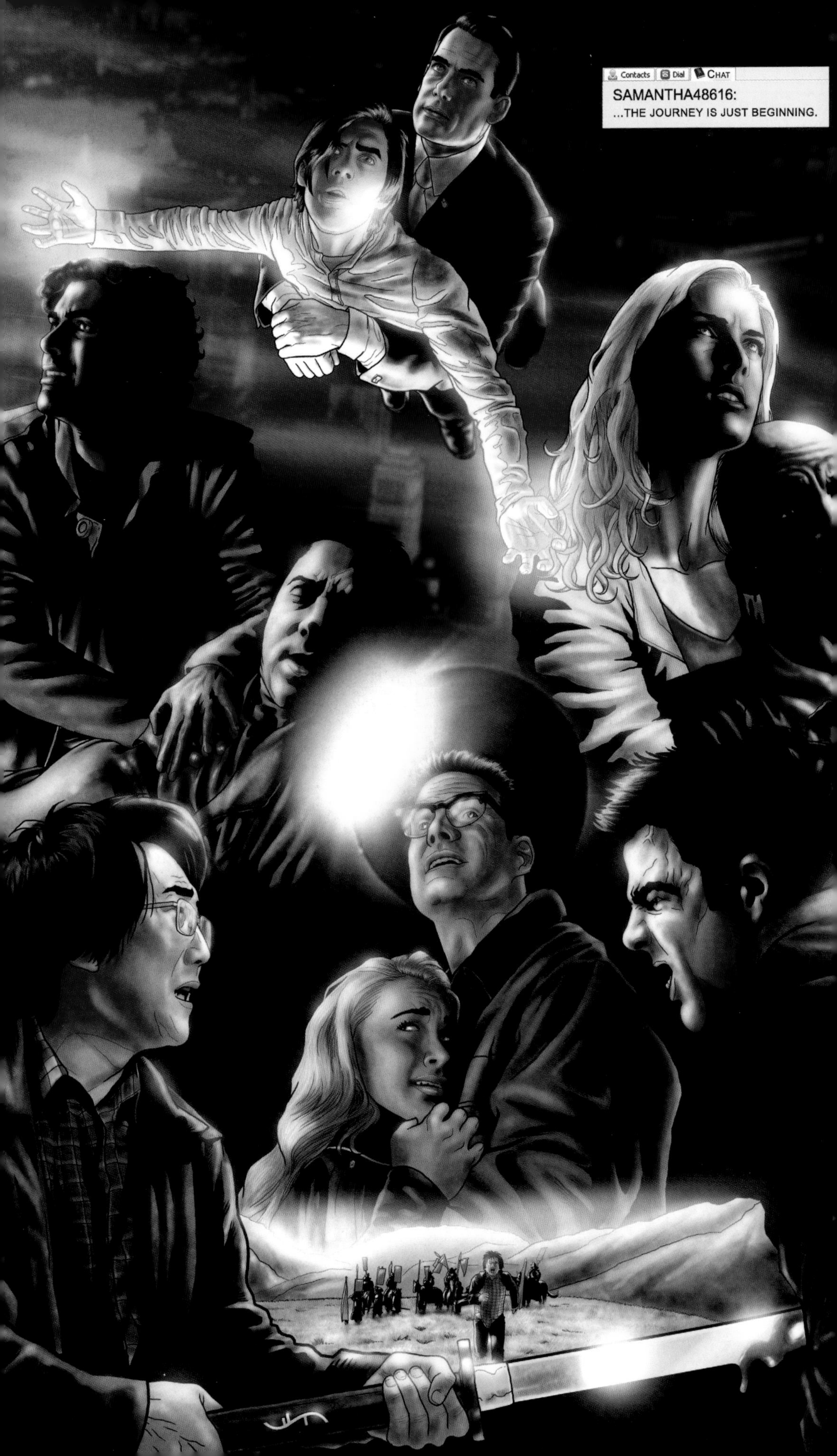
Contacts
Dial
CHAT
SAMANTHA48616:
...THE JOURNEY IS JUST BEGINNING.

THE HEROES INTERVIEW

EXECUTIVE PRODUCER **JEPH LOEB** TALKS WITH SERIES WRITERS **ARON ELI COLEITE** AND **JOE POKASKI**

JEPH: A comic book version of HEROES seems like a no-brainer, but how did it come about?

ARON & JOE: If Tim Kring was the general who ordered a strike on the American zeitgeist with this crazy show called "Heroes"—I guess you could consider us to be some of the first boots on the ground. Before the Pilot was even picked up, we talked extensively with Tim about the online component of the show. How to extend the storytelling from one hour on a Monday into an immersive fan experience.

The online comic was one of the first ideas that came to mind. We had so many stories to tell and there was only so much room in the TV show—so we decided that we could tell these alternate stories in the comics. The stories could be deeper, broader and reveal more secrets about our characters. It was also a way to tell stories that would be otherwise unproduceable on our show.

But this is different from traditional comics, right? It's online and only 5 or 6 pages a shot.

The goal was to put out 22 pages a month, like most comics, but to come out weekly like a television show. So the math dictated 5 or 6 pages per installment and we lucked into the perfect length for a Heroes Webcomic.

Like the scenes or stories in the pilot or in subsequent episodes—the webcomic would be what we called "Haiku," short but purposeful. Every panel meaning something.

It actually forced us to be better, more concise storytellers—we weren't allowed to ramble or wander. We had to tell unique, exciting and fulfilling stories in 5 pages.

You've filled in some of the gaps in the stories from the show. Do you feel like people who watch the show have to read these to know what's going on?

Not at all. In fact, our first rule going in was that you didn't have to read the comic to enjoy the show, but it created an enhanced experience if you did.

On the other side, we wanted people who did watch the show and read the comic to feel rewarded—that they were taking part of something larger and give them real emotional and important stories—not just fluff or filler.

Wildcat Pride!

Michael Turner, Phil Jimenez, Aspen, Nanci Quesada, Alex Ross, and Jim Lee—and those are just for starters. How did the comic book community get involved with what could otherwise be seen as just another licensed property?

For starters, we had a big gun—this guy named Jeph Loeb. It's not a stretch to call him a living legend. And on top of that, a ridiculously large amount of people in the industry who love him—and would jump in front of a train for him. We're not sure if it was that, or his ability to sell a good idea, but soon we had an amazing bullpen of writers and artists working for us.

The short format had a little to do with it too. Many comic book artists pour their hearts and soul onto each page. At 22 pages per comic that is a lot of soul pouring. It's easier to get a top-notch artist for 5 or 6 pages. It's like keeping a friend out at a bar by saying "one more drink." Who doesn't want one more?

Are there new writers we can look forward to next season?

We've already got a bunch of great writers from the show. We've also been joined by veterans like Steven Seagle, Joe Kelly and Duncan Rouleau. But, we've also been fortunate to get some young comic book scribes to join our crew like Mark Sable and Christine Boylen.

On top of that, we've got an amazing staff of up and coming brilliant minds that help us with the impossible task of writing one of these a week. Writers like Harry Wilcox, Oliver Grigsby, Chris Zatta, Jim Martin, Pierluigi Cothran, Timm Keppler and Andrew Chambliss. Watch out for these names—you will see them in the future.

And rumor has it that a certain writer whose name rhymes with SCHMEPH SCHMOEB will introduce a new character called "Rachel Red, Robogirl."

You had to start even before anyone had seen the show. What was that like?

In a lot of ways, it was liberating. As with the show, all we could do is tell the most exciting stories that you would want to experience yourself. Just go for it, because there was no audience reaction to be reactionary towards.

But of course, in the back of your head, for the show and the webcomic, there's the whole "what if you threw a Television Show and nobody arrives" concern eating at the back of your head.

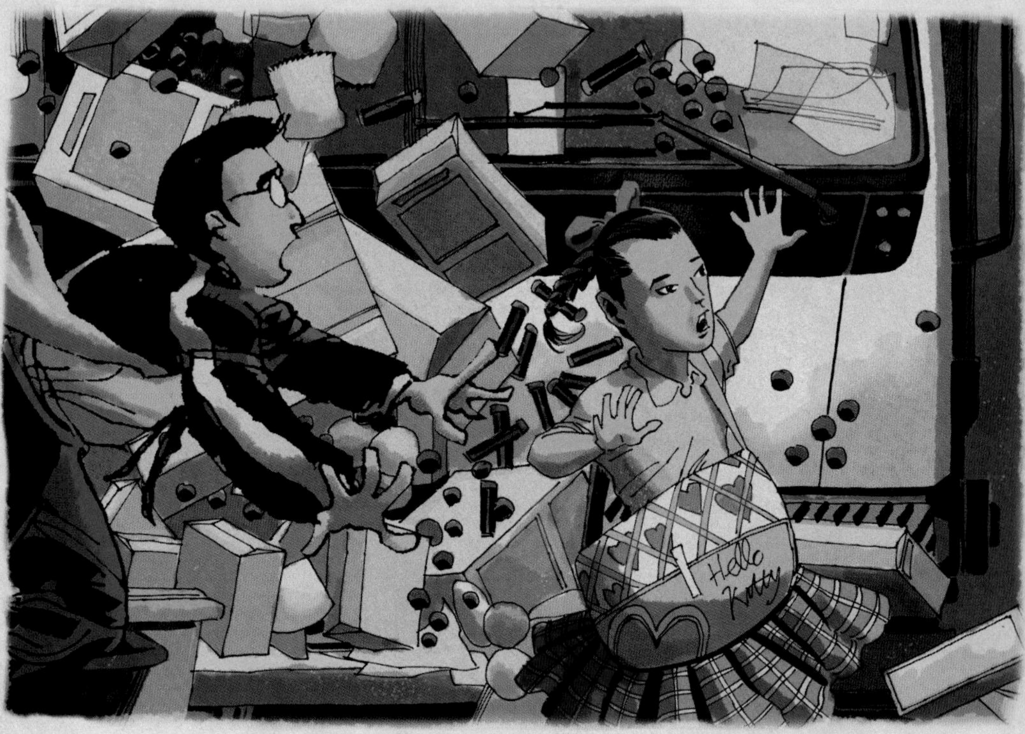
Hello Kitty

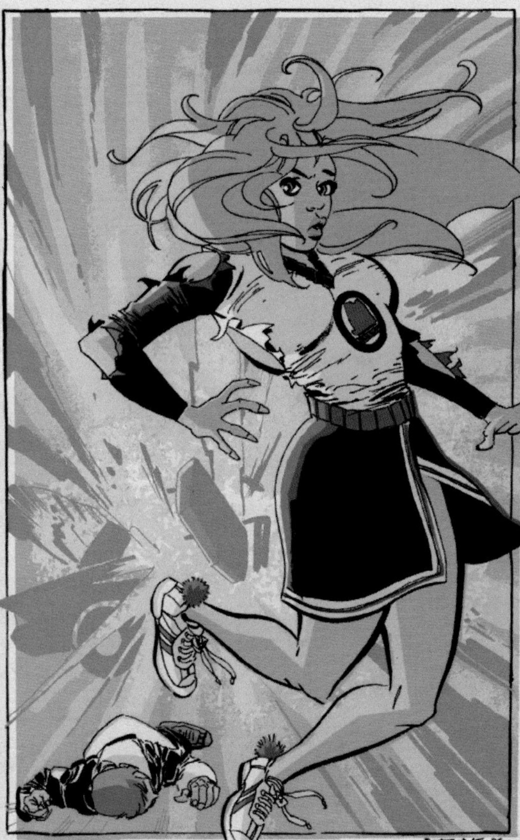

You're both pretty big comic geeks. What's it like now, creating your own universe? What do you read? Do you buy comics on a weekly basis?

Each Wednesday (ideally) we actually make our trek to the local store. A big shout-out to our friends at Meltdown who take good care of us every week. We read a lot of everything. Bendis. Millar. Johns. And of course everything that Loeb puts out. It's one of the rare pleasures in life to go to a comic book store with Jeph Loeb and see the fans pointing and whispering.

Are there stories that you can tell only in this graphic novel form?

There are certainly ones that are easier—because there are no production restraints. For example, when Hana Gitelman went to China to stow away on the Space Shuttle so she could spacewalk to a satellite and ride it down into the burning atmosphere. That would have been difficult to produce.

Fire. Space. Polar Ice Caps. Jungles of Africa. Battles with Indian gods and confrontations with Australian rock formations. There is no limit in this format. It's very rewarding.

Are there some stories you CAN'T or WON'T tell as comics?

We don't want to touch anything that should be seen on the television. For example, we were tempted to tell the webcomic of how H.R.G. got assigned to be Claire's father—but we knew that would be better served on the show—as everyone finally saw in "Company Man."

There's a new online story up every week! How do you do that when some monthly comics -koff-*Ultimates*-koff- sometimes can't make shipping!

Most of that lies with a guy named Mark Warshaw. And Chuck Kim. They keep the trains running on time. Sometimes we run right up to the wire and deliver the pages moments before they need to go live, but even so—we have yet to miss a deadline.

Fortunately we're able to line up the stories with the episodes so we can try to keep ahead of the curve and have scripts generated quickly and early.

If you could have a crossover with any of the DC characters, what would your dream team-up be?

I think everyone would want to see the Supergirl/Claire team up. A Peter/Superman throwdown might be fun as well. And of course Green Lantern/Ando would be a classic matchup.

So...are you comic book writers or graphic novelists? Remember, this is how you'll be defined for the rest of your lives...

Is there a third choice?

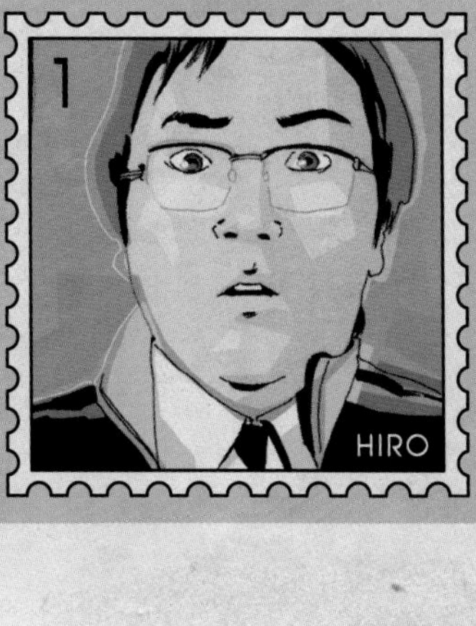
1
HIRO

THIS IS IT! YOUR

HEROES VALUE STAMP

FOR THIS ISSUE! CLIP 'EM AND COLLECT 'EM!

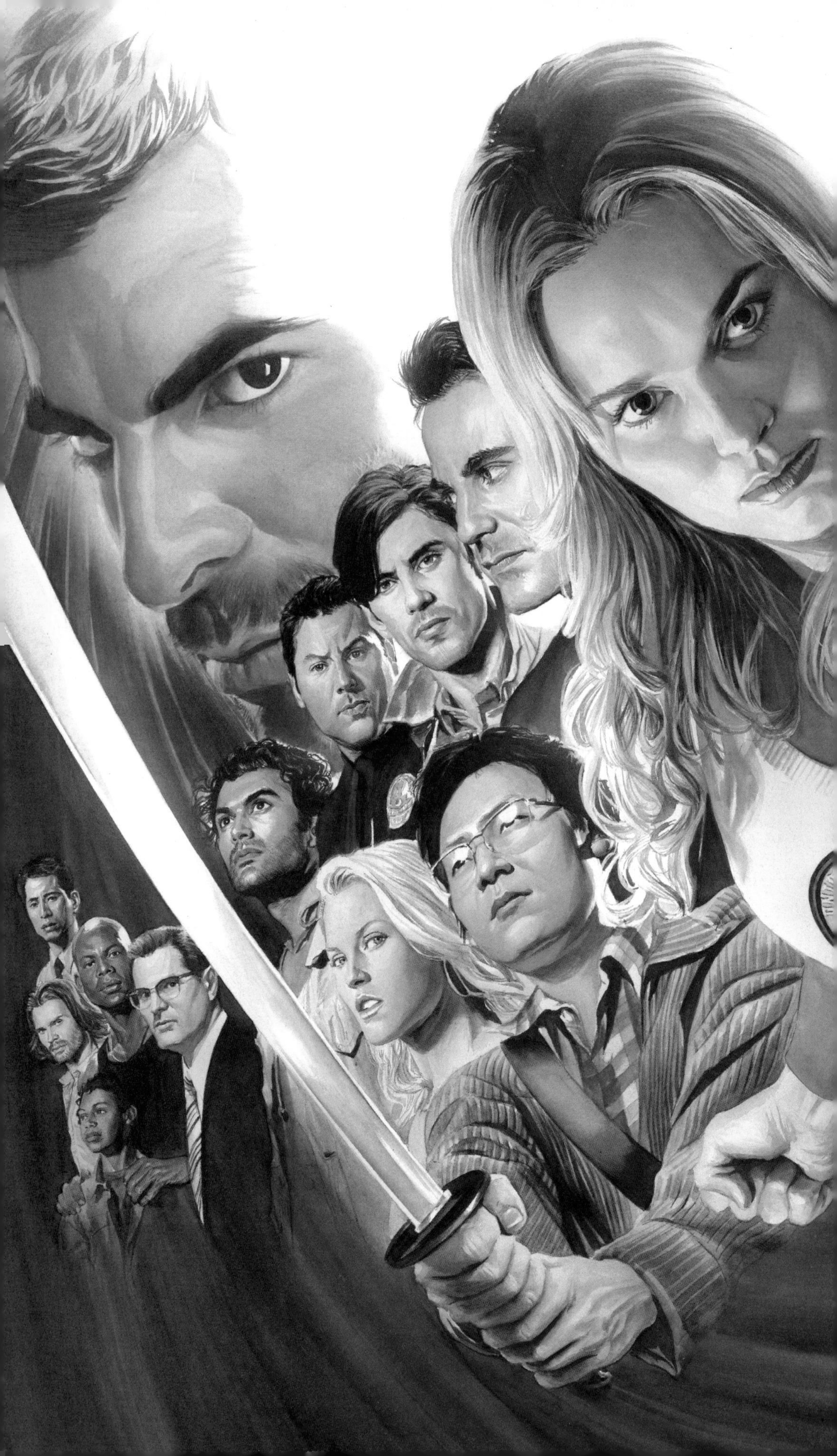

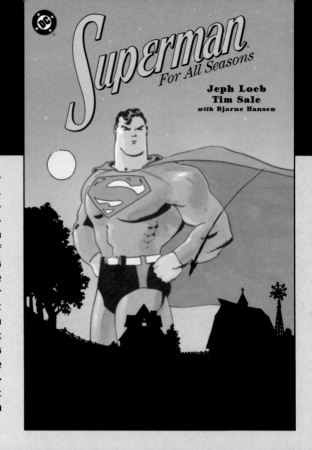

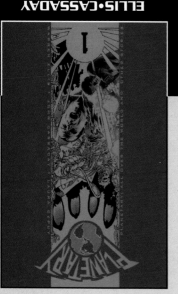
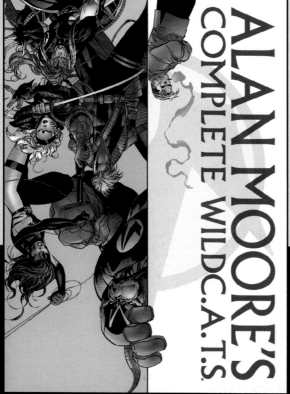